Hans Christian Andersen

HANS CHRISTIAN ANDERSEN

the story of his life
and work
1805–75

Elias Bredsdorff

Fellow of Peterhouse
Reader in Scandinavian Studies
at the University of Cambridge

Charles Scribner's Sons
New York

I am very grateful to three persons who have read the entire manuscript before it was printed, and who have helped me each in their way. Dr H. Topsøe-Jensen has carefully gone through each chapter, suggested various improvements and freely allowed me to pick his brains. Dr Alice Roughton has been untiring in discussing with me problems of language and style, thus preventing me from making errors which as a non-native writer of English I might otherwise have made. Anne Lise Bredsdorff, my wife, has discussed the manuscript with me chapter by chapter as I wrote it, has suggested valuable improvements of various kinds, and throughout the years I have been working on this book she has given me great moral and practical support.

E.BR.

Contents

Paper cutting by Andersen
incorporating many of his favourite
themes.

The tail-pieces throughout this book
are reproduced from Andersen's paper
cuttings. The items on the pierrot's
tray on the title-page represent some
of the stages in Andersen's life: his
birthplace in Odense, the old grammar
school in Slagelse, the windmill man
(a fairy-tale motif), Saint Canute's
Church in Odense, and the ugly
duckling transformed into a swan.

Preface

THE FIRST time I realized that Hans Christian Andersen was a person who had really lived, and was not just the title of a wonderful book of fairy tales, was when my grandmother, having read me one of Andersen's tales, told me how she had once met him, even danced with him at a party when he was an old man and she a young girl of seventeen. 'Weren't you proud?' I asked her. 'No,' she replied. 'In fact, I've never felt so humiliated in all my life. At the time I felt so ashamed when that ugly old man asked me to dance that I could have died on the spot. Moreover, he couldn't dance and kept on treading on my toes with his ridiculously long feet. It ruined the party for me!' Later in life she saw the scene in a different light.

Over the years Andersen has been seen by different people in many different ways. There were always those who saw him only as the vain egotist that he certainly *also* was. There have been others who saw him almost as a martyr or, with a phrase used by Georg Brandes, as 'the hounded animal in Danish literature', a genius ruthlessly persecuted at home and only grudgingly recognized after having been acclaimed by the world. To some extent Andersen himself is responsible for both over-simplifications. Some have seen him as a snob and a toady, others have stressed the element of sympathy for the underdog in his prose writings. There are biographers who have gone to such extremes in eulogizing him that they have even tried to explain away his egocentricity and his vanity. Many are the successful attempts to sentimentalize his life story, serving it to children with a thick layer of sugar-icing as a tear-sodden tale about 'poor little Hans' who succeeded in killing the giants of stupidity and envy, and ended by becoming rich and famous and living happily ever after.

The more one knows about Andersen the more one realizes how complex his personality was, and there are few writers who died a hundred years ago about whose life it is possible to know so much. He was obsessed with writing about himself and his own life and left behind a whole series of autobiographies and autobiographical sketches. He was also a prolific letter writer, and thousands of his letters are now available in scholarly editions, many of which have only been published in recent years. It is not only his own letters which have been preserved; he himself rarely destroyed a letter he received, so that in most cases both sides of the correspondence are available. Finally, during much of his lifetime Andersen kept diaries, which are now being published in full for the first time.

The autobiographies, the correspondence and the diaries are the main sources of information; but there are other valuable sources, the most important of which are listed in the bibliography.

Andersen's earliest autobiographical sketches were in four letters written during the years 1822–7, his last in scrappy drafts written less than a year before he died. 'Collecting and arranging material for the continuation of the fairy tale of my life,' he wrote in his diary on 22 November 1874, and on 18 January 1875 he wrote: 'Today I have been working on my life story.' His autobiographies proper are listed in the bibliography, and it will be seen that he wrote his first extensive autobiography (unpublished in his lifetime) before he was twenty-eight; the manuscript (referred to as *Levnedsbogen*) was found fifty years after his death and has only recently been made available in a scholarly edition. His first published autobiography, *Das Märchen meines Lebens*, was published in German in 1847 and immediately translated into English, but was not published in Danish in his lifetime. His definitive autobiography, however, was published in Denmark in 1855 as *Mit Livs Eventyr* – properly translated as 'The Fairy Tale of My Life' rather than 'The Story of My Life', though it has appeared in English under both titles. An American edition of this book was published in 1871, to which Andersen had added an account of the period 1855–67; in Denmark this continuation was only published posthumously.

However important the autobiographies are, they must be treated with a certain caution, especially the later ones, not only on account of what is said but also on account of what is left unsaid. Of the two, *Levnedsbogen* is more reliable, as far as it goes, than *Mit Livs Eventyr*, more candid and less apt to present events nicely and tidily 'arranged'. No autobiographer is objective, but Andersen was certainly less so than most, and it is excusable if readers of *Mit Livs Eventyr* get tired of reading detailed descriptions of every pin-prick, every humiliation and every adverse criticism of his works; conversely, they may also feel that the author might have been more sparing in his quotations of eulogies by famous as well as less famous people all over the world.

Dr H. Topsøe-Jensen, the greatest living authority on Andersen, supplied scholars with some invaluable tools when he published his outstanding annotated editions of the main autobiographies, and his important studies on Andersen as an autobiographer. Without the help of his works this book could not have been written. Equally, his many editions of Andersen's correspondence, especially the nine volumes devoted to that with the Collin family and the three volumes devoted to that with Henriette Wulff, are indispensable to anyone with a scholarly interest in Andersen. I am greatly indebted to all the editors and authors mentioned in the bibliography, but to none more than to Topsøe-Jensen.

There is still some unpublished material both in the Royal Library, Copenhagen, and in the Odense Museum, and I have consulted that which was most relevant to my study.

Andersen's diaries, whose publication is expected to be complete by 1976, are of course very important to anyone concerned with a study of his life. The earliest fragments date from 1825–6, when Andersen was still a schoolboy, and he wrote the last entries shortly before he died. Up till 1860, apart from the earliest fragments, the diaries are mainly concerned with his many journeys abroad, sometimes with his travels inside Denmark, and only occasionally with his life in Copenhagen, such as when events of great importance occurred. Otherwise daily events were briefly recorded in his almanacs from 1838 to 1871. From 26 May 1860, however, he kept a continuous diary all the year round.

Of the ten planned volumes of diaries only five had been published when the manuscript of this book was completed, but I have been fortunate enough to have had access to the entire material. My friend Dr Erik Dal very kindly arranged for me to see the page proofs of three and a half of the five unpublished volumes, and Dr Topsøe-Jensen was kind enough to lend me his own hand-written copy of the diaries for the remaining period after September 1872.

Of recent years the English-speaking world has tended to dismiss Andersen as a writer of literary importance and to relegate him to the nursery. Further-more, Andersen's tales have increasingly fallen a prey to unscrupulous publishers speculating in cheap, poorly translated and badly illustrated editions. The British and Americans have done to Andersen what the world has done to Swift and Defoe: they have pushed him into the nursery and locked the door on him.

This has not always been the case. There was a time when Andersen was accepted as a writer of great literary distinction both in Britain and in America, and it is an interesting fact that the first extensive biography was written by an Englishman, R. Nisbet Bain, whose *Life of Andersen* was published in 1895, ten years before the publication of the first Danish biography of Andersen.

It is also true that in this century there have been and still are people, both in Britain and America, who have taken and take Andersen seriously; they include Hilaire Belloc, G. K. Chesterton, E. V. Lucas, Robert Lynd, M. R. James, Hugh Walpole, Walter de la Mare, W. H. Auden, J. B. Priestley, Sir Michael Redgrave and Mrs Queenie Leavis; there have also been some good twentieth-century translators and some excellent illustrators. But the fact remains that most people in the English-speaking world are still surprised to hear that among his countrymen (as indeed in many other parts of the world) Andersen is considered a very great writer whose appeal is as great to adults as it is to children, in some cases even more so, and that he is not only a great master of style but also a great humorist.

This book falls into two parts, a biography of Andersen ending with an attempt at a characterization of his complex personality, and a discussion and critical appreciation of his fairy tales and stories, on which his claim to world fame is based. Andersen's novels, poems and other creative writings are discussed in the chronological context of the biography proper.

Elias Bredsdorff
Cambridge, 1974

for Anne Lise

In Sweden we don't say Hans Christian, we say Andersen, that's all, for we only know one Andersen, and that is Andersen. He is the Andersen of our parents, our childhood, our manhood and our old age. . . . I can remember a little quarto volume printed in Gothic type; I remember the woodcuts, the willow tree that went with 'The Tinder Box', 'The Top and the Ball', 'The Steadfast Tin Soldier', 'Willie Winkie', 'The Snow Queen' and the rest of them. And as I read and when I had finished, my life became embittered. This horrible everyday life with its bad temper and injustice, this dreary monotonous existence in a nursery where we young plants grew up too close together and pushed and squabbled for food and privileges – I suddenly found it all unbearable, for in Andersen's world of fairy tale I had learnt of the existence of another world, a golden age of justice and pity in which parents really fondled their children and did not just pull them by the hair, in which something I had never known before threw a rosy gleam over even poverty and meekness: that gleam which is known by the now obsolete name of LOVE.

It was Orpheus that he called to mind – this poet who sang in prose so that, not only animals, plants and stones listened and were moved, but toys came to life, goblins and elves became real, those horrible schoolbooks seemed poetic; why, he squeezed the whole geography of Denmark into four pages – he was a perfect wizard!

August Strindberg

Part one: Andersen

1 The swamp plant

1805-19

'MY LIFE is a beautiful fairy tale, rich and happy.' These are the opening words of *Mit Livs Eventyr*, Hans Christian Andersen's final autobiography, written for the whole world to read, and they are the underlying motif in all his autobiographical writings. For Andersen saw – and wished to see – his life as a romantic tale:

If, when I was a small boy, poor and lonely going out into the world, I had met a powerful fairy godmother and she had said, 'Choose your own course through life and your own destination, then I shall protect you and lead you according to the development of your mind and the way things must reasonably work out in this world', then my fate could not have been a happier one, nor more cleverly and well guided than it has been. The wonderful story of my life will say to the world what it says to me: that there is a loving God who directs all things for the best.

God, then, in Andersen's memoirs has been allocated the role of the fairy godmother responsible for leading this male Cinderella along the path from poverty to universal recognition and fame.

Poverty, yes, indeed! Andersen never disguised his background, although he was always eager to emphasize the respectable and almost idyllic character of his childhood home. He went out of his way to explain to the world that it was only accident and bad luck that had prevented his ancestors from rising to that higher class in society to which, in his opinion, they really belonged.

His first autobiographical sketch, known as *Levnedsbogen*, written in 1832 when he was twenty-seven, opens with the following statement:

My grandparents were well-to-do farmers on Funen. They suffered misfortune, the cattle were taken ill, the crop was a failure, my grandfather had *idées fixes*, became insane, though in a mild degree, and moved with his wife to Odense. My father was their only son, he was considered very bright and some of the wealthy citizens of the town offered his parents help in order to enable him to study; this was what he himself would have liked, but they did not like the idea, and his father insisted that he should learn the cobbler's trade. . . .

As soon as he had become a journeyman, when no more than twenty, he married my mother, a poor girl who preferred him to a rich distiller with whom she then served, or had served. They owned nothing at all but were very much in love with one another; they needed a bridal bed but the money did not stretch that far; a nobleman had recently died in the town, he was lying in state, a large wooden raised platform covered with black cloth carried the coffin, and when later there was an auction my father bought this platform, and being good with his hands, since he had amused himself as a boy dabbling in carpentry, he made a bridal bed out of this bed of state. (The fact that it was not all that gloriously made is proved by my remembering it having black borders of cloth at the bottom, for in the transformation these had not been removed.)

Where the nobleman's body had been lying in state, rich but dead, there lay the following year (on 2 April), poor but alive, a newborn poet, i.e. MYSELF, and it seems to me that there is really something poetic in this fact. I was very tiny, cried badly in the church when I was baptized, and the disgruntled parson became my first critic to indulge in personalities, for he is said to have called me 'a kitten'.

The factual information Andersen gives in his autobiographies about his parents and their background is very limited. He does tell his readers that his mother was 'some years older than her husband'. The latter is described as 'a strangely gifted person, a truly poetic nature', unhappy in his profession and frustrated by not having been allowed to attend a grammar school. He was a melancholy dreamer, fond of reading; among the books he owned were Ludvig Holberg's comedies and the *Arabian Nights*. His mother Andersen described as 'ignorant about life and the world, but with a kind and loving heart', and he makes it clear that she was extremely superstitious, unlike her husband who called himself a free-thinker.

His maternal grandparents are hardly mentioned, but he does say that as a little girl his mother had been sent out by her parents to beg, and finding herself unable to do so had sat weeping under a bridge for a whole day.

He is much more forthcoming about his paternal grandparents; they are the ones described above as having once been well-to-do farmers but later reduced to poverty by a number of tragic accidents, as a result of which his grandfather became insane. They lived in Odense 'in a house they had bought with the last remnant of their fortune', and the old grandmother, 'a quiet and most lovable old woman with gentle blue eyes and a fine figure', looked after her insane husband, who would occasionally go into the woods and come back decorated with beech leaves and garlands of flowers and walk through the streets of Odense singing at the top of his voice, the laughing-stock of the street urchins of the town. In *Mit Livs Eventyr* Andersen writes:

I was very much afraid of my mad grandfather. Only once did he ever speak to me, and then he made use of the formal pronoun *De*. He used to carve strange wooden figures, men with beasts' heads, animals with wings and wonderful birds; these he packed in a basket and then went into the country, where he was always well received by the peasant women, who gave him groats and ham to take home in return for the toys he gave them and their children. One day, when he was returning to Odense, I heard the boys in the street shouting after him; I hid myself behind a flight of stairs in terror while they rushed past, for I knew that I was of his flesh and blood.

As an old man, after he had lost his teeth, Andersen used to think he looked like his grandfather when he saw himself in a mirror.

A close examination of the facts uncovered after Andersen's death proves that much of what he told about his family background was pure fiction, though he may very well have believed some of it to be true; in certain respects he deliberately falsified his account (as so many autobiographers do), especially by omitting important information which, for obvious reasons, he wanted to keep from his readers.

It is therefore worth trying to establish the historical facts.

In 1805, when Hans Christian Andersen was born, Odense was the main town of Funen, the largest in Denmark after Copenhagen, with about five thousand inhabitants. It was a town of tremendous class differences, for although there were various groups of well-to-do citizens, such as the Funen nobility, army officers, civil servants, merchants and rich artisans, more than half the inhabitants belonged to the lower classes, and there was much severe poverty.[1] There were many fine houses, a medieval town hall, an ancient grammar school (or Latin School), a theatre after 1795, in which touring companies of actors performed, and a royal castle, built in 1720 and used as the official residence of the chief administrative officer of Funen; in 1816 Prince Christian Frederik (later King Christian the Eighth) moved there on his appointment as governor of Funen.

In the back streets and mews of Odense lived the many poor artisans, casual labourers, washerwomen, beggars and social outcasts, often in dire poverty. Social benefit was a concept almost unknown, though the more fortunate among the old people might be awarded a place in the Greyfriars Hospital. Criminals were put into Odense Gaol (*Odense Tugthus*) and the lunatics into the asylum.

Hans Christian Andersen was born in Odense on 2 April 1805, but nobody knows exactly where. He was born in wedlock, but only just. His parents' wedding took place two months before his birth, and they had only been engaged for a month. It seems probable that they did not have their own home until 1806; their names do not appear in the official register before then.

Hans Christian Andersen's father, whose full name was Hans Andersen, was a journeyman shoemaker, born in 1782. As a so-called *frimester* he belonged to the lowest class of artisans who were not admitted as members of the guilds and not entitled to employ anyone in their service. In 1781 his father, Anders Hansen Traes (*circa* 1751–1827), had married Anne Cathrine Nommensdatter (1745–1822), Hans Christian's grandmother. She seems to have been a pathological liar, and the pathetic story she told her grandson, that she and her husband had been reduced to poverty after having once been wealthy farmers, is pure invention. When and why Hans Christian's grandfather went mad we do not know, but we do know that before the couple moved to Odense he had been a poor village labourer and smallholder, and, like his son, worked for a time as a journeyman shoemaker. The grandmother's moving tale about her own maternal grandmother being a noblewoman of Kassel in Germany and eloping with an actor can also be dismissed as pure fabrication.[2]

Hans Christian Andersen's mother, whose maiden name was Anne Marie Andersdatter, was born about 1775, so she was probably twenty-nine or thirty when her son was born. Before she married she had been a servant in several Odense houses, and it is not quite true to say that she was 'ignorant about life and the world', for in 1799 she had given birth to an illegitimate daughter, whose father was a potter and grenadier by the name of Rosenvinge, a man who had previously fathered several other illegitimate children. Her mother, about whom Andersen is very reticent in his autobiographies, was called Anne Sørensdatter (*circa* 1745–1825). Before her eventual marriage to a tailor (an ex-convict) in 1783, she produced three illegitimate children: Anne Marie (Andersen's mother), born *circa* 1775, Christiane (his aunt), born 1778, and another daughter, born 1781, who died in infancy. In 1783 she was sent to prison for a week as a punishment for having given birth three times to illegitimate children. After her marriage she had a fourth child, who died shortly afterwards. When her husband died in 1790 she married a glove maker of thirty, and they lived in Odense until 1804, when they moved to another town on Funen, Bogense, where she died in 1825.

Hans Christian Andersen's aunt, Christiane (1778–1830), is believed to have gone to Copenhagen in 1799; in 1806 Andersen's mother was able to supply the poor-law inspector with the meagre information that she lived in Copenhagen, but whether she was married or unmarried she did not know. In his earliest autobiography Andersen says that he remembered this aunt coming back to visit them when he was a small child; she gave him a silver coin. His mother scolded her for showing off her riches and finery, and after that the two sisters were not on speaking terms. When the fourteen-year-old Hans Christian met his aunt in Copenhagen in 1819 she was running a brothel.

Andersen's half-sister Karen Marie Rosenvinge, who was six years older than he, is not even mentioned in the autobiographies. During a census held in 1801 she was reported to be living with her maternal grandmother in Odense, and it is unlikely that she ever lived with her mother and stepfather; only in that sense is Andersen correct when he states categorically that he was 'an only child'. She appears in the church register as having been confirmed at Odense in 1814, and she left for Copenhagen in the autumn of 1822. Andersen did his utmost to prevent anybody from ever knowing that he had a half-sister – 'my mother's daughter', as he called her.

In a candid letter to a friend who knew him and his background better than most, Andersen once described himself as a 'swamp plant'. It is a valid description. Andersen's background was, from a social point of view, the lowest of the low: grinding poverty, slums, immorality and promiscuity. His grandmother was a pathological liar, his grandfather insane, his mother ended by becoming an alcoholic, his aunt ran a brothel in Copenhagen, and for years he was aware that somewhere a half-sister existed who might suddenly turn up and embarrass him in his new milieu – a thought which haunted his life and dreams.

The mad grandfather and the beloved grandmother appear, usually idealized, in some of the tales (the grandfather for instance in 'Holger the Dane' and the grandmother in 'The Little Match Girl'); his parents may be recognized in many of his novels and tales (especially in 'Old Johanna's Tale' and in the story 'She was no good', his finest tribute to his mother). Even his sister Karen Marie, whose very existence he did his utmost to conceal from the world, still appears in some of his more important works, for instance in the novel *O. T.*, and in 'The Red Shoes', and 'The Girl Who Trod on the Loaf'. He often idealized the brother-sister relationship; one only has to think of Gerda and Kay in 'The Snow Queen':

In the middle of the town – where there are so many houses and people that there isn't room for everyone to have a little garden of his own, so most of them have to be content with flowers in flower-pots – there lived two poor children who did have a garden a bit larger than a flower-pot. They weren't brother and sister, but they were just as fond of each other as if they had been.

This is Andersen's way of compensating for the lack of love he felt for his sister Karen Marie: to invent a dream sister in a dream Odense.

Though nobody knows exactly where Hans Christian Andersen was born we do know where he spent most of his childhood; from his second to his fourteenth year he lived in a tiny house in Munkemøllestræde in Odense. In *Mit Livs Eventyr* he describes it in these words:

One single little room, almost completely taken up with the shoemaker's bench, the bed and the couch on which I slept, was my childhood home. But there were pictures hanging on the walls, and there were beautiful cups, glasses and knick-knacks on the chest of drawers, and above the bench, by the window, was a shelf full of books and poems. In the tiny kitchen, above the food cupboard, was a rack full of pewter plates. That little room seemed big and rich to me, and the door, whose panels were decorated with landscape paintings, meant to me as much as an entire picture gallery does today.

Most of the pleasures and excitements of his early childhood did not have to be paid for: excursions to the woods with his parents each year in May, when his mother put on her cotton dress, otherwise only used when she received holy communion; watching the traditional processions held by the local guilds through the streets of Odense; flautists and drummers welcoming the New Year with loud music in the streets; the beginning of Lent celebrated by the local butchers driving a big ox, decorated with flower garlands and with a little cupid mounted on its back, through the streets. After Whitsuntide there was popinjay shooting on the moors outside the town; and on Midsummer Eve Hans Christian used to go to a holy spring to fetch water for his parents.

His mother was a primitive, illiterate woman, with many superstitious ideas and practices, which she tried to pass on to her son. Sprigs of St John's-wort were stuck into the chinks of the beams to enable you to see whether your life would be long or short.[3] The boy was afraid of the dark, and terrified of walking past a churchyard. Occasionally he had to fetch buttermilk from a place near a demolished convent on a hill outside the town, and he knew this place to be haunted because a strange light came from it; only when he had crossed the river did he feel safe, for trolls and evil spirits cannot cross over water.

One of Andersen's earliest recollections in 1808, when he was only three, was seeing Spanish soldiers in the streets of Odense. In March of that year

Denmark, as an ally of Napoleon, had declared war on Sweden, and French and Spanish auxiliary troops under the command of Marshal Bernadotte were on their way via Denmark to Sweden. As a grown-up Andersen still remembered 'the almost black-brown men', the noise they made in the streets, and cannons being fired in the market-place and in front of the bishop's palace. He also remembered how one day a Spanish soldier picked him up and pressed a silver coin he was wearing round his neck against the boy's lips – to the horror and disgust of his mother, who strongly disapproved of this 'Roman Catholic nonsense'. On another occasion he saw a Spanish soldier being taken away to be executed for having murdered a French soldier.

From his earliest childhood he was impressed by the terrifying mystique surrounding Odense Gaol, not far from his childhood home. He describes how he was once taken there by his parents, who knew the porter, and how he was in a state of nervous excitement because the gates had to be unlocked to let them in and were then locked behind them. During the meal they were waited on by two prisoners, and the boy heard, or thought he could hear, the sound of the spinning-wheel and singing from the prison cells.

Another fascination was the garden of the old people's asylum known as Greyfriars Hospital, in which his beloved grandmother worked. Sometimes when she burned dead leaves and weeds she would take her grandson inside the enclosed area where the harmless lunatics walked about freely, and he was both excited and terrified at seeing the patients at close quarters. On one occasion he even ventured into the corridor leading to the cells where the dangerous patients were locked up, and peeping through a gap in a door he saw a naked woman sitting on some straw, her hair hanging down over her shoulders; she was singing in a loud voice, when suddenly she got up and with a wild scream rushed towards the door through which he was watching. The door was locked, but the little hatch for food flew open, and she stretched out her arms towards the terrified boy, who was half dead with terror when the attendant nurse came to fetch him.

In another part of the hospital, where the old female paupers had their spinning-room, he felt more at home. He could impress the simple-minded old women by entertaining them with improvised lectures on human anatomy and other subjects on which his ignorance was only surpassed by theirs. He was flattered and happy when they declared him to be a genius and exclaimed that such a clever child could not have very long to live.

He was obviously a very precocious child, and spoilt by his mother and grandmother, who encouraged him to believe that he was different from all other children. In two of his autobiographies Andersen describes his mother taking him out one day during the harvest season with some others to glean. An angry bailiff came running after them with a dog whip; Hans Christian could not run away quickly enough, and when the bailiff lifted his whip to strike him he exclaimed reproachfully, 'How dare you hit me when God can see it?' According to this story (which does not appear in the more reliable *Levnedsbogen*, and may well be apocryphal or at least somewhat embellished) the bailiff's expression suddenly changed, and he patted him on the head,

asked what his name was and even gave him some money. When Hans
Christian showed the money to his mother she told all and sundry that her son
was a strange and remarkable boy, 'Everybody is good to him. Even the
wicked bailiff gave him money!'

In a letter to his benefactor Jonas Collin, written in March 1825 shortly
before his twentieth birthday, Andersen wrote:

*From as early as I can remember, reading was my only and my dearest occupation; my
parents were poor, but my father was very fond of reading and therefore had some books,
which I swallowed. I never played with the other boys, I was always alone.*

A boy with no playmates, who spent most of his time indoors, reading books,
playing with all sorts of pictures, home-made toys, puppets and dolls – this is
the picture Andersen gives of himself in all his memoirs. He liked sitting at
home on a summer's day in the tiny courtyard protected by a 'tent' made out
of his mother's apron stretched from the wall over a broom-handle. Here he
could sit for hours, gazing at the leaves of the solitary gooseberry bush in the
yard, or making dresses for his dolls.

Although his parents were poor, Hans Christian must have been about five
when he was first sent to school. An old crone who was in charge of an infant
school taught him to read and to spell (though he never learnt to spell properly
and if he had lived in our time he would probably have been dubbed dyslectic).
Spelling was done by the whole class in a loud chorus. The school-teacher sat
in a high-backed chair, ready to use the birch whenever a child made a mistake
or misbehaved. Before sending her son to this school Hans Christian's mother
had made it a firm condition that he was not under any circumstances to be
subjected to corporal punishment, and so when one day the teacher did hit him
he immediately got up, took his book and left. His mother backed him up, and
he was sent instead to a school for Jewish children, most of them boys. Finding
it much easier to get on with girls he made friends with a little Jewish girl, Sara,
whose ambition it was to be a dairymaid in a manor house. Generously, Hans
Christian assured her that he would take her on in his own castle when he
grew up and became rich, and he was annoyed when she laughed at him. To
prove that he was serious he drew a sketch of his imaginary castle and told her
that he was really a changeling, belonging to a noble family, and that angels
came to talk to him when he was alone. Sara looked at him strangely and said
to one of the other boys, 'He's mad, just like his grandfather!' Hans Christian
was shocked and terrified at her reaction – their friendship was never the same
again.

The school closed in about 1811, and he was then sent to a third school,
which was open to the children of parents who could not otherwise afford to
send them to school. Housed in an old building, whose walls were decorated
with biblical paintings, the school taught reading, writing and arithmetic, but
the teaching seems to have been poor. Andersen later boasted that he very
rarely did his home-work until he was actually on his way to school, a fact
which his mother saw as yet another proof of his natural genius. The schoolmaster was a Norwegian by the name of Welhaven, who seems to have had a

certain talent for making the Old Testament stories come alive. Listening to the stories of Moses and Abraham, Hans Christian looked at the wall-paintings and lost himself in dreams and fantasies. He was often reproached for his lack of concentration but was otherwise the teacher's darling. Later in life he could claim that as a child he had never had a fight with anyone, but his relationship with the other boys was not very happy. He could not help inventing strange stories in which he himself invariably played the hero's part, whereupon they all laughed at him. The other boys in Odense also teased him on his way home from school. They would call out mockingly, 'Look, there's the playwright!' In his memoirs Andersen recalls: 'I went home and hid in a corner, cried and prayed to God.'

I was a very quiet child, never went out into the street to play with the other children; I only liked the company of little girls. I still remember a beautiful little girl of about eight who kissed me and told me she wanted to marry me; this pleased me, and I always allowed her to kiss me though I never kissed her, and I allowed no one else apart from her to kiss me. I felt a strange dislike for grown-up girls, or for girls of more than twelve; they really made me shudder; in fact, I used the expression about anything which I did not like touching that it was very 'girlish'.

Andersen's father plays an important part in his childhood recollections. He remembered him carrying him home from the country on his shoulders one summer's evening during a terrific storm, and reading aloud to him in the evenings from his favourite books, Holberg's plays and the *Arabian Nights*. He also made various toys for his son, including a toy theatre and a device whereby pictures changed into other pictures when a cord was pulled.

The rationalistic and sceptical shoemaker and his ignorant and superstitious wife must have made a striking contrast. He often read the Bible, but his comments used to horrify her. The boy remembered his father once closing the Bible with the words: 'Christ was a human being like the rest of us, but an unusual one!' and how shocked his mother was at hearing this; she burst into tears, and Hans Christian himself prayed to God to forgive his father for such blasphemy. It may have been this particular incident Andersen referred to when, as an old man, he told a young friend that once, after his father had declared himself to be an atheist, his mother was in such a state that she took her son into the wood-shed, where she threw an apron over him – presumably to shield him from evil spirits – saying, 'It was the Devil who was in our house and said this, it wasn't your father, and you must forget what he said, for he did not mean it.' Then they cried a little and said the Lord's Prayer together.[4]

On another occasion he heard his father saying, 'There is no other devil than the one we have in our hearts!' The cobbler was therefore regarded as a lost soul by his wife. Andersen says in his memoirs that when one morning his father woke up and found some scratches on his arm, both his wife and the neighbour's wife categorically declared that these were Satan's doings because Mr Andersen did not believe in the Devil. The true version of this story is probably the one which, again as an old man, Andersen told the same young friend, and according to which the scratches appeared on his father's dead body; Andersen's mother pointed to them and said, 'Look, Christian! The Devil grabbed him because he said those words about Christ.'

Sometimes an old woman from the hospital came to visit Mrs Andersen to be given some left-over food. She was looked upon with awe by Mrs Andersen, who regarded her as a 'wise woman' or even 'a witch', but her husband just laughed at her, thinking the woman a fraud. One day this woman was asked to tell Hans Christian's fortune. 'It will be better than he deserves,' she is reputed to have said; 'he will be a wild bird, flying high up and being grand. One day the town of Odense will be illuminated in his honour.' In spite of his father's scepticism Hans Christian was pleased, of course, and his mother was even more delighted and fully convinced that the old woman was right.[5]

Another story about Andersen's parents, also hearsay, is that once his mother, who had been out washing for a wealthy Odense family, came rushing home and told her husband that the son, just returned with a degree in theology from Copenhagen University, had tried to seduce her and had offered her a handsome sum of money. 'What did you do, then?' her husband asked, with clenched fists and a threatening expression. 'I ran away as quickly as I could,' she replied; 'I swear by Jesus Christ that I did. I ran straight back to you.' As an afterthought she added, 'But it certainly was a lot of money!' Hans Christian's father raised his fists and shouted, 'And such a one is going to be a parson – him a parson!'

On the whole his father seems to have kept himself very much to himself. Though he appears to have suffered from occasional depressions he was nevertheless very devoted to his son and insisted that the boy must never be forced to do anything he did not like. He was fond of walking in the country, either alone or with his son, and according to a story told in *Mit Livs Eventyr*, he had once hoped to be appointed shoemaker to one of the manor houses on Funen, a job which would have given him the advantage of having a cottage of his own, with a little garden and pasture for a cow. To prove his competence he had to make a pair of dancing shoes for the lady of the manor, who had supplied him with the necessary silk material. With great expectations Hans Andersen set off with the finished pair of shoes, but returned very angry: the gracious lady had rejected the shoes and complained that he had ruined her good silk. 'If you have wasted your silk, then I'll be content to waste my leather,' the cobbler is said to have replied, slashing the leather soles.

Meanwhile the war was raging in Germany, my father eagerly read the newspapers. Napoleon was his idol; we were the allies of the French; the troops marched off; he could not stay at home, he wanted to see Napoleon, he wanted to go to the war. The allied countries had also to join the war, he volunteered to enlist in the army as an ordinary soldier, convinced that he would be promoted in the war.

These are Andersen's words in *Levnedsbogen*. The truth is somewhat different.

In the spring of 1812 Hans Andersen enlisted as a musketeer, after having been offered a considerable sum of money to take the place of a farmer who was keen to get out of the army. Financial gain seems therefore to have played a greater part than any idealistic enthusiasm for Napoleon, though there was undoubtedly also an element of love of adventure behind the cobbler's decision. Hans Christian was in bed with measles when his father left home for the barracks. His mother, who did not like the army, cried bitterly after her husband had kissed the boy a passionate good-bye. The old grandmother was so miserable that she told Hans Christian that it would be a blessing were he to die at once, but God's will was always the best. 'It was one of the first mornings of real sorrow I can remember,' writes Andersen.

The regiment in which Hans Andersen had enlisted did not get further than Holstein; then peace was declared, and in January 1814 the shoemaker returned to his workshop in Odense. But his health had suffered and he only lived a few more years. Towards the end he was delirious and talked wildly of war and marching and Napoleon, from whom he thought he was receiving orders. In *Levnedsbogen* Andersen describes it in these words:

One morning he was feverish, had strong fantasies, spoke about Napoleon and wars; my mother could not think of anything better than to send me out to a so-called 'wise woman' at Eiby, a few miles from the town. She promised to come but first made some magic tricks, tied a woollen thread round my wrist and gave me a leaf of what she called 'the tree from which Christ's cross was made'. 'But will my poor father die?' I asked in tears. 'If he does,' she replied, 'then you will meet his ghost on your way home.'

When the boy reported to his mother that he had met no ghost on his way home she was reassured. But all the same, his father died two days later.

His corpse was left lying on the bed, and I slept on the floor with my mother; a cricket chirped throughout the night. 'He's dead already,' my mother told it. 'You needn't call him: the Ice Maiden has taken him,' and I understood what she meant. I remembered the previous winter when our window-panes were frozen over; my father had shown us a figure on one of the window-panes like that of a maid stretching out both her arms. 'She must have come to fetch me,' he said in fun; and now that he lay dead on his bed my mother remembered this, and his words occupied my thoughts.

Hans Andersen died on 26 April 1816, when his son was eleven. He was buried in a pauper's grave. Andersen remembered the funeral:

I walked closely behind the coffin, saw the parson at Saint Canute's Church throw sand on it, I was very sad. At home my mother sat wailing; only my old grandmother sat quietly, with wet eyes; she did not even sigh, but there was a strange suffering in her pale face which struck me, even though I was only a child.

After this he was left to himself even more than before. His mother went out as a washerwoman, while he stayed at home alone, playing with his toy theatre, sewing dresses for his dolls and reading plays. People told him later that he was tall and lanky, his hair was thick and of a light golden colour, and he always went bare-headed and usually wore wooden shoes.

His interest in the theatre was awakened early by the existence of the local theatre, which had a capacity of about 400; he·was first taken there by his parents, when only seven, to see comic operas and *Singspiele*, including

Ferdinand Knauer's *Das Donauweibchen* (The Little Lady of the Danube), and Holberg's *The Political Tinker* in a German vaudeville version. He collected theatre bills from the Odense Theatre and made friends with the man who carried them, Peter Junker. He supplied him daily with bills for distribution in his own neighbourhood, in return for which he was allowed to keep one for himself. At home he studied the list of characters and cast and let his imagination run riot. 'This was my first unconscious imaginative creation,' Andersen later wrote. In the previously quoted letter to Jonas Collin, his benefactor, he wrote in March 1825:

From the day I saw the first play my entire soul was burning for this art. I still remember how I could sit for days completely alone in front of the mirror, with an apron over my shoulders instead of a knight's cloak, playing Das Donauweibchen, *and that in German, though I hardly knew five German words. I soon learned entire Danish plays by heart (for then I found it very easy to learn things by heart), and I also began to write plays (my good mother scolded me properly for it, for she was afraid that all these commotions might make me mad).*

Like the German word *Dichter* the Danish word *Digter* has a much wider meaning than 'poet'. A *Digter* is a creative writer, and there is an element of artistic distinction linked to the word; all the romantic ideas of divine calling are embodied in it. Andersen first heard the word *Digter* being pronounced with awe, as if it were a holy profession, by a Miss Bunkeflod, who lived with her sister-in-law, the widow of a minor Danish poet, in the same neighbourhood as Andersen's parents. 'My brother, the *Digter*,' Miss Bunkeflod said with shining eyes. And in the home of these two ladies Andersen began to understand what a great thing it was to be a *Digter*; Miss Bunkeflod herself wrote comic verse and inspired the boy to write a few poems of his own, one about a field outside Odense, and another one called 'The Clouds'. Neither of these survive. He made the Bunkeflod house his second home, read aloud to Miss Bunkeflod and sang ballads and ditties for her. In return she lent him books; he read melodramas based on the stories of Ariadne and Medea, and J. H. Wessel's mock-heroic tragedy entitled *Love without Stockings*, at the end of which the stage is littered with corpses. He tried writing a play himself, and as he thought it had to end with universal death he was in great doubt as to how to kill off all the characters. An old Danish ballad about Pyramus and Thisbe supplied him with the plot for his tragedy, which he called *Abor og Elvira*. He introduced a hermit and his son, both of whom were in love with the heroine, and both of whom committed suicide when she died; the hermit's lines were more or less copied from the explanatory comments in Luther's catechism. He read his play to everybody and was deeply hurt when the neighbour's wife scornfully said that instead of *Abor og Elvira* it ought to be called *Aborre og Torsk* ('Perch and Cod'). But his mother consoled him: 'She only says that because her son didn't write it.'

A little later Hans Christian also began to read Shakespeare, though in a bad translation, which he borrowed from a lady in Odense who owned several books, and to whom he had introduced himself in order to borrow from her library. Among the plays were *King Lear* and *Macbeth*. They inspired him to begin writing another play, among whose characters were a king and a princess; but assuming that persons of that standing could hardly be expected to speak ordinary Danish he made inquiries to try and find out something about the language of royalty. No king had visited Odense for many years, but someone suggested that such people probably conversed in foreign tongues. By means of a multi-lingual dictionary Hans Christian managed to compose a 'royal language', based on a mixture of German, French, English and Danish; so the princess greeted her royal father, 'Guten Morgen, mon père! Har De godt sleeping?' Again he pestered everybody he knew by reading his play aloud to them.

Sometimes Hans Christian's acting so alarmed his mother that she had to tell him to stop, for at times even she thought he must be mad. When he performed an entire pantomime-ballet for her she threatened to send him as an apprentice to the Italian tight-rope walker Guiseppe Casortis, who was appearing in Odense in the winter of 1814–15, telling him that he would be fed on nothing but cod-liver oil to make his limbs lithe. But the boy was delighted with the idea, for there was nothing he would have liked better than to be a tight-rope walker. She had to threaten him instead with a spanking if he did not 'stop all that nonsense'.

In the summer of 1818 Andersen did see a real live king, when Frederik VI paid a visit to Odense. Astride a church wall he saw the King of Denmark drive past, but he was disappointed to find that he was dressed only in a blue cloak with a red velvet collar; he had expected him to be clad in a sumptuous costume of gold and silver.

Throughout his life Andersen was fond of singing, and he seems to have had a very beautiful singing voice as a boy. In *Levnedsbogen* he writes:

The peculiar tendency of my whole nature in comparison with other children in my social position, my zest for reading and my beautiful voice drew the attention of other people towards me. On a summer's evening I used to sit in my parents' tiny garden, which went right down to the river; on the other side water was rushing down the mill-wheel, among the elder trees I could see as far as Nuns' Hill, from which I was separated by the water – and consequently also from the trolls; over in the mill men ran up and down, and farmers drove over the bridge; in short, it was like a beautiful painting. Mr Falbe's garden was the one next to my parents', and nearby was the old Saint Canute's Church. While the church bells were ringing in the evening I sat in my curious reverie, looking at the mill-wheel and singing my improvised songs. Often the guests in Mr Falbe's garden used to listen; I often sensed the existence of an audience behind the fence and was flattered. This was how I became known, and people began to send for me to hear 'the little Funen Nightingale' as they called me.

After her husband's death Mrs Andersen was so poor that even she felt that her son should help her by earning money. The neighbour's boy went to work at a local cloth-mill, and Mrs Andersen suggested that her son might do the same. He did not like the idea: 'I always read stories, was very soft, cried my heart out at the story of Christ's sufferings and at reading about poor patient

Helen, whose hands were cut off and who was put to sea in a little boat. I wasn't suited at all to be put among other wild boys and girls.'

His grandmother entirely agreed. On the first day he went to work she saw him to the entrance of the cloth-mill, wept and kissed him at the gate, saying, 'this would not have happened if your father had been alive'.

The apprenticeship at the cloth-mill did not last long, though it began reasonably well. In spite of the rough atmosphere and the obscene jokes of the – mostly German – journeymen, the new apprentice made himself popular straight away by his singing. While Hans Christian sang, the other apprentices were working at more uncongenial jobs. When he had exhausted his repertoire he recited extracts from Holberg and acted scenes from Shakespeare to the astonished workmen. The next day he was told to do some work, which he did clumsily and badly. He blushed whenever the men began to tell dirty stories or sing obscene songs, and eventually began to cry. Having previously commented on his fine soprano voice some of the men grabbed him, calling out that he must be a girl, held him up and took off his trousers as if to convince themselves of his sex. Hans Christian struggled and screamed, and as soon as he was released ran straight back to his mother, who told him that he need never go back to the mill again.

After this he was sent to work at a tobacco factory, a modest firm which employed only one adult and a few harmless boys:

I was surrounded by tobacco plants, saw chewing tobacco and snuff being made, and was well treated myself. Here my voice also made me a success; people came into the factory to hear me sing, and yet the funny thing was that I did not know a single song properly, but I improvised both the text and the tune, and both were complicated and difficult. 'He ought to go on to the stage,' they all said, and I began to get ideas of that kind. Meanwhile I was taken ill, and my mother thought that it might be the tobacco which affected my chest, which it wasn't, however, for I have always had good lungs; so she removed me once again, saying that she was afraid I might die from it.

Once again the boy was left to himself, an eleven-year-old, so fair that he looked almost like an albino and with such small, half-closed eyes, that people sometimes thought he was blind. His appetite for books grew insatiable; and he began reading the lives of great and famous men. They made a great impression on him and increased his longing to become such a one himself.

In July 1818 Mrs Andersen, who was now over forty and had been a widow for two years, remarried. Her second husband was another journeyman shoe-maker; he was called N. J. Gundersen and only thirty-one. Andersen later described his stepfather:

He was in every respect different from my father and as far as character and mental development were concerned completely corresponded to my mother. He treated me well but would have no say in my education so that no one should be able to say that he was an 'evil stepfather', and consequently everything basically remained the same for me, following the same pattern as before. Only my poor old grandmother became more or less a stranger in our house; I was the bond which kept her there, and

I often cried with grief at her silent suffering, for she had suddenly turned old with sorrow.

In a month her hair had turned white, Andersen tells us.

Hans Christian Andersen was thirteen when he was formally entered for confirmation in Saint Canute's Church at Odense. This involved a choice, for there were two clergymen at the church who held preparatory classes, Dean Tetens and a curate, the Reverend Viberg. It was, however, more or less an unwritten law that Dean Tetens took the well-to-do children, whereas the curate took those from the slums. Hans Christian would normally have belonged in the curate's class, but being highly ambitious he went straight to the Dean and asked to be accepted in his.

Tetens could not refuse to accept me, and yet I am now fully aware, from small incidents which I remember, that he did not like the idea of me mixing with children of a class above my own; indeed, after I had recited one evening at Mr Andersen's, the chemist, some scenes from Holberg at a time when I was still attending the dean's classes, he called me to see him privately and severely upbraided me for what he considered unsuitable at such a time, and he threatened me that if I did not do my home-work properly he would expel me from his class.

Several prominent people in Odense began to take an interest in Hans Christian Andersen, including a Lieutenant Colonel C. Høegh-Guldberg, who took him to Odense Castle to introduce him to Prince Christian to whom he had previously mentioned him. 'If the prince asks you what you would like to do,' the colonel said, 'then you should say that you would like to become a student.' Having heard of the boy's talents Prince Christian asked to see proof of them, so Hans Christian acted a few scenes from a Holberg play and sang an improvised song. When the prince asked him what he wanted to do he naïvely replied that *he was supposed to say* that he would like to become a student but that *his real desire* was to become an actor or a singer. Prince Christian did not approve of this and told him that coming as he did from a poor home he ought to take up a good trade, for instance as a turner, and that he could help him in this. But the suggestion did not appeal to Hans Christian.

He was confirmed on 18 April 1819, shortly after his fourteenth birthday. This is his description in *Levnedsbogen*:

At Easter I went through the confirmation ceremony, and I was given the first pair of boots I had ever worn. A brown overcoat of my late father's was made into a smock for me by a woman; I considered myself to look extremely nice. In order that everybody should see that I was wearing boots I put my trouser legs inside the boots, and I was ever so proud as I stood there. My heart was beating with a holy awe towards God; I was innocent and pious, and yet a lot of worldly thoughts went through my mind, about my creaking boots, about my big shirt-frill; I thought they were ugly, sinful thoughts and asked God not to be angry with me.

His future had now to be decided, because boys of his class were expected to start working as soon as they had been confirmed. His mother wanted him to be apprenticed to a tailor or a bookbinder, but he wept and told her of the

many famous men of humble origin about whom he had read, and begged her
to allow him to go to Copenhagen to become an actor. He wanted to be
famous, he told his mother, and he knew the recipe for progress from poverty
to fame. 'First you go through terrible suffering, and then you become
famous.' He was convinced that for him the way to fame lay through Copenhagen, for there could be found the famous Royal Theatre where his histrionic
talents would soon be appreciated.

During the previous year his mania for the theatre had steadily increased.
In June 1818 a troupe of actors, actresses and opera singers from the Royal
Theatre had performed some operettas and tragedies in Odense. It was a great
event which everybody talked about, and Hans Christian would have given
anything to obtain tickets, but he could not afford them. In desperation he
went in at the stage door and told some of the actors about his love for the
theatre. They arranged that he could come back-stage to watch, and since he
was also keen to take an active part they allowed him to appear as a page-boy
in the operetta *Cendrillon*, where he even had a line. 'I was always the first one
to be there,' he later wrote, 'put on the red silk costume, said my line and
imagined that the entire audience thought only of me.' After that he had only
one ambition – to go to Copenhagen's Royal Theatre, where they also performed something called *ballets*, which were supposed to be even more
wonderful than plays and operas.

In July 1819 an actress called Miss Hammer came to Odense, and a local
actor, whom Hans Christian had met, took him to see her; she received him
kindly and used him as a kind of *postillon d'amour* for her various love letters.
He confided to her his plan to go to Copenhagen.

His mother reminded him that he did not know a single soul in the capital
and had no one to help him if he got into trouble. Hans Christian in turn
recalled the wise woman's prophesy, and also quoted his father's dictum, that
he should not be forced to do anything he did not want to do. In the end his
mother could not resist, especially as she considered it highly probable that he
might regret this madness when he got as far as the coastal town of Nyborg.
'He'll come back when he sees the water,' she said to herself. His stepfather
refused to be involved. To Mrs Gundersen's relief Miss Hammer promised that
Hans Christian could travel to Copenhagen with her free of charge, and that
in Copenhagen she would introduce him to a friend of hers, Miss Didriksen,
who was a ballet dancer at the Royal Theatre. But week after week went by,
and when it became clear that Miss Hammer had incurred so many debts that
it was impossible for her to leave Odense it was decided that Hans Christian
should travel on his own. In the course of one year he had managed to save
thirteen rixdollars (one rixdollar corresponded to 2s. 3d.), and it seemed to
him a fortune.

Neighbours and others who heard of his crazy plan to leave Odense and go
to Copenhagen insisted that he ought to carry a letter of introduction to
someone in Copenhagen; but who could supply him with such a letter? He
remembered having heard that an old Odense printer, Mr Iversen, knew many
of the actors and actresses in Copenhagen, and though he had never met him

he called on him one Sunday afternoon. As might be expected the old printer tried to dissuade him from carrying out his idea; he ought to take up a trade. 'That would really be a great pity,' the boy is supposed to have replied, and when Mr Iversen realized that he was determined to go, he agreed to give him a letter of introduction to someone in the Royal Theatre. But to whom would he like it addressed? Having heard of Madame Schall, the leading dancer of the Royal Copenhagen ballet, Hans Christian suggested her name. Even though Mr Iversen had never met her he agreed to give the boy a letter. Hans Christian was now convinced that nothing could go wrong. In the world of fiction with which he was so familiar there was always a happy ending.

His mother wrapped up a bundle of clothes and arranged with the mail-coach driver for her son to go with him all the way to Copenhagen without paying, in return for a bribe of three rixdollars.

On 4 September 1819 Hans Christian Andersen left Odense. His mother saw him out to the town gate, where he was to be picked up by the coachman, and there the boy's old grandmother was waiting to say good-bye; without saying a word she looked at him with tears in her eyes. He never saw her again, for she died three years later. There was one passenger in the mail-coach whom his mother knew, if only by sight, a Mrs Hermansen, and she asked this woman to keep an eye on her son.

In *Levnedsbogen* Andersen describes his journey in these words:

Now I rolled into the world with ten rixdollars, for the coachman had been given three. I had never been more than a couple of miles that side of Odense, and the new and changing landscape soon made me happy. I came to Nyborg, saw the sea; only when the ship sailed away did I begin to feel oppressed; it was as if I was sailing into the wide, wide world. When I came to Korsør I went behind a house, fell down on my knees and asked God to help me, cried a lot but was then happy again and drove during the night through the towns, not suspecting when I came to Slagelse that some years later I would be attending the grammar school there.

On Monday morning 6 September 1819, the very day when the theatre season began, I saw Copenhagen for the first time. When at Frederiksberg I first saw the towers of Copenhagen, for which I had longed so much, I burst into tears, feeling that I had now no one left except God in Heaven.

2 Hard times

1819–22

COPENHAGEN was in a state of uproar when Andersen arrived. What at first he took to be the normal bustle in the streets was, in fact, something far more sinister; on 4 September 1819 anti-semitic riots had broken out in Copenhagen and several provincial towns. They went on for ten days, during which period the mob attacked Jewish shopkeepers and others of Jewish origin. The riots originated in Western Germany and had spread from there to Denmark. This was the last pogrom in Denmark and was later described by Andersen in his novel *Only a Fiddler*.

The mail-coach dropped its unofficial passenger on the outskirts of the city. Carrying his bundle of clothes Hans Christian had to walk into the city where he found accommodation in a cheap lodging-house near the Western Gate. On his way to his first destination, the Royal Theatre, he saw the riots at close quarters. He tells us how his heart was beating as he stood outside the theatre which had for so long played such an important part in his dreams. He walked round the building, trying to take it in properly from the outside, fully convinced that this was going to be his future 'home', which had not yet opened itself to him. As he stood outside the theatre gazing at it, he was approached by a ticket tout, who asked him if he wanted a ticket for the evening performance. Never having come across a ticket tout before, the boy thought he was being offered a free ticket by a kind and generous gentleman, and cheerfully said yes, he would certainly like to have a ticket. The tout asked him where in the theatre he wanted his seat, and Andersen replied that he would be grateful for whatever he was given, whereupon the tout was furious and called him names for having made fun of him. Shocked and horrified Andersen ran away.

On the following day he put on his best clothes, the ones used for the confirmation ceremony, including the shirt-frill and a hat which was so big that it almost covered his eyes; he also wore the new boots, with his trouser legs tucked inside. Thus attired he went on his first important mission, which was to call on Madame Schall, the solo dancer, to whom he had a letter from Mr Iversen. He knelt down on the landing outside her apartment before pulling the bell-cord, praying to God that he might find help and assistance within; and at that very moment a maidservant came walking up the stairs. Seeing the kneeling boy, she smiled and gave him a penny. Hans Christian, who considered himself very well dressed, was appalled at being taken for a beggar and tried to explain that he was *not* a beggar, but the girl just said 'Keep it!'

At last he was admitted to Madame Schall's apartment; she thought he was slightly off his head. She had never heard of Mr Iversen. And when she asked Hans Christian if it was true that he was good at acting he immediately offered to prove it by playing the part of the leading lady in *Cendrillon*, which play, although he had seen it twice in Odense, he had never read, nor had he learnt any of its tunes. To impress the dancer he chose a scene which included dancing; he took off his boots, and while improvising both text and tunes danced in his socks, using his big hat as a tambourine. Small wonder that Madame Schall thought him mad and wanted to get rid of him as soon as possible. She held out no hope for him, and when he burst into tears and urged on her his wish to join the theatre, the only thing she did was to offer him a free meal once in a while – an offer he never took up. As he left in tears, however, she did say something about asking Bournonville, the ballet master, if he could use him.

After another fruitless visit, this time to a well-known Danish writer and critic, Hans Christian presented himself at the office of the director of the Royal Theatre, Colonel F. von Holstein, who had already received a letter from Colonel Høegh-Guldberg. But Holstein could not hold out any hope for him either; he was ungainly and too thin, he said, to which the boy replied, 'Oh! if only you would employ me at a salary of a hundred rixdollars I would soon be fat.' This was not well received and he was told that the Royal Theatre only employed educated people. In despair Andersen asked if there might be an opening for him in the ballet. No, was the reply, no one was taken on before May, and even if he were accepted then, he would not initially receive any salary.

Things were looking very bad indeed, and Andersen went to ask the advice of Mrs Hermansen, the woman with whom he had travelled from Odense. She told him that he had better go back there as soon as possible; but he could not face the thought of ridicule if he returned home as a failure. He even contemplated suicide, but the knowledge that this was a mortal sin dissuaded him.

So far he had not even seen a play at the Royal Theatre, and so, though he had very little money left, on 16 September 1819 he bought a ticket in the gods and saw an operetta entitled *Paul and Virginie*. This is how he describes it in *Levnedsbogen*:

I was deeply moved by the play; it seemed to me that there was something similar to my situation in it. I thought Paul looked like me, and Virginie was to him what the Theatre was to me. So when in the second act Paul was torn away from Virginie I burst audibly into tears; this was like me whom they also wanted to separate from my beloved, namely the Theatre. The people sitting near me noticed my violent weeping, offered me some apples and spoke kindly to me. I thought they were such nice people all of them, was completely ignorant of the world, regarded them all as good and decent people, and therefore completely naïvely told the entire audience in the gods who I was, how I had travelled all the way over here, and how terrible it was that I could not get on to the stage, my fate being like Paul's down there. People looked at me in astonishment, and they whispered to one another. The happy ending of the play made an equally great impression on me: I was filled with courage and happiness and considered it impossible that I should not succeed.

Further visits to Colonel Holstein and Madame Schall were equally fruitless, nevertheless he was still firmly resolved not to go back to Odense. After paying his bill at the lodging-house he had only one rixdollar left, and so he bought a newspaper to see if anyone wanted a young boy. In the *Adresseavis* for 17 September he found an advertisement from a Mr Madsen, a Copenhagen joiner. Andersen went to see him, told him that he came from Odense and wanted to learn the joiner's trade and applied for the job without mentioning his fruitless efforts to become an actor. Mr Madsen wanted to see his birth certificate and also insisted on a reference from Odense; if and when these documents arrived he would take him on for a period of nine years and give him board, lodging, and clothes. Since Andersen was unable to produce the desired documents immediately, and since he was by now completely penniless Mr Madsen agreed, conditionally, to employ him at once, which would also give him a chance of seeing if he liked the work.

Next morning at six o'clock Andersen turned up at the workshop, along with several other boys and journeymen. But he was shocked and embarrassed at their language, and was teased for his prudishness. Before the day was over he was dissolved in tears and told Mr Madsen that he did not like the work and wanted to leave immediately.[6] Mr Madsen tried to persuade him to stay a little longer, but Andersen had made up his mind: he thought of going all the way back to Funen by boat in the hope that the ship would sink and he would be drowned.

But, of course, the ship might *not* sink, and then he would be the laughing-stock of everyone in Odense. He tells us that he was at his wits end and prayed to God for help. Then he remembered that in Odense people had admired his singing, and he had read in the papers that an Italian tenor called Giuseppe Siboni had recently been made head of the Royal Choir School. He found out Siboni's private address and went straight to his apartment, where he arrived at four o'clock in the afternoon, and, as on his first visit to Madame Schall, he knelt down on the landing outside Siboni's door, saying a prayer before ringing the bell.

Siboni's housekeeper answered the door and told him that Siboni was busy; there was a dinner-party going on. But Andersen was not so easily put off; he told her not only that he wanted Mr Siboni to employ him as a singer but also his entire life story. Apparently she was moved by this and went in to speak to her master, to whom she must have repeated the story, for after a while Siboni and all his guests came out into the hall to see this strange creature. Among them were two prominent Danes, C. E. F. Weyse, the composer, and Jens Baggesen, the poet. Andersen was taken into the drawing-room and asked to sing. He cheerfully accepted the invitation and sang an aria from a *Singspiel* he had heard in Odense, and he also recited some poems and a few scenes from a Holberg play. He was heartily applauded and felt certain that he had convinced everybody of his talent. 'I predict,' Baggesen is supposed to have said, 'that he will get somewhere.' To Andersen he added, 'But don't get too vain when the audience show their approval!' Siboni told Andersen to return another day, so that they could discuss his future. As he left, Andersen asked the housekeeper, who let him out, whether she thought that he would now be employed at the Royal Theatre as a singer; she said she did not know but that he would be well advised to call on Mr Weyse the next day for he had spoken the most sympathetically about him.

There is reason to believe that Andersen's visit to Siboni took place on 18 September, and on the following morning he went straight to Weyse's apartment. There he was told that Weyse had exploited the enthusiasm and sympathy shown by the guests at Siboni's dinner-party and had collected the sum of seventy rixdollars for Hans Christian Andersen. The money would be held in trust by Weyse, and from now on Andersen could collect ten rixdollars each month from him. Siboni had promised to give him free singing lessons, but since Siboni did not speak Danish Andersen would have to learn at least some elementary German. And here again Mrs Hermansen, Andersen's mail-coach acquaintance, proved a useful contact, for she put him in touch with a language teacher, who agreed to give him free German lessons.

Full of enthusiasm and optimism Andersen wrote his first letter home, which his mother proudly showed to everybody she knew.

As soon as Andersen had acquired a smattering of German, Siboni opened his house to him, sang some scales with him and gave him free meals in his house, where he spent most of the day, chatting with the maidservants and running errands for them. He was also occasionally allowed to attend the singing lessons which Siboni gave to members of the Royal Opera. He was terrified whenever Siboni flew into a rage; but in his broken Danish Siboni would tell him not to be afraid and gave him a few pence, saying, 'Wenig amüsieren!' with a kind smile.

Meanwhile Andersen had moved out of his lodging-house into a cheap room belonging to a Mrs Thorgesen, a midwife, who had inherited from her late husband a house in one of the least reputable streets in the centre of Copenhagen. Andersen had not the faintest idea that the street was famous for its prostitutes and brothels. The room Mrs Thorgesen let him was very small, unlit and off the kitchen.

While staying at Mrs Thorgesen's Andersen remembered that he had an aunt, his mother's sister Christiane, who was supposed to live somewhere in Copenhagen. True enough, she and his mother had quarrelled when he was a small boy, and since then there had been no contact between the two sisters. But she *was* after all his aunt, his one and only relative in Copenhagen, and he must have remembered having heard that she was now the widow of a rich sea-captain by the name of Jansen, for he did manage to find her address and went to see her. In *Levnedsbogen* he describes his visit to his aunt in these words:

The inside of her house was quite elegant, and she received me tolerably well, but she was very hard on my poor mother, whom, in the presence of a well-dressed lady in the room, she scolded for being uncivilized and coarse, and lacking in education, and she finished by saying, 'And look, after having behaved so badly towards me, she now saddles me with her child! And a boy at that – if only it had been a girl!' Shortly afterwards a gentleman entered; 'He's the young girl's sweetheart,' my aunt whispered and told me to follow her. We went up to the attic where she kept on talking about her income and said that I could come and see her once in a while. But the way in which she talked about my mother, and the presence of the young lady and her lover made a strange impression on me, and when I told Mrs Thorgesen about it I became horrified, because now I realized how my good aunt lived.

In Andersen's later autobiographies this story is missing, in fact there is no mention of the existence of his Aunt Christiane. Even in the first, from which the above quotation is taken, Andersen says that he cannot remember her name; he writes, 'I found out her address quite accidentally, and have never since been able to remember her name nor ever met her again; she has probably died by now.'[7]

Andersen only had his private singing lessons with Siboni once or twice a month, and one day in the spring of 1820 Siboni called him in to tell him that neither his appearance nor his manners were suitable for the stage; his voice was beginning to break and seemed to be deteriorating; it would be at least three or four years before it would be possible to get him into the theatre and he could not possibly have him in his house for such a long time. He suggested that Andersen should go back to Odense and take up some trade. It would seem that he had lost all interest in his protégé. Andersen appeared to be back where he had started in September 1819.

But he still refused to go back. He asked Mr Weyse if he could not get him apprenticed to a watchmaker. Then he remembered that Colonel Høegh-Guldberg, who had been kind to him in Odense, had a famous brother in Copenhagen, a poet called Frederik Høegh-Guldberg; so Andersen wrote to him, told him his story and explained his plight. Having thus paved the way he went to see Professor Guldberg (as he was called). He was well received, for Guldberg had already heard about him from his brother; and having seen from Andersen's letter how bad his spelling was, he offered to give him lessons in both Danish and German, for though Andersen claimed to have learnt some German in order to talk to Siboni, Guldberg tested him and found that his knowledge was extremely poor. The money which Weyse had collected having now run out, Guldberg appealed to various people to contribute to a fund to keep Andersen alive, and succeeded in collecting about eighty rix-dollars, to be paid to Andersen in monthly instalments.[8]

Andersen told his landlady all about the money that had been collected for him and asked her if, from now on, he could have full board as well as lodging at her house. Mrs Thorgesen said she was very willing to accept him as a boarder, and since there was no window in his room he could sit in her drawing-room whenever he liked; but she insisted on a payment of twenty rixdollars per month – and payable in advance. She also told him how grasping many other landladies were, and how well he would be treated in her house. Andersen was horrified at the price she asked, and he begged her to reduce it to sixteen rixdollars per month; but she insisted on twenty, and if he would not pay that, he would have to find somewhere else. What happened next is described by Andersen in *Levnedsbogen*:

What was I to do? I burst into tears and asked her to accept the ten rixdollars I had, and then wait for a fortnight for the next ten, then I would try to find the money. 'I want twenty rixdollars,' she insisted. 'You have eighty rixdollars with Mr Guldberg, that is your money, and he cannot keep it from you. For this you can live for four months, and after that he is sure to find ways and means. Now I'm going out shopping, and if you do not get hold of twenty rixdollars before I return, you can go away!' She left, and I sat there crying in her drawing-room, bereft of all hope. On the wall hung a portrait of her late husband; while lying weeping in front of it it seemed to me that the picture looked at me in a kindly way, and in my childish innocence I prayed through the picture to the dead man that he would soften his wife's heart for the sake of me, poor child that I was; indeed I took my tears and smeared them on to the eyes of the portrait to make him feel how bitterly I was crying.

Exhausted by pain and grief I sank into a half-dozed sleep which continued until the landlady returned. She was in a more kindly mood, and now that she realized that it would have been impossible for me to produce the sum on that same day she accepted the ten rixdollars on condition that I gave her another ten within two weeks, and so on: ten on the first day of the month and ten a fortnight later.

The story reveals how close Andersen was to primitive magic.

In the German autobiography, written thirteen years later, Andersen retold the story but in an improved and embellished fashion which is also to be found in *Mit Livs Eventyr*; for there the landlady also begins by asking for twenty rixdollars, but when she returns after he has performed his primitive invocation she relents and reduces the price to sixteen rixdollars per month – 'and I was happy, grateful to God and the dead man'. As so often, there is little doubt that *Levnedsbogen* is less literary and far more reliable than the later autobiographies, which were written for the whole world to read.

Andersen had promised to pay his landlady twenty rixdollars every month, but since his monthly allowance from Guldberg amounted to only ten rixdollars, he had to find the remaining ten elsewhere. Once again Weyse, with the help of some of his friends, guaranteed him a sum of money every quarter, but this was still not enough. Andersen then remembered a young girl who had been kind to him in Odense when they both attended Dean Tetens' religious instruction in preparation for their confirmation. He knew that she had since moved to Copenhagen where she now lived with her wealthy uncle, and he went to see her and told her his story. She gave him some of her own pocket-money and collected some more for him from friends and relatives. In this way Andersen was able to pay Mrs Thorgesen her twice ten rixdollars every month.

The earliest documents in Andersen's handwriting and signed with his full name: Hans Christian Andersen, are two almost identical petitions to 'noble benefactors', dated, respectively, 2 June and 3 July 1820. In these he explains his sincere love of acting and says that he considers himself 'entirely born to serve Thalia'. He mentions the support given to him by Weyse, Siboni 'and other noble-minded persons', states his age as being 'a little over fifteen', and mentions the fact that he is 'being employed in the Theatre at the ballet', but at an extremely small salary, 'and the only extras I shall receive are shoes and stockings'. Since 'because of their poverty my parents cannot give me any support' he asks noble-minded benefactors to give him a small monthly allowance. Another petition of a similar kind was sent to the King of Denmark on 6 August 1820.

Andersen's statement that he had been employed at the Royal Ballet School was, in fact, quite true. As soon as he was installed in Mrs Thorgesen's house, he went to see Antoine Bournonville, the head of the Royal Ballet; but he was in Paris with his son (later the famous August Bournonville). During his absence Carl Dahlén, the leading solo dancer in the Royal Ballet, was in charge, and so it was he whom Andersen saw. Dahlén, who had already heard rumours about this strange boy, received him kindly and accepted him as a pupil in the school, which was at that time housed in the old Court Theatre. Andersen went through all the complicated training of a would-be ballet dancer during the entire season 1820–1, but Dahlén could not hold out any hope that he would ever distinguish himself in this field. Nevertheless the Dahléns opened their hospitable house to Andersen, who felt at ease with these kind people and their daughters, and for a time came to regard their house as his home.

On 24 August 1820 the board of directors of the Royal Theatre declared:

When the suppliant presented himself before the board about nine months ago with a wish to be employed in the Theatre, he was found, after having been tested, to lack both the talent and the appearance necessary for the stage. None the less Mr Siboni had the kindness voluntarily to give him lessons in singing in the hope that it might be possible soon to train him to serve in the choir of the Theatre, but even this he was forced to abandon. He then took refuge in Mr Dahlén's dancing school to be trained in this subject for which, according to Mr Dahlén, he also lacks the ability and outward appearance.

In view of the fact that the board regard it as their duty to advise against employing him in any subject in the Theatre, they cannot recommend that he be given any financial support from the Theatre's chest.

Even though his prospects of ever becoming a solo dancer were minimal, Andersen felt that the world about which he had been dreaming for years had now opened itself to him. As a pupil at the ballet school he had access backstage to the Royal Theatre, and he could watch any performance free of charge from a box in the third tier which was reserved for the dancers.

His first appearance on the stage happened more or less by accident in September 1820, during a *Singspiel* in which there was a scene with a huge crowd of people. Supernumeraries, pupils from the ballet school and even stage-hands, were invited to join in, and one of the ballet dancers asked Andersen if he would like to come on to the stage with all the others. He was quickly made up, and with beating heart went on to the stage, happy and elated. But his happiness was short-lived. One of the actors, who saw him in his threadbare and ridiculous confirmation dress, took him by the hand and congratulated him on his début with the words: 'May I present you to the Danish people!' Andersen, who was extremely self-conscious about his appearance, was very upset at the mockery of this remark. He tore himself away and ran offstage with tears in his eyes.

Four months later Andersen appeared in the ballet *Nina* by V. Galeotti, dressed as a musician. He describes it in *Levnedsbogen*:

There were two musicians in it who are asked to play for Nina, but she is not satisfied until they play the tune that reminds her of her lover. Two of the tallest pupils at the ballet school were chosen to play the two musicians, and I was one of them. This was my début. I was there already at four o'clock in the afternoon and was dressed. In the ballet we two musicians were placed at the front of the stage. Madame Schall danced the part of Nina, and I was overjoyed that she took most notice of me (I probably made a very comic appearance).

During the winter of 1820–1, after Andersen had been at the ballet school for about six months, Guldberg asked an actor called Ferdinand Lindgreen whether he would give Andersen tuition in acting. Lindgreen gave him an audition and told him that he had some talent for comic parts, but unfortunately Andersen wanted to play tragic or sentimental parts. Lindgreen was adamant, however: 'Good gracious, my dear child, your appearance is against you. People would only laugh at such a lanky hero!' All the same he allowed him to learn Correggio's monologue from Oehlenschläger's tragedy. When he played it to Lindgreen, Andersen was so moved by his own performance that he burst into tears. Lindgreen pressed his hand and said, 'You have a heart, and by God you also have a head, but you mustn't go on wasting your time here. You ought to study! You're no good as an actor, but there are other wonderful things as well as acting.' Andersen, who had previously learned some comic parts, was in despair. 'Am I no good at all?' he said. 'Not even for the comic parts? O God! I'm so unhappy! What's going to become of me?' Lindgreen comforted him and told him that he ought to learn some Latin; perhaps Mr Guldberg would be prepared to help him. Andersen was quite willing to learn Latin but asked to be allowed to remain in the theatre, for that was the world in which he really felt at home.

Saturday, 12 April 1821, was a great day for Andersen. On that day, for the first time, his name appeared in print. Dahlén had composed a new ballet for the Royal Theatre, called *Armida*, in which Andersen was given a part which appeared on the programme: 'A troll . . . Hr Andersen'. In his memoirs he describes his feelings:

It was a great moment in my life that my name now appeared in print; it seemed to me there was a halo of immortality about it. I had to look at the printed letters all day, I took the ballet programme with me to bed in the evening, lay in the candlelight staring at my name, put it away only to take it up again: this was sheer bliss.

Andersen's copy of the printed programme for the ballet *Armida* (first performed on 12 April 1821) in which his name appeared as one of the trolls. The additions in ink were made by Andersen later in life. Outside his own name he has put an asterisk and added the initials 'H.C.' One of the cupids in the ballet was a little girl called Johanne Pätges (mis-spelt 'Petcher'), who was later to become famous as the great actress Johanne Luise Heiberg.

Personalet i Balletten Armida.

Armida, Mad. Schall.
Ismene, hendes Fortrolige, Mad. Jansen.
Rinaldo, Herr Funck.
Ubaldo, — Dahlén.
Fortuna, Jfr. Skaarup:
Amor, Jfr. Lina Schall.

Armidas og Ismenes Følge:
Jfr. Bruun.
— Volstrup.
— Larcher.
— Johnsen.
— Høyer.
— Weile.
— Hinck.
— Sannes.
— Evanemann.
Mad. Brandt.
— Bechman.
— Freiman.

Amoriner:
Theodor Scharff.
Andreas Füssell.
Josephine Fredstrup.
Ida Andersen. X
Sophie Møller.
Andrea Møller.
Jensine Weiner. X

Amoriner:
Johanne Petcher.
Amalia Petcher.
Adelaide Børresen.
Henr. Charpentier.
Antoinette Block.
Henriette Schumann.

Onde Aander:
Herr P. Larcher.
— E. Weile.
— Jacobsen.
— Benzen.
— Holm.
— Stramboe.
— E. Petersen.
— Hammer. XXX
— Friis.
— W. Petersen.
— E. Lund.
— Nehm.

Trolde:
Herr Fredstrup.
— Lundgreen.
— Villeneuve.
— P. Poulsen.
— Hamberg.
— Aagaard.
✳ Andersen.
— Wilhelm Scharff.

Handlingen foregaaer paa Armidas fortryllede Øe.

In May 1821 Andersen saw Mr P. C. Krossing, the Royal Theatre's singing master, who had already heard about him and who for some reason was angry with Siboni. He decided that Andersen's voice was still good and accepted him as a pupil at the singing school, so that he was now a pupil at both the ballet school and at the singing school of the Royal Theatre. He became a member of the choir and appeared on the stage in various guises, as a footman, a page-boy, a peasant lad, a shepherd, a brahmin, a halberdier, and a Norwegian warrior.

Andersen was still very immature, and he still loved to recite poems to anyone who was prepared to listen. Through some of his benefactors he had met the lady-in-waiting to the crown princess of Denmark and been invited to Frederiksberg Castle, where the crown princess herself came in to see him, and at her request, without the slightest embarrassment, the boy immediately agreed to sing and recite in front of the princess, who praised his voice and gave him sweets, grapes and peaches, and a gift of ten rixdollars. In his earliest autobiography Andersen describes his reaction:

I sat down in the park under a tree, ate some of the things I had been given but wanted to save up half of it for my landlady, as indeed I did. Out of sheer happiness I began to sing in a loud voice. I had not seen any summer landscape in Zealand before, and I was strangely moved by seeing the green, fragrant trees; I sang, but in an improvised way, addressing flowers and birds, for I had no one else to express my happiness to. While I was sitting there a stable boy came along and asked me if I was mad, where-upon I sneaked away, silent and embarrassed.

At Mrs Thorgesen's he spent most of his time reading; he borrowed books from a lending library with whatever money he could scrape together, bought some paper to write on, and some second-hand books whenever he could afford them. With his talent for getting to know all the people who might be useful to him he also made the acquaintance of the university librarian, who allowed him to use the library and borrow books.

His room was so small that when he wanted to read or write he had to go to bed, which he often did at about six o'clock. He then had a candle brought in, and his supper, and wandered into his dream world. In *Levnedsbogen* he writes about this period:

The memory of my little toy theatre in Odense now became alive with me, and I wanted to make a similar one. I immediately began doing so and lay in my bed as a boy of sixteen sewing dolls' dresses. In order to get pieces of material for them I had the idea of going into the shops in Østergade and asking for samples of silk and velvet, which I then sewed together and made into beautiful dresses. I also made my own stereoscope and thus spent a year of my youth playing.

On one occasion, early in 1821, when the money collected by Guldberg was running out and Andersen did not know how he was going to pay Mrs Thorgesen, Guldberg published a pamphlet of verse and prose, the proceeds of which were to go to Andersen, or, in the words of the preface: 'to a hopeful young scholar deprived of almost any other support'. And so for a time he was again able to survive.

At about this time another lodger moved in; a young lady, Miss Müller, whose old father, Mr Müller, visited her frequently, but only in the evenings. Andersen sometimes had to let the old man in through the kitchen door, and was told that Mr Müller always had tea with his daughter in her room, and as he was very shy they must in no circumstances be disturbed. Some years later, when Andersen was moving in high society in Copenhagen, he met a distinguished elderly gentleman at a party, whom he recognized as 'Mr Müller'. He then realized what had really been going on, but at the time he was so innocent that he accepted what he was told at face value.

Mrs Thorgesen also had a lover who visited her regularly, a tailor's cutter, and when they decided to get married and move to the West Indies, she arranged for Andersen to move one floor up in the same house, to a Mrs Henckel. Here, too, he had a room without windows, and to save money it was agreed that he should only have breakfast and supper there. Sometimes he had his main meal at noon in a cheap basement eating-house called The Plane, but often he had to go without a hot meal and spent his lunch-time in one of the parks, bitterly cold in the winter, for he had no overcoat, as he tells us, and his boots were badly in need of repair.

Time and again it was suggested to Andersen that he ought to have further education, and Lindgreen was not the only one to tell him how important it was to learn Latin and study Latin grammar. Andersen was quite prepared to do so, as long as it did not interfere too much with his life in the theatre, and though he had no idea what the word 'grammar' meant, he asked Guldberg if he would teach him; but Guldberg refused. So, once again Andersen turned to Mrs Hermansen, his former travelling companion, for he knew that her son had recently become a student and gave private lessons. He wondered whether this son might be willing to teach him Latin free of charge. But Mrs Hermansen replied that her son might have been willing to teach him German, but 'Latin – that is such an *expensive* language'. In the end Guldberg found a student who volunteered to give Andersen Latin lessons once or twice a week; unfortunately he found it terribly dry and boring.

One evening in September 1821 Andersen was told that Guldberg was angry with him for having neglected his Latin lessons. What happened next is described in *Levnedsbogen*:

As soon as I heard this I was frightened and sad, left my toy theatre and immediately ran out to his house in Nørrebro to beg his forgiveness; but he was excited, called me a bad person who did not want to do what was good for himself, and firmly told me that he would have nothing more to do with me. I was broken-hearted, begged him to forgive me and not let me be completely unhappy. 'Oh! you're just play-acting in front of me,' he said. 'If you desert me I shall have no one left! I have been wrong, but by God I will be more diligent, I didn't see what it might all lead to and had no idea of what Latin was until I came to you.' These were more or less my words. – 'You unhappy!' he repeated. 'What a tirade of a comedy! I've read that before. I'll do nothing more for you. I still have thirty rixdollars belonging to you, and of that sum you can still collect ten each month, but our relationship is over!' And he slammed the door in my face. I realized that it was wrong of me to have neglected the Latin lessons on those occasions but felt all the same that he was too hard on me. I walked homewards full of despair. He had told me that I was 'a bad person', and that affected me terribly. I stood for a long time by the Peblinge Lake and saw the moon shining into the water. There was a cold wind, and the horrible thought struck me: 'Nothing good can become of you! You aren't good any longer! God is angry, you must die!' I looked into the water, and then thought of my old grandmother, who would certainly not have thought that my life was going to end in this way. This made me cry bitterly, but it relieved my mind, and in my heart I begged God to forgive me for my errors and for my sinful thought of jumping into the water.

Andersen then went to the student who taught him Latin and asked his forgiveness; he explained that he had been involved in so many plays in the theatre that his mind had not been on Latin grammar, but he was now going to mend his ways. The student was not in the least angry and Andersen went home greatly relieved. He no longer neglected his Latin; but for a long time Guldberg remained irreconcilable.

Shortly before Guldberg broke off all relations with him Andersen had begun his first literary work. As part of his Danish lessons he had been told to copy out one of Guldberg's poems every week and learn it by heart. For a change Andersen had asked Guldberg if he might be allowed to write a tragedy based on a German story which he had read in a Danish magazine; Guldberg had agreed on condition that it was only regarded as an exercise in written Danish and must not be submitted to the theatre. The play (which still exists in manuscript) was called *The Forest Chapel*; it was written in blank verse, a very naïve and immature imitation of German *Schreck-Romantik*, or in the words of Mr Thiele, a young contemporary Danish writer, 'some terrible phantasmagoria, taken from bad German novels', though Thiele was generous enough to say that 'in spite of everything the play had its bright points'. Andersen later admitted that at that time he was still so childish that, 'when I went out to Guldberg to ask him if I might attempt such a thing I was in two minds whether I had better give up this idea and instead make a bigger toy theatre for myself'.

He read his play to all and sundry, and every kind word he heard convinced him of his own literary talent. He went to the great, recognized Danish writers and was given kind words of encouragement by Oehlenschläger, Ingemann and Grundtvig. He now began to believe in himself as a *Digter*, and wanted everybody to read his play. When someone suggested that he should submit it to the Royal Theatre he rushed straight out to ask Guldberg's permission. The latter had sufficient good sense, however, to forbid it. At the time Andersen attributed this to envy because Guldberg himself had never been successful as a dramatist.

After Guldberg had broken with him, Andersen was more eager than ever to be given a good part, so that he would come to everyone's notice and might earn a decent salary. There was still so much of his mother's superstition in him that he was fully convinced that what happened to a person on New Year's Day would decide what happened to him during the rest of the year, and since it was still his dearest wish to appear as often as possible on the stage of the

Royal Theatre, he wanted desperately to appear on New Year's Day 1822. It so happened that no performance was to be given on that evening, and the theatre was closed. But the stage-door was not, so he went in, sneaked past a half-blind old custodian, and with beating heart went past curtains and wings on to the empty stage; facing the orchestra pit he sank down on his knees, but could not think of anything to recite; then a thought occurred to him, and in a loud voice he said the Lord's Prayer – and left the theatre fully convinced that he would be successful as an actor in 1822.

He wanted to be an actor, and he wanted to be a writer, and wherever he went he wanted to recite, either poetry or his own first literary product. It was at that time that one of the actresses in the Royal Theatre gave him the nickname '*der kleine Declamator*'[9] – and the name stuck.

The favourable reception of his first attempt made him decide to write a new tragedy, this time secretly, because he wanted to submit it to the Royal Theatre. Following the example of Schiller he wrote a play about robbers, which he called *The Robbers of Vissenberg*; it was based on a Danish legend, but the plot was his own. The play took him only two weeks to write and was full of both grammatical and spelling mistakes. A fair copy in someone else's handwriting was anonymously submitted to the Royal Theatre in March 1822, and filled with great expectations Andersen now eagerly awaited the reply from the board of directors.

But in the spring of 1822, before he knew of the fate of his play, Andersen was 'dismissed from further service in the theatre', which meant that both his singing and dancing career had come to an end. This was a terrible blow, and more than ever he now pinned his hopes on becoming a successful playwright. So he decided to write yet another play for the theatre. This time he took his subject-matter from a story entitled 'Alfsol' in a collection of *Nordic Short Stories*. In this five-act tragedy Andersen used a number of lines from his own previous plays, and he was so enthusiastic about his new play that he went to see Captain P. F. Wulff, Denmark's leading translator of Shakespeare, to whom he is said to have introduced himself with the words: 'You have translated Shakespeare. I like him very much too, but I have written a tragedy, may I read it to you?' Wulff asked him to sit down and have lunch first, but Andersen was so eager to get on with his reading that he began then and there. According to Wulff Andersen said something like: 'Don't you think I'll get somewhere? I do hope so.' We do not know what Wulff thought of the play, but when he left he asked him to visit him again, to which Andersen replied that he would come as soon as he had written another tragedy. Well, said Wulff, then he wouldn't be seeing him for quite a while. 'Oh, I think I shall have another one ready in a couple of weeks,' Andersen is reputed to have replied.

The wife of a Danish writer later remembered how Andersen read one of his own plays to her at this time. After having listened to the first few scenes she exclaimed, 'But there are entire paragraphs which you have copied word for word from Oehlenschläger and Ingemann!' To which he simply replied, 'Yes, I know, but aren't they wonderful!'

Another extremely influential person was Jonas Collin, among whose many official appointments was that of being a member of the board of directors of the Royal Theatre.[10] Already on 2 April 1821 – his sixteenth birthday – Andersen had sent a little autobiographical poem to Jonas Collin, which he ended by expressing the hope that he might find 'a modest place in the Garden of Art'. While he was still a pupil at the Royal Theatre he had once called on Jonas Collin, who at that time seems to have been completely ignorant of the boy's existence and felt unable to help him. Following Dean Gutfeld's advice, Andersen now went to call on Mr Collin at home, but the visit did not look very promising. As Andersen later explained, he only saw the businessman in Collin, 'He did not say much, and his speech was serious and almost severe, it seemed to me; I went away without expecting any sympathy from that man.' Andersen then regarded Jonas Collin more as an enemy than as a friend, and neither of them knew how closely associated they would later be, nor that Collin was to become Andersen's most important benefactor and the person responsible for changing his whole life.

On 16 June 1822 *The Robbers of Vissenberg* was rejected by the Royal Theatre as being immature and unsuitable and giving evidence of the author's lack of elementary education. Nevertheless one scene of the play was printed in a journal called *The Harp* on 9 August 1822. This was the first time anything was printed over the name Hans Christian Andersen.

By this time he was already engaged on a new literary work. Among the novels he had borrowed and read with enthusiasm was Scott's *The Heart of Midlothian*, which had appeared in a Danish translation in 1822. In direct imitation Andersen wrote a story about 'Mad Stine', which he called 'The Ghost at Palnatoke's Grave'. One of the actors at the Royal Theatre introduced him to a compositor in a Copenhagen printing firm, and this firm agreed to print his story and the tragedy *Alfsol* in a book called *Youthful Attempts*, for which Andersen chose the *nom de plume* 'Villiam Christian Walter', i.e. Andersen himself (Christian) flanked by his two literary heroes, Shakespeare ('Villiam') and Scott (Walter). Andersen wrote to Mr Guldberg to ask if he might dedicate the book to him, but received a very cold refusal: 'If you think you owe me some consideration you can only show it by *completely* abandoning your intention of dedicating to me a book you are intending to have printed.' Guldberg went on to say that Andersen could hardly annoy him more than by doing this. He had missed his great chance of showing his gratitude by learning something, and Guldberg was not interested in being mentioned to a handful of readers. How deeply this hurt Andersen is shown by the fact that he put it in verbatim in his novel *The Improvisatore* years later.

There was an advance notice of *Youthful Attempts* in the newspaper *Dagen* on 12 June 1822, and Andersen tried to enlist subscribers, but hardly any of the printed copies seem to have been sold. To recover some of their money the printers sold all the remaining copies to a bookseller, who tried to sell them with a new title-page in 1827, but he was equally unsuccessful, and eventually all the printed sheets were used as wrapping paper or sold as pulp. Very few copies of the book have survived.

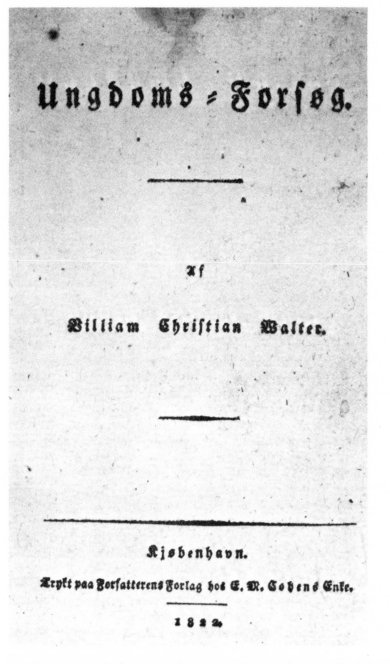

Ungdoms ≠ Forsøg.

Af

William Christian Walter.

Kjøbenhavn.

Trykt paa Forfatterens Forlag hos E. M. Cohens Enke.

1822.

The title-page of Andersen's first book, *Youthful Attempts*, published in 1822 under the *nom de plume* of Villiam Christian Walter. 'I loved *William* Shakespeare and *Walter* Scott, and then I also loved myself, of course, so I took my name *Christian*, and thus I had the pseudonym: William Christian Walter,' Andersen writes in *Mit Livs Eventyr*.

Before the publication of *Youthful Attempts* in the autumn of 1822, Andersen's life had changed its course completely.

On Andersen's behalf Dean Gutfeld had submitted his tragedy *Alfsol* to a member of the board of directors of the Royal Theatre. On 3 September 1822 the play was rejected as being 'a collection of words and tirades without any dramatic action, without plan, without character . . . in short, completely unsuitable for the stage.' But in spite of this damning criticism it was recommended that the young author of this play ought to be sent to a grammar school to acquire at least the elements of education. This recommendation was repeated at a meeting of the board of directors on 6 September, and it was agreed that Hans Christian Andersen should be called to appear before the board on 13 September. On this occasion he gratefully accepted the offer to be sent to a grammar school at public expense for the next three years, which would eventually enable him to enter Copenhagen university, and the board left it to Mr Collin to take whatever further measures were necessary. Since the money had to be provided from a royal fund Jonas Collin went straight to the king, and after having received his verbal agreement it was decided on 18 October that Andersen should be admitted as a pupil at the grammar school of Slagelse, fifty-six miles west of Copenhagen. There a new headmaster, Dr Simon Meisling, had recently been appointed, and there Andersen went on 26 October 1822.

Before leaving for Slagelse he went to see Jonas Collin privately and was told that he could always turn to him with any problems he might have. From now on Jonas Collin took it upon himself to be *in loco parentis* to Hans Christian Andersen, who in turn promised to write regularly to his 'father'.

Andersen's mother, who could neither read nor write, sent him a letter, dictated to a literate neighbour, in which she told him how happy she was that he was now to be a pupil at the Latin school and how happy his old grandmother would have been, had she known it. The grandmother had, however, died shortly before, on 29 August.

From one point of view Andersen's three years in Copenhagen had been a complete failure. His love-affair with the theatre had been an unhappy one; he had been rejected as a singer, as a dancer, as an actor, and as a playwright. He was clumsy and 'different', and his appearance was unfortunate in every way, and to make things worse he had grown out of his suit without being able to afford to buy a new one. His coat was too short, so he tried to pull down his sleeves all the time, his trousers too short and too narrow, and his heels trodden down. He moved awkwardly in a vain attempt to cover up the many defects in his clothing. His whole behaviour was often ridiculous. This is how he was described in a letter, written in Copenhagen less than four weeks before he went to Slagelse by Mrs Collin's niece (and the sister of the great-grandfather of the author of this book), Miss Eline Bredsdorff, to her sister Hanne in Funen:

Ask Ottilie if she can remember the little shoemaker's son from Odense, who used to act out plays before them; he is now here in Copenhagen and writes tragedies and stories, which once in a while he comes and reads aloud to us; there are a few nice parts in them, but generally speaking it is the most terrible nonsense. Tomorrow he is coming again to read, and I am quite looking forward to it if only I could stop myself laughing, but it is almost an impossibility, for he behaves so foolishly.

But there was more to it than that. In another sense the three years in Copenhagen were not wasted at all, for Andersen's extraordinary talent for making other people interested in him had resulted in the fact that 'the little shoemaker's son' could now look forward to a number of years without any financial worries, for, at the age of seventeen, he was going to begin life as a schoolboy again.

3 In the grammar school

1822-7

ANDERSEN arrived in Slagelse on 26 October 1822 and the following morning presented himself before Dr Simon Meisling, his future headmaster. Dr Meisling received him kindly and invited him to spend the evening at his house together with two boys from the top form. Eager to show off his talents Andersen entertained the party by reading aloud first his play *Alfsol* and then his story 'The Ghost at Palnatoke's Grave'. *Der kleine Declamator* had moved to Slagelse with a vengeance.

On Monday 28 October Andersen took his place behind a desk in the second form, where he towered above all the other boys, whose average age was eleven; he was seventeen, and they all looked at him in astonishment. His knowledge of Latin was almost non-existent, and many subjects were new to him: Greek, geometry – even geography; he had to admit that he did not know how to find Copenhagen on the map.

Most of the teachers were kind and helpful, especially Mr Snitker, the Latin master, and Mr Quistgaard, the divinity master; the latter came from a poor family and was the one who best understood Andersen's situation. The history master, Andersen tells us, was always bad-tempered and said of Andersen that he was so tall that 'one could cut him in half and make two puppies out of him'. Meisling, who was a classical scholar, only taught Andersen's form once a week, but he was a man of violent temper and changing moods and had developed an extraordinary talent for sarcasm and mockery. Before long Andersen was so scared whenever the headmaster's lesson approached that he prayed that some catastrophe or other might prevent him from coming. At times Andersen seems to have been almost paralysed with fear of Meisling, who could so distort even a correct answer from Andersen that the other boys would laugh at him.

In private life Meisling could be friendly and cheerful, and he often invited Andersen to his house on Sundays and even allowed him to go with the top-form boys to the compulsory church service on Sundays.

Andersen boarded with a Mrs Henneberg, a widow, and he shared a small bedroom and a sitting-room with another boarder, who from time to time came home drunk. When this happened Andersen fled upstairs to his land-lady's flat where he spent the night on the sofa. On the whole he seems to have kept himself very much to himself and, as before, would often sit alone singing in the garden.

Slagelse itself was a small, unexciting provincial town; on his arrival Andersen had been told that the main attractions of the town were 'Pastor Bastholm's library and the new English fire engine'. To his delight he found

that it also had a small, primitive theatre, in a converted stable, where performances were given every fortnight, and in order to ensure an audience for
the dress rehearsals grammar-school boys were given free tickets.

When the Christmas holidays began Meisling hired Slagelse's one and only
coach, into which were packed Dr and Mrs Meisling, their three children, their
maid and Andersen, plus a goodly supply of pancakes and sweets, and a big
eiderdown to cover them all. They played cards all the way from Slagelse to
Copenhagen, while Mrs Meisling sang arias from Mozart's *Don Juan*. In
Copenhagen Andersen stayed with an elderly lady whose acquaintance he had
made when he lived in the city, and for the first time he was invited to have
dinner with the Collin family. He found Mr Collin a kind, benevolent,
fatherly man, who expressed satisfaction with Andersen's mark book, and
encouraged him to write every month to let him know how he was getting
on, telling him always to be frank about his feelings.

When Andersen returned to Slagelse after the holidays his relations with the
headmaster began to deteriorate, and he was often very unhappy. When
Meisling discovered that he still went on reading his own play to anyone who
would listen, he categorically forbade him to do so and insisted that he must
stop writing. In this, however, Meisling was not alone; Collin also impressed
upon him the necessity of sticking to his school work and not indulging in
imaginative writing. Other correspondents did likewise, so that Andersen
almost came to regard writing poetry as sinful. During his first year at Slagelse
he did his utmost to keep his promise not to *digte*. When he heard that Dean
Gutfeld had died, however, he wrote a poem in memory of his benefactor and
sent it to the local paper, where it was printed on 1 February 1823. The editor,
Pastor Bastholm, sent him a letter: 'I must admit that God has given you a
lively imagination and a warm heart – what you still lack is education of the
mind.' But Pastor Bastholm also told him to continue with his school work
and put aside any other ambitions for the time being.

Another occasion for writing poetry arose in July 1823, when Meisling was
formally installed as headmaster at a ceremony presided over by the Bishop
of Zealand; at the request of the singing master Andersen had written a song
for the occasion. He sent a copy to Collin, who wrote back to say that he liked
the song but hoped that 'this not unsuccessful attempt may not tempt you to
others, which would not be very suitable for your present occupation'.

After he had arrived in Slagelse Andersen received several letters from his
mother, invariably in somebody else's handwriting (and one suspects that
occasionally the scribes put into her letters what they thought she ought to
have dictated rather than what she did, in fact, dictate). In the first extant letter
(undated) she complained that Hans Christian had not replied to her previous
one, 'for I do think a mother is worth a reply'. She told him that 'your sister
came here last Sunday and was angry that I would not give her your address';
if he gave it to her she would be spared any more reproaches. In a subsequent
letter (2 November 1822) she thanked him for his reply and added, 'Your sister
has travelled over to you [presumably meaning to Zealand], but against my
will', followed by some cryptic words to the effect that Hans Christian must

Dr Meisling, a contemporary caricature.

let Lieutenant Martens read the letter and ask him to fulfil his promises. The implication seems to have been that a certain Lieutenant M. F. Martens, who had lived in Odense from 1817 to 1821, had been Karen Marie's lover, and that she had now left Odense for Copenhagen in order to try and find him.

In December 1822 Andersen's mother told Hans Christian how proud she was that he was now a pupil at 'the learned school', and she went on to say that 'many a secret tear of joy runs from the mother's eye, for how could I, poor woman that I am, think or hope that our Most Gracious Paternal Monarch would bestow this immense grace on a boy who falls headlong into the great world?'

About Karen Marie she wrote:

Your sister is in Copenhagen, I do not know at what address, but there is no need for you to worry about either her virtue or her youthfulness, for it has all been well preserved here in Odense, though I do certainly hope for and long to see a few words from her quite soon.

Andersen, who had not seen his mother for almost four years, asked Meisling's permission to go to Odense during the Easter holidays 1823 and was told that he could go for a week, but not more, because Meisling was going to Copenhagen and wanted Andersen to play with his children while he was away.

Leaving Slagelse at three o'clock in the morning Andersen walked to Korsør, went by boat across to Funen, and walked from Nyborg to Odense. When he saw the tower of Saint Canute's Church he fell on his knees and wept with joy. 'Everything was like a dream to me when I entered the town,' he says in his autobiography, 'in the first street I met my mother, she wept but could not really understand my happiness.' He visited old acquaintances, including Colonel Høegh-Guldberg, Mr Iversen and Miss Bunkeflod. People who had known him as a child looked at him in astonishment and called him 'Mr Christian', being uncertain of his surname. His mother was so proud of him that she wanted to show him off all the time; on one occasion she even went to fetch him from Colonel Guldberg's house because a servant girl of her acquaintance wanted to see him; Hans Christian came home, the girl curtsied and looked at him, but they hardly said a word to one another and she left. His mother's pride was boundless when she saw him in a boat on Odense river with the colonel and the bishop and members of their families.

Returning to school was a terrible anti-climax. He found Latin and Greek increasingly difficult and Meisling increasingly unpredictable. When the first annual examination approached in the autumn of 1823, Andersen was very pessimistic and wrote a letter to Mr Quistgaard, his divinity master, telling him of his anxiety and unhappiness. After beginning, true to form, with a brief account of his life, he declared that he wanted to prove himself worthy of the generosity shown him, but that he was now beginning to doubt his own capacity, for in spite of hard work his Greek and Latin masters were often dissatisfied with him, and he himself felt that his progress was far too slow. Recently, however, there had been some progress, and both his teachers and his benefactors in Copenhagen had expressed their satisfaction with him, which doubled his desire to continue. 'But I am already more than eighteen, and I grow older day by day.' The crux of the matter was his fear that he might fail the examination because of bad marks in Latin composition; this would mean 'utter despair, for then I shall never reach the goal, then my efforts will have been in vain'. Andersen practically implored Mr Quistgaard to tell him that he thought he would get into the third form, adding, 'You may object that I ought to speak to the headmaster about all these matters; but I don't think he likes me as much as he did during the first few days.'

Despite very poor results in Latin and Greek, and mediocre results in several other subjects Andersen was moved up into the third form and given an encouraging report by Meisling. 'This made me unspeakably happy,' Andersen writes. 'My friends wrote me encouraging letters, Collin expressed his satisfaction. I was youthfully happy and felt as if reborn. The crown princess sent me some pocket-money, and when I went to Copenhagen for the Christmas celebrations I had a marvellous time, but could only stay there for a week. I had to go home and play with Meisling's children; this he insisted on.' The mail-coach from Copenhagen to Slagelse only went on weekdays, and as he wanted to see a play in Copenhagen on Saturday evening Andersen had to set off early on Sunday morning on foot, walking in frost and drifting snow the fifty-six miles to Slagelse, where he arrived at one o'clock on Monday morning.

Andersen wrote regularly to Jonas Collin and among his other regular correspondents in Copenhagen were Mrs Wulff (the wife of Captain P. F. Wulff) and Mrs Birgitte Andersen, an actress in the Royal Theatre. In October 1823 there had been a reconciliation between Professor Guldberg and Andersen, and from then on Guldberg also wrote to him regularly.

The main cause of his misery was still Meisling, whose outbursts of anger nearly drove him to despair. One of Meisling's nicknames for Andersen was 'Shakespeare with the vamp's eyes', and his mockery could make him burst into tears, whereupon Meisling would tell one of the other boys to fetch a brick with which Andersen could wipe his eyes. In his first autobiography Andersen describes the state he was in:

I sank into a melancholy mood, all my letters were full of whimpering and wailing; Guldberg in Odense talked to me like a father, kept on telling me that I had intelligence and talent; I doubted it, for Meisling constantly behaved in the same way towards me. I progressed so well that for a time I was the top boy in my form, but then I was placed nearer to him and he took the chance to tease me even more when in my state of fear I gave my replies in a confused order.

One day another boy had written a silly verse on the binding of my Homer. Meisling read it and was choleric. I replied, 'But it is not mine; the handwriting, you can see, doesn't look like mine.' 'But the *spirit* does!' he replied. 'You're a stupid boy, who'll never be any good. When you begin to stand on your own legs you may scribble a lot of nonsense, but no one will read what you write, and it will be sold as pulp. – For God's sake, don't start weeping, you overgrown fellow!' – This was his way of educating me. He probably meant well, for in Copenhagen he spoke well of me, and he allowed me to visit him on Sundays; but it was not the right kind of education.

It certainly was not the right kind of education. In his despair Andersen wrote another letter to Mr Quistgaard, who tried to comfort him and encourage him not to give up. 'You will probably win the favour of Meisling, who uses stronger expressions than is customary both when he approves and when he disapproves,' Quistgaard wrote back. This gave him encouragement, but only for a short while, and after some further clashes with Meisling, Andersen took his courage in both hands and wrote to Meisling himself:

I hope you will peruse my letter, for I promise you never to trouble you with suchlike again. You are angry with me, and especially because I am supposed to have smiled when I was unfortunate enough to receive bad marks, but I swear to you by God (and I think you will never have found any untruthfulness in me) that never, either in the school or on my way home, did I show any sign of being satisfied with myself, that is a behaviour which is beyond me.

He went on to say that he found all grammar except Danish difficult, and assured Meisling that he did not read 'entertaining books' or neglect his home-work. He appealed to Meisling:

Please, be patient with me for yet a while, and if during the next three months I am incapable of making any progress then I promise you to withdraw from a place where I cause nothing but dissatisfaction.

Meisling's reaction to this letter is not known, but it was not long before Andersen was in disgrace again, this time for having recited a poem at a private party in Slagelse. He was summoned before his headmaster, who told him that it would have to be reported to Mr Collin, that Andersen might have to be expelled, that he was no good anyway, and that Meisling could not tolerate him any more. Andersen took it very seriously, confessed everything in letters to Collin and his other friends in Copenhagen, telling them that this was the end, and that he intended to emigrate to America. Collin and Guldberg sympathized with him, some of his other correspondents scolded him for behaving like a child, and it was with the greatest anxiety that he sat for his examination in the autumn of 1824. The result was not outstanding, nor was it abysmally bad, for he was fifth out of eight, but only those above him were admitted to the fourth form; Andersen remained in the third form, where he was now the top boy.

During 1824–5 the relations between Andersen and his headmaster improved somewhat. In December 1824 Andersen wrote to Collin, 'This year the headmaster treats me much better (I am, of course, also less bad this year), and sometimes he says nothing for several days though I am tested almost every day.' In January 1825 he wrote: 'Since my return the headmaster has treated me with extraordinary gentleness. I wish he would stay like that.' But in his next letter Andersen was again puzzled and worried about Meisling: 'Sometimes he is angry with me, at other times very kind.' In subsequent letters

Andersen reported on his improved relations with Meisling, and the good relationship culminated in September 1825, when Andersen was called in to see Mrs Meisling, who told him that her husband hoped soon to be appointed headmaster of Elsinore grammar school, where he had previously been a classics master. If this were to happen Meisling would wish Andersen to move with him to Elsinore and finish his education there. The Meislings would take him into their own house as a boarder at the same payment as Mrs Henneberg received, and if he found Latin and Greek difficult Meisling would give him private tuition, so that it would be to his advantage to stay in the headmaster's house. As Meisling might be called upon to move to Elsinore at any time it was suggested that Andersen should move in with them as soon as the quarter for which payment had been made to Mrs Henneberg ran out. So on her husband's behalf Mrs Meisling asked Andersen to write to Mr Collin and suggest that he should move at the end of October 1825. Andersen was both flattered and worried at this proposal – flattered because it was an indication that he had won Meisling's favour, worried because he knew Meisling's violent temper and was aware of the fact that at any time he might fall into his disfavour again. He therefore left the decision entirely to Collin, and Collin being in favour of the proposal it was arranged that Andersen should live with the Meisling family.

In a small provincial town such as Slagelse every traditional festivity, such as Shrovetide amusements and the poppinjay shooting in the summer, was a great event for all the schoolboys. Participation in a local choir was, however, forbidden, since the ladies of the town, in whose homes the singing master organized the choir practice, did not want Mrs Meisling to take part, and so her husband retaliated by prohibiting his pupils from joining in. On Sundays and during school holidays Andersen often walked to the neighbouring town of Sorø, where the poet B. S. Ingemann and his wife always received him very cordially. Andersen was secretly planning to write an historical novel entitled *Christian II's Dwarf*, and he discussed his plans with Ingemann, whose historical novels were then very popular.

An unusually exciting event took place in April 1825 when three convicts were publicly executed on a hill between Slagelse and Skælskør. A girl of seventeen had persuaded her lover and another man to murder her father, because he would not allow her to marry her lover by whom she was pregnant. After the murder had been committed the three were found guilty and sentenced to death. The senior grammar-school boys were given the day off so that they could witness the execution, and Andersen was among those who went. In *Levnedsbogen* he gives a detailed description of the gruesome event, which made a terrible impression on him but seemed to leave most of the spectators unmoved; indeed he overheard some of the peasants say to one another that it was a pity that the good clothes of the three beheaded people should be wasted. A local tailor had written a ballad about the murder and earned so much by the sale of his broadsheet that he gave up his trade and became a towncrier.

During the summer holidays in 1825 Andersen went to Odense again and stayed with Colonel Høegh-Guldberg. A few months previously his mother had been given a free place in Doctors Boder, a charitable institution for old people. Andersen and his mother had corresponded at irregular intervals since he went to Slagelse, but none of his letters have survived. She had told him that his mad old grandfather had been taken into the Greyfriars Hospital, apparently against his will; and that when his house and belongings were sold they brought in about 110 rixdollars, half of which Hans Christian was to have; although the old man did not in fact die till 1827.

It is clear from Andersen's letters during this period that he was firmly convinced he was going to be a *Digter*, and a great *Digter* at that. In the spring of 1823 he wrote to Mrs Andersen, the actress: 'If anyone can become a *Digter* through the events of his childhood, then I will become one. Not a minor one, however, there are plenty of those. If I cannot become a great one I shall strive to become a useful citizen in the community.' And to Ingemann he wrote in May 1826: 'So, courage! *aut Cæsar, aut nihil* shall be my slogan.' He must have written along the same lines to Mrs Wulff, for in one of her letters to him she writes: 'You think, my good Andersen, that you were born to be a great *Digter*. No, this is not so, and least of all you yourself must think so.' She continued later in her letter: 'Most important of all, my dear Andersen, do not flatter yourself that you will be an Oehlenschläger, a Walter Scott, a Shakespeare, a Goethe, or a Schiller, and do not ever again ask which of these you should take as your model – for you will not be any of them.'

Andersen's letters to Collin (or those that have been preserved) often reveal much about himself, for he felt free to speak openly to Jonas Collin. In a letter dated 27 March 1823 he concluded after one of his usual detailed accounts of his life story: 'It is only now that I know myself; my character is quite good-hearted, but I am confused and airy-fairy. Without God and the kindness of other people I would be nothing at all.' On 19 June 1825 he wrote to Collin: 'I certainly feel that I am too childish, for a mere smile or kind word will make me overjoyed immediately, whereas a cold face can cause the deepest misery in my soul.'

While a schoolboy at Slagelse he kept a private diary, some fragments of which have been preserved. The earliest part dates from the period immediately after the suggestion that he should move into Meisling's house; this was also just before the annual school examination, which was crucial to Andersen that year, for if he failed to get into the fourth form he might have to leave the school altogether.

The following extracts from his diary are from September 1825:

18 September *No letter from Collin. Went to see Mrs Meisling, she hoped we would be going to Elsinore, wished me luck in the exams.*
19 September *O Lord! O Lord! Thy will be done, pay me according to my diligence over the year, not more! . . . Unfortunate person! – did badly in Latin, you won't get into the fourth, will have to leave school, your destiny will be that of an artisan or a dead body, my God! my God! are you really there? – All the same, 'Praised be thy name!' – Did better in Latin grammar, maybe a tolerable mark, also in German. – I*

do not understand your will, O Lord, oh! let me not lose hope that you govern every-thing, give me courage to face my destiny, I see it, O Lord! Good-bye all my hopes and dreams, indeed, they were but dreams, oh! if only I had the courage – death, you are not so frightening. . . . God! I could become great, respected by other people, create happiness, already the winding road was going that way, I could become an angel or a devil, the scales don't know what way to turn – O Lord! you're the one who decides the fate of the person in despair.

20 September *What could become of me? and what will become of me? My strong imagination is bringing me to the point of the lunatic asylum, my strong emotions are turning me towards suicide, and before, united, they would have made me into a great Digter, O Lord! are your ways really also the ones down here on earth? – Forgive me, Lord! for being unreasonable to you who have done so unspeakably much good to me, oh! forgive me, Lord! and please continue to help me. – (God! by my everlasting peace I promise you never again to doubt your fatherly guidance if this time I get into the fourth* AND TO ELSINORE.)

28 September *God! I promise you solemnly and sacredly, by my everlasting peace, not to grumble even if my time in the fourth form will be very hard, so long as I get there.*

29 September *Accidentally tore off a spider's leg. – Did wonderfully well in maths.*

On 1 October, when his agony was culminating ('God! my God! do not desert me. My blood runs sharply through my veins, my nerves are trembling. O Lord! almighty God! help me!') Mrs Meisling whispered to him that he had passed the examination and would get into the fourth form. His entry then continued: 'And I got there. – How strange, my joy was not so overwhelming as I had expected.'

On 27 October Andersen moved into the Meislings' house ('was a little sad, found everything better than I had expected'), and on 31 October he confided to his diary: 'I'm much better off here than at Mrs Henneberg's, O Lord! how good you are, if only I could keep the headmaster's kindness, I hope I may be able to please him, O Lord! how overjoyed I am, I'm doing very well at school.'

But on 3 November he was worried again, though this time for a different reason: 'The Meislings have taken on a maid from Copenhagen, I have a premonition that it is my sister; they say her name is Maria.' But on the following day he was reassured: 'This time my premonition was wrong, I don't know the girl at all.'

Andersen's new home was a very curious place and Mrs Meisling, his new landlady, a very curious person. She was a fat woman with false, red curls, constantly at war with her servant girls, with whose morals she was much concerned, though she herself was suspected of being unfaithful to her husband whenever opportunity arose. In order not to be disturbed by his children Dr Meisling had his bedroom on the top floor; he usually went to bed at eight o'clock after making punch, which he drank in bed while his wife read one of Scott's novels aloud to him. Sometimes when she did not feel like reading she would pick a quarrel, whereupon he sent her away, which was what she wanted. Then she would make herself a strong punch, for which the maid had to steal rum from Meisling, and when he complained that it was running short she told him that she suspected the maid of stealing it. Occasionally when her husband was asleep she would lock his bedroom door, dress herself up as a peasant girl and sneak out of the house; she told Andersen that once she had been out and amused herself with some of the officers of the local regiment. When they came back there was such a noise that Meisling woke up, but he did not recognize her in her disguise, and she walked past the house – and later sneaked in unobserved. One evening when there were visitors and everybody was staying up late she was entertaining them by singing. Suddenly somebody knocked on the window-pane, and Meisling sent Andersen to find out what was going on. Andersen innocently reported that there was an officer outside but that he had gone away as soon as he saw him. Meisling did not believe this, and Mrs Meisling was furious. 'How could you be so naïve as to say such a thing,' she told him the next day. 'You don't know how jealous Meisling is.' In his first autobiography Andersen writes:

It was a very strange world which gradually opened itself before me. I was truly still so much of a child that I tended to blush, probably at more than was reasonable, and Mrs Meisling also used to say, 'You're not really a man!' – One evening she came into my room, told me that she was beginning to lose weight and her dress was hanging quite loose round her body, asked me to feel it. I bowed many times before my headmaster's wife; she gave me some excellent punch, was extremely kind and good – but, I don't know, I was on tenterhooks, I might be wrong in my suspicions, I thought at the time, but she made me think badly of her, and I hurried away as soon as I could, my body shaking all over. I had been infected by the local gossip about her character, I probably did her an injustice, but from then on I was suspicious.

The house seems to have been unbelievably dirty. Meisling himself hardly ever washed his hands, and his fingertips were only clean when he had squeezed a lemon into his punch. The privy served both as a larder and a pigsty (the pig died while Andersen was there and was given a fine funeral in the garden), and when there were some left-over meat balls Mrs Meisling would put them into the drawing-room cupboard, where nails and starch and all sorts of other things were kept, so that the maids should not get hold of them before the Meislings and Andersen could have them for supper.

On Sundays Meisling was often in a good humour and would play with the children's tin soldiers and toy theatre, and he would get Andersen to join in. During school hours he was still unpredictable and easily lost his temper. He treated all the teachers very arrogantly and could play nasty tricks on them. Thus he would ask Mr Snitker to dictate French texts to the boys in the top form, and he and his wife would stand outside the classroom door, half choked with laughter – the joke being that Mr Snitker had never learnt French and therefore mispronounced every word. (For a period Mr Snitker gave Andersen private tuition in Latin, and whenever Andersen made a mistake Mr Snitker would beat his son Georg, saying, 'He is my own flesh and blood, so I'm allowed to punish *him*.')

A few more entries in Andersen's diary of 1825 should be quoted as they reveal much about himself:

20 November *Stayed at home all day, read Byron's biography, oh! he was just like me, right down to his fondness for scandal, my soul is ambitious like his, happy only when admired by everybody, even the most insignificant person who refuses to do so can make me unhappy.*

23 November *Some of the other pupils glance into their books, in fact G. reads everything straight out of them. This annoys me, but I wonder if I wouldn't have done the same if I hadn't been so afraid of the disgrace of being caught, and yet I wish the teacher would catch the others, this is a nasty thing in me.*

5 December *Yes, he* [Meisling] *treats me kindly, O God! if only I could show some progress but I'm scared of the exam, I'm balancing somewhere between the two bottom marks, and he must and will be angry, he must think that either I'm very stupid or I don't do my home-work, O Lord! you know me, I won't be afraid, the demon of pride has taken his seat inside me, I believe myself to be possessed with the spirit of a* Digter, *think that I shall reach a high place, and while thinking so another feeling inside me shouts horribly that this is a mad notion, O God! O God! do not forsake me.*

Having been appointed head of the naval academy in 1824 Captain P. F. Wulff had moved into Amalienborg Castle, and his wife, who was one of Andersen's regular correspondents at this time, invited him to spend the Christmas holidays of 1825 as their guest, an invitation he accepted with enthusiasm. He arrived in Copenhagen on 19 December, was cordially received by the Wulffs, had a bedroom and a warm sitting-room and found as a present from Captain Wulff his translation of Shakespeare's plays in three volumes. When he looked out on to Amalienborg Square below he felt like Aladdin in Oehlenschläger's play, and he wrote in his diary: 'Five or six years ago I, too, was walking down there, didn't know a single person in this city, and now I can enjoy my Shakespeare up here with a lovable and respected family – oh! God! you are kind, a drop of the honey of joy makes me forget all bitterness, oh! God will not forsake me – he has made me very happy.'

The next morning Andersen went to see Jonas Collin, who praised his diligence at school. He also spoke to Mrs Collin and met some of the children, Ingeborg, who was about his own age, and Edvard, who was a few years younger, and whom he did not like because he did not speak to the visitor.

During the next few days Andersen was busy visiting old friends and acquaintances, including Adam Oehlenschläger and his daughter Lotte, H. C. Ørsted and his wife (with whom he spent Christmas Eve), Mr and Mrs Dahlén, Professor Guldberg, Mrs Andersen (the actress), and the lady-in-waiting to the crown princess. Whenever he had a chance to do so he would read aloud extracts from his unfinished historical novel or some of his own poems. He was given several theatre tickets, and on 23 December he was invited to the Naval Cadets' Ball in the Wulffs' apartment, but he felt ill at ease and badly dressed, for everybody was dressed up for the occasion since the royal family and members of Copenhagen's high society were present. Andersen's dark blue coat looked very shabby compared with the uniforms and tails, and when he saw Captain Wulff whisper something to his wife, he suspected that they were criticizing his appearance, and he asked Mrs Wulff if his coat was unsuitable. 'It would be better if you had a tail-coat,' she replied, and so he hurried up to his room and changed into the only tail-coat he had, which was made of grey homespun and was the one he used every day at school. Having brushed it almost to pieces he reappeared and then realized that everybody else was wearing *black* tails and he was conspicuous as the only one in grey. 'No one spoke to me except Oehlenschläger, he walked right through the crowds and held out his hand to me, that made me proud.' But he was too embarrassed to enjoy the evening and was afraid of being taken for a waiter. It was especially painful for him that Lotte Oehlenschläger should see him thus attired; for he had decided that he was in love with Lotte, although he later admitted to himself that it was only because she was the daughter of the great *Digter* whom he admired so much. At nine o'clock he sneaked up to his own rooms and (according to his diary) 'went to bed, cursing my fate at having no nice clothes'. Next morning he told the Wulffs that he had had a headache and had therefore had to leave the party before the dancing began.

Andersen was careful to call on Meisling, who was also in Copenhagen, every single day; for Meisling, who wanted to use him as an errand boy – and did so – had insisted on this. When he called on him on 23 December he was told to arrange to go back to Slagelse within a few days, 'for you must get back to your Greek and Latin and start working again'. Andersen's comment in his diary is this: 'That seems to me to be going a bit far, I'm here for a few days, he knows I want to go back and yet he torments me, in strange contrast to the way I'm received by others, every day I come back to him, and even so he doesn't look kindly at me, I would like to love him truly, but I'm not responsible for my own feelings.'

On Boxing Day, when Andersen went to call on Meisling, he was not at home but had left a note for Andersen. It read:

I have nothing to tell you at my departure but must most emphatically request that from the day you arrive in Slagelse you do not spend your time writing stories and poems, with which, to their great amusement, you have entertained certain people – but spend it on school matters. Orally I shall speak to you about the way in which you frustrate my efforts by wasting your time in such a fashion when I thought you were reading your prescribed texts, and I shall supply you with certain facts which may possibly have a cooling effect on you. I do not wish you to take any part in the decoration of the children's Christmas tree, crèches, mascarades, or goodness knows what other things have been planned, seeing that you employ your time badly enough anyway.

MEISLING

Andersen immediately wrote to Meisling explaining that the poem he had read aloud was one he had written during the holidays, and that he worked as hard as he could at school.

Meisling's letter ruined the whole day for him; in the evening he read a new play entitled *William Shakespeare* to Captain and Mrs Wulff; the play was by a

Danish writer called C. J. Boye, and in his diary Andersen wrote:

In the evening I read to the Wulffs Boye's William Skakspear [sic]. *The author has described him quite like me, in act one William's lines agree entirely with my feelings, he has a premonition that he is going to be a* Digter, *he decides not to write poetry, oh! tears came into my eyes.*

By 29 December he was back in Slagelse. Meisling had not yet arrived, but had written to Mrs Meisling that after three days in Copenhagen Andersen had still not collected his books, and that he was lazy. Andersen wrote in his diary: 'A hell is awaiting me; despair – oh! he is too severe, too severe.' On New Year's Eve he went to bed at eight o'clock, Meisling still not having returned; furthermore it was obvious that he had told his wife that Andersen must not play with the children, for they just sat, looking at one another, without saying a word. On New Year's Day 1826 Andersen wrote in his diary: 'God! must the whole year be like today? I'm suffering from anxiety and despondency, wrote some bitter letters to the Collins and the Wulffs. O God, let this be my last New Year's Day!'

On 5 January Andersen was tempted to write a tragedy about Leonardo da Vinci – 'but go away, go away – I daren't, I mustn't.'

When Meisling eventually returned to Slagelse he admitted that he had written his letter in a fit of bad temper; the ominous 'facts' which might have had a cooling effect on Andersen turned out to be a remark by Oehlenschläger to the effect that Andersen took every smile to be a smile of appreciation. And that Andersen might as well have shown his poem to Meisling as to Oehlenschläger, for Meisling was also a poet. Andersen, who feared he had been sent back to the third form, was relieved.

The mood of Andersen's diary followed Meisling's mood. Here are some extracts from the beginning of 1826:

26 January *M. kind and good.*
8 March *M. quite cheerful.*
25 March *M. irritable, I melancholy . . .*
1 April '*However bad my thoughts are of you, you still manage to be worse,*' he said. *Bad mark in Greek. – Dejected. – No! No! I'm no good; I cannot express my feelings. How unhappy I feel, and yet my dissatisfaction gives me pleasure. – I'm burning with a kind of fever! – O Lord! what a strange creature I am.*
2 April *My birthday was quite pleasant. – God knows whether it will be my last one.*

In May the entire Meisling family, their maid, Andersen and another pupil travelled by carriage from Slagelse to Elsinore, where Meisling took over as headmaster of the grammar school.

In a letter to one of his friends Andersen gave a long, detailed description of the journey through Zealand, and he was so pleased with it that he copied it verbatim and sent it to several other friends and acquaintances. Unfortunately one of them, Mr Nyerup, the university librarian, arranged for it to be printed (anonymously) in a Copenhagen paper under the title 'Fragment of a Journey from Roskilde to Elsinore', as a result of which some of his friends in Slagelse sarcastically thanked him for a letter which they had received and later read in print.

On the day after his arrival in Elsinore Andersen wrote to Jonas Collin to say how happy he was to be there. 'Seen from the outside Elsinore did not look very promising to me,' he wrote, 'but now that I am here it seems to me a little Copenhagen. What traffic! What liveliness on the quay, here some fat Dutchmen speak their hollow language, there I hear harmonious Italian, further down coal is being unloaded from an English brig so that I think I can almost smell London.' He was delighted with the scenery; the coastline was like Naples, he was told, and the hills of North Zealand like Switzerland – 'and I felt unspeakably happy; oh! this beautiful landscape must make one into a poet or a painter. Oh! My Benefactor! Thank you, thank you! for every happy moment. After all, life is wonderful!'

The first few months at Elsinore seem to have been happy and harmonious. Andersen got on well with his new school friends and with his new teachers; on 2 July 1826 he wrote to Collin: 'If the teachers continue the humane treatment they have begun, then I can hope for the best and hope that everything will go well; I think Meisling will continue, as he has begun, to take an interest in me.'

Immediately before the school summer holidays Meisling sent Collin a very favourable report on Andersen, whom he considered perfectly worthy of continued public support: 'His natural aptitude is extremely good, indeed in certain spiritual disciplines even brilliant, his diligence constant, and his behaviour, due to his lovable good-naturedness, of such a kind that it may serve as a model to the pupils of a school.'

Andersen's main difficulties were still Latin and Greek, which Meisling continued to teach. He also found Hebrew and French difficult but to his own surprise did far better in mathematics than he had done at Slagelse.

Meisling, who had previously been a teacher at Elsinore (1808–12), had not been well liked by the townspeople then, but now that he was headmaster of the local grammar school all the distinguished ladies of the town came to pay their respects to his wife. Her reaction is described by Andersen:

'I can't tell you how pleased I am,' she said, 'to have come here. Slagelse is such a terrible town, with lots of nasty gossip, no decent woman escapes it.' And then she would tell them all the scandalous things people did in fact say about her. The poor ladies would blush and curtsy and I went off into a reverie while listening to these confessions. As soon as they had left I asked her why she wanted to tell them such things. 'It is better,' she said, 'that I should tell them than for them to hear it from strangers. Coming from my mouth they won't believe it.'

Andersen's obsessional analysis of himself and his shortcomings continued. In a letter to Collin on 2 July 1826 he wrote:

Day by day I make an effort to get to know myself, but as far as ability and strength are concerned I am not very successful, for I feel that my nasty vanity creeps in, and if in a dark moment I judge myself a little too harshly, then I prefer to think better of myself; but Meisling has made me realize that there is a kind of nasty airy-fairyness in me, something restless and hasty in my soul which makes it twice as difficult for me to get to grips with languages.

Colonel Høegh-Guldberg had invited Andersen to spend the summer holidays as his guest in Odense, but as Meisling had promised to give him extra tuition in Greek, he stayed in Elsinore and only made brief visits to Copenhagen. One morning in July he got up at three a.m. and walked all the way to Copenhagen, where he stayed at Amalienborg Castle with Captain and Mrs Wulff. He was so inspired by the scenery on that beautiful summer's day that next day he wrote his first descriptive poem, called 'Evening', and in this poem, for the first time, there is a humorous element.

He also visited the Collin family, but must have felt shy and embarrassed, for after his return to Elsinore he wrote to Jonas Collin (27 July 1826): 'I don't know why but I can speak much more freely and cordially to you by letter than by mouth; I don't feel half so embarrassed.'

The relaxed and relatively happy atmosphere of the first few months at Elsinore did not last. After the summer holidays everything changed for the worse again. Meisling was irritable and would fly into tantrums; Mrs Meisling managed to make her new home as filthy and unpleasant as her house in Slagelse had been, and the quarrels with her servant girls continued. She scolded them for using too much butter, and to prove her point she made a wager that in a week or a month she could manage with just so little, and so the tub was moved into the library where Andersen and the other boarder had their beds; late at night she would creep in and steal butter from her own tub in order not to lose her wager. It was not long before the rumours about Mrs Meisling's affairs were as bad as they had been in Slagelse. Meisling himself quarrelled with some of the teachers, and Andersen was constantly being told that the two hundred rixdollars paid annually for his board and lodging was far from sufficient, and that Meisling regretted ever having taken him with him to Elsinore.

Andersen must have written to Collin in despair soon after the summer holidays were over, for on 19 August 1826 Collin wrote back:

Be sensible and don't get upset, Andersen, take things the way they are in this world and not the way you imagine they ought to be. One may come across unpleasant experiences in any walk of life, but this is no reason for leaving it. Especially one mustn't give up one's school career. The written report the headmaster sent me about you was extremely advantageous, so don't lose either your head or your courage when he speaks to you in a serious, indeed probably harsh tone of voice; he is your closest superior, and you must obey him.

Andersen must also have written to Mrs Wulff telling her how unhappy he was, for on 25 August 1826 she wrote to him to say that she was worried having seen from 'both your two recent letters' how sad and miserable he felt. She told him to be patient, and added, 'The fact that in his violent temper Meisling tells you that you are *mad* etc. cannot surprise you very much – you've heard that from him before!' She admonished Andersen to follow the example of Christ and put his trust in him: 'Christ is our Redeemer! – but there are others as well in this life, look for them and follow their examples! Take also fictional images, look at little Cinderella, how she was hated and persecuted by her father and sisters, who *ought* to have loved her, but patiently she put up with her lot, and what a reward she got.'

It is doubtful how much comfort Andersen found in the story of Cinderella, for Meisling did his utmost to crush his hope of a happy ending. That was what worried Andersen most of all – Meisling's deliberate effort to kill in him even the dream of ever becoming a *Digter*, for if that dream could not be realized he saw no point at all in having to endure all this suffering. 'Every day he told me that nothing would ever become of me, that I was stupid, that I would get nowhere,' Andersen wrote in his first autobiography. He wished to die, he said, 'that was my thought when I went to bed in the evening, and I woke up with it in the morning'. It was not only that Meisling wanted to prevent him from writing poems or stories as long as he was at school; he rammed down Andersen's throat that he was no good at all and would *never* be more than a fifth-rate writer. The extraordinary thing is that it was in a mood of sadness and despair caused by such remarks that Andersen wrote the poem which was the first one to give him fame both at home and abroad, 'The Dying Child'. By trying to kill the poet in him Meisling had released his poetic talent.

To present-day readers the poem may seem sentimental, but it undoubtedly gives a genuine expression of Andersen's melancholy mood at the time, and its popularity was extraordinary and lasting. The poem is given here in full in an English version by R. P. Keigwin:

> Mother, I'm so tired, I want to sleep now;
>   Let me fall asleep and feel you near,
> Please don't cry – there now, you'll promise, won't you?
>   On my face I felt your burning tear.
> Here's so cold, and winds outside are frightening,
>   But in dreams – ah, that's what I like best:
> I can see the darling angel children,
>   When I shut my sleepy eyes and rest.
>
> Mother, look, the Angel's here beside me!
>   Listen, too, how sweet the music grows.
> See, his wings are both so white and lovely;
>   Surely it was God who gave him those.
> Green and red and yellow floating round me,
>   They are flowers the Angel came and spread.
> Shall I, too, have wings while I'm alive, or –
>   Mother, is it only when I'm dead?
>
> Why do you take hold of me so tightly,
>   Put your cheek to mine the way you do?
> And your cheek is wet, but yet it's burning –
>   Mother, I shall always be with you . . .
> Yes, but then you mustn't go on sighing;

When you cry I cry as well, you see.
I'm so tired – my eyes they won't stay open –
Mother – look – the Angel's kissing me!

In his despair Andersen identified himself with a dying child, for in the poem everything is seen through the eyes of that child. Later in life, at a more mature age, Andersen was able to treat the subject of a dying child from a different angle; for in his masterly 'Story of a Mother' everything is seen through the mother's eyes. When he wrote 'The Dying Child' he was still a child, in spite of his age.

By this time he had come to regard writing poetry as a sin:

After I had written it I had the most terrible pangs of conscience; for writing poetry was something I was not allowed to do. So it eased my mind considerably when I copied it in a letter to Collin, whom I assured that it was something I could not help, that it had come entirely by itself, and that I hadn't wasted any time in writing it. I even showed it to Mr and Mrs Meisling, for it did seem to me that I had committed a sin by writing a poem when this was forbidden.

Following Høegh-Guldberg's advice Andersen decided to have it out with Meisling himself, and in the autumn of 1826 he wrote a letter, which began as follows:

I must talk to you. I haven't the courage to do so personally, therefore I am writing these lines, which I hope will not increase your dissatisfaction with me. I am fully convinced that your intentions concerning me are honest and good, otherwise you would never have taken me with you here. I cannot repay your kindness in the way an intelligent person would be able to, the only thing I can do is to have full confidence in you, and I intend to do that. For more than four weeks you have shown yourself dissatisfied with me, this has increased day by day, and I see no possibility of improving this situation and am despairing about myself.

He went on to give an account of his background, talked about his life before coming to Slagelse, and described his present state of mind:

If you ask me a question my blood starts boiling in my head and for fear of giving the wrong answer I often reply without really knowing what I am saying, and whenever this has happened the desperate idea comes to my mind: nothing will become of me, I am good at nothing, and then I remain completely silent.

He assured Meisling that he was not lazy, and that sometimes he wished he had never been born. He implored Meisling not to be impatient with him and not to despise him for appealing to him in this way.

Andersen's letter had a certain temporary effect, for Meisling told him not to lose courage; he was severe, he said, only to get good results for Andersen in his final examination.

But the relief was shortlived. At the annual examination in the autumn of 1826 Andersen did so badly in Latin composition and Greek that Meisling began to treat him worse than ever before. On 24 October Andersen wrote a long letter to Collin from which the following extracts will give an idea of Meisling's behaviour:

Every day he expresses his dislike of me and when I bring him my Latin composition on Sunday mornings every mistake makes him shatter my soul with the most terrible truths. I dare not doubt that he means well, but everything arouses his dislike of me, and I live in the most terrible tension. . . .

I shall tell you Meisling's words to me during the last fortnight, almost the very ones he used, and I am sure you will forgive me for being dejected. – Last Sunday I brought him my composition and being angry with my mistakes he then said, 'I'm despairing about you when I think of the final examination. At examen artium *such a composition would result in a nought. You think it doesn't matter about a single letter, that it's the same whether you write* e *or* i. *If I had thought of that I would never have taken you with me to Elsinore. You are the most narrow-minded person I have met, and all the same you believe yourself to be something. If you were really a poet then you would drop your studies, devote yourself entirely to poetry. If you couldn't make a living out of it in Denmark, then there's the whole of Germany for you. But you are no good at all! You may be able to write an occasional drinking song, make some rhymes about the sun and the moon, but such things are nothing but pranks. I, too, can write, probably just as well as you can, but it is only tomfoolery . . .'*

'You are lazy,' he says, 'an intolerable monkey, a mad person, a stupid numskull!', etc.

It was too late for him to become an artisan, Andersen concluded his long letter to Collin, but there were other possibilities, 'at least I am honest, and that is something', and perhaps he might get a clerical job in an office, in Jutland, or Norway, or the West Indies, 'but, please, don't throw me over! I have only got you! You must give me life or death.'

Two days later Collin wrote back:

Do not lose heart, my dear Andersen, compose yourself, calm down and be level-headed, then you will see that everything works out all right. The headmaster means well. Maybe his method is somewhat different from that of others, but it will lead to the desired goal all the same. Maybe more some other time, for now I am pressed for time. May God give you strength!

To an old school friend in Slagelse, Emil Hundrup, Andersen wrote on 31 October:

You will never see me happy again. Oh! Emil, do not read the Digtere, *the dream world you find in their works is to be found nowhere in this world. I wish my father had burnt every book I ever got hold of and had forced me to make shoes, then I would never have become mad, would never have had to disappoint my benefactors.*

The situation was now so critical that Mrs Wulff realized that something had to be done, so she went personally to discuss the matter with Jonas Collin, and on 16 November she wrote to Andersen in confidence that she and Collin had worked out a plan to improve his condition at Elsinore: within a few days

Collin would write to Meisling but in such a way that Andersen could not be blamed for it.

On 24 November Collin did write to Meisling. He said that he had not heard from Andersen for a long time and was worried because his last letter had been a very melancholy one. He then continued:

This, together with some words I heard at a party a couple of weeks ago, and to which at the time I did not pay much attention, has created in me an anxiety, maybe completely unfounded, that you had become dissatisfied with him and he, in consequence thereof, had lost heart altogether (in which case my hope of his progress is soon finished), an anxiety which I had not previously had, satisfied as I was with the excellent report you gave him in the autumn.

Collin ended by politely asking Meisling to give him some information concerning these matters.

Meisling reacted by writing immediately a furious and deeply insulting letter to Collin in which he suggested that he was a busybody who tried to interfere in matters for which Meisling alone was responsible, and that he was acting irresponsibly on the basis of mere gossip; he ended by saying that he was quite prepared to leave Andersen's final education in the hands of others.

Next morning in a fit of rage Meisling asked Andersen why he had complained to Collin and tried to find out from him who was 'the gossipmonger' in Copenhagen. He told Andersen to write immediately to Collin to ask whether he wanted him to stay with Meisling for the remaining part of the quarter for which advance payment had been made, for he could certainly not stay in Meisling's house any longer than that.

Andersen did as requested and ended his letter to Collin:

O God! this, then, is the end! Is there no possibility that I can get private tuition? The meals I can get somehow, and the money which is saved could then be used to pay a teacher. That I will be diligent goes without saying, for my life is at stake.

Jonas Collin wrote back to say that there might be a change of some kind, in which case he would be informed later on where to go. He wrote a very cool letter to Meisling ('from your reply I learn that you have not considered yourself obliged to answer me politely'), refuting the accusations of interfering or listening to gossip. He concluded his letter: 'If you do not want Andersen to remain in your house I hope I shall be informed about it some weeks in advance.'

And what happened after all this? However strange it may seem, the answer is: nothing at all. When Meisling had calmed down again he did not want Andersen to leave; Collin thought it was best for Andersen not to change school once again; and Andersen accepted the decision.

Once again there was a temporary improvement in the relations between Andersen and his headmaster; a letter from Andersen to Collin written 1 February 1827 is quite cheerful and relaxed. But, as usual, it did not last long. On 24 February Mrs Wulff wrote to Andersen: 'It makes me very sad to see from your last letters that once again you are unhappy.'

Collin told Andersen that if he wished to do so he could go back to his old school in Slagelse, and Andersen wrote to his friend Emil Hundrup, who advised him strongly against doing so.

Early in March he must have been on the point of a break-down and sent Mrs Wulff a desperate letter, for she wrote back on 8 March: 'My dear, good Andersen, for heaven's sake, calm down! Why is "everything lost"? Be calm until Councillor Collin informs you of his decision.' This time she scolded him for depicting the situation as if everybody had let him down:

'You certainly do your utmost to tire your friends, and I can't believe it can amuse yourself – all in consequence of your constant concern with YOURSELF – YOUR OWN SELF – THE GREAT DIGTER YOU THINK YOU'LL BE – *my dear Andersen! Don't you realize that you are not going to succeed in all these ideas and that you are on the wrong road – supposing I had the idea that I wanted to be Empress of Brazil and I found that all my attempts went wrong, that no one was interested in them, would I not then have to do my utmost to summon enough reason and thought to see: I am Mrs Wulff – do your duty! and don't be a fool! – would the conviction not have to be accepted that it is greater to be good at something small than bad at something great? – because I had had such a silly idea – and don't for a minute think that you ever will be, my dear Andersen!'*

As H. Topsøe-Jensen has said: 'It was not easy for Mrs Wulff to realize that she was speaking to a future Emperor of Brazil.'

According to Andersen's autobiography, Meisling complained that he ate too much, and Mrs Meisling liked to embarrass him in front of the servant girls – 'in short, it was detestable, unhappy, I was on the point of being destroyed and succumbing to Meisling's scorn and erroneous way of treating me,' Andersen wrote.

This time the help came from a teacher, Christian Werliin, a young man of Andersen's own age (twenty-two), who had seen at close quarters how Meisling treated Andersen, to whom he had himself taken a liking. Werliin went to Copenhagen with Andersen in the Easter vacation 1827 and encouraged him to see Collin and tell him how bad things really were. This Andersen did on the morning after he had arrived (he was staying as usual with the Wulffs at Amalienborg Castle), but Collin appeared still to be firmly convinced that Andersen ought to stay on with Meisling at Elsinore. When Werliin heard this he went himself to see Collin and had a long talk with him. Nobody knows what he told Collin, but whatever it was (and it may well also have had something to do with Mrs Meisling's morals) it made Collin decide there and then that Andersen should leave Elsinore and have private tuition in Copenhagen during his final year, and he at once wrote a letter to Meisling to that effect.

'How happy I was,' Andersen writes in *Levnedsbogen*. 'I could breathe and live again! My old happy spirits returned, I could hardly sleep the following night.'

It was decided that Andersen should go back to Elsinore by steamer on Easter Sunday and take leave, properly and politely, of Mr and Mrs Meisling. When he arrived Meisling was away, and Andersen did not dare tell Mrs

Meisling of Collin's decision before her husband's return. However his mood was such that one day when a boy from his class happened to pass by Andersen shouted out of the window, 'I'm going to leave school, I'm going to Copenhagen,' and nearly jumped out of the window for joy.

Meisling returned on the Wednesday after Easter. When he saw Andersen he said coldly, 'Haven't you left? When are you going?' 'Tomorrow with the mail-coach,' was Andersen's reply. Nothing more was said. On the following morning when Meisling came into the library Andersen went up to him and said, 'I would like to say good-bye and thank you for all the kindness you have shown to me.' Meisling's reply was, 'You can go to hell!'

On Thursday morning, 18 April 1827, Andersen left Meisling's house and Elsinore. What he later referred to as 'the darkest, the bitterest time of my life' had come to an end.

Ten years later he happened to meet Meisling in Copenhagen. He gives an account of the meeting in a letter to B. S. Ingemann written on 5 January 1838:

I had one joyful experience at Christmas: Meisling approached me in the street and said that he must tell me that he had not been kind to me in the school but had misjudged me, for which he was sorry, and that I was high above him, as he expressed himself; he asked me to forget his hardness and said about himself: 'The honour is yours, the shame is mine!' Oh, I was moved!

According to what he told another friend Andersen also ran into Mrs Meisling in Copenhagen one day several years after he had left her house. She was very outspoken about her unhappy marriage to a man whom, she said, she had detested for a long time and to whom she felt that she owed no obligation. Now she had her liberty and had come to Copenhagen on a little excursion and lived alone in a lodging-house in Vestergade, and if Andersen would like to pay her 'a tender visit' he would be very welcome. He did not accept the invitation and never saw her again. He was reminded of her, however, when he was in Switzerland in 1833, for according to his diary he went into a privy at Simplon, and inside the privy were two cupboards with jars full of jam – 'and I thought I was in the Meisling house'.

Meisling himself haunted his dreams for the rest of his life as can be seen from these extracts from his diaries:

30 January 1834 *Last night I dreamt something about the Pope and Meisling.*
8 June 1857 *Very unsettled sleep; again dreamt myself back in Meisling's house.*
26 July 1860 *Dreamt again last night that I was with Meisling at the school in Slagelse, was supposed to take a degree but wouldn't, couldn't, knew nothing; felt terribly dependent on old Collin, also on Edvard whom I tried to confide in.*
1 January 1865 *Dreamt about Meisling whose school I wanted to leave.*
15 February 1866 *Nasty dreams with Meisling in them.*
14 May 1866 *Slept restlessly, dreamt about Meisling.*
28 October 1867 *Slept restlessly; nasty dreams, felt oppressed by Meisling and dependent on Collin, both on old Collin and Edvard; afraid of what they would say because I had left Meisling.*

4 June 1870 Slept badly last night. My dream was again about being dependent; I ran away from Meisling, was afraid of old Collin, for they were not satisfied with me in the new school.

13 July 1871 Dreamt that I had to be examined by Meisling during the visit of the royal family; I didn't want to be, for I knew that I couldn't do the Latin translation and so would be laughed at, then I woke up.

30 July 1874 A painful dream about Meisling, in front of whom I stood miserable and awkward.

The last time Meisling's name is mentioned in Andersen's diaries is on 9 December 1874, eight months before he died; then his dream was of a different kind:

The morphia must have had a strong effect, I had lovely dreams and in particular a pleasant one in which I was sitting for my examination in good spirits when Meisling entered, and I told him he mustn't hear me being examined, for then I should feel very oppressed in case I gave a stupid answer, as in fact I did. A little later I went for a walk with Meisling; he was in his kind of good spirits, I felt happy and contented, we soon began talking about art and all sorts of beautiful things, and in the end we became great friends, he seemed to be fond of me and I of him. When I woke up I was quite pleased about this dream of reconciliation.

4 'He's either mad, a lover, or a poet . . .'

1827-33

IN HIS book about Andersen and the Collin family, written after Andersen's death, Edvard Collin discusses the contrasts in Andersen's personality and mentions the 'split personality' of the young man who went to school at Slagelse and Elsinore: half a *Digter*, half a schoolboy, a person who at times felt like a caged bird, but at others could think of nothing but his school reports. Edvard Collin then adds the remark, 'He was diligent, he read much; but how did he read? He learned many things, but "he never learned to learn properly".'

Edvard Collin was a man who had learned to learn properly; he was in many ways an almost predictable product of class and education, and his words undoubtedly echo a resigned sentiment shared by the other members of the Collin clan. Jonas Collin's purpose in rescuing Andersen and sending him to a grammar school was not to make a great writer out of him but to enable him to become a useful member of the community in a social class higher than the one into which he was born. The grammar-school system was devised to teach boys to learn properly, to mould them into the desired finished products, to make them grow up to be like their fathers.

When he was sent to Slagelse grammar school in 1822 Andersen was desperately in need of basic education, and without it he could never have achieved what he eventually did. But fortunately the school never succeeded in 'breaking him in' completely; fortunately he resisted the attempts to mould him into a set shape, and therefore, in the eyes of Meisling, he left Elsinore a complete failure.

Many people would have shared Meisling's view and regarded the five years Andersen had spent at the grammar schools of Slagelse and Elsinore as completely wasted, for he had not passed any final examination, nor had he any certificate of any kind to show the world. The sole aim of his education had been to enable him to pass the important *examen artium* which automatically qualified its holder to become a student in the University of Copenhagen, and Jonas Collin would undoubtedly have been reluctant to allow him to leave Meisling and Elsinore if it had meant abandoning that goal.

But fortunately, when he had spoken to Collin and urged him to take Andersen away from Meisling, Werliin had a trump card up his sleeve, for he had an answer to the question Jonas Collin would inevitably put to him: What is going to happen to Andersen's *examen artium* if he leaves Elsinore? For Werliin, who was a student of theology and taught Hebrew at Elsinore, had a friend and colleague, L. C. Müller – nicknamed 'the Hebrew Müller' – who was prepared to act as Andersen's private tutor in Copenhagen and prepare

him for his *examen artium* during his final year. This arrangement was acceptable to Collin. Andersen rented a small attic room in a widow's house in the
centre of Copenhagen, and for his dinners he went on a regular rota among his
various friends and benefactors: on Mondays to the Wulffs, on Tuesdays to the
Collins, and so on. Sunday was the only day without a regular appointment
for dinner, so that on that day he was able to accept invitations from others.

To begin with Andersen felt most at home with Captain and Mrs Wulff and
their daughter Henriette, who became one of his closest friends. It took him
quite some time to feel at home among the members of the Collin family,
about whom he writes in *Levnedsbogen*:

I was in some way really afraid of the father, though I loved him with all my heart;
my fear was due to the fact that I regarded him as my life's destiny, indeed, my entire
existence depended upon him. The eldest daughter was married and had left home,
she was the one who had spoken to me most, the other children did not do so at all,
in fact, Edvard seemed to me so cold, so forbidding, that I really believed that he
could not stand me, that he was arrogant, and even my enemy. That is what I
believed of the man who later on became infinitely dear to me, and whom I now
know to be my first, my most reliable friend.

Müller taught Andersen every subject except mathematics; for Andersen had
suddenly begun to understand mathematics and was able to do that on his own.
He liked Müller and they got on very well, except for one thing: Müller was
an orthodox evangelist, and they clashed irreconcilably on matters of
theology, for Andersen was and remained throughout his life an unorthodox
believer, firmly convinced of the existence of an almighty God and a believer
in the immortality of the soul but (like his father) a disbeliever in the Devil
and in the existence of hell. Unlike Andersen, Müller believed every word in
the Bible to be true, and he was both hurt and shocked when he found that
Andersen did not share that belief.

Though in principle he was still under a moral obligation to refrain from
writing poems and imaginative prose Andersen spent most of his free time
doing so. He was delighted when he met Johan Ludvig Heiberg for the first
time at his Friday dinner with H. C. Ørsted. He was the poet and playwright
who at that time might have been said to be the dictator of literary taste in
intellectual circles in Copenhagen. Heiberg took an interest in Andersen and
printed some of his poems in his journal, *Kjøbenhavns flyvende Post*, in 1827
and 1828.

The German poet Ludolph Schley, whom Andersen had met at Elsinore,
had translated his then unpublished poem 'The Dying Child' into German,
and in Schley's translation it was first published in a German newspaper, but
without any mention of the author's name. This resulted in the Danish original
being printed, alongside the German translation, in *Kjøbenhavnsposten* in
September 1827, and the poem, which had a popularity almost unequalled by
any other poem by Andersen, was reprinted by Heiberg in *Kjøbenhavns
flyvende Post* in December 1828.

When L. C. Müller moved to the Copenhagen district called Christianshavn on the island of Amager, Andersen had to walk there twice daily to have his lessons. In the evenings he did his home-work in his attic, though time and again he was tempted by what he called 'The Rhyme Devil' (an expression he used as the title of one of his poems). These daily walks from the centre of Copenhagen to Christianshavn also inspired him to begin writing his first major prose work, *Journey on Foot to Amager*, extracts from which were printed in Heiberg's journal in 1828.

From an educational point of view Latin composition was still Andersen's weakest point, and very bad marks in that subject could still deprive him of his *examen artium*, which he was due to take in October 1828. 'The examination is only six weeks away and I know I shall fail,' he wrote to Henriette Wulff on 14 August.

When Andersen eventually presented himself in the university it so happened that Adam Oehlenschläger was the dean of the faculty of arts that year. In this capacity he had to receive all prospective students and when Andersen handed him his birth certificate and other documents Oehlenschläger kindly took his hand and wished him luck. Andersen did reasonably well, except in Latin, but the result there was not bad enough to fail him. During the oral examination he was so nervous that he spluttered ink from his pen all over the face of one of the examiners, who was kind enough, however, not to say anything but just to wipe the ink off his face.

Andersen had now passed the final examination which Meisling had told him time and again he would never pass. It had taken him six hard years to qualify as an academic citizen. But he was not aiming at a university degree. He was now fully convinced that he wanted to be a *Digter*. And even the Collins had to resign themselves to this fact.

In the period preceding his *examen artium* and in the year immediately following it Andersen developed a wry humour and a youthful irony which is clearly noticeable in some of his poems and prose works. To some extent this may perhaps be seen as a reaction against the melancholy mood which had predominated in his years at Slagelse and Elsinore. But the light-heartedness and irony, including irony at his own expense, which are characteristic of this period of his life, were not entirely new. His poem 'The Evening', which he wrote during an excursion from Elsinore to Copenhagen in 1826, ended with a stanza clearly intended as a humorous self-portrait, here quoted in a literal translation:

> Look, yonder on the hill a lanky person,
> His face as pale as that of Werther,
> His nose as mighty as a cannon,
> His eyes are tiny, like green peas.
> He sings a German song with a *'woher?'*
> And longingly stares at the sunset.
> I wonder why he's standing there so long.
> Well, bless my soul! I'm not omniscient;
> Yet one thing is certain, if I'm not mistaken:
> He's either mad, a lover, or a poet.

There is also reason to believe that Andersen's sense of humour was further developed under the influence of Henriette Wulff, the intelligent and spirited but physically handicapped girl, with whom he developed a close friendship which lasted as long as she lived. She found 'The Dying Child' a sentimental poem and to some extent infected him with her own humour.

A direct result of his new mood was his prose work *Journey on Foot to Amager*, which was published at his own expense on 2 January 1829 after he had turned down the offer of a Copenhagen publisher to buy the rights for seventy rixdollars. The venture proved successful, for a first edition of 500 copies was soon sold out, after which the same publisher offered him better terms for the right to print a second, enlarged edition, which came out in April 1829. On the whole the book was well received both by the critics and the public.

Journey on Foot to Amager takes place, according to the sub-title, 'in the years 1828 and 1829', the joke being that it takes place from a few hours before midnight on New Year's Eve until a few hours after midnight. It is an exuberant, fantastic and youthful arabesque in the style of E. T. A. Hoffmann, who was Andersen's literary idol at the time. The main character is a young poet (Andersen himself, of course) to whom all sorts of fantastic things happen on his nightly journey: he meets the Lyrical Muse; he is carried three hundred years forward in time to the year 2129; he hears Hoffmann's book *Die Elixiere des Teufels* telling its own story; he meets a giant who is really a Tom Thumb from the planet of Sirius; he meets Saint Peter, who has the keys to the gate of Amager, and borrows his spectacles, which enable him to see many things invisible to other mortals; he meets Ahasuerus and borrows his hundred-league boots, etc., etc.

There is also an oblique reference to Meisling in the book; for at one point the poet meets the Devil in the disguise of a schoolmaster: 'He looked horrible. His hair stood out bristling and uncombed round his purple face; his eyes had a greenish shine, and the entire person showed itself to belong in the pool.' Those who knew Meisling immediately recognized the headmaster whom his pupils at Slagelse and Elsinore had nicknamed 'the Monster'.

Andersen was also in the mood for writing parodies, and when he re-read his own immature tragedy *The Forest Chapel* he found it utterly ridiculous and was inspired to write a mock-heroic vaudeville entitled *Love on Saint Nicolas' Tower*, which was produced in the Royal Theatre. Apparently it did not worry either the author or the public that he was flogging dead horses, for the satire was directed against a kind of tragedy which was a thing of the past.

In his autobiography Andersen writes about the first performance:

When the play was staged it was received by my fellow students with enthusiasm, they shouted, 'Long live the author!' I neither thought nor saw further on, I was overwhelmed with joy, I attached far more importance to it than it had; I was bursting with happiness, rushed out of the theatre, into the street, into Collin's house, where only his wife was at home. Nearly fainting I threw myself into a chair, sobbing, crying hysterically. The sympathetic woman had no idea what it meant

Andersen's self-portrait, drawn in a
letter to Henriette Wulff on 29 April,
1835.

and so began to comfort me with words such as, 'Don't take it so much to heart.
Oehlenschläger and many other great writers have also been hissed off the stage.' –
'But they didn't hiss at all,' I interrupted her, sobbing; 'they applauded and shouted
"Long live!"'

The account is probably somewhat exaggerated, for we know from other
sources that there was in fact a certain amount of hissing and booing, and the
play was only performed three times.

The two foreign poets most admired in Denmark at that time were Byron
and Heine, and in the spring of 1829 Andersen went through what might be
described as a Heine fever, for he and a student friend read and recited Heine all
the time, especially his love poetry which particularly appealed to Andersen.
In his autobiography he writes that there were only three writers who
'spiritually have gone into my blood and with whom I have lived completely
for a time', namely Scott, Hoffmann and Heine.

Andersen had decided to enter himself for an examination in philosophy and
philology which students of all faculties had to take as a prerequisite for an
honours degree; the examination, which consisted of two parts known as
Philosophicum and *Philologicum*, was usually taken one year after *examen artium*.
In October 1829 Andersen passed both parts of the examination and was now
entitled to call himself *candidatus philosophiæ*. One of his examiners was
Ørsted, whose initial questions he had answered satisfactorily, but then came
the final question: 'Please tell me what you know about electro-magnetics.'
'I don't even know the word,' Andersen told the discoverer of electro-
magnetism, 'there is no mention of it in your textbook on chemistry.' Ørsted
admitted that this was true but added that he had talked about it in his lectures.
'I have attended all of them except one,' Andersen said, 'so you must have
talked about it at the one I missed.' Later, in Ørsted's house, Andersen asked

him to explain about electro-magnetics, and for the first time he heard about the important discovery on which H. C. Ørsted's fame is still based.

In January 1830 a volume of poetry by Andersen, entitled *Digte*, was published; this included many of his recent humorous poems. After this he again took up the idea of writing an historical novel, set in Denmark at the beginning of the sixteenth century, and to be published under the title *Christian II's Dwarf*. He began a systematic collection of historical material for his novel, and in this connection decided to visit some of the places connected with his story. In the summer of 1829 he had visited various places on Zealand and Funen, and now he decided to go to Jutland, where he had never been. So having saved up a small sum of money he set out on a more extensive tour of Denmark, went by steamship to Aarhus, saw the Jutland moors and visited several Jutland towns; to his delight he found himself received everywhere as a budding author whose name was already known, mainly due to his *Journey on Foot to Amager*. From Jutland he went to Funen, saw his mother whom he had also visited the year before, and spent ten days as the guest of Mrs Iversen (whose husband had died in 1827) at her country house near Odense. Surrounded by Mrs Iversen's granddaughters and other young girls who admired 'the poet', Andersen felt happy and at ease. Eager, however, to get to know some of the other towns on Funen he went on to Svendborg, where he toured the neighbourhood. Andersen's diaries for the years 1827–31 are entirely lost, although the contents of a small fragment, covering 4 and 5 August 1830, when he was staying at Svendborg, are known (though no longer extant). The entry for 5 August ends with these words:

Almighty God! I have only got you, you govern my destiny, I must give myself to you! Please give me a living! Please give me a bride! My blood wants love, as my heart wants it.

Two days later Andersen met a young girl with whom he fell in love.

What happened was this. On 6 August, he arrived at the little provincial town of Faaborg, where one of his fellow students lived, a young man called Christian Voigt, who had invited him to come and visit him at the house of his father, a wealthy local merchant. Andersen found a room at an inn, and from there he sent his visiting card to his friend, who came round immediately and invited him to spend the next day at his parents' house.

When Andersen arrived the next morning his friend Christian was still asleep, and the person who received him was the eldest daughter, Miss Riborg Voigt, a girl of twenty-four, who had read his *Journey on Foot* and some of his poems. This is how Andersen described her in *Levnedsbogen*, written in 1832, two years after the event:

The eldest daughter received me with great kindness, blushing every moment when she spoke to me; otherwise she seemed gay and lively. She had a very lovely face, with much childishness in it, but her eyes looked clever and thoughtful, they were brown and very much alive. She wore a simple, grey morning dress which was very becoming; in fact, her entire simplicity and this face of hers won me over for her immediately. Her interest in my poems, indeed the very fact that she seemed to have a kind of respect for me, tickled my vanity and immediately made me interested in her. She made jokes about her brother's sluggard manners, proved herself possessed with so much spirit and humour that I, too, felt a desire to make myself interesting – I don't know why, but it was almost immediately as if the two of us had known one another for a long time, and it gave me a tremendous pleasure the whole day to please the young girl.

Andersen was persuaded to stay for a couple of days at Faaborg, and with the Voigt family he went on boating trips and excursions in the neighbourhood, and even to a dance at the house of one of their friends. Riborg was fond of dancing but on hearing that Andersen did not dance she sat down next to him and entertained him all evening. Before leaving he went for a walk with Riborg and her younger sister and jokingly told Riborg that he would name the heroine of his next novel after her. When she asked him to give her one of his own poems in his own handwriting he copied out for her his poem 'Avis aux lectrices', the point of which is that the poet wants a wife but she will have to praise all his poems, for if she doesn't he will break off the engagement.

From Faaborg Andersen wrote on 9 August 1830 to Edvard Collin:

The ladies in this town are the most good-looking I have come across so far, Jutland included, and one of Mr Voigt's daughters is even beautiful and, what I like particularly, very natural.

On the following day he went back to Mrs Iversen's country house, but the young girls there found his behaviour so much changed that teasingly they told him that he must have fallen in love. In *Levnedsbogen* Andersen described his reaction:

The first time I heard this it was as if a fire went through my body, and I put it off as a joke but could not help thinking about it. I myself was struck by the way I behaved, by the manner in which I had acted during the few days I had spent with her. I began to long for her; the others made jokes about me; I did not like it and wanted to get these thoughts out of my head altogether. I found it ridiculous that I, who had always spoken mockingly about love and *Schwärmerei*, should now fall a victim to it myself.

Though he was twenty-five Andersen had never been in love before – 'my own person had given me enough to think of, without thinking of anybody else,' as he candidly admitted.

He tried to forget the whole incident, he says; in Faaborg he had heard it said that Riborg was more or less engaged to a son of the local apothecary, but he had also heard the rumour that her parents were against the engagement. When he was back in Copenhagen, however, he visited his friend Christian Voigt much more often than he had done before. One day he was told that Riborg had soon to come to Copenhagen, and had told her brother that she hoped to see Andersen again. They did in fact see one another several times during her three weeks stay, and when Andersen read to her part of a libretto on which he was working at the time he felt that the lovers' dialogue contained a message to her. When she gave him her hand he pressed it to his lips and now realized, he says, that he was deeply in love with her. He gave her some of his own handwritten poems, including a recent one entitled 'To Her' as a secret message of love. Andersen also began to make enquiries about the young man to whom Riborg was 'unofficially engaged' and was told, he says, that he was unworthy of her and unwilling to give her up because she was rich.

One evening he went to see Christian Voigt alone and confided to him his secret love for Riborg. Christian pressed Andersen's hand and told him that this did not come as a surprise to him; but all he could say was that he knew that Riborg *liked* Andersen. Andersen had hoped for a private meeting between Riborg and himself but nothing came of it. So in his despair Andersen wrote a letter to her; it was dated Copenhagen, 30 October 1830, and began:

It is impossible for me to find an opportunity to speak to you about something I must tell you, something you must know before leaving. Least of all did I want to put this on paper, but this is my only, my last resort, and in my heart I am convinced that you are possessed of a pure, female emotion, that my profound confidence in you will not be scorned, and that no one else will see these words. Promise me not to put this paper away until you have read everything, and let me at least find a sisterly heart the first time I really open mine to someone else.

Andersen then went on to say that Riborg had shown him more than what was usually called 'social kindness', but when he first met her he did not know that she was engaged. He then continued:

NOW *your brother has told me about your engagement, and consequently I ought to withdraw in resignation but – I think you have already sensed my feelings, I am not enough of a man of the world to be able to conceal my heart, and I dream of a hope, without which my life is lost.* DO YOU REALLY LOVE THE OTHER MAN? *I do not know him at all, cannot have anything against him, and I dare say he has his good sides since you have chosen him, but do you really love one another?*

If this was so, then Andersen would wish all the best for both of them and hope they would be happy, and she should regard his letter as nothing more than a poetic attempt; 'but if you do not love him as much as God and your eternal bliss, if you are not quite certain – ? Then do not make me unhappy!' Andersen assured her that he was prepared to do anything she and her parents might demand from him. 'You are my one and only thought, my everything, and a poet's heart beats stronger than any other heart.'

Andersen's love letter ended on a pessimistic note, however:

If you really love the other person, then forgive me! Forgive me for having dared do this, which will then be an effrontery. I wish you will both be happy! and please do not forget someone who can never, never forget you. If you have not been insulted by this letter, then give me permission to see you once more, and then I shall read my destiny in each of your expressions. I rely on your female heart that you will destroy this letter or give it back to me. Now you know everything! – Bless you! Maybe good-bye for ever!

And in a postscript he added:

Do not, for God's sake, believe that all this is one of my poetic dreams! For three months my heart and my thoughts have been obsessed with it, now I cannot live in this uncertainty any longer, I must know your decision. But forgive me, please forgive me! I was unable to act otherwise. Good-bye!

Hans Brix has – rightly, I think – characterized this love letter as 'a warning against the thought of their engagement' and maintained that the method used by Andersen was bound to lead to a result exactly opposite the one at which he was apparently aiming.

In the detailed account in *Levnedsbogen* Andersen says that he heard (presumably from Christian Voigt) that when she read his letter Riborg had burst into tears and said that it was her duty to be faithful to the other man, and that she would make him unhappy if she broke off her engagement to him, for he really loved her. Andersen saw her in the Royal Theatre the same evening, where she sat in the audience with her father and sister; 'her eyes sought mine, she was deathly pale and yet very beautiful, extremely beautiful,' Andersen writes. She did not see Andersen alone, but she and her family spent the next evening, which was her last in Copenhagen, in the Royal Theatre again, and when they left the theatre Andersen stood outside to say good-bye.

On the following morning Riborg's brother gave Andersen a note from her:

Good-bye, good-bye! I hope Christian will soon be able to tell me that you are as calm and happy as before.
With sincere friendship,
RIBORG

One must presume that his love letter to her was enclosed with this letter. Six months later Riborg Voigt married her fiancé.

Andersen tried to convince himself that in spite of everything Riborg really loved him, and that it was only her sense of duty and loyalty to the man to whom she was engaged that prevented her from accepting his proposal. In this he was probably wrong. In an undated letter to her brother, Riborg wrote: 'I cannot, of course, give him my love since it has for a long time belonged to someone who fully deserves it; but my friendship he can have. I shall be pleased to be his sister, his friend, if he considers me worthy of it.' These are not the words of an unhappy girl unable to marry the man she loves.

There can be little doubt that Andersen was in love – but he was also in love with being in love. Was not some of Heine's best poetry about unhappy love? And was not unrequited love an almost compulsory part of the equipment of a true romantic poet?

During the following months Andersen wrote a large number of melancholy love poems, the best of which were collected under the title *The Melodies of the Heart*. The most famous of them is given here in an English translation by the late R. P. Keigwin:

> Two brown eyes I did lately see –
> A home and a world lay there for me.
> With goodness and childlike peace they shone;
> I'll never forget them while life goes on.

It is also clear from the many letters he wrote to his friends during the ensuing months that he did not want to leave them in any doubt about his sad state of mind and the reason for it. When Henriette Hanck (Mrs Iversen's granddaughter) wrote to him in November 1830: 'You are not as unhappy as you would like to imagine,' he was hurt and wrote back: 'So you think I *imagine* myself being unhappy, well, you have reason to think so, and the world will agree with you, but remember that many scenes are enacted not only in one's heart but in real life, something no one knows about and which I *dare* not reveal.' But later in the same letter Andersen could not refrain from writing in pretended surprise: 'People are struck by my latest poems, just fancy, they think I'm in love; everybody thinks so; I have already heard the names of several about whom they are guessing, perhaps it will amuse you and your family, some say it is', and then he mentioned the names of six girls, of which the last one was 'Miss Voigt', about whom he then added, 'It is quite foolish to include the last-mentioned person, since she is engaged, and I am almost ready to swear that *she* doesn't mean more to me than I to her.'

In January 1831 a new volume of poems by Andersen was published under the title *Fantasies and Sketches*; in this were included all his love poems to and about Riborg Voigt, without mentioning her name, of course. As a characteristic example the following is quoted, again in R. P. Keigwin's translation:

> There is a legend wonderful to tell:
> Each mussel shell
> That deep within the salty sea doth lie,
> Once it hath formed its pearl, must surely die.
> O love, thou art the pearl my breast did pray for –
> And now with life must pay for!

Ingemann, to whom Andersen had sent a copy of the book, commented on the melancholy mood to which many of these poems bore witness. About one, 'Life is a Dream', Ingemann wrote that if this poem truly reflected something Andersen had experienced, then life had indeed put him to a hard test, but he warned him against turning life into an unhappy dream, as he warned him against studying 'Byron's poetry of despair', from which he thought he could trace a certain influence. Andersen replied on 31 January 1831:

Indeed, my poems are not fantasy, they are based on something real, oh! it is so sad that it hardly looks real. By my soul and my thoughts I am attached to one single person, a spirited, childlike being whose like I have never seen; ... but oh! it sounds terrible, I feel it: she is engaged, is going to be married next month. My friends and acquaintances make jokes about my poems, they do not realize that it is a profound, a sad truth, oh! their jokes make me suffer. ... I met her for the first time last summer, her family was the most respected in the town and her brother a student friend of mine, I only spent three days in the house, and when I felt what I have never felt before and heard that she was engaged I left immediately. But here in Copenhagen we met again (three weeks). ... Oh! I don't know, God really is too hard on me. If only I were dead, here I shall never be happy!

On 2 March Andersen again wrote to Ingemann about Riborg:

We never write to one another, it would not be right, and yet I know that she thinks of me often, that she really loves me, though I cannot understand how she can then MARRY *someone else – I could not do it!*

He also wrote that he was now beginning to think that he was a *Digter*, 'I hope it is not too vain of me, though it is the most wonderful thing I can dream.'

To a young friend Andersen wrote: 'Last year I was a happy, fluttering being, ready to mock all Wertherianism, and this year I am almost *such* a fool myself!' Half wanting to give a clue he added, 'Every day I visit my dear Christian Voigt, the one I feel most attached to of all.'

Levnedsbogen, Andersen's first autobiography, written in 1832 when he was twenty-seven, ends (incomplete, in the middle of a sentence) with a long and detailed account of the Riborg Voigt story, in which the name of Faaborg and her family name have been deliberately omitted; her first name is only mentioned once, almost as if by accident. Henceforth his German autobiography, *Das Märchen meines Lebens ohne Dichtung* (1847) and the more expanded and definite version of it, *Mit Livs Eventyr* (1855) are our main sources of information about Andersen's life – fortunately supplemented from other sources, including his diaries and letters.

In his important study of Andersen as an autobiographer H. Topsøe-Jensen has pointed out that the account Andersen gives of events in the period 1830–3 in his two autobiographies is completely misleading, for he gives the false impression that he was constantly persecuted, ridiculed and slighted by almost everybody in Copenhagen during that period, whereas in fact there is plenty of evidence to show that at that time he was much more esteemed both by literary critics and the general public than he would himself allow.

It is true that there were some attacks on him. In January 1830 Carsten Hauch, another Danish writer of the Romantic period, published a comedy in which Andersen is portrayed as Pierrot, who boasts about 'having built a madhouse on the flat land' and of 'having wandered humoristically on my feet to the beach of Dragør' – an obvious reference to Andersen's *Journey on Foot* – and of being able to 'write vaudevilles, without rules, without restraint' – an equally obvious reference to Andersen's *Love on Saint Nicolas' Tower*. Deeply hurt Andersen replied with a long poem in *Kjøbenhavns flyvende Post*.

Another attack, which Andersen took much more greatly to heart, was contained in an anonymous publication entitled *Letters of a Ghost*, which appeared in December 1830. It consisted of six rhymed letters purportedly sent from paradise by the late Danish poet Jens Baggesen. The author, who acknowledged all his anonymous publications in 1832, was Henrik Hertz, a distinguished playwright and poet, who intended his *Letters of a Ghost* to be a poetic manifesto, in which he criticizes contemporary authors for being concerned more with content than with artistic form. In one of the letters Andersen is taken to task for the way in which, 'intoxicated by the ale of fantasy', this young writer rides on 'the Muse's night-old foal, a Slagelse jade with paralysed sides', regarded by the mob as 'a prophet of a poet'. If Andersen had been guilty of such grammatical howlers in a class for backward children as the ones he constantly commits in his published works, the rhymed letter continued, then he would have been spanked and given the dunce's cap.

Andersen was unable to take such attacks lightly, and they embittered him for a long time.

In April 1831 he wrote to a friend that he felt that he had become sickly and sentimental of late, and as a cure for this he wanted to travel, 'so I have decided to go at the beginning of May via Hamburg and Brunswick to the Harz Mountains and from there via Leipzig to Dresden and finally via Berlin and Hamburg back again.'

On 16 May Andersen went by steamship from Copenhagen to Lübeck, then by mail-coach to Hamburg, across the Lüneburg Moor to Brunswick and Goslar. Then he walked in the Harz Mountains from Goslar across the Brocken to Eisleben, and from there went via Halle and Merseburg to Leipzig, and then via Meissen to Dresden. He made a three-day excursion on foot into Saxon Switzerland and returned to Dresden on 8 June. There he visited the poet Ludwig Tieck, to whom he had a letter of introduction from Ingemann. He went to a recital where Tieck read *Much Ado about Nothing*, and in his diary he described how he and Tieck took leave of each other on 10 June:

At three o'clock I went to Tieck, he wrote a few farewell words, pressed me to his heart and kissed my cheek, I couldn't help weeping, even at the door he pressed me to his breast and told me to go courageously the way to which I had been born. – I shall never see him again!

The last sentence was not true, for Andersen did in fact see Tieck again, in 1844 and 1846; he later spoke of him as having been the poet outside Denmark who gave him 'the kiss of initiation'.

From Dresden Andersen went to Berlin, where he called on Adalbert von Chamisso, the renowned author of *Peter Schlemihls wundersame Geschichte*, to whom he had a letter of introduction from Ørsted. On 12 June he wrote in his diary: 'Chamisso was a tall, heavily built, thin man; a greyish-brown dressing-gown and long, grey locks; he looked like a hermit from the desert; there was a multitude of children; he said that these were not the times for a poet to be read, the world wanted action.' Chamisso could read Danish, and he later translated some of Andersen's poems into German.

In June Andersen was back in Copenhagen again and immediately began to write a book about his travels in Germany, *Skyggebilleder*, a deliberate mixture of *Dichtung* and *Wahrheit*, of prose and poetry, a work clearly inspired by Heine's *Reisebilder*. Among the fictional elements in imitation of Heine is a vision in Brunswick Cathedral of a wedding; the expression on the face of the bride is a mixture of happiness and sadness, and while walking up to the altar she seems to be looking for someone – for the man who *really* loves her, and who, if it had been a cheap novel, 'would probably have been standing, pale as death, behind a pillar watching the wedding, but here it was real. He was not there but where – ?' In this and the ensuing poem about the rejected lover and his desire to die Andersen is alluding to Riborg Voigt's wedding, which had taken place shortly before he left Denmark.

All the same, he was not in love with her any more, as he admitted in a letter to her brother on 9 June 1831: 'Every time I think of her I feel an unspeakably profound pain, but I cannot cry, and I do not love her any more, *that is certain*, but now I am suffering *more* at the memory of her, I feel an emptiness – O God! Christian! I hope you will never feel what I am feeling now.'

Skyggebilleder was published in September 1831 and was reasonably well received. By now Andersen's melancholy mood had more or less worn off; in October he wrote to a friend, 'You blame me for being too gay – you couldn't pay me a greater compliment.' Once again he began working on his historical novel, and to the same friend he later wrote about the novel, 'on which I'm now working hard', and added, 'if this work doesn't make me immortal then I shall never be so'. But Andersen's immortality is not due to his historical novel, for it was never in fact completed.

Andersen, who had been to Odense in the summers of 1829 and 1830, went there again in the summer of 1832, and it can be assumed that he visited his mother on all these occasions.

How regularly they corresponded over the years we do not know. None of his letters to her exist any more, but it is known from other sources that she used to allow others to read his letters against a cash payment, and that she gradually became more and more addicted to alcohol. Among the letters from her which have been preserved several contain requests for money, while others express gratitude for sums of money he had sent. In May 1829 she wrote that she hoped sometime to be able to see her son's play *Love on Saint Nicolas' Tower*, and on his twenty-fifth birthday, 2 April 1830, she wrote about 'this day which is the happiest in my life', and assured her son that 'if you had not been so kind to me I should have been dead, for how can you live on twenty-four skillings a week?' In one letter she asked for money to buy a pair of new shoes, and in another she complained that he had sent money to her via Colonel Høegh-Guldberg instead of direct to herself; the Guldbergs had bought her a shift made of coarse material. She added cryptically, 'That which you ask me not to do I won't do, but I cannot help being described in bad terms by envious people.' (The clue to this statement is probably to be found in what Andersen told a friend many years later: that he had asked his mother not to uncork the bottle in the cupboard too often. 'I should be very sorry to hear from my friends and acquaintances in Odense that people made fun of my dear old Mother.')

In December 1831 Andersen wrote to Mrs Iversen's daughter in Odense that he had arranged for his mother to be able to fetch meals from an eating-house at his expense; she herself would rather have the money, but Andersen asked his Odense friend to tell her in a friendly way that this was the best arrangement, adding, 'She knows that I shall send her whatever I can, and she will certainly hear from me at Christmas.' A week later Andersen's mother wrote to him: 'I'm in need of money at the moment,' and in February she wrote again: 'My good Christian, if it is possible for you to send me a small help I hope you won't forget your frail old mother.'

In the summer of 1832 Prince Christian (later Christian VIII) visited Doctors Boder in Odense, and he asked to see Hans Christian Andersen's mother, whom he knew to be living there. When he saw her he said, 'Your son does you great honour!' which made her very happy, especially since all the others present heard these words.

Andersen himself saw his mother for the last time in July 1832, and she was then in the last stages of alcoholism, constantly intoxicated and sickly senti-mental. Without directly mentioning his mother or the state she was in Ander-sen wrote from Odense to Edvard Collin that his friends there did everything to entertain him, 'and all the same I feel in bad spirits here, all the memories of my childhood, every spot has a dark influence on me'.

In December 1831 a new volume of poems by Andersen was published, and in order to earn some extra money he translated a couple of French libretti for the Royal Theatre and, in close cooperation with Danish composers, wrote libretti for operas based on foreign plays and novels. The one based on Sir Walter Scott's *The Bride of Lammermoor* was a success and led to his being approached by one of his earliest benefactors, C. F. Weyse, the composer, who suggested that he should write a libretto for an opera based on Scott's *Kenil-worth* for which Weyse would then compose the music. This Andersen did, but Weyse objected to the unhappy ending and suggested that Amy Robsart should be allowed to marry Leicester. 'But this is against history!' Andersen protested. 'And then what do we do about Queen Elizabeth?' – 'She can say: "Proud England, I am thine!"' Weyse said. Andersen agreed and allowed the opera to end with these words.

In 1832 a new volume of poems by Andersen was published, *The Twelve Months of the Year*, and the year after came his *Collected Poems*. But at the time that the latter was published Andersen was on a long journey abroad.

It was early in 1832 that he began to think of spending a year or two abroad, but this could only be done if he was given a grant from the Royal Foundation *ad usus publicos*. Jonas Collin supported the idea but knowing that Henrik Hertz was also going to apply for a travel grant expressed the opinion that the latter's application might take precedence over Andersen's. *The Twelve Months of the Year* was dedicated to King Frederik VI, and therefore Andersen himself had to present the king with a copy; this seemed to Jonas Collin an excellent opportunity for Andersen to tell the king that after his *examen artium* he had managed to make a living as a writer without any support from public funds, and that he thought a journey abroad might broaden his horizons and be of value to him as an author; the king would then ask him to submit a written petition, and this he should have ready to hand to the king then and there. Andersen did not like the idea of asking a favour during an audience whose purpose was to give a present, but he was told that the king knew perfectly well that Andersen was only giving him the book in order to ask a favour of him. In *Mit Livs Eventyr* Andersen describes what happened:

My entry must undoubtedly have been very funny; my heart was beating with anxiety, and when in his peculiar fashion the king briskly stepped towards me and asked me what kind of a book I was bringing him, I replied, 'A poetic cycle.' – 'A cycle, a cycle – what do you mean?' Then I became quite disconcerted and said, 'It is some poems about Denmark.' He smiled, 'I see, I see, well, that's all right! Thank you! Thank you!' and so he nodded and dismissed me. But as I had not yet begun on my real errand I told him that there was much more I would like to say, and without further ado I told him about my studies and how I had managed to live. 'That's very praiseworthy,' said the king – and when I came to the bit about wanting a stipend to go abroad he replied as I had been told, 'Well, then send me your petition!' – 'Yes, Your Majesty,' I exclaimed in all simplicity, 'I have it with me, and this is what I find so terrible that I should bring it along with the book; but I have been told to do so, told that this was the right way, but I find it so very distasteful, I don't like it at all – !' Tears came into my eyes. The good king laughed heartily, nodded in a friendly fashion and took my petition. I made a bow and hurried away in great haste.

Andersen's application to the foundation *ad usus publicos* is dated 7 December 1832; it had been drafted by Jonas Collin, who as past secretary of the foundation knew exactly how such an application should be worded. To give it more weight he had told Andersen to get supporting letters from some prominent Danes, including Ingemann, Ørsted, Oehlenschläger and Heiberg. The application was favourably received, for on 13 April 1833 Andersen was given a stipend of 600 rixdollars per annum for two years – and this was supplemented a year later by an extra grant of 200 rixdollars.

At this stage it is necessary to say something about Andersen's relationship with the Collin family, and particularly about his friendship with Edvard Collin, who was between three and four years his junior.

To Andersen Jonas Collin became the beloved, respected and indeed revered father figure, on whose kindness, loyalty and sympathy he knew he could always rely. Jonas Collin's attitude was paternal but not patronizing, and he came to regard Andersen almost as an adopted son. In his letters Andersen invariably referred to Jonas Collin as 'the Father' and to the Collins' house in Copenhagen as 'the Home of Homes'. After his *examen artium* he went there every single day, and the Collin children came to regard him almost as a member of the family. At times Andersen was deeply grateful for being thus accepted in this tightly knit and, in many respects self-sufficient, patrician family; at other times he suffered pangs of grief at all the 'almosts': *almost* a son, *almost* a member of the family, *almost* a brother, and saw himself as a homeless outsider.

Jonas Collin was the dominating force in the house, the paterfamilias, whom no one ever contradicted, but who was deeply respected for his sense of justice and fair play. Mrs Collin, who was almost deaf and later became almost blind as well, played a less important part in the family life. There were five children, two daughters and three sons. Ingeborg Drewsen, the eldest daughter, was witty and outspoken and could tease Andersen in such a way that he never got angry with her. Louise, the youngest daughter, was a child of thirteen when Andersen moved to Copenhagen in 1826. Edvard, to whom Andersen originally had taken a dislike, helped him with his Latin composition in the final period before his *examen artium*, and it was only in 1827 that their close relationship began. In his book on Andersen and the Collin family Edvard Collin writes:

I had certainly often seen Andersen during his first period in Copenhagen, but his picture is somewhat blurred in my memory from that time; I can only dimly remember a lanky boy with an oblong, old face, pale eyes and pale hair, and a pair of yellow nankeens reaching only to the middle of his shins. But when he came to Copenhagen again I remembered well his previous appearance and was surprised to observe the change for the better which had taken place as regards his physical development.

In almost every respect Edvard Collin was Andersen's opposite: a cool, reserved person, reluctant to show his emotions, socially secure and firmly rooted in his milieu, a young man with a traditional upper-class education who took it for granted that people with whom he associated 'knew their classics' and wrote grammatical and correctly spelt Danish, a student of law who would develop into an excellent administrator, a firm believer in the *status quo*. Edvard shared the general Collin conviction that Danish literature had reached its peak with the works of Oehlenschläger and Heiberg; the Collins disliked Grundtvig, regarded Kierkegaard as a rebel and never really appreciated Andersen as a writer.

No wonder that the friendship which developed between these two men was laden with conflict, and desperately though Andersen needed this friendship it was the cause of some of the bitterest and unhappiest moments of his life.

In June 1830 Andersen wrote to Edvard Collin: 'There is no one to whom I feel attached more closely than to you, and if you are prepared to forget the conditions of birth and always be to me what I am to you then you will find in me the most candid and cordial friend.' And he was delighted when shortly afterwards Edvard, whose letters were often very businesslike, signed himself, 'Your sincere friend'. Andersen replied:

It was the first time you signed yourself as my 'friend', though you have often proved yourself to be that in real life, and this little circumstance was infinitely dear to me for the very reason that I feel drawn to you, not only out of gratitude but from the depth of my heart, and it is my most sincere wish that I may never give you any cause for our friendship, if I may be allowed to use that expression, to be loosened. I shall always approach you with the most sincere confidence, and I am bold enough to hope that you will not push me away even when you are in bad humour, and if you do I shall realize that it is not your friendship for me that has diminished but that it is due to circumstances of the moment.

To Edvard Collin's credit it should be said that he was untiring in rendering Andersen all kinds of practical services: he looked after his financial interests, helped him negotiate contracts with publishers, discussed his work with him and often corrected monstrous spelling mistakes. Unfortunately he also regarded it as one of his more important duties to go on 'educating' Andersen by telling him home truths, however unpleasant they might be.

Thus in July 1830 Edvard considered it his duty to inform Andersen by letter that 'a person in this town' had said that he was selfish to an unforgivable extent and so conceited that he considered himself more original than Oehlenschläger and Ingemann. Having reported this statement Collin added, 'You are entitled to expect that being your friend I should defend you against this bitter accusation. But as your friend I must this time draw your attention to the partial truth of this judgement. Were I to go by outward criteria alone then I should have to agree with it; but your way of thinking and, in one word, your relationship to me, would always prevent me from doing so.'

Andersen sadly replied that he would never dream of considering himself more original than Oehlenschläger, or even as his equal. His most vain ambition was to regard himself as being the most promising among the young poets of the period, 'and I believe that with God's help circumstances will allow me to take my place among the good writers, but at a place far below Oehlenschläger and far removed from Ingemann'.

One of the things Edvard Collin objected to most of all was Andersen's fondness for reciting his own poetry whenever he had a chance of doing so. In *Mit Livs Eventyr* Andersen mentions an occasion at a private party at which he had been asked to read some of his own poems and had agreed to do so when Edvard Collin went over to him and said aloud, 'If you recite so much as a single poem I shall leave!' It was similar motives which made him write to Andersen in the summer of 1830 that he ought to get rid of manners which were harmful to him; whenever Andersen's name came up people would talk about the way he would keep on reading his poems aloud to others. The only way to stop such remarks, Collin added, was by removing the reason for them. 'If apart from me you have a single true friend who is not reluctant to tell you his true conviction, then ask him and you will see that you get the same reply,' he wrote.

Andersen did his best to accept Edvard Collin's advice. He wrote back, 'Avidly I swallow every letter I receive, even though it may occasionally taste like medicine, but then medicine is supposed to help the sick person, and if handed by a friend one accepts it gratefully. Please believe me that I myself am aware of my many mistakes and shortcomings, but it is impossible for me to correct all of them at once. I do believe, however, that there has been an improvement during the last year, or, in the terms of the world, that I have become more polished.' At the same time he admitted that he was still tempted to read his poems aloud; but then, did not every young person want to please, he asked, 'and since I cannot please with my appearance I take refuge in whatever is at hand'. Proudly he reported that he had, in fact, just refused an invitation to read his poems at Odense Theatre: 'Believe me, it was hard to resist, and quite honestly, I would have liked to do it very much – again my sinful vanity! But your letter made me decide to refuse the invitation categorically.'

Some of Andersen's letters are almost declarations of love. In August 1830 he wrote to Edvard Collin: 'I repeat what I have told you before that you are the only person I regard as my true friend, and my heart is sincerely attached to you. This is something I might never be able to say to you personally, but you can rest assured that I attach the greatest importance to your every word, so please do not ever push me away – but I am becoming sentimental; you will understand what I mean.'

During his first journey abroad in the spring of 1831 Andersen plucked up courage to suggest to Edvard Collin that they should abandon the formal *De* in favour of the more familiar *Du*; but he had to be as far away as Hamburg before sending his pathetic cry to be accepted as a friend and equal:

Of all human beings you are the one I regard as being my true friend in every respect, please be that to me always, my dear Collin, I do so much need an open heart. But my friend, the person I am able to love, must also possess a spirit, I must be able to respect him in that way, and that is really missing in the few others I like – you alone are the one person of my own age to whom I feel closely attached. I have an important request, perhaps you will laugh at me, but if sometime you really want to make me happy, to let me have true evidence of your respect – if and when I deserve it – then – oh! please do not be angry with me – say 'Du' to me! Face to face I should never have been able to ask you that, it must happen now that I am abroad. If you have any objections, then please do not ever mention this matter to me and I shall never ask you again, of course. From the first letter I receive from you I shall be able to see whether you have wanted to make me happy, and I shall drink your toast and do it very sincerely. – Are you angry with me? – You have no idea how my heart is beating while I am writing this, though you are not here.

It is hard to understand how Edvard Collin could bring himself to reject Andersen's outstretched hand, but he did, amicably, coolly and politely in a letter dated 28 May 1831. Having first dealt with some other points in Andersen's letter he continued:

I am now coming to a point in your letter which – well, how shall I make myself fully understood to you, my dear friend? I shall not succeed in convincing you by giving reasons, and maybe reasons are out of place here, but you must take my word for it, you must be firmly convinced that there is a trait in my character which I shall now reveal to you truthfully. Otherwise it will be impossible for you not to misunderstand me, something I would be very fearful of. What I am aiming at are my feelings regarding the question of saying 'Du' to one another, and this is something I would like to make clear to you. As I have already said, Andersen, you must take my word for it that I am being honest with you. If at a merry party among students etc. someone suggests to me that we should be on Du terms then I agree, partly for lack of consideration at the moment, partly in order not to insult the person concerned who thinks that by so doing he will establish a more friendly relationship with me. I only remember one single occasion when, having on such an occasion been through the ceremony of drinking Du with a young man at his insistence, I have afterwards, on closer consideration, continued to address him as 'De', and however sad I was to insult this person I never later regretted doing so. Why did I do it? It was someone I had known for a long time and whom I liked very much! There was something inside me which I cannot explain that made me do it. There are many insignificant things against which people have what I believe to be an inborn dislike; I have known a woman who felt such a dislike against wrapping paper that she was sick whenever she saw it – how are such things to be explained? – But when I have known for a long time someone whom I respect and like and he invites me to say 'Du', then this unpleasant and inexplicable feeling arises in me.

Collin went on to tell a story about someone who had been a close friend of the Danish poet Jens Baggesen for many years, but when the latter suggested that they should address one another as *'Du'* it made such an unpleasant impression on the former that he almost began to dislike Baggesen. But, of course, Collin did not want to suggest that this might happen between him and Andersen. He then continued:

My Du acquaintances mainly date from my earliest boyhood, partly also from such gay moments which did not leave me time for serious consideration, partly also from the fact that I was too embarrassed to refuse the invitation. But I am proving how candid I am to you by the very fact that I express myself to you as I have done here however easily this might be misunderstood, rather than concealing my true nature to you. But no, Andersen! You will not misunderstand me! And why should we make this change in our relationship? Is it in order to give others an outward sign of our relationship? But that would be superfluous and of no consequence to either of us. And is not our relationship very pleasant and useful to both of us as it is? Why then restart it in a new fashion, a fashion which, I suppose, is of no importance in itself but for which I have, as I have told you, a feeling of dislike; I admit to being a curious person in this respect. But as it has grieved me that this matter should be raised altogether, as certain am I that our relationship must be the way you wish it to be, provided this is no more than a haphazard idea, for by God! I do not want to insult you. But once again, Andersen, why should we make such a change? Let us speak no more of it. I hope we shall both forget these mutual exchanges. When you return I shall be in Jutland, so we shall not see one another till the winter. There could never be any question of my being angry at your request. I shall not misunderstand you, and I hope that you will not misunderstand me either.

Andersen received Edvard Collin's letter in Berlin, and from there he wrote back humbly, almost gratefully: 'Yes, indeed, I love you like a brother, thank you for every line. No, I shall not misunderstand you, I am incapable of being sad, for you open your heart in such a kind way to me. If only I had your character, your entire personality! Oh! I certainly do feel how deep below you I am in many respects, but please remain always what you are now, my true, perhaps my most sincere friend, I really need it.'

In the same letter Andersen told Edvard Collin about his unhappy love affair: 'You will sympathize with me and find that life may have treated me very badly. Last summer I got to know a wealthy, beautiful, high-spirited girl who feels the same for me as I do for her; she was engaged, and certain considerations forced her to marry a man who took her only because of her fortune; she was married shortly before I went away; all I have from her are a few words in which she asks me, as a sister, to forget everything. That was the reason why I wanted to go away, had to go away, oh! I have been crying like a child. It was unwise of me, poor person that I am, to fall in love; it is true that she had fortune enough for both of us, but then people would have said that it was a speculation on my part, and that would have hurt me deeply.'

In letter after letter Andersen kept on telling Edvard Collin how much he loved him but also how much he disliked his cool, condescending and patronizing manner. In August 1831 he wrote: 'I long to speak to you from the heart and in friendship, alone . . . but please! Do not look so serious – so – what shall I call it? – so terribly sensible as you sometimes do, thus causing me to jump away like a shuttlecock to write many a dark and bitter poem.'

For almost five months Andersen refrained from bringing up the painful subject of the rejection of his suggestion that they should say '*Du*' to one another, but he did not forget the humiliation he had then suffered. In November 1831 he wrote: 'Once you wrote to me, when I became too intimate with you, that you had developed an inexplicable coldness towards people who wanted to say '*Du*' to you. You know that it was something which burst from my heart, a long nourished wish, and I hope that the fact that I expressed it in words will not mean that your feelings are now such that you are unable to meet me in the way I would like you to? Please be frank with me!'

In July 1832 Andersen again wrote: 'We shall always remain close friends. Even though we may not address one another as '*Du*' we shall do so in our hearts, and I trust you will be proud of me. . . . Oh! How I wish you were my brother in the blood as you are indeed in my heart and my soul, then perhaps you might be able to understand my love for you!' In the same letter Andersen implored Edvard not to moralize to him: 'Occasionally there has been in your letters something – something solid – something about the future, etc., etc., which has made me quite miserable, and I swear to you that it makes me sick, it really does make me sick. Please be my dear and kind Edvard as you are indeed every now and then! Just because I love you so sincerely, just for that very reason do I attach such great importance to your every word.'

Edvard Collin replied: 'You tell me not to moralize to you. However easily this request might be misunderstood, be assured that I did not misunderstand you when I read your letter, for I know you very well, indeed, perhaps better than myself – and from your subsequent words that I should be your dear and kind Edvard I immediately understood that I had not misinterpreted you. That is what I am, my dear and good friend, and I shall remain so, in spite of occasional momentary misunderstandings, and I am equally certain that I have and will always have in you the most sincere and faithful friend, even though we do not address one another as "*Du*".'

It was unusual for Edvard Collin to have expressed himself so warmly in a letter, and of course Andersen was delighted. He wrote back: 'Your letter made me very happy indeed, I cannot love you more than I do, and yet I would like to very much, for I see and I feel and know that you love me too! Oh! My dear Edvard, my heart must always be open to you, for thus, and only thus, can true friendship exist.'

While Andersen was touring Funen in the summer of 1832 Edvard Collin wrote: 'We here at home long for you at least as much as you long for us.' Andersen was overjoyed and wrote back: 'The word "to long" threw the sunshine of a whole summer into my heart.' But in the same letter he complained about being an outsider: 'However kind people are to me I am and remain "a stranger".' And he added, 'Your home I almost regard as mine. That is all right, isn't it?'

Having been unable to discuss his unhappy love for Riborg Voigt with Edvard, Andersen had opened his heart to his sister, Louise, who listened patiently and tried to comfort him. And gradually as the wound was healing Andersen realized that he had now fallen in love with Louise, who was no longer a child but, in 1832, a girl of eighteen. It is impossible to say to what extent he imagined himself in love with Louise, or to what extent this infatuation was linked (subconsciously) with his desire to become an 'accepted' member of the Collin family. It is more than doubtful that he ever proposed to her directly, and she certainly discouraged him from doing so. When Louise and her family suspected what Andersen's feelings were, they informed him that every word he wrote to Louise would also be seen by her elder sister Ingeborg. Most of Andersen's letters to Louise Collin and all her letters to him were later destroyed; but a few have survived from the crucial year 1832 when she occupied Andersen's thoughts particularly.

Enclosed with one of the earliest preserved letters to Louise Collin was a poem by Andersen, entitled 'The brown and the blue eyes' (i.e. the brown-eyed Riborg and the blue-eyed Louise) and ending with the lines:

> Det Brune vinker ned, det gjør mig svimmel,
> Det Blaae mig aabner Kjærlighedens Himmel.
>
> (The Brown beckons me downwards, makes me dizzy,
> The Blue opens to me the Heaven of Love.)

In September 1832 Andersen wrote to Louise and told her how difficult it was to be 'a stranger and lonely in this world'. He asked her to imagine that she had no parents and no brothers and sisters, and then continued: 'Thank you for all your kindness, for the sisterly friendship you have shown me recently. By God! I do appreciate it, I think of you more than you believe – or can believe, but one hardly dare say such things to a young lady.'

When he had more or less finished the manuscript of his first auto-biographical sketch (*Levnedsbogen*) he gave it to Louise Collin to read, so that she should understand him and his background better. Then he wrote to her on 27 October 1832:

You told me that it pleases you to read my letters, even after you had read the last one I wrote, and in it I allowed my heart to express itself so strongly that it quite frightened me; I think it was something very strange I wrote. – You have now read the story of my childhood, full of confidence I have shown you everything, and yet you appear to me more of a stranger than before. I thought of you while writing it, oh! So far you have not said a kind word to me about it. This has made me very sad; many a night when you are soundly asleep I am very sad, very unhappy. – They call this being hysterical, I know! – Why have you not spoken to me at all since I showed you my entire youth, not a single word about it? Is there in me something which makes me so repulsive, so unworthy of your – friendship? – YOU and Edvard are the two persons in whom I place most confidence in your dear home, you do not mind my saying so, do you? There is nothing wrong in that. O God! I have become so fearful of any expression of my feelings, I am always scared that it will bring me into trouble, that it will make me unhappy. – To me it seems that I have not spoken to you for an eternity! You are always surrounded by so many others that I cannot speak seriously to you. I feel terribly shy, I would like to talk to you like a brother, find comfort and courage.

Later in the same letter Andersen wrote: 'O God! my dear Miss Collin, I feel very unhappy – indeed, I must go away, far away! If only it could happen next spring.' She did not realize how much she could influence him, he continued: 'You have taken an interest in me, then be to me a sister, I trust you, give me courage, please! If you *can* then let me feel that I have not misjudged you.'

On 1 November Andersen again wrote to Louise Collin: 'Now that I am alone with your spiritual ego I want to gossip, you have allowed me to do so – and after all, your sister is our censor in this cipher conversation. My God! How embarrassed I am even about this censorship!' Andersen then went on to speak about his love for Edvard and continued: 'You, too, must be kind to me, my dear Miss Collin! I have great confidence in you, I trust you as I trust Edvard – you do not mind my saying that, do you? After all, we have known one another for many years! – You may not think so but it is true: It seems to me that there are eternities between every time I see you, and then when I come it is strange to realize that it was the previous day I was there. – This is due to the fact that I am very lonely, have no home and look for it in the family which is dearest to me.'

Finally an undated letter should be quoted in full:

Sunday morning

Andersen is always the one who is wrong; this also makes him suffer the most in his loneliness, let that be his punishment! In another world, in which everything will be more intelligible to us, I am sure he will eat more humble pie, though there he may need his friends less than here. Please accept his apology for having once in a while regarded you as a sister and for having forgotten that he himself is only

H. C. ANDERSEN

Miss L. Collin

On New Year's Day 1833 Louise Collin was formally engaged to a Mr W. Lind, whom she married in 1840. Andersen appears fairly soon to have resigned himself to his fate; it is doubtful, in fact, whether he ever really expected to marry Louise Collin.

But his stormy friendship with Edvard Collin continued. After being reproached by Oehlenschläger for not having shown sufficient gratitude to

Jonas Collin, Andersen wrote in December 1832 to Edvard Collin a letter filled with self-reproach and misery:

I feel so slavishly humiliated that I cannot speak to you properly – face to face I cannot express to you my grief. I love you like a brother, O God! Edvard, and yet you are far too highly placed that I dare cling to you – a relationship has arisen between us which makes me infinitely sad, I feel all too well the truth of Oehlenschläger's words about my subordinate position, now I see clearly how right you were when you did not give in to my childish demands that we should say 'Du' to one another, the way friends usually do. It has often made me cry, I have been more grieved than you think, but now I clearly see that it would not have been appropriate.

It was in a different mood that Andersen sent the following undated note to Edvard in 1833: 'I feel a desire to be rude to someone, I must have air! Would you do me the truly friendly favour of insulting me a little this evening, so that I may have cause to give vent to my rage, there's a kind soul! After all, I'm not asking something very difficult, am I?'

Early in March 1833, at a time when Edvard had recently succeeded his father as secretary of the royal foundation *ad usus publicos*, Andersen sent him the following letter:

Dear Collin,
You have very often told me your sincere opinion, and even though this may have – I won't say hurt me, but saddened me, I have always been truly devoted to you. Now for once allow me to speak to you in these terms. – I am, as you know, highly over-excited, and it is due to this fact that I have been able to fool myself into believing that it is possible for intimate friendship to exist in this world. There was something in you which attracted me at an early stage, many things I respected and found very attractive; you showed an interest in me, and I wanted this interest to grow, I wanted to win you as a friend, of a kind of which only few exist, and I have done everything towards that end, have acted according to your wishes even when your views were contrary to mine. Now I realize that I am not to you that which you need and for which you are entitled to ask; every day you remove yourself more and more from me – just now that so much affects my life and has a disturbing influence on my soul, now that I really need a friend, you hardly speak to me. I feel there is something begging, something degrading in this constant demand for pity, but my pride succumbs because of my love for you. I am so unspeakably fond of you, and I am in despair that you cannot, will not be to me the friend that I would be to you if the situation were reversed. – Is it possible that your new office will affect your life so much that it makes you uninterested in the most sincere affection? – What have I done, then? What is there in my character that you dislike? Tell me, please! Is it the same inexplicable feeling which you explained to me once upon a time in a letter in reply to an unfortunate request, which keeps you away from me? Do tell me, I must get accustomed to lose! Anything which gets near my heart is ruined for me immediately. You cannot send me away or put me into a new circle of friends, but as a friend you could more than any other person have comforted me, and I am sure you would have done so if your feelings for me amounted to more than mere interest. Do not believe that I am being completely unjust to you, that it is my sickly

nature which spins out these threads with which I fasten my crazy ideas! No, Edvard, of late you have been somewhat less kind to me. Indeed, my doubts about you are already so strong that I believe that I have destroyed your last vestige of kindness to me by these outpourings of my heart. But one day you will get to know me truly and will fully understand how much I was to you even though your poor friend was never able to prove it. I wish you well! In your future position you will have many friends but not one who will love you as I do.

Yours,

ANDERSEN

Behind the desperate craving for an intimate friendship, a *Blutbruderschaft* of the kind D. H. Lawrence later dreamt about, are Andersen's feelings of insecurity and social inferiority.

Often a few kind words could change his mood completely. When he left Copenhagen to go abroad on 22 April 1833 he wrote in his diary: 'I saw tears in Louise's eyes at my departure, Ingeborg was also sad. They do like me after all! Those dear, very dear people.' On the same day Edvard Collin wrote a farewell letter to Andersen which he asked the captain to give him next morning. In it Edvard Collin wrote: 'Believe me, I am truly saddened by your departure, I shall miss you terribly, I shall miss not seeing you any more coming up as usual to my room to talk to me; I shall miss you on Tuesdays at your place at the table, and yet, you will miss us even more, I know, for you are alone.'

Edvard Collin's letter made Andersen cry, and he wrote back:

Please forgive me for every time I have done something against your wishes, forgive me for every bitterness I have felt, for I have been unjust to you! The fact that you refused to say 'DU' to me made such a deep impression on me that I began to doubt whether you had anything more than mere interest in me. I thought you foresaw that in time it might be awkward to you in the position you might then hold that we were on DU terms, and for two years my heart has been grieved, I will not conceal it; but now my thoughts are quite different, and I admit that it was wicked of me, please do not be angry with me for it! Now I understand you better, my dear, dear friend!

Andersen had now left Denmark on a long journey which was to become a turning point in his life. But the conflicts inherent in his friendship with Edvard Collin followed him abroad.

5 Travels – despair – success

1833-5

AFTER travelling from Copenhagen via Lübeck to Hamburg Andersen spent twelve days in Germany. He visited the German composer Ludwig Spohr, and in Frankfurt the Jewish ghetto, which made a great impression on him; in his diary he describes how he walked 'through the well-known narrow Jewish Street where all the Jews live, it looked dark but not dirty, everywhere Jewish heads peeped out, and in the front rooms some old crones were sitting; trading was going on. In this street lives the mother of the wealthy Rothschilds, she has not allowed herself to be persuaded to leave this neighbourhood, for in her pious superstition she believes that if she were to do so good fortune would desert her sons. One of them lives a short distance away in a big, green corner house. In the doorway were footmen in livery, and on the ground floor large offices.' Andersen later used the Rothschild theme in his *Picture Book without Pictures*.

He went on to Paris, and arrived on 10 May 1833. His first impression was not inspiring; he wrote to Henriette Wulff: 'Paris – ! I did not like it. It made an almost ugly impression on me. One did not see it for dust until one was there. The houses were thrown helter-skelter, the streets narrow, and we were immediately visited by eight or ten police constables who looked for someone in our carriage in vain.' But a revised impression comes a few lines further down: 'The next day when I got the sleep out of my eyes and came into the city – Pardonnez, sancta Paris! What a city! A wonderful, proud city! A world in itself! I like it, I like it very much indeed.'

Andersen stayed in Paris for just over three months. He met a number of compatriots and visited churches, museums and art galleries. The climax of a visit to Versailles is recorded in his diary in these words: 'Went to the Great and the Small Trianon, went to see Napoleon's bedchamber, everything was as he had left it. Yellow covers and yellow tapestries, some prints, there was a little ladder up to his bed, I placed my hand on the steps and on his pillow. Saw myself in the mirror which has often reflected his face. How insignificant I looked! If the others hadn't been there I would have knelt down.' Andersen still worshipped his father's idol, and he was deeply moved when he saw a statue of Napoleon being unveiled on top of the Vendôme column.

The unveiling of Napoleon's statue was a part of the celebrations of the third anniversary of the July uprising. He described these in a letter:

On the first day (Saturday, 27 July) guns were fired from the Hôtel des Invalides; these salutes were repeated every quarter of an hour during the day. In the various places in the city where those fallen during the July days had been buried memorial monuments had been erected and music was played. Each person who went past them threw his bunch of immortelles on the graves, several citizens went in and placed their wreaths on the columns. I came to the grave of a boy whose poetic story was that he was killed by a bayonet stab inside the Tuileries; bleeding he dragged himself into the Throne Room, where he collapsed on the throne; he was wrapped in the velvet drapery, and thus the poor child died on the throne of France.

Andersen also used this theme in his *Picture Book without Pictures*.

He went to the theatre as often as he could afford it, and at the Paris Opera attended a performance of Auber's *Gustave III, ou le Bal masqué*, an opera based on the murder of Sweden's Gustavus the Third. He was enthusiastic about the realism of the performance and wrote to a friend called Ludvig Müller: 'It is only now that I know what décor is. My God! You should have seen it! In the third act we saw the surroundings of Stockholm in moonshine, the moon reflecting itself in the water. Light clouds were floating in the sky, and we really looked up into God's blue heavens! The stage floor was covered with snow. This wasn't décor, no! reality, great, beautiful reality!'

There were some aspects of Paris that shocked him: 'The most sensuous pictures, often highly titillating, are displayed in the streets. What I find most offensive is the fact that even sacred things are made vile.' But he hurried to add: 'I'm not at all prudish, do not mind a frivolous picture; but in sensual matters a certain amount of decorum ought to be observed.' And to Christian Voigt he wrote:

I can tell you that Paris is the most lecherous city under the sun, I don't think there is an innocent person there, things go on in an unbelievable way; publicly in the street I have been offered during the daytime in the most respectable streets 'a lovely girl of sixteen'; a young lady with the most innocent face, the most acceptable behaviour, stopped me and Schwartsen [a Danish actor] yesterday and in the most lovely manner asked us to visit her, saying that she would subject herself to any kind of examination first, that there was nothing the matter with her, etc. Everywhere there are bawdy pictures, everywhere lasciviousness is referred to as something demanded by nature, etc., so that one's modesty is almost deadened. All the same I can say quite candidly that I am still innocent, though it is hardly believable to anyone who knows Paris.

Some Danish actors in Paris told him that he had changed. 'The actors find me somewhat paler but more like a gentleman.'

For more than a month he received no letters from Denmark, and when one eventually came it was an anonymously printed lampoon, anonymously sent. This was one of the many pin-pricks which Andersen never forgot and which take up an inordinate amount of space in *Mit Livs Eventyr*. Worst of all was the fact that he had not heard from Edvard Collin, to whom he had written from Hamburg: 'You must always love me as you do now, otherwise I shall feel very unhappy.' And in Mainz he wrote in his diary: 'Oh, Edvard! If only you were here!'

On 11 June Andersen wrote to him from Paris: 'Your silence has awakened in me a strange feeling which I have not known before; it is a kind of anger just about to change into love and sadness.' Edvard had recently become engaged to a girl called Henriette Thyberg, and Andersen added: 'O God! Edvard, I feel so lonely, you have your Jette, your sisters and all the dear ones at home. I have no one, absolutely no one here, and for a whole month you have let me feel my loneliness.' Andersen must also have written to Jonas Collin about this, for the latter wrote at the beginning of July: 'Be convinced, dear A., that in him you have a faithful friend whose heart beats warmly for you, even when he appears cold, and one who will show it whenever there is an occasion to prove it in deeds.' He added reproachfully: 'And do I not have reason to be angry if you can think that we have forgotten you? No, Andersen, you were too dear to all of us for that; we often talk about you and we often miss you in our little circle.'

When Edvard Collin did finally reply in July he was apologetic: 'You are quite right, my dear friend, to complain that so far you haven't received any letter from me, and I am very sorry about it. Quite unexpectedly I went on a journey, which prevented me from writing.' Edvard Collin admitted that for a short while he had been slightly jealous because of Andersen's close friendship with Ludvig Müller, and he was relieved to have been told that Andersen was more fond of himself than of Müller. He wrote:

Quite frankly, I knew it, I was convinced of it; that friendship is, as you yourself remark, too much a child of the moment. You were a mature person when you got to know him, whereas I have known you as the poetic caricature whom we used to call 'the clamator', who came and read his 'Forest Chapel', etc., aloud to us. I have known you as the schoolboy who went through an ordeal, I have known you as a young student, I have followed you on your course of education, and finally, I have got to know in you the true poetic talent, the uncorrupted, natural heart, I have learnt to respect the former and love the latter. During your career as a writer I have faithfully shared with you your joys and your sorrows, though I may often not have appeared to you in a very clear light because with my lesser degree of enthusiasm I was not always able to share your views about other people's behaviour towards you. – Here is my hand, Andersen, we are old friends.

These were indeed soothing words for Andersen, who wrote back from Paris: 'Thank you for your handshake of reconciliation; I have noticed that we often quarrel, but that is perfectly natural, for our hearts are so close to one another.' And in a subsequent letter he wrote: 'You have no idea how much I long for you! Indeed, Edvard, you are infinitely dear to me! Your Jette can, in her own way, not be fonder of you than I am. You are always in my thoughts, and I know that you are and will remain faithful to me.'

To Jonas Collin Andersen wrote from Paris: 'My dear, dear Father, – May I be allowed to call you that? I know of no other word which better expresses what you really are to me.'

Andersen's talent for meeting interesting people did not fail him in Paris either. Soon after his arrival he visited the Italian composer Luigi Cherubini, and on 26 June he wrote to Christian Voigt about another acquaintance he had made on the previous day: 'I have been introduced to "*Europe littéraire*", a kind of Athenaeum for the belletrists of Paris. I had decided not to call upon Heine, but fate would have it that he was the first person I met there; he approached me quite kindly, talked very decently about our literature and said loudly, for everybody to hear, that he thought Oehlenschläger might well be the first poet of Europe.' Later in the same letter he said that Heine had tried to visit him and given his name to the concierge; but, Andersen added, 'I won't cultivate his friendship, I think one ought to be careful about him.' To Mrs Læssøe, one of his motherly friends in Copenhagen, he wrote: 'I don't like Heine as a person; I have no faith in him whatever; I don't think he is any good!' But then these words were written to an extremely prudish lady who was known to disapprove of Heine's 'immorality'.

Three weeks later, while he was walking along one of the boulevards of Paris, somebody tapped his shoulder and took his arm; it was Heine. Andersen then had a long talk with him, because Heine had asked him for information about Baggesen and Oehlenschläger for a book he was intending to write. Before finally leaving Paris Andersen went to say good-bye and spent a couple of hours with Heine, who wrote some kind words in German in the album in which Andersen collected famous autographs.

He had hoped to meet Victor Hugo in Paris, for he was a writer he greatly admired and whom he had often discussed with Henriette Wulff, who had a portrait of Hugo on her wall. When shortly before his departure he still had not met Hugo, Andersen decided to call on him in spite of the fact that he had no letter of introduction. He described what happened in a letter to Henriette:

I was told he was not at home, but I said, 'I'm leaving tomorrow!' and then I was received. He resembled the portrait you have, only he is thinner and looks younger. In the hall was a picture of Notre Dame, and a little gipsy brat, probably the good Victor's, was running about on the floor. We sat down together, talked about Danish literature, but he did not even know of Oehlenschläger. I believe I could become fond of him as a person; there was something about him I really liked. During our conversation I often thought of you and wished that you had been sitting there next to your favourite author. . . . Victor was in a dressing-gown and slippers. I would have liked to have asked him to write a poem in my album, but then I was a complete stranger to him; modestly I therefore only asked for his autograph (so that you could see it), and he scribbled it among the other laurels in my book. He said he understood me, but then I think he is very clever.

On 15 August Andersen left Paris for Geneva and Lausanne, whence he made an excursion to Vevey to see the Castle of Chillon, which he knew from Byron's poem, 'The Prisoner of Chillon'. He continued up into the Jura mountains, where he showed his patriotism by singing the Danish national anthem. A Swiss watchmaker, related by marriage to a Copenhagen watch-maker, had invited Andersen to spend three weeks as his guest in the little town of Le Locle in Neuchâtel, a few miles from the French border. Andersen had a happy time there, enjoyed the beautiful scenery of the Jura mountains and improved his French, for the family spoke nothing else. 'Here there are also lovely girls who nod kindly to me when I'm out walking; if they knew that I was a poet I'm sure they would give me a kiss,' he wrote to Ludvig Müller.

Above The centre house in this drawing, by J. H. T. Hanck, 1839, was where Andersen spent most of his childhood.

Below The centre of Odense at Andersen's time, with Saint Canute's Church in the background and Odense grammar school on the right.

An amateur painting of the centre of Odense at Andersen's time. 'I always felt a strong desire to approach the grammar-school pupils . . . when they were playing in the churchyard I used to stand outside the wooden fence, peeping in and wishing I were among the fortunate ones.' *Mit Livs Eventyr*

Top right 'The gods' in the Royal Theatre, Copenhagen. On 16 September 1819 Andersen watched a performance of the *Singspiel: Paul and Virginie* from such a so-called 'Hucksters' Box'.

Right The Royal Theatre, Copenhagen, where Andersen went immediately after his arrival in Copenhagen on 6 September 1819. 'I walked round it, looked at it from all sides, and prayed sincerely to the Lord to let me gain admittance and become a good actor,' Andersen writes in *Levnedsbogen*.

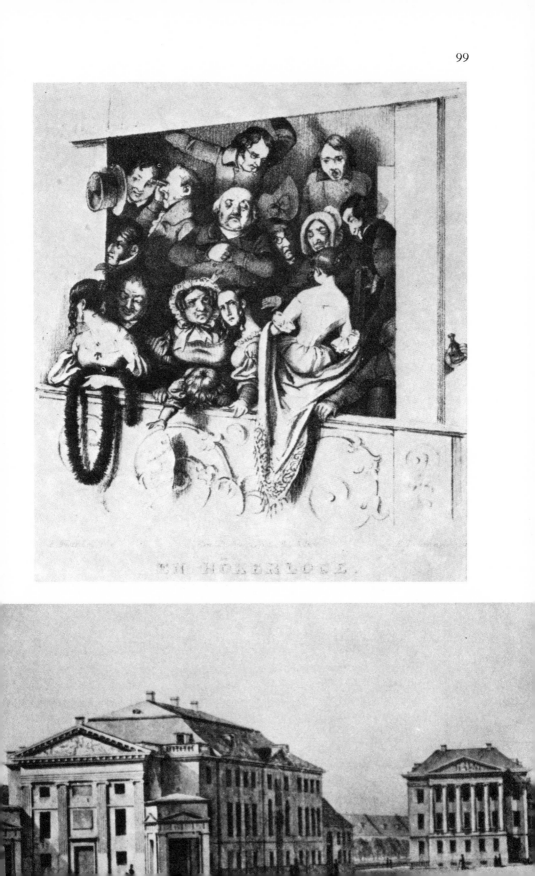

EIN HÖKERLOGE.

On the left the grammar school at Elsinore, to which Andersen moved in 1826, when Meisling was appointed headmaster there. Andersen remained a pupil until April 1827. Simon Meisling, Andersen's headmaster both at Slagelse and Elsinore is shown in a contemporary painting on the right.

Elsinore harbour, with Kronborg Castle in the background. 'What traffic! What liveliness on the quay, here some fat Dutchmen speak their hollow language, there I hear harmonious Italian, further down coal is being unloaded from an English brig so that I think I can almost smell London,' Andersen wrote to Jonas Collin in May 1826.

The earliest known picture of Hans Christian Andersen. The drawing was made by the ten-year-old Fritz Jürgensen in 1828. Length of body and size of nose are, as ever, the features that stand out.

Andersen's self-portrait, drawn in 1830. One finds in this portrait the same irony at his own expense as in his poem 'The Evening', in which he describes himself in these words:
'His nose as mighty as a cannon,
His eyes are tiny, like green peas.'

Riborg Voigt, Andersen's first love. From a contemporary daguerreotype.

Jonas Collin, Andersen's benefactor and fatherly friend. Painting by J. V. Gertner, 1839.

Louise Collin in 1833. She was Jonas Collin's youngest daughter and Andersen fell in love with her.

The back of what Andersen called 'The Home of Homes', Jonas Collin's house in Bredgade, Copenhagen.

In Le Locle Andersen finished writing a new dramatic poem, *Agnete and the Merman*, which had occupied his thoughts for more than a year, and which he had begun writing in Paris. He had sent the first part to Edvard Collin. The inspiration came from an old Danish ballad about Agnete, a girl strangely drawn towards the sea; when a Merman proposes to her she accepts and agrees to live with him at the bottom of the sea, and in the course of eight years she has seven sons by him. Then one day she hears the sound of church bells ringing and nostalgically asks the Merman's permission to go back to her homeland and visit the church. This he allows on certain conditions, but, having returned, she breaks all her promises, reveals the story of her secret marriage to her mother, and, when the sad Merman finally comes to fetch her back to himself and the children, she refuses to go.

Andersen's letters from Switzerland show how completely taken up he was with his *Agnete*; he was firmly convinced that this poem was going to be his break-through. 'She is my northern Aphrodite arisen from the sea,' he wrote to Edvard Collin, and on 30 August he wrote in his diary: 'I'm very tired, but *Agnete* is finished; these last four days I have been in a kind of ecstasy such as I've only experienced at home momentarily when I've written a lyrical piece. Gracious Lord, see to it that my *Agnete* will be a work that gives me joy and honour! Look after both of us, dear God!' A few days later he wrote: 'In Denmark they have said about me that I was "a young poet who *used to be* promising", even after I had progressed. These words hang like drops of poison in my heart; I hope *Agnete*'s good fortune may throw in some sunshine which can make these drops vanish.'

Unfortunately Edvard Collin did not much like the first part of *Agnete*, and he told Andersen so in a long and not very diplomatic letter, in which he spoke of the many trivial thoughts the poem contained, of its long, hackneyed tirades and its imitative character; lack of objectivity he saw as the main fault. When he had read this letter Andersen wrote in his diary: 'Had a long letter from Edvard, it was a kind of opposition to *Agnete*. I will no longer go on giving in to him, I will not be treated like a child by somebody younger than myself, even though he is a friend. A tone such as the one used by Edvard demands opposition, and yet I love him sincerely.'

Andersen did his utmost to control himself when he wrote back: 'Praise, infinite praise, as I have said so often, will have the most beneficial effect on me. You cannot give it to me, all right, I shall not drop my head, nor shall I burst into tears, but I shall keep it all in my heart while I proceed along the way I must and shall take.' He then recalled an earlier humiliation: 'With the confidence of a child I offered you my brotherly *Du*, and you refused it! Then I wept and kept silent – it has always been an open wound.' All the same, he realized Edvard's good intentions: 'I know you give me wormwood to cure my bad stomach.' But in a later letter he warned: 'Even the child one chastises out of too much love becomes stubborn.'

By the time these letters were exchanged Andersen was already in Italy. His first reactions were somewhat mixed. From Milan he wrote to Henriette Wulff: 'France and Germany do not count for much! No, behind the Alps is

'Le Locle, from my window.'
Pen sketch by Andersen, 1833.

the Garden of Eden with marble gods, music, and God's clear sky.' A few days later he wrote from Genoa: 'Today it is five days since we left Milan and travelled here in two and a half days with a *vetturino*, after having tried all the plagues and outrages to which a traveller is subjected in Italy. The purpose of everything is to swindle him, everything is dirty to a degree you cannot possibly imagine; we have had to threaten to call in the police, have had to guard our luggage, have seen robbers being dragged away by soldiers, etc., etc.'

In Genoa Andersen had an experience which he also described in his letter to Henriette Wulff:

From the Admiral of Genoa we obtained permission to see the Arsenal. There we came to a place where there were 600 galley slaves, most of whom had the most horrifying faces one could imagine, we saw them chained together two and two as if they were only one body, we went into their dormitories; along the walls they were lying, chained, and they took off their caps when we entered; we saw the sick room, three of them were lying with yellow-greenish faces, long black hair and glazed eyes, waiting to die; it made a terrible impression on me, I heard that we were being locked in with them. One of these beings observed my weakness, and when he saw me closing my eyes he laughed in a terrifying way while shaking his chains like a wild beast. In the courtyard a young man was walking, dressed like the others but in very fine material, he was a rich man

'The River Tiber in Rome.'
Sketch by Andersen, 1834.

from Genoa who had robbed and swindled the city, and so he had been sentenced to remain here in the galleys for ten years; true enough, he did not work, and he ate very luxurious meals, but at night he had to sleep with the others, chained to his plank bed! If it had been me I should have died with shame or killed myself!

Via Pisa Andersen went on to Florence, where he spent much time in the art galleries. 'Titian's *Venus* is mortal beauty in all its fullness; but the *Venus de Medici* is heavenly beauty! I have been sitting in front of her for more than an hour.'

He progressed slowly southwards with one *vetturino* after another. In October he arrived in Rome, and immediately wrote to Henriette Wulff: 'Oh, Italy is wonderful – and yet, on my journey to Rome I have been wishing that I had never arrived here. – You're surprised? Well, listen to my reasons, though you will not be able to believe them: the filth and dirt exceeds one's most dirty imagination! Out of six nights we only slept one night, and the bugs forced us into the stables.'

His first experience in Rome was to attend Raphael's second funeral. With the Pope's permission Raphael's coffin in the Pantheon had been opened to disprove a popular theory that his head was somewhere else. When his skeleton was found to be intact he was reburied with religious pomp and ceremony.

During the following months Andersen often saw Thorvaldsen, the Danish sculptor, and they became friends. Andersen remembered how he had greeted Thorvaldsen deferentially in the streets of Copenhagen in 1819 when he had just arrived from Odense, and how Thorvaldsen had then turned round and asked him, 'Where have I seen you before? Don't we know one another?' On 7 November Andersen wrote in his diary: 'Visited Thorvaldsen's studios, saw a most wonderful *Psyche* in plaster of Paris, and a marble *Byron*; he is sitting with a book, has a cloak loosely round his shoulders, places his foot on a broken Corinthian column; next to him is a human skull; meant for London.' This is the statue which is now in the Old Library of Trinity College, Cambridge.[11]

But there were many other Danes and fellow-Scandinavians in Rome; for to Scandinavian artists and writers Rome was then the Mecca of Beauty to which all made their pilgrimage. Andersen was soon an accepted member of the Scandinavian colony in Rome, whose regular meeting place was the Café Greco in Via Condotti. Among the semi-permanent Scandinavian residents was Ludvig Bødtcher, the Danish poet, whose intimate knowledge of the city and its surroundings proved extremely useful to Andersen. With eight others he went on a three-day excursion to Frascati, Nemi, Albano and Monte Cavo; later he also spent a day at Tivoli.

Andersen was not very impressed with the theatres in Rome. He attended a performance of Bellini's opera *La Sonnambula* and wrote to Christian Voigt about it: 'The noble Roman ladies in the chorus were disagreeably ugly: veritable Funen milkmaids, in fact one of them had a hare-lip, one was blind, and a third had something wrong with her nose.'

Henrik Hertz was expected in Rome soon, and this worried Andersen, who regarded the author of the *Letters of a Ghost* as his enemy. But when Hertz did arrive he turned out to be very friendly and Andersen got on with him very well. From Rome he wrote to H. C. Ørsted:

Chance would have it that it was I among the compatriots whom Hertz first met; he approached me with kindness, and a handshake easily makes me forget my bitterness. I walked about with him the first day, found rooms for him with which he is very pleased, and if we had not had any previous conflict in Denmark I would have said that he is a kind-hearted and pleasant person. Some of our compatriots have told me that I ought not to be too kind to him, since he might take that as an expression of fear; but this is not the case; I am pleased to turn an enemy into a friend.

In Rome Andersen saw all the sights: the Colosseum, the Capitol, the Catacombs, Saint Peter's and all the other famous churches, including the Lateran ('where in the cloisters we saw the height of Christ, which corresponded to mine'), the Vatican, with the Sistine Chapel, museums and art galleries. He tried to sum up his impressions in one of his letters: 'Rome is a three-headed chimera: one head is antiquity with its crown of temples and the evergreen of memory; the second one is a cowl surrounded by a smell of incense and singing monks; and the third one is a merry Parisian child playing between the other two.' To Henriette Wulff he wrote: 'Rome has opened my eyes to beauty.'

'My bedroom in Rome.' Pen sketch by
Andersen, 1834.

Shortly before Christmas he received a letter from Jonas Collin informing
him that Edvard had not been able to find a publisher for *Agnete* but was
arranging for it to be published privately. 'I hope it will not meet with too
severe criticism, for the form, my dear Andersen, the form, to which you do
not pay sufficient attention, leaves much to be desired,' wrote Collin and
continued: 'Immediately after Edvard had written his last letter to you, we
received the news of your mother's death. I dare say you have already been
informed about this and have composed yourself after the news, which must
upset a good son.'

Andersen, who had heard nothing, wrote back:

*My dear, dear Father, – Now I am completely alone in this world! Your letter, which
I received yesterday, informed me of the death of my old mother. It was a blessing of the
Lord, she was frail and helpless. You do not know how many tears her situation has
made me shed, for I could do almost nothing to alleviate it; I have often prayed to God
to take her home to Himself. She will not have received my last letter from Rome, but
I know that in her last hour she prayed for me and blessed me. My first thought when
I heard that she had departed was: God! I thank you! But as yet I have not been able
to get accustomed to the strange situation of being so completely alone. Here I feel it
doubly, and therefore I am writing these words, for then I'm talking to you. – Please be
kind to me as always if you can! So far I hope I haven't been unworthy of it?*

About *Agnete* he wrote: 'Edvard's criticism of part one of *Agnete* and yours of the neglected form are the only words I have heard so far from home about a work into which I have put great hopes and much happiness, and so your utterances have affected me deeply.'

Andersen celebrated Christmas Eve in a house in the Villa Borghese Gardens with other members of the Scandinavian colony, and on New Year's Eve he thought of all the events of the past year, including his love for Louise Collin. He wrote to Henriette Wulff: 'Just think how much the dying year brought me! At its beginning it allowed me to dream of a passion which I shall never be able to satisfy. He who is not handsome or rich will never win a woman's heart.'

The first few days of 1834 were happy days for Andersen. But on 6 January his whole world collapsed.

For quite some time he had been expecting a letter from Edvard Collin who must by now have read the whole of *Agnete*, and Andersen hoped and prayed that he would now appreciate the beauty of the poem. 'I do wish there was a letter for me today,' he wrote in his diary – and the same day a letter from Edvard Collin did arrive, dated Copenhagen, 18 December 1833. It began with some trivial information about recent events in the Collin family and then went on to inform Andersen that his mother had died – obviously Edvard did not know that his father had already given Andersen the news; he added: 'I cannot comfort you, my dear friend. The thought that you have always been a good son who did not forget his poor old mother in the new sphere into which you came must be of great comfort to you.'

The remaining part of Edvard Collin's long letter was about *Agnete* and must be quoted fairly extensively:

You are not aware of the fact, Andersen, as I am and as others are who are well intentioned towards you and sincerely fond of you, how people – in fact, almost everybody, it is shocking how few exceptions there are – how people talk, 'Has he been scribbling again?' – 'I have been fed up with him for a long time!' – 'It is always the same stuff he's writing!' – in short: it is incredible how few friends your Muse has at present. What is the reason? You write too much! While one work is being printed you have half-way completed the manuscript of another; due to this mad, this deplorable productivity you depreciate the value of your works to such an extent that in the end no bookseller wants them even to give away as presents. Aren't you already again – according to your letter to Father – thinking of writing another travel book? Who do you think wants to buy a book in several volumes about your journey, a journey which a thousand people have made, and two thousand eyes cannot have missed so much, I suppose, that you can fill up two volumes with new and interesting material. – It really is extraordinarily selfish of you to assume such an interest in you among people, and the fault is undoubtedly yours, for the reading public have certainly not given you any reason to think so, and the critics least of all. – If I know you well, Andersen, you will reply quite calmly and with great confidence in yourself, 'Well, but when people read my Agnete *they will change their opinion, and then you will see how my journey has improved things, made me more mature, etc.' These, more or less, are the contents of*

your recent letters. But you are wrong, Andersen, you are sadly mistaken. — Agnete
is so entirely the old Andersen, both in the beautiful childish passages, such as we know
them from his earlier works, and in those desperately deformed, nay, formless passages
which we know equally well from his earlier works. While reading the proofs I have
often been on the point of crying because I met with so many old acquaintances in
Agnete whom I did not want to meet again; usually annoyance suffocated my tears. —
When you have read this you will say that I am unreasonable, etc. Therefore I shall
tell you the following story. I confided my distress concerning your proofs to a man
who takes a great interest in you, and whom you respect highly, and to whose judge-
ment you attach great importance, and I also asked him to go through the manuscript,
so that Agnete could appear to the public in a reasonably decent shape. I gave him the
manuscript for a provisional first reading and had the following response from him: 'It
had been my intention to spend this evening reading Andersen's Agnete; but I cannot
stand it! I find it painful to read such a mediocre product of his, and I must ask your
forgiveness, for it is not possible for me while reading it to think of correcting small
mistakes, so long as what I have read so far only very rarely offers a single bright spot.
If we have the benefit of our absent friend at heart, then there is no other course left than
preventing it from being published altogether; this in my opinion would be a true act of
friendship towards him. Unfortunately Oehlenschläger once upon a time sent home
from Paris works of great merit; this is presumably the reason why this has been
scribbled down in such a hurry. I return the manuscript to you and wash my hands of it —
you ought to do the same thing! In time we may regret having acted as godfathers to this
baby.' — From this you will see, first that what I have said above is not my opinion
alone; unfortunately you will realize in due course that it is the opinion of almost
everybody. — For God's sake, for the sake of your honour as a writer, stop writing for a
time, at least for six months! Spend half your journey studying and amusing yourself,
and spend the other half in the same way.

He went on for some time in this vein until he concluded: 'Here the unpleasant part ends. In the next letter you get from me I shall do my utmost to
use a kinder and calmer tone, for in this one I have been slightly irritable.'

Slightly irritable. What an understatement! This must have been the most
insensitive and brutal letter Andersen ever received. And to make things even
worse it also contained the information that Andersen's poetry had recently
been subjected to the most damaging criticism by C. Molbech in one of the
leading literary journals of Denmark, *Maanedsskrift for Litteratur* — criticism so
vicious and nasty that even Edvard Collin wrote: 'But, truly, you do not lose
by being criticized in that way.'

Andersen's reaction to Edvard Collin's letter can be seen from his diary,
which for more than a month is completely dominated by agony and despair
and suicidal thoughts. The day he received it he wrote: 'It shook my soul
profoundly, I was so overwhelmed that I became emotionally quite numb and
lost my faith in God and in other people; the letter made me despair.' The next
day was equally bad: 'What a night I have spent, there was fever in my blood,
I tossed in my bed. How near I was to putting an end to my unhappy life! May
God forgive my thoughts! May God forgive those who have brought so

much distress to me!' Again the next day: 'Last night I had a little more sleep, but my mind cannot find its balance again, I am sick. All Danes tell me the same thing. I have now written a serious letter to Edvard, he must use the language of a friend, I cannot any longer put up with his hectoring if we are to remain friends; but I did not want to distress the Father, to whom I owe so much, therefore I sent the letter to him; he can give it to Edvard if he wants to. Maybe I shall lose both of them. – But the Father is a clever man, he cannot be angry with me. May God govern and direct all for the best!'

On 9 January Andersen noted in his diary that he had now sent a letter to Jonas Collin and enclosed his letter to Edvard. 'It is difficult to tear oneself away from old oppressions, but better late than never! I will not be dominated by Edvard any longer,' he wrote, concluding the day's entry with the words: 'The bitterness of one's enemies chastises with whips but that of one's friends with scorpions.'

Here are some further extracts from Andersen's Rome diaries, all of which prove how much he was still smarting under the wounds of Edvard Collin's letter:

10 January *An unsettled night! – God forgive my enemies and my friends!*

13 January *My heart is longing for a kind and loving letter from home. – No, nothing came.*

16 January *O God! Shall I never know the young happiness of youth again?*

17 January *In very low spirits. Edvard, you are to blame! I don't think we shall ever be friends again!*

18 January *In the afternoon my gloomy spirits returned. Either Edvard has invented the letter he quotes or he has spoken to the other person in such a way that he could feel his unfriendly attitude. Nobody would write like that to his best friend. Only an enemy writes like that about an enemy.*

19 January *Edvard, the more I consider everything, the more I see your supreme selfishness, the terrible injustice I am suffering. There is a rift between us of your creating which can never be bridged. Everybody is false, even she who cried, who was so very pious, so sisterly – false, false, like everybody else in this world.*

25 January *My friends are becoming bitter enemies. Eternal God, make it possible for me never to see the Home again, I have come to hate it. – What is my reward for being decent? Nothing! nothing! All right, then I will be a devil, I have been brought to despair. Man is evil, evil! Still no letter today. I walked through the streets, almost out of my mind, poison and hatred filling my veins, I could have torn my enemies to pieces.*

26 January [during a visit to Saint Peter's] *In my heart I prayed to God to guide and direct me, make my soul kind and soften the hearts of others towards me. Thought much of Edvard.*

27 January *Today there must be some letters or I have no friends left. Kind and loving letters there must be or I shall break every bond imposed on me by my weak good-naturedness. Today I must get a letter from my most candid friend.*

[Later the same day no letter having come] *A fever went through my limbs; tears came into my eyes, but I could not weep.*

28 January *Am not feeling well today, my rage against E. and certain others at home*

waxes greater and greater. They have killed my peace of mind, my happiness, here where I could have been so very happy.

31 January *So this month ends today. Since I lived at the Meislings' I have not experienced such a destructive feeling every morning as now. Then I was broken-hearted, now it is rage and misery. My God! Edvard, what a creature you are – and the others also! You are killing me!*

2 February *I was shivering as with a fever, B[ødtcher] thought it was homesickness, oh no! no! I'm only shivering because of the Home, nothing good awaits me there, from there comes no joy, there they have scorned me, insulted me, fooled me. She – he – all of them.*

5 February *My spirits are low, I'm longing to go on travelling, always to travel further on! – Imagination, idealism, everything I possessed before seems to have been killed in me by recent events. I am inactive and – therefore unhappy.*

At long last, on 20 February, letters arrived from both Jonas and Edvard Collin. Jonas Collin wrote:

Your last letter, of the 9th ult., made me extremely sad because of the misunderstanding that had arisen between you and Edvard, and because I could clearly visualize your mood. I knew nothing of Edvard's letter and had no idea that it contained anything which might be unpleasant to you. I burned your letter immediately. Not that I reproach you for a single word in it, but I am afraid it might have had an effect which would have grieved me sorely – i.e. a break between you and him. And as you do not deserve all his reproaches, thus he does not deserve all the anger you expressed in your fit of rage; for he really is extremely fond of you, and he is your warmest defender whenever it is needed.

Later in the same letter Jonas Collin wrote about Edvard:

I do not condone his constant lecturing to you. But, my dear Andersen, do not judge him too severely; each person has his weak spot, and that is his; we must be tolerant of one another. I did not show him your letter to me but only said that his last letter had made you very unhappy because it had hurt you. He took that to heart and said he would write to you by this mail. So, when you get a letter from him, please tear up your bad letter; one should not keep such memories.

Edvard Collin's letter (dated 29 January) began:

At this moment Father called me down from my study and told me that he had received a letter from you, which disclosed an extremely sad, indeed almost despairing, mood on your part, and that this was caused by my last letter to you. My dear Andersen, is your character still so soft? I should have thought it had been somewhat hardened by the many attacks on your kindness which you have had to suffer from many sides. I cannot recall any more what I wrote in that letter which was so terrible; but I know that I was annoyed. How far I had good reason to be so you must judge for yourself.

He then went on to reiterate the complaints that Andersen was merely repeating himself all the time, that he was smug and complacent and insensitive to criticism. While Edvard Collin was doing his utmost to try and find ways of covering the expenses of paper, printing, etc., Andersen wrote to him happily calculating on a profit of some 200 rixdollars, and this to Edvard was like a slap in the face, 'and can't you imagine that one gets annoyed when one is being slapped in the face by the hand of a friend? If it is the hand of an enemy one strikes back.' Then he stopped himself: 'But I do think, God forgive me, that I am getting annoyed once again. That was not my intention; for on the whole I am in very good spirits and feel happy. I can tell you that I have never been more fond of you than I am now. I can furthermore tell you that I am still hopeful that you won't regret having published *Agnete* privately. And furthermore again I can tell you that I have indeed come across several people who *liked Agnete.*' The letter ended: 'May you thrive, my dear friend, and do not get me wrong for having previously been your annoyed friend, for now I am your honest friend, E. Collin.'

Andersen's immediate reaction can be seen from the entry in his diary on the day he received the letter: 'Edvard's letter did not satisfy me altogether, but then, of course, he did not know *my* letter.' Jonas Collin's letter on the other hand he found 'cordial and kind'.

Andersen wrote back to Edvard from Naples, but there was none of his usual warmth in his rather formal letter:

I cannot be sufficiently grateful for your very great interest in me, your concern and worry for the work I have sent home to you. Unfortunately, my position is and remains such that I shall not be able to return it. But please rest assured that I feel quite deeply how much friendship you give me, how much I am in your debt.

To Jonas Collin he wrote:

My loving, dear Father, – God bless you for your love for me. I wish I could express to you what my heart feels. What a comfort and healing power there was in your letter to me. That mine should have caused you grief I ought to have foreseen, but – I have suffered infinitely. – All the bitterness shall be forgotten, and I know I shall love Edvard again as before; I only want to see his good, his many good sides. I only wish I didn't have to feel obliged to him all the time, it does do damage to our friendship, it puts a chasm between our hearts.

When the carnival festivities began in Rome early in February Andersen's mind was to some extent taken off Edvard's letter, and he did his best to throw himself wholeheartedly into the merry-making, which he described in a letter to Henriette Wulff:

Then we had the Carnival in Rome, and this was something marvellous. I fought with confetti so that Hertz had to take refuge at a shoemaker's shop, where he took a pair of boots and threatened to hit me with them instead of the confetti, of which he had run out. The ladies emptied whole basketfuls over us. Rome was a masquerade hall, Il Corso a surging torrent. A thief stole my purse with 3 scudi in it and filled my eyes with confetti, that was the drawback of the Carnival. Every day there was horse racing and in the theatre brilliant festinoes with and without music. While dancing and music was going on someone was murdered in a theatre box.

As soon as the carnival was over Andersen, with Hertz and others, travelled to Naples. 'My God, my God! What a stepmotherly treatment we get in the North. Here, here is Paradise!', Andersen wrote in his diary after he had spent a week in Naples, and from there he wrote to Henriette Wulff:

I am sitting in my room, it is almost midnight, I have told my waiter to bring me a bottle of Lacrymae Christi, it is the first time I have tasted it, there's a smell of Vesuvius in it. SKAAL! my dear sister! Listen, now they're singing serenades in the street, they are playing the guitar. – Oh, this really is too good! My soul is full of love, for a long time I haven't been so happy as at this moment. My distress is crushing when I suffer, but my joy when I am happy is also unspeakable. – The warmth of the South is in my blood, and yet I must – die in the North. – It says in the Bible that he who has tasted bread from heaven can never be satisfied with earthly bread, and so I shall never be satisfied in the cold land where I am forced to belong. But thank God that at least I HAVE seen and felt heaven; I shall dream about it, I shall sing about it.

From Naples Andersen went to Herculaneum and climbed Mount Vesuvius with Hertz. Later he went on a six-day excursion to Pompeii, Paestum, Salerno, Amalfi, Capri (where he visited the recently discovered Blue Grotto) and Sorrento; another excursion took him via Lake Agnano (and the Dog Grotto) to Ischia. He left Naples reluctantly to celebrate Easter in Rome, and on 1 April he began his four-month journey home.

While in Innsbruck he met a young Scot who was reminded of his native country while they were walking together in the mountains; the sounding of the Angelus made him burst into tears from homesickness. Andersen, who reported this incident in a letter to Henriette Wulff, wrote: 'I felt very angry with myself for not knowing this beautiful feeling.' Then he added, 'Now I know it! This side of the Alps homesickness has awakened in my soul, deep and powerful! I am longing for my home where the oranges grow, where the endless blue sea expands with its swimming islands, Vesuvius with its red lava, and the entire life there. Oh! If only I had died in Naples, if only I could live there always! – Rome isn't enough for me, there nature has died, a burnt out crater, and I cannot live without the sea, I am tied to it like Agnete – my poor, jilted Agnete. "That desperately deformed work", as my *best* friend called it.'

Andersen had not heard from Edvard Collin at all since he wrote to him from Naples in February. The fact that Edvard had been silent for nearly three months made Andersen increasingly anxious. In Munich on 14 May he wrote in his diary: 'Today there must be a letter!' – and a little later: 'No letter. Feverish. Have been lying on the sofa all afternoon and evening. – If only I was dead! Life holds no joy for me. She, youthful desire, Italy, all is gone! – Oh! I'm ill, both body and soul, if only I could sleep, sleep quite soundly, never to wake up again in this world.'

On 25 May a letter came from Edvard complaining that Andersen had punished him by not writing for a long time, which he ascribed to wounded pride, 'because I once wrote the unfortunate words that you wrote too many letters, in which I was quite right at the time whatever you may say'. Andersen replied that it was monstrous to think 'that my silence – that is, my waiting for a reply – was due to "wounded pride". – O God! my dear friend, how little you know me! My pride should have been wounded because at one time you said that I wrote too many letters? No, my pride is not so sensitive, you are wrong in this.' Andersen then went on to say that it was almost eighteen months since they parted, and he hoped that when they met again it would be with the same feelings as before his departure. He added, 'You have your parents, your brothers and sisters, and a wonderful girl who loves you, I am completely alone in this world. Your heart may be able to do without me, mine will not be able to do without you, and yet I may lose you, I am seized by a strange fear, a fear which tells me how infinitely dear you are to me, and how unhappy you can make me in the Home. May God's will be fulfilled! I shall never touch on this subject any more, it leads to a whimpering which is unworthy of a man.'

On the day he received Edvard Collin's letter Andersen wrote in his diary: 'At long last a letter from Edvard . . .; his letter was of the usual type, the mighty person to his subject.'

From Munich, where he met Schelling, the German philosopher, he went to Salzburg and then to Vienna, where he made the acquaintance of Franz Grillparzer, the Austrian playwright, and saw Johann Strauss the Elder conducting an orchestra in one of the suburbs.

He arrived at the Bohemian town of Collin (Kolin) in July, and from there he wrote a letter to Edvard ('a kind of letter from Collin to Collin', as he put it), in which he told him that he had learnt so much of the language that he was able to shout from inside his coach to the young girls they passed on the road: 'Krásné děvče, já té miluji!' (Beautiful girl, I love you!). Then he continued: 'We shall soon meet again. I wonder whether you look older? I wonder whether – well, please, forgive me! – whether you will please me even more than before? – I don't think I am so passionate and soft as before, that was a mistake and has been corrected, I wonder whether you will like me better then? – Do please approach me in a kind and brotherly way, I beg you, then you will see how amicable I can be! Indeed, I am serious about this!'

Andersen continued to Prague and Dresden, where he fell in love with Raphael's *Madonna* ('She is innocence personified, the others say they could not fall in love with but only show respect to such a woman; indeed, I could love her, love her blissfully in my mind and spirit, with hot kisses and embraces,' he wrote in his diary).

The nearer he approached Denmark the more he dreaded his homecoming. He wrote to Ludvig Müller saying he hoped his friends would stop lecturing to him the way they used to do. 'I won't tolerate it! Now I will and must break old habits, otherwise these will persist for the rest of my life.' And immediately before going to Copenhagen he wrote to Henriette Wulff: 'Well, now I am flying towards my Gethsemane, to Judas kisses and cups of bitterness; but this, of course, is quite poetic; as a poet I am held to be a butterfly, and they are supposed to be most beautiful when wriggling on the pin.'

In fact his homecoming turned out to be much better than he had expected. He arrived in Copenhagen on 3 August 1834, and two weeks later, when he was staying with the Ingemanns at Sorø, he wrote to Mrs Iversen:

Back in Copenhagen I moved in to Commander Wulff's apartment at the Naval Academy, where my belongings are still deposited, and the same evening I called on the Collins, who were celebrating Louise's birthday. They all received me in a very fatherly and brotherly way; I even saw tears in the dear old councillor's eyes; I was a child come home into the dear circle. The king was also very kind to me.

In September Andersen moved into his own small apartment in Copenhagen, and he wrote to Henriette Wulff, who was now in Italy, to say that he did not make the same demands on his friends and acquaintances as before, and therefore everything was going quite well: 'For a long time I haven't been in such good humour as I am now; I feel the point where I myself stand, see better than before the value of people around me, and if once in a while a didactic preacher turns up, one of those who previously used to be so eager to educate me, then I first listen to find out if it is nonsense, and if I find that it is I snub him.' He went on: 'Nobody shall treat me like a boy any more, that is something I have only experienced once after my return.' The person who had 'treated him like a boy' happened to be Mrs Wulff, Henriette's mother, against whose lecturing Andersen reacted so sharply that their relationship was never quite the same again.

In the same letter Andersen told Henriette about his relationship with Edvard Collin:

I have told Edvard how angry I was with him, and by mutual information we have learnt to judge and appreciate one another rightly. He is my faithful friend, I do appreciate his many good qualities, and now that I am no longer so womanlike and soft in my feelings everything goes well, it never occurs to him to lecture to me, now we are ON EQUAL TERMS, and I am quite fond of him as a tested friend.

To Andersen Jonas Collin's house was still his real home. In November he wrote to Henriette Hanck: 'I visit the Collins daily, but that is almost the only place I go. . . . My home is at the Collins; the small grandchildren there call me uncle, and the councillor is as much a father to me as his children are my brothers and sisters, so I must feel at home there.'

But, of course, his friendship with Edvard still had its ups and downs; in October he wrote in a postscript to a letter: 'My apologies for having been a little too sensitive, you don't like it, but I was not feeling well – and by and by I shall be cooler.'

A month later he again wrote:

In the evening I become over-sensitive; last night I wrote a poem to you which you won't get. Do not think this is my old sensitiveness, no! It is, as my Signora from Naples says, the fact that one's heart longs for something outside oneself, and then I have an ideal Edvard, a very kind friend, and I stretch out my arms towards him, it isn't you at all, you have far too many shortcomings, drawbacks and bad jokes to make me dream of you.

'My Signora from Naples' was a sensuous Junoesque Italian lady by the name of Santa, a character in a novel which Andersen had just completed. He had secretly begun writing the novel in Rome in December 1833, continued it in Naples, and when he arrived in Munich had read a number of books on Italy, for his novel was entirely set in Italy. He wrote to Henriette Wulff from Munich:

I have read a lot of books about Italy – how empty they all are. Heine's little jump down to Lucca [in *Reisebilder*] *might just as well have been written in Hamburg; there is no trace of Italian scenery in it.* [Madame de Staël's] *Corinne is a boring guide full of novel gossip and criticism; Goethe* [in his *Italienische Reise*] *is the only one to give something true, but it is very fragmentary. Is it not possible, then, to express this tremendous impression?*

This was his ambition: to express in novel form his own tremendous impression of Italy. After he had completed the manuscript in Denmark he wrote that anyone could write a travel book and describe what they had seen, but his book was going to be something different: 'You will see what I have seen, experienced, felt and dreamt in the two most interesting places in Italy, Rome and Naples, but as Walter Scott, if I may say so, described the Highlands and the people there, I shall depict the scenery and the people of Hesperia.'

The novel was published in two volumes in April 1835 under the title *Improvisatoren*. It was well received by most of the critics and became a great success both at home and abroad. Indeed, this was the first work to make Andersen's name generally known in Europe. It was soon translated into German (as *Jugendleben und Träume eines italienischen Dichters*, 1835), Swedish (1838–9), Russian (1844), English (1845), Dutch (1846), French (1847) and Czech (1851). No other Danish work of fiction had had a comparable success.

The reason for this is obvious: with its mixture of poetic realism and picturesque romanticism it gave a multi-coloured and many-sided picture of Italian scenery and Italian people from the lowest to the highest; among its characters are robbers and witches, beggars, peasants, artists, priests, academics and members of wealthy patrician families. Antonio, the hero of the novel, is an Italian boy, born in the slums of Rome, but by his poetic nature predestined to become something great. Members of the distinguished Borghese family take an interest in this unusual boy, who is sent to a Jesuit college, and, thanks to his poetic temperament and genuine talent for improvisation, he is gradually accepted by the new social class into which he has moved – except that his friends and benefactors have an unfortunate desire to criticize and 'educate' him, which causes him much suffering.

The women in Antonio's life are: Domenica, a primitive peasant woman who looks after him after his mother's death, and whom he loves like a mother; Annunziata, a great Spanish-Italian singer,[12] with whom he is unhappily in love, believing (wrongly) that she loves his friend Bernardo; Santa, a married woman in Naples who falls in love with him and tries (unsuccessfully) to seduce him; Flaminia, a young girl whose unworldly love for him is that of a sister; and Maria, a beautiful girl whom Antonio knew previously as Lara, the blind girl, and with whom he is eventually united in a happy marriage.

Even this brief sketch is enough to make it clear that Antonio, the Italian *improvisatore*, is really Andersen's idea of himself and the novel a thinly disguised piece of autobiographical fiction, transplanted from Denmark to Italy. The more one knows of Andersen's own story, the more one recognizes elements from it in the book. Habbas Dahdah, the head of the Jesuit college, is a composite picture with elements of both Meisling and Molbech, the literary critic; Santa's attempt to seduce Antonio is clearly reminiscent of Mrs Meisling's attempt to seduce Andersen at Elsinore; the influential members of the Borghese family, Antonio's benefactors, are composed of elements in which the Collins, the Wulffs and even Mr F. Høegh-Guldberg would immediately recognize themselves; the warm-hearted description of Domenica, the illiterate peasant woman, must be seen as Andersen's tribute to the memory of his mother; and Antonio is scared of his uncle, the crippled beggar called Peppo,[13] just as Andersen used to be scared of his mad grandfather in Odense.

'Every single character,' Andersen admitted, 'is taken from real life, *each one*, not a single one is made up. I know and have known all of them.'

Even the title of the novel has its background in Andersen's own life story, for in a report on Andersen as a playwright J. L. Heiberg had once called him (in a slightly pejorative sense) 'a lyrical improvisator'. Andersen now took the term 'improvisator' and used it (in a complimentary sense) about Antonio, his own *alter ego*.

Andersen also smuggled his real ego into the book in a way which would only be discovered by a very few readers. The final chapter takes place on 6 March 1834 on the island of Capri, where Antonio and his wife Lara/Maria have arrived with their baby daughter, Annunziata. There they meet two foreign gentlemen, who turn out to be Danish, one of them 'tolerably tall and somewhat pale, with strong features, and dressed in a blue frock coat', the other 'a grave little man, with an intelligent look, and dressed in a white surtout'. This is so to speak Andersen's secret signature; for the two Danes are Hans Christian Andersen and Henrik Hertz, who visited the island of Capri together on 6 March 1834.

The novel was dedicated to 'Councillor Collin and his excellent wife, in whom I found parents; their children, in whom I found brothers and sisters; to the Home of Homes I bring, with a filial and fraternal heart, this the best which I possess.'

In *Mit Livs Eventyr* Andersen tries to make it look as if the book became a success *in spite of* the attempts of the critics to kill it by their silence; he writes: 'The book was read, sold out and republished; the critics were silent, the papers said nothing.' He goes on to say that 'finally' an appreciative review of the novel appeared. But the review in question appeared ten days after the book was first published, and it was followed by other highly appreciative reviews. Andersen's own happiness is borne out by a letter to Henriette Wulff at the end of April 1835, in which he wrote apropos of the publication of *Improvisatoren*: 'Everybody is so kind, so pleasant towards me, many even tell me that they

120

Eventyr,

fortalte for Børn

af

H. C. Andersen.

Første Hefte.

Kjøbenhavn.

Forlagt af Universitets-Boghandler C. A. Reitzel.
Trykt hos Bianco Luno & Schneider.
1835.

The title-page of the first slender
volume of *Eventyr, fortalte for Børn*,
published in 1835.

hadn't expected anything like that from me. I am "on the crest of a wave", but
my heart is full of gratitude to the Lord from whom I feel everything to be a
gift.'

Andersen was still hopelessly in love with Italy and found it difficult to
reconcile himself to life in Denmark. He wrote to Henriette Hanck: 'I do not
belong here in the Northern countries and regard it as one of my earthly
accidents that I was born and brought up on the corner of Greenland and
Novaja Sembla.' And to another friend he wrote: 'I love Italy with the
whole of my youthful soul; I only think of her blue sky, her handsome people
and her sacred ruins. If I had only three years to live I would gladly give away
two of them to stay in Naples. There my thoughts are dreaming, there my
memories live.'

After he had finished *Improvisatoren* and while it was being printed Andersen
began to write some tales for children. On New Year's Day 1835 he wrote to
Henriette Hanck: 'Now I am beginning to write some "Fairy Tales for
Children". I want to win the next generations, you see.' He added: 'People
will say this is my immortal work! But that is something I shall not experience
in this world.' In February he also mentioned them in a letter to Ingemann,
saying that he thought he had been quite successful in finding the right form:
'I have written them completely as I would tell them to a *child*.' And in March
1835 he wrote to Henriette Wulff: 'I have also written some fairy tales for

children, and Ørsted says that if *The Improvisatore* will make me famous, the fairy tales will make me immortal, for they are the most perfect of all my writings; but I myself do not think so.'

On 8 May 1835 an insignificant and modest little unbound volume was published, entitled *Eventyr, fortalte for Børn*, by H. C. Andersen. The words 'Første Hefte' on the title-page indicated that it was the author's intention to continue with some more tales later on. The first volume contained only four tales, 'The Tinder Box', 'Little Claus and Big Claus', 'The Princess on the Pea' and 'Little Ida's Flowers'.

Very few people would have agreed with H. C. Ørsted's prophetic words; but an event of great importance had occurred. Hans Christian Andersen had arrived.

6 'Would I were rich . . .'

1835-40

IN JANUARY 1836 Andersen wrote to Henriette Hanck:

No other winter has passed as quietly and happily as this one. The Improvisatore has gained me respect among the noblest and best of people, even the general public have come to show me more respect; fortunately I have no pecuniary anxieties, and latterly I have been able to enjoy a pleasant existence. The publishers send me magazines, Reitzel [Andersen's publisher] sends me books and prints, and then I sit with my gaily coloured slippers in my dressing gown, with my legs put up on the sofa; the stove purring, the tea urn singing on the table, and I enjoy a smoke. Then I think of the poor boy in Odense wearing his wooden shoes, and then my heart melts, and I bless the Lord. Now I have reached my zenith, I feel. Later on it will go downwards.

A few weeks later he wrote to Henriette Wulff:

My years of writing began with my return from abroad; I may have another four or six years in which I shall still be able to write well, and I must use them. This I am doing comfortably at home before a crackling fire, and then my Muse comes to visit me; she tells me strange fairy tales, shows me funny characters from daily life – peers as well as commoners – saying, 'Look at those people, you know them; depict them and – they shall live!' This is asking a lot, I know, but that is what she says.

In December 1835 the second instalment of *Eventyr* had been published (containing 'Thumbelina', 'The Naughty Boy' and 'The Travelling Companion'); this was followed by a third instalment in 1837. A new volume was begun in 1838 with the second and third instalments appearing in 1839 and 1842. In December 1839 Andersen's *Picture Book without Pictures* (in English sometimes called *Tales the Moon Can Tell*), containing the first twenty 'Evenings', was published; the remaining ten 'Evenings' followed in 1840.

The first review of *Eventyr, fortalte for Børn* appeared in a journal called *Dannora* in 1836. The anonymous reviewer's attitude may be judged from this extract:

Among Mr Andersen's tales the first three, 'The Tinder Box', 'Little Claus and Big Claus' and 'The Princess on the Pea', may well amuse children, but they will certainly not have any edifying effect, and your reviewer cannot answer for their being harmless reading. At any rate, no one can possibly contend that a child's sense of propriety is increased by reading about a princess who goes riding off in her sleep on a dog's back to visit a soldier who kisses her, after which she herself, wide awake, tells of this incident as 'a curious dream'; or that a child's idea of modesty is increased by reading about a farmer's wife who, while her husband is away, sits down at table alone with the parish clerk, 'and she kept filling up his glass for him, and he kept helping himself to the fish – he was very fond of fish'; or that a child's respect for human life is increased by reading about episodes like that of Big Claus killing his grandmother and of Little Claus killing *him*, told as if it were just a bull being knocked on the head. The tale of the Princess on the Pea strikes the reviewer as being not only indelicate but quite unpardonable, in so far that a child may acquire the false impression that so august a lady must always be terribly sensitive.

The reviewer concluded by expressing his hope 'that the talented author, with a higher mission to follow, will not waste any more of his time in writing fairy tales for children.'

Another review appeared in *Dansk Litteraturtidende*. Andersen was taken to task for not using a sufficiently literary style: 'It is no empty convention that one must not put one's words together in the same disorderly fashion as one may do perfectly acceptably in oral speech.' A recent collection of fairy tales written by C. Molbech was praised at the expense of Andersen's tales for clearly teaching a moral lesson, something which, the reviewer objected, Andersen's did not do.

Some of Andersen's friends also received his first tales with a certain amount of reservation.

When Andersen sent the second instalment of his *Eventyr* to B. S. Ingemann he wrote in an accompanying letter: 'I hope you will be more satisfied with these than with the previous ones. Strangely enough, many people place these even above *The Improvisatore*; others, on the other hand, wish, as you do, that I had not written them. What am I to believe?' In his reply Ingemann declared that he very much approved of the second instalment and had in fact given these tales as a present to several children. He added, 'I have told you what my objections to the first part were; and to the best of my knowledge I have told you how much I liked the second part.'

Carsten Hauch wrote to Andersen about the first instalment:

In my opinion 'The Princess on the Pea' is an amusing as well as apposite little satiric tale, and many a mother arranges her daughter's marriage on grounds no better than the ones given here. The delicacy of the queen is indescribably great, and no bornée lady of the nobility could possess a greater one. The story of 'Little Claus and Big Claus' is also, as far as I can see (in spite of anything refined members of the reading public may object) the true creation of a childlike, but by no means small imagination. The fact that the images are grotesque and therefore strongly marked is no objection – on the contrary, they must be so in such a story.

On the other hand Hauch did not like 'the moral indifference' which he found characteristic of 'The Tinder Box', and he found it objectionable that without any moral scruples the soldier should have killed the old woman who had helped him, even though she might have done so from purely selfish motives. 'Little Ida's Flowers' he found too much in the style of E. T. A. Hoffmann. Like Ingemann he also preferred the second instalment, especially 'The Travelling Companion'.

After the publication of the second instalment Henriette Hanck wrote: 'You will certainly win posterity for you.' She was able to report that a girl of eleven had told her that Andersen's *Eventyr* was the most wonderful book in the world.

In January 1837 Andersen wrote to Henriette Hanck: 'I wonder what Aunt Augusta, who doesn't like my tales for children, will say when she hears that Heiberg declares them to have a place high above *The Improvisatore* and *O.T.*, and that the fairy tales, rather than the novels, will give me the greatest name in our literature.' Andersen reported Heiberg's statement to several of his friends; he wrote to Ingemann: 'Heiberg says they are better than anything else I have written. I am sure you will like my most recent tale, "The Little Mermaid". It is better than "Thumbelina" and, apart from the story of the little abbess in *The Improvisatore*, the only one of my works which moved me deeply while writing it. Perhaps you will smile? Well, I don't know how other writers feel. I suffer with my characters, I share their good and bad moods, can either be evil or good, according to the nature of the scene with which I am concerned.'

The most important verdict of all came from those for whom the tales were intended, namely the children. In June 1836 Andersen wrote to Henriette Wulff: 'Wherever I go and there are children they ha 'e read my fairy tales, and bring me the loveliest roses and give me a kiss, but the girls are very small, and I have asked some of them if I cannot be allowed to draw the capital with interest in about six or seven years time.' Two years later he could joyfully report that his *Fairy Tales for Children* were going to be published in German, with illustrations.

Andersen's conquest of the world had begun.

Meanwhile he had continued writing novels. Soon after the publication of *The Improvisatore* he was busy writing his second: 'It describes our time from 1829 to 1835 and is set in Denmark. I think the fact that the author describes what he knows, the surroundings in which he lives, will be of value and give the work a special interest. In years to come people will have a true picture of our time, and if I have succeeded in giving that, well, then the book will increase in interest with age.'

Andersen's new novel was published in two volumes in April 1836 under the title *O.T.* – and to the reader it soon becomes clear that the initials are those both of the hero of the novel, Otto Thostrup, and of *Odense Tugthus* (Odense Gaol).

Otto Thostrup is a melancholy Byronic hero whose past holds dark and sinister secrets which haunt his life and prevent him ever being happy. A vague memory of having spent his infant years in a kind of factory with a sister, of whose fate he is ignorant, turns eventually into the firm conviction that he and his unknown sister were both born and brought up in Odense Gaol, where his mother was a convict. When tattooing his initials on his shoulder 'German Heinrich', the villain of the novel, tells him the other possible meaning of these letters. To make matters worse Heinrich makes Otto believe that Sidsel, a hateful and evil girl, is his lost sister. In the end, however, everything is satisfactorily resolved, and it emerges that Otto Thostrup's mother was not a criminal but a martyr, who assumed the guilt of her lover to save him from the wrath of his well-to-do father; Sidsel is not Otto's sister but Heinrich's daughter; Otto's real sister turns out to be the beautiful and angelic Eva, a girl so ethereal and frail that she dies before being united with her brother; and finally, Providence sees to it that both 'German Heinrich' and his daughter Sidsel are drowned in a storm.

O.T. is not a good novel, though better than this brief summary would indicate. On the one hand Andersen was trying to write a folkloristic novel about life in Denmark in the early decades of the nineteenth century; on the other he very much wanted to write a psychological novel about 'interesting' characters, and in both respects he was trying to imitate Scott, whose novels he had always admired but whose greatness as a novelist he never equalled. Both Heinrich and Sidsel (whom one of the female characters calls 'my Meg Merrilies') are attempts at recreating Scott's characters, and so is Peer the Cripple (referred to by the same character as 'my little Dickie, my boy from Kenilworth'). Otto Thostrup is one of the many melancholy and 'interesting' heroes of the novels of the 1820s and 1830s, a type whose origins are to be found in the general worship of Byron on the Continent at that time. It is no coincidence that Otto Thostrup is also a remarkable swimmer.

In this failure of a novel there is, however, a great deal of Andersen's own life and experience. Otto Thostrup is one aspect of Andersen himself, his friend Baron Vilhelm is clearly inspired by Edvard Collin (even the question of *De* or *Du* plays a part in their friendship), and the account of Otto's supposedly low origin clearly reflects Andersen's feelings about his own origin as 'a swamp plant', and more especially his uncertainty about the fate of his 'lost' half-sister Karen Marie, whose very existence he had kept secret even from his most intimate friends. In *O.T.* Andersen tried to overcome some of his secret fears about his own past. Read as a personal document, therefore, *O.T.* is extremely interesting and revealing.

Shortly after its publication Andersen wrote to Henriette Hanck: 'I want to be Denmark's foremost novelist! In my remote corner of the world the few individuals around me must recognize me as a true *Digter*. Had I been French or English, then the world would know my name. But I shall fade away and my songs with me, no one will listen to them in poor, remote little Denmark!'

On this occasion Andersen was already thinking about his third novel, about which he wrote to Henriette Wulff in June 1836: 'I have sung about Italy and written a Danish novel, now I want to write a novel for my own pleasure.' While writing this new novel Andersen wrote to Ingemann:

In O.T. I had a precise plan before writing a single word, but this time I leave every-thing to the Lord. I have two definite characters whose life stories I want to tell; but how they are going to end up – let me confess this to you – I do not yet know myself, though part two is approaching the end . . . this time I do not write a single word without it being GIVEN *to me, almost forced upon me. It is as if the memory of an old tale has come to my mind and I had to tell it. If it weren't too profane to say so I would maintain that I have understood the biblical quotation: 'The entire Writ is inspired by God'.*

The new novel, *Only a Fiddler*, was published in three volumes in November 1837.

The title character is called Christian (as was Andersen as a boy), and no contemporary reader could be in doubt that a large number of autobiographical features had been used in the portrait of Christian and the description of his development – indeed, in a sense *all* Andersen's novels are about himself. Christian is the son of poor parents on Funen (though born at Svendborg, not at Odense), and in many ways his parents resemble Andersen's. Christian has a talent for music, but unlike Andersen, he is not given the right kind of help and encouragement, and so instead of becoming a great and famous musician he ends up as a mediocre village fiddler. So many details from Andersen's own life are woven into the story that the novel has (wrongly, in my opinion) often been regarded as a valid source of information about unknown or little known aspects of the author's own childhood and youth. Some of the people Andersen liked or disliked are unmistakably portrayed or caricatured in the novel, including Dr and Mrs Meisling (in the guise of an Odense schoolmaster, Mr Knepus and his wife) and C. Molbech, the unkind and unappreciative critic whom Andersen disliked intensely.

Almost as important as Christian is the Jewish girl Naomi, Christian's contrast in every respect, daring where he is timid, sensual where he is puritanical and ascetic, cynical and sophisticated where he is naïve and prone to tears. Naomi and Christian were childhood friends, suddenly separated at an early age, and when they meet again it is impossible to bridge the gap caused by the differences in their social status, temperament and mind, though Christian cannot forget the love he had for Naomi. He is too pedestrian and unimaginative for her, and eventually she elopes with Ladislaus, a worthless but seductive Polish riding master (another of Andersen's Byronic characters). The humiliations to which she is subjected turn her love for Ladislaus into hate; she leaves him and eventually marries a marquis and lives unhappily ever after. At the end of the novel Naomi returns to Denmark with her unfaithful husband just in time to see through the windows of her carriage a pathetic funeral procession in a Funen village. It is the funeral of her boy friend Christian, the poor fiddler whose hopes of fame and greatness had never materialized.

Two contrasting philosophies are formulated in *Only a Fiddler*, one with which Andersen disagreed violently, and one which was his own basic philosophy. The former is expounded by a haughty nobleman who tells Christian to remember that he is but a poor boy and only time will show whether he has true musical genius; he then adds: 'If there is genius in you it will come out all right, even if you have to spend another year as a sailor boy. *Per aspera ad astra!* Hardship and adversity are essential for the purification of the genius.' Andersen's own philosophy, on the other hand, is expressed in the words: 'Genius is an egg in need of warmth, in need of the fertilization of good fortune, otherwise it will only be a wind-egg.'

In 1846 Andersen wrote of *Only a Fiddler*: 'I wanted to show that talent is not identical with genius, and when the sunshine of good fortune is missing, then the former perishes in this world, though noble and good nature does not.'

The novel is, therefore, really about the way in which social conditions and general adversity are able to destroy talent. But it is not the story of how genius is destroyed, for, in his optimistic moments at least, Andersen believed in the romantic theory that true genius will always be victorious in the end – a philosophy he expressed most clearly in another autobiographical story, 'The Ugly Duckling'.

Both *O. T.* and *Only a Fiddler* met with a favourable reception from the reading public and were soon translated into a number of European languages. In England the two novels were published together in 1845 under the title *Only a Fiddler! and O. T. or, Life in Denmark*; the German translation of *Only a Fiddler* (*Nur ein Geiger*) contributed more than any of his other novels to his increasing recognition in Germany.

In Denmark a twenty-five-year-old student of theology, Søren Kierkegaard, devoted a whole book, his first published work in fact, to a devastating criticism of *Only a Fiddler*. Kierkegaard's book, which was published in September 1838, had the strange title *From the Papers of a Person Still Alive, Published Against His Will*; the sub-title was 'On Andersen as a Novelist, with constant regard to his most recent work, *Only a Fiddler*'.

Kierkegaard's book (the only one which has never been translated into English) is the work of a young, brilliant, and somewhat arrogant person eager to demonstrate his own super-intellectual qualities; the author's style and his use of Hegelian terminology make the book almost unintelligible to the ordinary reader. Its main argument is summed up in the following statement:

What perishes in Andersen's novel is not a struggling genius but a sniveller whom we are told is a genius and who shares with a genius only the fact that he suffers a little adversity, as a result of which he succumbs.

There are, as one might expect with hindsight, many brilliant and pregnant observations in Kierkegaard's book on Andersen, or as Kierkegaard calls him – in a literal translation preserving the typically German incapsulation of words: 'the by a fairly extensive literary production not disadvantageously known writer Hr H. C. Andersen' ('den af en temmelig betydelig literair Virksomhed ikke ufordeelagtigt bekjendte Digter Hr H. C. Andersen'). But Kierkegaard's treatment of *Only a Fiddler* is unjust for two reasons, firstly because the hero of Andersen's novel is not necessarily to be regarded as a genius, and secondly, because Kierkegaard's discussion of the novel emphasizes its sentimentality while completely disregarding other important aspects, for instance its humour and irony, its boldness in including subject-matter which was at that time usually considered taboo, and its good descriptive writing.

Andersen must have heard rumours about Kierkegaard's book before it was published, because on 30 August 1838 his almanac contains the following entry: 'Suffered torment of the soul at Kierkegaard's not yet published criticism.' A week later he wrote: 'An outrageous letter from Wulff and immediately thereafter Kierkegaard's criticism. Edvard gave me a sedative. Been as in a haze.' The two last sentences have often been interpreted as being directly linked with Andersen's impression of Kierkegaard's book. I very much doubt if this is the case, and agree with Topsøe-Jensen who thinks that the main reason for Andersen's torment on this occasion was the 'outrageous letter' he had received from Admiral (as he was now) P. F. Wulff; there are good reasons for believing that the agony caused by that letter overshadowed everything else. Wulff, one of Andersen's earliest benefactors, in whose house he had been accepted as a son ever since his schooldays at Slagelse, had sent Andersen a highly insulting letter in which he accused him of slander while at the same time preventing him from defending himself, the letter ending: 'Finally I shall ask to be excused from any further oral or written explanations', which amounted to saying that all relations were broken off and Andersen was never to be allowed to cross Wulff's threshold again. This at least was how Andersen interpreted the letter, for he wrote to Wulff's son Christian: 'After a letter I received from your father this morning I can never again enter a house where for eighteen years I have felt myself to be at home.' Three weeks later Admiral Wulff realized that the whole thing was based on a misunderstanding and came to ask Andersen's forgiveness, begging him to come to his house as before. During those three weeks Andersen had suffered unspeakably, and it seems much more reasonable to believe that the entry for 6 September was due to Wulff's letter rather than to a criticism written by an unknown student and for which he was already prepared. Posterity has tended to see this event in the light of the fame Kierkegaard later acquired, and so the importance of his criticism at the time has often been exaggerated.

After having read Kierkegaard's book B. S. Ingemann wrote to Andersen:

I suppose Kierkegaard's criticism has made you sad. I do not find any bitterness or desire to hurt in it, however. His intentions towards you are probably much better than expressed by him. The end of the book suggests such an – admittedly strangely repressed – kind attitude, but it is one-sided and unreasonable only to express one's censure loudly while whispering one's praises and appreciation, to register one's disapproval in printer's ink and one's thanks and approbation in invisible ink.

Why did Kierkegaard devote the whole of his first book to a criticism, not of Andersen as a writer generally, nor of Andersen as a novelist, but of one single novel, *Only a Fiddler*? To this question his own book gives no clear answer, but various conjectures about personal animosity may be entirely rejected since there is every reason to believe that Kierkegaard was telling the truth when he stated that he 'hardly knew Andersen personally', though they may have met once or twice in the Students' Union in Copenhagen, of which they were both members. In his book on Kierkegaard Georg Brandes suggests that what annoyed Kierkegaard in *Only a Fiddler* was what he took to be Andersen's basic philosophy: that a genius needs kindness, warmth and appreciation in order to blossom; and so Kierkegaard, whose own philosophy was exactly the opposite, namely that a genius grows through adversity, protested in the firm conviction that, being a genius himself, he had a right to protest. What Kierkegaard felt wanting in Andersen was a consistent philosophy of life – which he himself had lacked until a short time before. It was therefore partly his earlier self he was criticizing in the book, but this was a secret to which he did not wish the world to be privy, and this was why he attacked Andersen. Brandes' explanation appears to me to be the most acceptable among the many that have been advanced.

Kierkegaard's book does not seem to have been widely read. It was jokingly said that Kierkegaard and Andersen were the only two persons who had read it from cover to cover.

During the first few years following his return to Denmark in 1834 Andersen found it very difficult to make both ends meet, and the success of his novels only gave him brief periods of respite. In spite of his assurance to Henriette Hanck that he had no pecuniary anxieties, he was often deeply worried about his financial situation. In May 1835 he was so downcast that he wrote a despairing letter to Jonas Collin from whom he occasionally had to borrow money. He spoke of his financial insecurity and his dislike of being dependent on others:

I am poor and feel my poverty more oppressive than that of the lowest beggar, and it cows my spirit and my courage. I know too much about the realities of life to be able to dream of better times to come. I see before me a sad future for which I have hardly the courage to wait. The time will come when I shall have to look for a miserable teaching post in the country, or a job on the coast of Guinea. – If you die I shall have no one left to take an interest in me, and talent does not count, except in propitious circumstances.

Collin immediately replied with a brief but reassuring note:

Relax this evening and sleep well! Tomorrow we shall have a talk and think of resources. Yours C.

In November 1834 Andersen had applied for a post in the Royal Library, Copenhagen, and Ørsted wrote in support of his application, but the librarian told Andersen that he was much too talented for such a post, and it was given to someone else. Another attempt to supplement his income was equally unsuccessful, and he again had to turn to Jonas Collin. In *Mit Livs Eventyr* he describes the situation:

At that time Councillor Collin was my help, my consolation, my support, in whom I took refuge reluctantly and only in the most pressing circumstances – something I do not like talking about here. I thought, however, as I did in the years of my boyhood, that our Lord brings us help when things seem to be worst for us. I have a star of fortune, and that is God.

Andersen was still dreaming about going back to Italy if only he could afford it; on a wild and rainy day in July 1836 he wrote to Henriette Wulff: 'O Danimarca cativa! I should very much like to be a patriot, but I cannot be a Tartuffe and praise a climate which belongs to the marshes of Lapland.' In the autumn of that year he was so keen to go abroad again that he wrote to H. C. Ørsted, asking him to use his influence with the King of Denmark to get him another travel grant:

My best school is life. The more I can move freely about in it, the more mature my spirit will become, the more powerful my activities. Unfortunately I was born in a small country in which, even if my works are read by a fairly large public; I can hardly earn more than sufficient to exist, and it is certainly impossible for me to gain that which will most effectively benefit my further education: to be able to travel for a short while again. But then Denmark is also the country which helps the needy artist more than any other country. This help I must seek, with all my soul I am trying to catch it!

He had received a travel grant too recently, however, to qualify again for another. True enough, he went on his first journey to Sweden in 1837, but he did not get any grant for this, and in Stockholm he wrote in his diary on 1 July: 'Today I begin to fear for my money, calculation on top of calculation, thus the miser must suffer, I suppose. Oh! This Purgatory is punishment enough on this earth for every sin.'

How painful Andersen's situation was at that time may be seen from the letters he wrote in the early part of 1838 to Mrs Læssøe, one of his motherly friends in Copenhagen. In one he writes: 'Now I am often forced to think of a branch of the bread tree and must therefore let go of the laurel tree.' In a letter to her son:

No one can detest talking about money and livelihood more than I – . . . but here and for the nonce let me tell you: there is a nuisance of a goddess called Need who is to blame for most of my wants. You have no idea what a battle I have been fighting! My childhood passed without my learning anything. I have grown up in surroundings of grinding poverty and inanity; no one guided me, no one gave any direction to my spiritual power: it burned like a will-o'-the-wisp. When finally I went to school I was treated so harshly and mechanically that it was a miracle that I did not succumb. Publicly, in front of the audience, I have made every step of my poetic career; it has been a performance in which the plate has been sent round to get food for the artist. All the same, I have managed to get a name for myself, indeed, even outside my native country the shadow of a name. But I am still as poor, as helpless, as when I walked through the Western Gate of Copenhagen carrying my bundle of clothes, and less happy; for then my soul was full of beautiful dreams, now, on the other hand, of a reality, of an understanding which tells me what I am missing and the near impossibility of obtaining it.

If only the King of Denmark would grant him an annual allowance, such as Oehlenschläger and Heiberg had had for years. This was his hope. But he also knew that one had to have influential friends who could suggest it to the king, and Jonas Collin seemed unwilling.

Then the miracle happened. A nobleman from Holstein, Count Rantzau-Breitenburg, who was a Danish cabinet minister, wrote to Andersen to say how much he liked *The Improvisatore*, whereupon Andersen sent him a copy of *O.T.* A few days later Count Rantzau asked if he might call on Andersen, but instead Andersen went to call on Rantzau, who from then on became one of his patrons and protectors. When Rantzau asked him if there was anything he could do for him, the latter did not hesitate to impress upon him how difficult it was to exist as a writer in Denmark, and Rantzau promised to use his influence with the king. In January 1838 a petition was sent to Frederik VI, and in May Andersen was officially informed that he had been given an annual grant of 400 rixdollars. This was a great relief, and Andersen always looked upon it as a turning point in his life. When he told Ingemann the good news he added: 'Now I have got a little bread tree in my poet's garden and will not be obliged to sing at everybody's door to get a crumb of bread any more!'

We get a glimpse of Andersen's routine existence immediately before he was awarded the annual grant from the following extract of a letter to Henriette Hanck:

I shall give you a plan of my week, but first the usual order of the day. At eight o'clock: coffee; then I read and write till eleven or twelve o'clock, when I go to the Students' Union to read the newspapers, then I have a bath, go for a walk and pay visits until three o'clock; then rest. At four to six dinner, and the remaining part I spend at home working or reading. If there is something new in the theatre then I am THERE, and nowhere else, in the evening. My dinners are as follows: Mondays at Mrs Bügel's, where the dinner is always as if for a big party; Tuesdays at the Collins', where the eldest son and his wife also dine on that day, and therefore we get something special; Wednesdays at the Ørsteds', who always invite their guests on that day; Thursdays again at Mrs Bügel's; Fridays at the Wulffs', where Weyse always comes on the same day and plays his fantasies on the piano after dinner; Saturday is my day off, then I dine wherever I happen to be invited, or at Ferrini's [a Copenhagen restaurant]; Sundays at Mrs Læssøe's, or in the Students' Union if I do not feel well enough to make the long walk. There, that is how my week goes!

In the summer of 1835 Andersen wrote from Odense to Edvard Collin that Jette, his fiancée, should say as a message from Andersen: 'Jeg elsker Dig!' ('I love you!'). He added: 'She will not be afraid of saying "*elsker*" nor of using the *Du* form; in a man it is sentimental, and that is something I have finished and done with.'

But, of course, he had not finished with it at all. In August he sent Edvard another letter which he described as 'a letter coming from my soul, just the kind of letter I shall afterwards regret having written. One of the letters in which I place emotions as Number 1 and reason as Number 16. Does that annoy you?' Andersen's letter was in fact a love letter:

I'm longing for you, indeed, at this moment I'm longing for you as if you were a lovely Calabrian girl with dark eyes and a glance of passionate flames. I've never had a brother, but if I had I could not have loved him the way I love you, and yet – you do not reciprocate my feelings! This affects me painfully or maybe this is in fact what binds me even more firmly to you. My soul is proud, the soul of a prince cannot be prouder. I have clung to you, I have – bastare! which is a good Italian verb to be translated in Copenhagen as 'shut up!'

Later in the same letter a few lines reveal how much importance Andersen attached to the social difference between Edvard Collin and himself:

Oh, I wish to God that you were very poor and I rich, distinguished, a nobleman. In that case I should initiate you into the mysteries, and you would appreciate me more than you do now. Oh! If there is an eternal life, as indeed there must be, then we shall truly understand and appreciate one another. Then I shall no longer be the poor person in need of kind interest and friends, then we shall be equal.

The nagging question of the formal *De* versus the informal *Du* kept cropping up in Andersen's letters to Edvard Collin. In June 1836 Andersen wrote: 'Whether we say "*De*" or "*Du*" to one another in this world, whether you will end up as Prime Minister and I remain plain Mr H.C., we shall still remain friends, as faithful and devoted to one another as friends can be.' Edvard, who thought that these words were to be taken at face value and that Andersen had in fact arrived at the conviction that the question of a formal or a less formal mode of address was immaterial, was delighted: 'Your reasoning about the *De* and *Du* matters I found amusing. This was said from my soul; it has taken you a long time to realize this.' He continued:

Your last letter pleased me more, I think, than usual. There is such a human tone in it, I am tempted to call it – please, do not be angry: grown-up. All the same, there is of course as usual a mixture of good-natured kindness and pretence, stemming from the fact that you have not made up your mind which of these parts suits you better, or which is the more becoming to you.

Andersen, who resented the patronizing tone of Edvard's letter, wrote back:

Your last letter pleased me more, I think, than usual. There is such a human tone in it, I am tempted to call it – please, do not be angry: childish. All the same, there is of course as usual a mixture of kindly cordiality and hectoring level-headedness, stemming from the fact that you have not made up your mind which of these parts suits you better, or which is the more becoming to you.

He signed his letter: 'Your "grown-up" friend, who has "such a human tone".'

When in a subsequent letter Edvard called Andersen 'skikkelig', an adjective meaning 'inoffensive', 'harmless', 'good-natured', Andersen was furious: 'Why do you call me your *skikkelige* friend? I do not want to be *skikkelig*! It is the most vapid, the most tedious word you can use.'

In August 1836, a few days before Edvard's wedding to Henriette Thyberg, Andersen wrote: 'My dear, dear Edvard, – God bless and accompany you! Indeed, you will be happy, and you deserve it.' In these opening lines Andersen used the informal *Du*; in the remaining part of the letter he used the pronoun *De*. He went on to say that domestic bliss was something he himself had to imagine:

Like Moses I stand on the mountain looking into the promised land which I shall never reach. . . . My feelings are as strong as yours; as you love your Jette, thus I have loved too. Twice I have loved but it was only self-deception, though I dare say the self-deceived person is the one who suffers most. I shall not forget it, but even you and I will not talk about it. This is one of the sufferings one cannot discuss even with one's most intimate friend.

He had to find consolation elsewhere, Andersen continued, exclaiming: 'Italy is my bride!'

One of the things that worried him increasingly was the fact that the Collin family did not appreciate him as a *Digter*. He wrote to Edvard in August 1837: 'I know that you all like me as a person, indeed in the Home I am like a brother to you. Sometime you will also have to recognize my worth as a writer, which has no high place in your family and ranks below that of Hertz and Heiberg.'

Andersen wanted the Collins to be proud of him, and this was a most difficult thing to achieve.

One of the main driving forces in Andersen's life was, and always had been, his ambition to become famous. He never forgot a derogatory or humiliating remark, and *Mit Livs Eventyr* is marred by the self-pity with which he recounts trivial (though admittedly often stupid) remarks made about him either verbally or in writing.

In November 1835 Andersen wrote in a letter to Henriette Hanck:

I cannot get rid of the idée fixe *that the writer about whom* Maanedsskriftet *at one time said that he showed promise but that this hope had been given up, the boy to whom one of our most promising men said that he must remember that he was but a poor boy, and who was told by Bishop Mynster twelve years ago that it was a very special privilege that he was allowed to study – that one day he will get a name as famous as theirs. This is what I want! If it doesn't happen now, then I must see about it in another world where we are all to be regarded as children of the same father, that is to say, we are equals.*

To Mrs Iversen in Odense he wrote in January 1837:

The poor washerwoman's son who ran about with wooden shoes on his feet in the streets of Odense, has got so far that he is now treated like a son in the house of one of Denmark's most highly respected men and has friends among worthy and brilliant people. I MUST *be mentioned among the* GOOD *writers of my age; but I want more than that! May God give me strength towards it: I want to be ranked among the* FOREMOST *of Denmark's writers, I want to be mentioned with Holberg and Oehlenschläger. But there is still quite a distance to jump, a long jump indeed; I feel it well, though I do not like talking about it. The Lord must lift me up by the arms: it is no good that I lift my legs. But never say die! A great* Digter *in this world, and an even greater one in the next, that is what I hope to be, and it is a bad soldier who doesn't dream of becoming a general.*

In September 1837 Andersen wrote to Henriette Hanck:

My name is gradually beginning to shine, and that is the only thing for which I live. I covet honour and glory in the same way as the miser covets gold; both are probably empty, but one has to have something to strive for in this world, otherwise one would collapse and rot.

In 1836 he had the good fortune to meet a French writer called Xavier Marmier, who was spending some time in Scandinavia. Marmier became very interested in Andersen and, based on his conversations with him, wrote a biographical sketch entitled *Une vie de poète*, which was published in the *Revue de Paris* in October 1837 and later reprinted in Marmier's *Histoire de la littérature au Danemark et en Suède* (Paris 1839). Marmier's sketch of Andersen contributed greatly to his international fame at the time, and not only in France. In 1838 Andersen was able to report to Henriette Hanck that Byron's widow had sent him a greeting. Lady Byron had read *La vie d'un poète*, Andersen wrote, and added, 'and you know, ce poète, c'est moi!'

As already mentioned, Andersen went on his first trip to Sweden in the summer of 1837. On the boat he happened to meet Fredrika Bremer,[14] the Swedish novelist who had already won a name for herself both in Europe and America, and they became friends for the rest of their lives.

During a visit to Uppsala Andersen wrote in his diary: 'Went up to Castle Hill, a large plain open on all sides. Sang out the name of the woman I love, the cold northerly wind carried it away.'

The woman Andersen loved at this time was neither Riborg Voigt nor Louise Collin but H. C. Ørsted's daughter, Sophie, whom he had known since she was a child and who was now (like Louise Collin) a young girl.

But Andersen had little hope of marrying Sophie Ørsted. After his return from Sweden he wrote to Christian Wulff: 'I have become very suntanned during my Swedish journey and am supposed to look handsome in so far as this is possible. I have a burning desire to be married, but I need a fortune which will yield an annual interest of 3000, otherwise I cannot live with a wife and children.'

This time he was most cautious not to reveal the secret even to his most intimate friends. When Henriette Hanck suggested to him that he might be secretly engaged to somebody he denied it categorically:

I assure you I think it will never happen that I shall become engaged! I am far too clever to take such a rash step (may the Lord always keep me like that!) I can only make a tolerable living and have no prospects at all! My wife would have to live the way she was accustomed to in her family circle, so you can see that I shall never be engaged. I shall die alone like poor Christian in my novel. . . . Well, if I had a fortune, if I had some hope of earning one or two thousand a year – then I would fall in love! There is a young girl who is beautiful, spirited, kind and charming, she belongs to one of the most distinguished families in Copenhagen, distinguished in spirit, that is; but I have no fortune and – I shall not fall in love. Furthermore, she is exactly half my age! – Thank God she has no idea that I do more than like her, and she treats me like an elderly gentleman whom she has known for many years. She has full confidence in me and may well tell me one of these days: 'Andersen, you must congratulate me, I have become engaged!'

And this was exactly what happened. At about the same time as Andersen wrote this letter he entered in his diary:

Today Sophie was engaged. Last time after I had dined there with Marmier he said: 'You are in love with her, I know that! I can see it. Why don't you propose to her?'

A silhouette of Sophie Ørsted, the daughter of H. C. Ørsted. She was sixteen and he thirty-two when Andersen fell in love with her.

I pondered all evening how wrong it would be because I am poor. Last Saturday when I was there she was very kind, and yet in the evening I felt that it was quite possible for me to live alone.

In fact, he went on, he had decided that he did not want to fall seriously in love with Sophie Ørsted, and he then added: 'I shall never be engaged, and it would be a great misfortune if it ever happened. God has arranged all for the best.'

Andersen had promised to read his autobiography to the Ørsted family that same evening, but having heard about Sophie's engagement he felt unable to do so. The entry continues:

For the first time I took her hand. I pressed it twice, and I was in fine spirits, I was convinced of that, for I didn't suffer and was supremely relaxed. – Now I'm at home, I'm alone as I shall always be! I think I might have told her at Christmas, but it would never have been good for her. Now I shall never be married, no young woman grows up for me any more, day by day I shall become more of a bachelor. Oh! Even yesterday I was young among the young – this evening I'm old. God bless you, my dear, my beloved Sophie! You will never know how happily I could have lived with you if I had had the money!

It was in the same mood that he wrote to Ingemann: 'Oh, I have grown old, *youth* has deserted me.' And having mentioned H. C. Ørsted's name he added: 'His daughter, the most beautiful, the most charming girl, who used to sit on my lap and kiss me to make me tell her stories when she was a child, has become engaged – indeed, I'm getting old!'

As an epitaph to this little love story let me quote a letter which Andersen sent to Mrs Læssøe in March 1838. In it he copied the poem entitled 'Would I were rich!' from his (as yet unpublished) tale 'The Goloshes of Fortune'. It is given here in R. P. Keigwin's translation:

'Would I were rich!' I prayed with all my might
When still a child and scarce a yard in height.
'Would I were rich! An officer I'd be
With sword and uniform adorning me.'
Time passed; an officer I grew to be.
But riches? Not a sign of these to show –
Good heavens, no!

I sat one eve, a gay and happy youth,
And kissed a seven-year maiden on the mouth;
For I was rich in tales – romantic, funny –
Yet poor as could be when it came to money.
All that she begged was tales – romantic, funny.
Though rich, it was not gold I had to show,
Good heavens, no!

'Would I were rich!' is still my prayer to heaven,
Though now my maiden is much more than seven.
She is so pretty, and so kind and good . . .
But I am poor, my tongue alas! is stilled.
So God hath willed.

Would I were rich in calm and solace, too!
My grief would ne'er be written down for you.
You whom I love, if you can comprehend
Read this as something that my boyhood penned.
And yet 'tis best you should not comprehend,
For I am poor, my future hopes are drear.
Heav'n bless you, dear!

Having copied out the poem in his letter to Mrs Læssøe Andersen added: 'It is an old story, that is: hardly a year old. My own heart was getting a little too hot, but no one noticed it, not even you, my dear friend; but then it was one of the *minor* infatuations! Now it has cooled off, and the only outcome of that eruption is this little poem which may pass for a nice little lava-cast.'

Indeed, Andersen's infatuation for Sophie Ørsted was certainly a minor one, in which the prospect of becoming H. C. Ørsted's son-in-law may well have played an unconscious part – just as the prospect of becoming Jonas Collin's son-in-law might well previously have played a part when Andersen was in love with Louise Collin.

He certainly seems to have recovered fairly quickly. In April 1838 he was again mainly in love with himself. He wrote to Henriette Hanck:

Do you know what my most gallant friends are saying? That Andersen has become marvellously foppish, the greatest dandy! He wears an overcoat worth sixty rixdollars, with a velvet lining, a hat like an umbrella, and his figure – well, he is becoming more and more handsome every day. Jette Wulff says, 'Before you were wonderfully original, now you look like a groom-in-waiting or a lieutenant, ugh! a refined, noble gentleman!' Mrs Drewsen says, 'Our friend is becoming handsome in his old age, but he is the same silly old fool as before. Is he supposed to be a célèbre poète? Well, if only you knew him the way we know him,' etc.

Andersen liked quoting Ingeborg Drewsen's jokes at his own expense. With obvious delight he reported to Henriette Hanck Mrs Drewsen's comment when he had been ill for some time and was beginning to recover after taking the waters: 'It is not the well-water that cures Andersen, no! It is the extra-ordinary good fortune he has had this winter,' whereupon she went on to enumerate three new Danish plays, written by three of Andersen's rivals (Heiberg, Paludan-Müller and Hertz), all of which had been failures on the stage.

In the spring of 1839 Andersen wrote to Henriette Wulff: 'I have recently amused myself by playing a trick on my friends. . . . I have written a criticism of myself, sharp without being exaggerated, and I have carefully pointed to shortcomings in myself as a writer, shortcomings which no one else has noticed so far.' Dr Topsøe-Jensen found the manuscript of this 'criticism' and published it in Danish. It begins:

H. C. Andersen has a poetic nature which shows us what a difference there is between having originality and being possessed with a rich imagination, for no one can deny the existence of the latter in him; he knows how to embellish and arrange thoughts and feelings, but he lacks creative power. This will strike his friends as being a harsh and somewhat unreasonable statement, since he has written altogether three novels which would appear to be unusual, indeed, at a first glance they do not compare with any others we know; but if we look somewhat more closely then it is nothing more than a poetic embellishment of experienced facts that have been arranged in the three books.

The 'criticism' continued in this vein, about his novels, his poems and all his other writings – and about himself, 'our Improvisator, our good-natured, childlike, vain Andersen, whom one cannot deny, however, possesses a certain talent.'

Pretending that this was a genuine piece of criticism Andersen read it aloud to some of his friends. H. C. Ørsted found it too harsh, but written all the same in a lucid style by an intelligent critic, and the Collins found themselves in agreement with much of what was said. They were all surprised when Andersen revealed that he had written it himself, for they had thought him incapable of such self-analysis. 'He is a true humorist,' Ørsted said.

In the summer of 1839 Andersen again went to Sweden, but this time only to the southern part. On his way to the steamship for Malmö he met C. Molbech, his old enemy, and the following exchange took place (according to a letter from Andersen to Henriette Wulff):

'Herr Andersen,' Molbech said crossly, 'are you also going to Scania?' – 'Yes,' I replied, 'to Baron Wrangel's.' – 'Well, I don't want to know whom you're going to visit!' he replied, showing his tusks.

Andersen stayed as the guest of Count Wrangel at the Manor of Hyby, and through him met another Swedish nobleman, Count Barck, his son and his two daughters, Louise and Mathilda. In his diary he wrote: 'Count Barck's daughters Louise and Mathilda pleased me, the elder sister was a young lady of the world, we spoke about Paris, music and poetry, and half-way in love we parted after arranging to meet at their uncle's, Count Beck-Friis's.'

Three days later Andersen wrote to Henriette Hanck:

At Torup I made the acquaintance of Count Barck and his family, and one of the daughters made a great impression on the poet's heart. We met again during a visit to Börringe at Count Beck-Friis's, where I read The Mulatto *and was much applauded, but I also noticed that my heart was doing very well, since it was leaning now towards Mathilda Barck, now towards Louise Barck.*

To Henriette Wulff he wrote on 3 July: 'One of the Countesses Barck has been in Paris for a long time, is young, lively and beautiful, alas! my old heart – if only I had enough money I should fall in love in my old age.'

So Andersen again thought he was in love though he was not quite certain which of the two sisters was the true object of his love. In the end, as we shall see, he decided on Mathilda.

In the autumn of 1839 Andersen was writing his *Picture Book without Pictures*, in which the moon tells its tales of what it has seen and experienced. On the sixth evening the moon tells the story of what it saw one evening in Uppsala, among the mounds of Old Uppsala:

'Up there stood a man, a poet. He drained the meadhorn with its wide silver brim and whispered a name which he begged the wind not to betray, but I heard it and recognized it. A count's coronet sparkles above it, and therefore he did not say it aloud. I smiled, for a poet's crown sparkles above his own. The nobility of Eleonora d'Este clings to the name of Tasso. I, too, know where the rose of beauty blooms!'

Thus spoke the moon, and a cloud came in front of him. May no clouds come between the poet and his rose!

Now that he had become infatuated with Count Barck's daughter rather than Sophie Ørsted Andersen allowed himself a slight falsification of history; for when he was in Uppsala in 1837 he did not even know of the existence of Count Barck's daughters, and it was Sophie Ørsted's name he had 'sung out' on the hill of Uppsala Castle, and no coronet sparkled above *her* head. But the sixth evening in *Picture Book without Pictures* (published in December 1839) was intended as a kind of love letter to Lady Mathilda Barck.

Andersen returned to Scania in the spring of 1840, when the climax of his visit was a banquet given in his honour by the students of the University of Lund, complete with speeches, toasts and serenades. It was very unusual for a Danish writer to be honoured thus abroad, and the news was received with somewhat mixed reactions at home. Jonas Collin wept tears of joy, but others treated the whole thing as a joke. Heiberg remarked sarcastically to Andersen: 'Next time I go to Sweden you must come along with me so that I, too, can be paid homage.' To which Andersen replied: 'If you take your wife with you you will get it much more easily.' At that time Fru Heiberg was the leading actress in the Royal Theatre, Copenhagen, famous all over Europe as the greatest actress Scandinavia had ever produced.

Andersen used his visit to Scania to renew his acquaintance with Count Barck and his daughters, and when he left Malmö for Copenhagen both Mathilda and Louise were on the quayside to wave good-bye to him.

After his return to Denmark Andersen wrote a letter to Mathilda, for whose beauty and charm he had now fallen. He thanked her for having so kindly seen him off at Malmö and told her that he had made a sketch of her and her sister going by carriage across the plains of Scania: 'If only I had been able to draw portraits, then this picture would have had the most beautiful figures.' He expressed his hope that he might see her again: 'Oh! Come soon across the sea to us! Unfortunately I daren't go to Sweden again too soon, people are far too kind and attentive to me for that.' He asked Mathilda to think of him with kindness, 'indeed, only to be half as fond of me as I am of you'. Two months later he wrote to her again, regretting that he had not been able to say a kind 'Hello!' to her in Copenhagen. He longed for his Swedish friends, and wanted his letter to be regarded as a bouquet of greetings, 'the best of which is intended for you'.

At the end of August Andersen wrote once more. He was then about to leave Denmark to go on a long journey abroad, and he began:

Dear Countess,
I must once again send you a few words before I leave Scandinavia. I am leaving in a sad mood. The South with all its warmth, all its splendour, will not breathe sunshine into my spirit. Bring my loving greeting of departure to your parents, your sister and your brothers. I wonder whether we shall meet again – much can happen in a year. My heart's prayer is to die abroad, or to return home in order to produce a work which will bring honour to me and to Denmark. You are in my thoughts more often than you may think; the sisterly and gentle kindness with which you met me gives me hope that you may make me happy by writing a letter, indeed if you are kind to me, then I shall get a little letter from you already in Munich, so if you write at the beginning of November and address it Munich 'poste restante', then I shall get it before I cross the Alps. Please show me whether Sweden in her heart means well towards me. To me YOU *represent the entire country. But please do not write unless you really want to make me happy. Then you will get a letter from me, it will come from Rome.*

For some unknown reason this letter, dated 25 October 1840, only reached Mathilda Barck on 6 January 1841. That this is so can be seen from a letter Louise Barck wrote on 1 February 1841 to her parents, and in which she wrote:

On the thirteenth day of Christmas Mathilda received a nice but very sad letter from Andersen, dated 25 October, in which he says good-bye before going abroad and asks her to write early in November to Munich, which was not possible, of course, so instead she has now written to him in Rome. I do wish the letter may reach him, especially since he is said to be terribly melancholy, indeed on the point of a breakdown, which would be sad if it were true.

As a postscript to her sister's letter Mathilda Barck added these lines:

My beloved Father and Mother, a letter to Andersen prevents me from writing to those dearest to me, and so this time my letter will be a short one.

Mathilda Barck's letter was a kind and encouraging one of three densely written pages. In it she told Andersen that she often thought of him and that it was her sincere hope to see him again. Now that he was away, Copenhagen held no attraction for her; she spoke of his 'beautiful soul' and his 'rich imagination' and assured him that 'the Danish *Digter* is often the subject of our conversations and thoughts'. But this letter did not reach Andersen in Rome, where he was waiting impatiently for it. It reached him in Copenhagen almost three years after it was written.

What happened was this. In order to ensure that Andersen got her letter as quickly as possible Mathilda Barck gave it to a Danish lady whom she knew to be going to Rome, and she asked this lady to give it to Andersen personally in Rome. But the lady forgot and only found the letter among her belongings in the autumn of 1843, when with sincere apologies for the delay she called on Andersen and delivered it. The letter arrived much too late for by the time it reached him Andersen was deeply in love with another Swedish lady, Jenny Lind, while Mathilda Barck was engaged to the Belgian ambassador in Copenhagen and a year later died at the age of twenty-two.

In *Mit Livs Eventyr* Andersen says 'for a number of years the theatre caused much bitterness in my life.' This is certainly true of the years 1839–40.

Andersen had never lost his early love of the theatre, and it was his ambition also to be recognized as a playwright. An important incentive was the income he might derive from a successful performance of one of his plays at the Royal Theatre. Having already written a number of libretti as well as an original vaudeville, he wrote a double-bill *Singspiel* entitled *Parting and Meeting*, which consisted of two separate one-act plays, *The Spaniards in Odense* and *Twenty Years Later*. These were first staged in April 1836 and were quite well received. A far greater success, however, was his next vaudeville, *The Invisible Man on Sprogø*, which had its première in June 1839 and ran successfully for quite a while at the Royal Theatre.

Andersen's next work for the stage was 'an original romantic drama', *The Mulatto*, whose plot he had taken from a French short story, 'Les épaves', by Fanny Reybaud. It is a five-act play in rhymed verse, and it was rejected by C. Molbech, who was then one of the three directors of the Royal Theatre, but accepted by the two others, and it was arranged that the play should have its first performance on 3 December 1839. Unfortunately that day Frederik VI died, and as part of the official mourning the theatre was closed for two months. *The Mulatto* therefore had its first performance on 3 February 1840, and two days later it was published as a book, dedicated to the new King of Denmark, Christian VIII, to whom Andersen had read the play a few days before the death of Frederik VI.

The Mulatto was Andersen's greatest dramatic triumph so far, for it was very popular and had many performances. But when a Copenhagen journal published a Danish translation of the French short story on which the plot was based, then there were murmurings that *The Mulatto* was not really an 'original romantic drama', and unfortunately Andersen's own acknowledgement of his indebtedness to the French author had been omitted by the printers for technical reasons, and so he felt his position as an original dramatist in question. To make matters worse, Heiberg, who was still the literary dictator of taste in Copenhagen, did not like the play, and his critical judgements were echoed by his many admirers – including members of the Collin family.

Andersen now decided to show the Danes that he was quite capable of writing an entirely original serious drama, and in August 1840 he submitted to the Royal Theatre the manuscript of a new play, entitled *The Moorish Girl*. This melodramatic and fairly unimportant play was immediately accepted by the directors, and the première fixed for 18 December. But the negotiations about the play nearly drove Andersen crazy. He had written the title part of Raphaella, the Moorish girl, with Fru Heiberg in mind, and in March, before he had even finished writing the play, he had called on her to discuss it. The day before he submitted the play to the Royal Theatre he called on Heiberg, to whose views he attached the greatest importance, and two days later he wrote in his almanac: 'Been told that Heiberg will not accept *The Moorish Girl*, am absolutely furious.' Eleven days later Andersen was told that the play had, in fact, been accepted, and the next day he called on Fru Heiberg. His almanac reveals what happened:

29 August *Written to Fru Heiberg. Read the play to Fru Heiberg at one o'clock, she called it* [i.e. the title part] *a male one and said it was turgid. Rejected my abject entreaty to play the part. Reply tomorrow. Furious.*

Fru Heiberg was adamant, and the part of Raphaella was eventually given to another, far less popular actress. Unfortunately Andersen was unwise enough to speak ill of Heiberg to all and sundry. As we shall see, he was a dangerous man to have as one's enemy, and it was not long before he took his revenge. But by that time Andersen had left Denmark.

In *Mit Livs Eventyr* Andersen gives a long and detailed description of all the troubles and tribulations he suffered in connection with the staging of *The Moorish Girl*, and he sums up thus:

The wrong may be on my side or not – no matter: a party was opposed to me, the public were not in favour of me, I was conscious of being overlooked and badly treated all the time, I felt hurt, a combination of unpleasant circumstances occurred: I felt ill at ease at home, was half sick – was unable to stand all this any longer – and I left my play to its fate; in a suffering and melancholy mood I hastened to go away. In this mood I wrote a preface to *The Moorish Girl*, a preface betraying my sickness of mind far too obviously, and, of course, it was held up to ridicule!

It was indeed an extremely unwise preface, full of self-pity and bitterness at having been so badly treated.

He did not even wait to attend the first performance of his own play. On 30 October 1840 some of his young friends and older benefactors (including Jonas Collin, Adam Oehlenschläger and H. C. Ørsted) arranged a farewell party for him in Copenhagen, and the next day he left for his second long journey abroad.

7 The traveller

1840-3

'MY MIND was sick when I left Denmark,' Andersen wrote to Henriette Wulff. He was deeply moved when he said good-bye to the members of the Collin family, who saw him off as he boarded the steamer to Kiel. 'Edvard C. was the last person of whom I took leave, he pressed a kiss on my mouth. Oh, it was as if my heart was going to burst!' he wrote in his diary, and the next day he wrote from Germany to Jonas Collin:

My very kind, beloved Father, – Never have I felt so much for the Home as yesterday when I left it, and by the Home I mean your house and everybody in it, and also Edvard's and Gottlieb's. No son, no brother, can suffer more than I do – but it is just as well that I am leaving: my soul is unwell. Even to those dearest to one, one dare not express that which weighs heaviest on one's mind. – Oh, how you let me feel your love these last few days! I love you like a father, please be that to me always, and I shall realize that I have gained much in this world.

Andersen spent nearly nine months abroad, and this time his travels took him further than ever before, even beyond the European continent.

The first month he spent in Germany. He stayed for a few days at Breitenburg Castle in Holstein as the guest of his new friend and benefactor, Count Rantzau-Breitenburg. From there he went to Hamburg, where he heard a piano recital given by Franz Liszt, as he records in his travel book, *A Poet's Bazaar*:

As Liszt sat before the piano, the first impression of his personality was derived from the appearance of strong passions in his wan face, so that he seemed to me a demon nailed fast to the instrument from whence the tones streamed forth – they came from his blood, from his thoughts; he was a demon who would liberate his soul from thraldom; he was on the rack, his blood flowed and his nerves trembled; but as he continued to play, so the demon vanished. I saw that pale face assume a nobler and brighter expression: the divine soul shone from his eyes, from every feature; he became as beauteous as only spirit and enthusiasm can make their worshippers.

A railway line had recently been opened between Magdeburg and Leipzig, and Andersen ventured to travel by train for the first time in his life. The following extract from a chapter entitled 'The Railroad' in *A Poet's Bazaar* describes his experience:

The first sensation is that of a very gentle motion in the carriages, and then the chains which bind them together become taut; the steam whistle sounds again, and we move on; at first but slowly, as if a child's hand were drawing the little carriage. The speed increases imperceptibly, but you read your book, look at your map, and as yet do not rightly know at what speed you are going, for the train glides on like a sledge over the level snow-field. You look out of the window and discover that you are careering away as with horses at full gallop; it goes still quicker; you seem to fly, but here is no shaking, no pressure of the air, nothing of what you anticipated would be unpleasant.

What was that red thing which darted like lightning close past us? It was one of the watchmen who stood there with his flag. Only look out! and the nearest ten or twenty yards you see, is a field which looks like a rapid stream; grass and plants running into one another. We have the impression of standing outside the globe, and seeing it turn round; it pains the eye to keep it fixed for a long time in the same direction; but when you see some flags at a greater distance, the other objects do not move quicker than they appear to do when we drive in an ordinary way, and further in the horizon everything seems to stand still; one has a perfect view and impression of the whole country.

This is just the way to travel through flat countries! It is as if town lay close to town; now comes one, then another. One can imagine the flight of birds of passage – they must leave towns behind them thus.

Those who drive in carriages, on the by-roads, seem to stand still; the horses appear to lift their feet, but to put them down again in the same place – and so we pass them.

When in Augsburg Andersen came across another new invention; he saw daguerreotypes for the first time. He told Edvard Collin that a Swiss painter had shown him 'a collection of excellent daguerreotypes, in fact portraits of living persons taken in 5–10 minutes. They were in all sizes and looked like etchings on steel plates; the hair was beautiful and the eyes quite distinct, including the shining point in the pupils.'[15]

During his stay in Munich Andersen wrote a sad letter to Jonas Collin, a letter in which he told him that his thoughts were entirely in the Home, 'and by the Home I only think of your house; that is the place which can give me homesickness, otherwise I never want to see Denmark again, where I have felt more unhappy than happy'. He added, 'Please do not judge me too harshly for this statement, there are many sorrows, much which may lie hidden in one's soul, something one cannot even express to oneself.' According to his diary he began to weep while writing this letter. His sadness may have had something to do with the fact that Louise Collin was soon to be married; although his love for her was an old story it was still not completely forgotten, though he had sent the following message to be conveyed to the bride and bridegroom on their wedding night: 'Andersen wishes both of you as much happiness as a brother can wish you.'

In a bookshop in Munich he saw a volume of the German translation of *The Improvisatore*. He went in and picked it up. His diary relates what happened:

'But that's only Part One,' I said. 'That's the lot,' said the bookseller. 'No,' I said, 'it's only the first part.' 'But I read it yesterday,' said the bookseller. 'Didn't it seem to you to end rather abruptly?' I asked. 'Yes, indeed, like the new French novels; they end in a sophisticated way.' 'But all the same, it is only Part One,' I said. 'But I tell you, I read it,' he said. 'But I wrote it,' I replied.

Via Innsbruck and the Brenner Pass he went on to Italy; but this country, to which he had looked forward so much, was to some extent a disappointment. 'The North of Italy is a pigsty, later on one becomes so accustomed to it that it doesn't matter,' he wrote to Henriette Wulff, and in a letter to Henriette Hanck he described the six-day journey, travelling with a *vetturino* from Florence to Rome:

I had as one of my travelling companions an Englishman who was churlish and intolerable to such an extent that I can still feel the salt in my blood at the mere thought of him; but at the same time he was such a character that in a novel he would be as amusing to the reader as he was a nuisance in real life. He always took the best seat in the carriage, was always being awkward and inconvenient, took the food from our plates if he saw a good morsel we had been given, plundered the kitchen in every inn so that there was a constant row, and demanded a subservience which out of foolish kindheartedness I gave him the first two days, whereas later on I sent him about his business.

The chapter entitled 'Travelling with a Vetturino' in *A Poet's Bazaar* gives a very amusing picture of this English traveller in Italy.

In Rome, where he arrived in mid December, Andersen often felt lonely and miserable; the weather was cold and he suffered from toothache. His diary reveals that on New Year's Day he went into Saint Peter's, where he prayed under the cupola: 'God! Grant me an immortal name as a writer, give me health, and give me thy peace!' Two days later his diary records: 'Went home and in my loneliness I thought of my wish to die, away from home. Thought of the dear ones at home and felt sad.' And on 13 January: 'Melancholy and sad: I thought of my lost rose in Denmark.' By the 'lost rose' he undoubtedly meant Louise Collin, or as she now was: Mrs Lind.

The Moorish Girl had its first performance in Copenhagen on 18 December 1840, but Andersen had to wait anxiously for a whole month before he heard anything of its fate. To some extent it was better received than he had anticipated, for both the public and the critics received it politely at the première, though not with any kind of enthusiasm. But financially it was a catastrophe, for it failed to attract an audience, and after three performances it was taken off. It was a letter from Edvard Collin which gave Andersen this news, and as one can see from his diary his first reaction was one of relief. But as the days went by his spirits sank more and more. On 3 February he wrote: 'I should like to die, there is nothing left to live for. – I cannot pray to God, I know that my prayers will not be answered. Oh, I'm tired, body and soul, so please let the flame be extinguished, let the body rot! – Oh, where shall I go in this distress? – I went into a church in the Corso, a baby was christened Eduardo. My Edvard might think of me if only I had received my christening: the three shovelfuls of earth on my coffin.' Six days later he had worked himself into a fury 'at the icy coldness of Edvard's previous letter'.

One passage in Edvard Collin's letter contributed more than anything else to Andersen's increasing bitterness, namely this one: 'But if you think that the unfavourable criticism of *The Moorish Girl* has left any lasting impression in your disfavour, then you are wrong; for it has already been forgotten. Another important literary *Erscheinung* has taken its place, namely Heiberg's *New Poems*, of its kind and by its brilliant form a most remarkable product.' This was perhaps not the most tactful remark, considering the recent animosity between Andersen and Heiberg.

But unfortunately, Andersen was also informed shortly afterwards, by another correspondent in Copenhagen, that Heiberg had held him, Andersen, up to ridicule in his new book. He was not told how, which made matters far worse, for as Andersen writes in *Mit Livs Eventyr*: 'It is doubly painful to be mocked when you do not know what aspect of you is being mocked. Like molten lead the news dripped into an open wound.'

It was only after his return to Denmark that Andersen found out what Heiberg had in fact written about him. The *New Poems* included a brilliant 'apocalyptic comedy' entitled *A Soul after Death*, a contemporary satire directed against the 'average' Copenhagener, who finds himself after death being refused admittance to heaven as well as to Elysium, whereas he is freely admitted to hell. He feels completely at home there, for hell is not a place of fire and brimstone but merely a repetition *ad infinitum* of the soulless existence he had always been living. In hell, so Mephistopheles reassures the Soul, everything he is accustomed to is to be found, including theatres, and it so happens that on the night he arrives both *The Mulatto* and *The Moorish Girl* are being performed, and Mephistopheles talks about Andersen's European fame which extends from Scania to North Germany – and even as far as Constantinople, where the grand eunuch reads *The Mulatto* aloud to the sultan's harem and *The Moorish Girl* to those about to be strangled. And for good measure a few remarks were thrown in about Andersen's desire to be known – at any price.

In Rome, before knowing the contents of Heiberg's satire, Andersen wrote him a satirical rhymed letter; according to his diary 'it put me in good spirits, and I've felt more lively and more satisfied all day'. But a Danish colleague found it 'too nasty', and Andersen later tore it up. His public reply to Heiberg came in his travel book, *A Poet's Bazaar* (1842), in the chapter in which he describes his sufferings in an East-European quarantine camp:

In *this* hell, I dreamt that I was shut down in *that* of Heiberg's; and there, just as he has related, they only performed my two pieces; and that was very agreeable to me; nay, as a Christian, particularly pleasant to learn, as he has also told us that the condemned, after having seen my pieces, could lie down with a good conscience. Even there, at least, I had effected some good by my works. I heard, however, down there that, besides my two pieces in one evening, they had also determined to give Heiberg's *Fata Morgana* as a concluding piece; but the lost spirits had protested against it – after all, one can make hell too hot, and there must be a limit!

So thus the account was settled, and Andersen was generous – or clever – enough to add in a footnote that he regarded Heiberg's latest book as his most outstanding work.

From Rome Andersen went on to Naples where his health deteriorated to such an extent that he thought he was going to die, and he had to be bled. He had abandoned all hope of being able to continue to Greece when suddenly the good news reached him that the King of Denmark had given him a grant of six hundred rixdollars to enable him to go on.

So now the most adventurous part of his journey began. From Naples he sailed on a French steamer, first to Malta, and then to the Greek island of Syra (Siros), where he boarded another steamer, which took him to Piræus. On 24 March 1841 Andersen arrived in Athens. In a letter to Carsten Hauch he records his first impressions:

One can almost say that Athens grows hour by hour; houses and streets shoot up from the gravel; several streets look exactly like the booths we see on a fair-ground: tents are put up, all sorts of goods are displayed, and the selling is done by handsome, squatting Greek boys. Some parts of the city are no more than heaps of gravel, and in the middle of them one sees a hole; that is the entrance to a dwelling. One must look where one goes all the time, for suddenly one is standing on the edge of a well without the slightest kind of railing; scattered around are capitals, broken marble bas-reliefs, and all round ruined churches with gaily coloured pictures of saints on the walls; the Turks have scratched out every single face and shot bullets through the eyes and mouth of Christ. I walk up to the Acropolis every day. The view is marvellous and the place itself a ruined fairy world; wild cucumbers grow over the steps of the Parthenon; scattered round are unburied skulls of Turks and Greeks; here and there are whole bombs from the time of the Venetians. I have been to Socrates' prison: two small holes in a rock near Athens; at the entrance grew lovely red flowers, I picked one of them, thinking of Oehlenschläger – will you give him this flower from me?

He had planned to go to Parnassus on his birthday, but the weather forced him to stay in Athens where instead he heard two of the so-called rhapsodists, itinerant musicians, singing their traditional Greek songs. He visited the monastery of Daphne, and in Athens he celebrated both Independence Day (6 April) and the Easter festivities, and was invited by King Otto of Greece and his queen to an evening party at the royal palace.

After a month in Greece he sailed, again via Syra, to Smyrna and then through the Dardanelles, past Gallipoli and through the Sea of Marmara to Constantinople. He even crossed the Bosporus to Asia Minor to see the dancing dervishes in Scutari and Pera; and one of the most fascinating chapters in *A Poet's Bazaar* is the one in which he first describes the horrific, wild, almost obscene dancing of what seemed to him to be some completely insane dervishes from Scutari, and then the strangely beautiful dance of the dervishes at Pera – 'each of them wrapped in a large, dark-green cloak; a white felt hat, certainly two foot high, and entirely without brim, covered the head'. Moving slowly they circled round an old dervish:

They now threw off their cloaks, and each appeared in an open, dark-green jacket, with long, narrow sleeves; a long skirt of the same stuff and colour hung down to their ankles, and fell in large folds round their legs. They extended their arms and turned, always to the same side; their skirts stood out in the air like a funnel about them.

In the centre of the circle stood two dervishes, who continued to turn the same way round, and always on the same spot; the others turned round about them in a whirling dance; the eldest, with a long beard, walked quietly between those that formed the outer circle and the two in the middle. The dance was intended to represent the course of the planets.

The dance of the Pera dervishes, Andersen says, 'appeared to me like a sort of ballet, whereas the dance of the dervishes in Scutari remained in my memory like a scene in a madhouse'.

In Constantinople he had to decide whether to return by the safe route via Greece and Italy or to 'sail up Europe's royal river', the Danube. The latter was tempting because it would take him through parts of Eastern Europe he had never seen before; but on the other hand there were rumours in Constantinople about violent uprisings in Rumelia and Bulgaria, and he was told that thousands of Christians had been massacred. After a sleepless night he decided to go home via the Danube – in spite of all the dangers.

Normally, no one would call Andersen courageous, least of all himself. But what he wrote about Christian, his own *alter ego* in *Only a Fiddler*, was true of himself: 'In small matters I am no hero, and of this I am not ashamed. But believe me, when it's a matter of important things, then I have courage.' Andersen was afraid of dogs, he suffered from agoraphobia, he was hysterically obsessed with the thought of suffering an untimely death by fire or drowning, or as the victim of murderers; he was constantly afraid of being robbed, of being seduced, of losing his passport, and so on. But his zest for travelling, his desire to see new parts of the world was such that he could overcome his fears and anxieties, even when they were well founded.

Edvard Collin, who was not easily impressed, *was* impressed that Andersen had even got as far as Constantinople; for on receiving a letter from the Turkish capital he wrote back: 'You are a damn good traveller! The way you have managed to carry through this journey is something not many others could have done, and if you haven't got courage then at least you have shown a firm determination, which is equally good; that certificate will be given to you by yours faithfully, who is not in the habit of flattering you.'

This statement is the more remarkable in view of the fact that the Collins were unable to understand why Andersen was always wanting to travel. While Andersen was still in Italy Jonas Collin had written: 'Your journey to Greece will probably come to nothing, and this I do not regret, for goodness knows what you want to go there for.' His daughter, Ingeborg Drewsen, wrote: 'Heaven knows why you do not stay at home to see the many lovely things we have here! What is the pleasure of being cold in Rome? It would be better to be cold in Copenhagen.'

As soon as Andersen had made up his mind about the return journey he was perfectly calm, and so, after having celebrated Mohammed's birthday in Constantinople, he went by steamer through the Bosporus into the Black Sea as far as Kustendje (Constanza), and from there he continued by a carriage drawn by Wallachian horses across Tartary to Czernawoda. Here he boarded another steamer and sailed up the Danube, passing Wallachia, Bulgaria and

Serbia, through the Iron Gate to Orsova, a town on the border of Wallachia and Hungary. Here Andersen and all the other passengers coming from Constantinople were obliged to spend ten days in quarantine.

One of Andersen's fellow-travellers was a British explorer, William F. Ainsworth, a cousin of W. Harrison Ainsworth, the novelist; he was returning from a journey to Kurdistan and later published a book about his travels. Andersen and Ainsworth shared two rooms in the quarantine camp at Orsova and became friends. Five years later Ainsworth described Andersen in an article in the *Literary Gazette* as 'friendly and cheerful in conversation, although restless and *pré-occupé*' and spoke of the 'extreme simplicity in manners and confidence in others' that made Andersen so likable. He was 'a tall young man, of prepossessing appearance, pale colour, yet somewhat delicate; brown hair, and sharp nose and features, with a very very slight slouch in his gait, and the sidling movement of an abstracted man'. Mentioning the quarantine at Orsova Ainsworth wrote that he 'rejoiced very much in the good fortune that had given me so pleasant, and in every respect so gentlemanly a companion in durance vile'; he also mentioned Andersen's skill in cutting out paper, and revealed that 'the drawing of the Mewlewis, or turning dervishes, in my Asiatic travels, are from cuttings of his'.

From Orsova he travelled by carriage to Drenkova, and from there another steamer took him as far as Budapest, where he and Ainsworth parted company. The journey from Constantinople to Budapest had taken him just under a month, including the ten days quarantine.

After a few days in Budapest he continued along the Danube to Vienna, where he renewed his acquaintance with Grillparzer, once again heard Johann Strauss the Elder conducting, and visited the pianist and composer Sigismund Thalberg. He went on to Prague and down the Elbe to Dresden, then by railway to Leipzig, where he met Ottilie von Goethe, Goethe's daughter-in-law, and called on Mendelssohn-Bartholdy whom he had visited once before. He arrived back in Denmark on 13 July 1841, spent some time on Funen and was back in Copenhagen on 22 July.

On his return journey Andersen had had some evidence that his fame was beginning to spread in Europe, as the following extracts from his diary show:

Budapest, 31 May *Read the German newspapers and in an encyclopedia of the theatre and a general encyclopedia saw my own biography.*

Budapest, 1 June *Saw my* Improvisatore *in a bookshop; later bought two copies.*

On board the steamer *Bohemia* between Prague and Dresden, 28 June *A doctor from Prague looked at my name on the trunk and asked me if I was the 'vielberühmte Dichter Andersen'; another man came enthusiastically towards me, a Dr der Rechte from Schleswig; he went down to his cabin and wrote a German poem to me and my palm stick.*

On board the steamer *Hamburg* between Magdeburg and Hamburg, 7 July *A lady was reading my* Improvisatore *and adored the author; she introduced me to her daughters, Berliners; there I am supposed to have the largest public, and I dislike Berlin.*

In Hamburg Andersen had met some Danes, including an elderly lady, who asked him: 'Tell me, Hr Andersen, have you ever, on all your many and long journeys abroad, seen anything as beautiful as our little Denmark?' – 'I certainly have,' he replied. 'I have seen many things more beautiful.' – 'Shame on you!' she said. 'You are not a patriot!'

One of the immediate results of Andersen's Oriental journey was the travel book he wrote on return. It was published in April 1842 under the title *A Poet's Bazaar*. This inspired mixture of fact and fiction – for it includes chapters which were later incorporated into his *Eventyr og Historier* – is by far the best of all his travel books and was soon translated into several languages; an English translation in three volumes was published in 1846. It is a brilliant piece of journalism and demonstrates Andersen's extraordinary talent for communicating his own visual experience. But *A Poet's Bazaar* is certainly not political journalism; for in no way does the book prepare its readers for the upheavals of 1848.

When *A Poet's Bazaar* was published it was not received as well as it deserved by the Danish critics. One journal, however, M. A. Goldschmidt's radical, republican *Corsaren*, while recognizing many of the good qualities of Andersen's book, pointed out – and quite rightly – that there was something missing, 'something we had expected, particularly from H. C. Andersen, whose origin was in the people, who has fought the bitter struggle of poverty against richness, who knows what suppression and subjugation are: from him we had expected a feeling for the people, for their poverty, for their suppression.' But the reviewer (undoubtedly Goldschmidt himself) went on: 'H. C. Andersen has depicted the light of the sun and the lustre of the sea and the greenness of the plains and the splendour of the mountains; indeed, he has given life to dead stone. Only the life of the people has been for him dead stone.'

Certain events in Andersen's life in 1842 make it desirable to discuss his attitude to the problem of class generally.

Speaking in modern terms Andersen was a man born in the '*Lumpen-Proletariat*' but completely devoid of 'class consciousness'. In his novels and tales he often expresses an unambiguous sympathy for 'the underdog', especially for people who have been deprived of their chance of success because of their humble origins, and he pours scorn on haughty people who pride themselves on their noble birth or their wealth and who despise others for belonging to, or having their origin in, the lower classes. But in his private life Andersen accepted the system of absolutism and its inherent class structure, regarded royalty with awe and admiration and found a special pleasure in being accepted by and associating with kings, dukes and princes, and the nobility both at home and abroad.

He was certainly not a social rebel nor a champion of political reform. In *Mit Livs Eventyr* he even makes a point of the fact that he was totally uninterested in political matters and held the view that artists and creative writers should steer clear of politics altogether. With arguments acceptable to even the most conservative supporters of the *status quo* he writes:

Lady *Politica* is the Venus who entices them into her mountain, where they perish. The fate of the songs of such poets is like that of newspapers: they are eagerly caught, read, praised and – forgotten. In our age everybody wants to rule. The power of subjectivity is strong; but many people forget that much of that which is *theoretically possible* may not be *practicable*; they forget that the view as seen from the top of the tree is different from the view as seen from below, at its roots. I respect whoever is motivated by a sincere and noble conviction, be it the prince or be it the ordinary man; I respect whoever strives to achieve that which is for the common good and who has the ability to do so. Politics is not for me to dabble in; I have nothing to do there. God has given me a different task; I feel it and I have felt it.

Andersen, the social climber, rejoiced whenever he was able to spend his time in the company of those who enjoyed 'the view as seen from the top of the tree', and his own social insecurity was such that in the presence of royalty or titled persons he could be quite obsequious. Heinrich Heine, who *was* a political rebel, full of contempt for snobbery, gave a cruel picture of this unpleasant aspect of Andersen's character when he wrote:

Andersen called on me some years ago. I thought he was a tailor: he really does look like one. He is a tall thin man with hollow sunken cheeks and his manner reveals the sort of fawning servility that princes like. That is why princes have given Andersen such a brilliant reception. He is a perfect example of the type of poet princes like to see. When he visited me he had adorned his chest with a large tie-pin; when I asked him what it was that he had got there on his chest, he replied with great unction: 'This is a gift which the Electress of Hesse was graciously pleased to bestow upon me.' In other respects Andersen is a very admirable character.

Already in the 1830s Andersen had often enjoyed the privilege of being invited to some of the manors owned by members of the Danish aristocracy. In the summer of 1842 he spent two months as the guest of Count Danneskiold-Samsøe, Count Moltke, and Count Moltke-Hvidtfeldt at the manors of Gisselfeld, Bregentved and Glorup. With obvious delight he noted in his diary that when he went to bed the man-servant at Gisselfeld wished him 'a most humble goodnight!' After a few days at Bregentved he returned to Gisselfeld for the sole purpose of meeting the Duke and Duchess of Augustenborg, who had come for a few days. It gave him great pleasure that both the duke and the duchess invited him to visit them one day at Augustenborg Castle.

While staying at Gisselfeld Andersen wrote in his diary: 'I was sad, against my will, walked at random in the woods and fields, felt ill at ease. Had the idea of "The Story of a Duck", this helped my sunken spirits.' Three weeks later, while staying at Bregentved, he wrote: 'Began "The Cygnet" yesterday.' Both references are clearly to the story which eventually had the title 'The Ugly Duckling', one of Andersen's most famous tales. The final scene of the story is set in a large garden or park, like those of Gisselfeld and Bregentved, where the ugly duckling meets three white swans swimming towards him in one of the moats or streams of the manor:

Some little children came into the garden and threw bread and grain into the water, and the smallest one called out: 'There's a new swan!' and the other children joined in with shouts of delight: 'Yes, there's a new swan!' And they clapped their hands and danced about and ran to fetch father and mother. Bits of bread and cake were thrown into the water, and everyone said: 'The new one is the prettiest – so young and handsome!' And the old swans bowed before him.

In a famous essay on 'Andersen as a writer of fairy tales', written in 1869, Georg Brandes complained at 'The Ugly Duckling' ending as it does, with a tame swan being fed by the children of the manor, he was annoyed to see the duckling ending up as nothing more than a domesticated animal. 'Let it die if necessary,' Brandes wrote; 'that is tragic and grand. Let it lift its wings and fly soaring through the air, jubilant at its own beauty and strength.' To Brandes' romantic demand there is, however, an obvious reply: such an ending would have been untrue. Andersen, who is, of course, the ugly duckling ending up as a beautiful swan, was in real life a domesticated bird and not a wild eagle. He did eat the bits of bread and cake most graciously thrown to him by high-ranking persons, and it would have been false to pretend otherwise.

In Danish society of the early nineteenth century it was almost impossible to break through class barriers. Almost the only exceptions were a few individuals with unusual artistic gifts: Bertel Thorvaldsen, Fru Heiberg and Hans Christian Andersen. And even they had occasionally to be put in their place and reminded of their low origin. Jonas Collin's brother-in-law, a well-known professor of botany, once told Andersen that he should not have accepted an invitation from the King of Denmark to a grand *bal paré* at Christiansborg Castle in view of his humble origin. Andersen was of course furious at the insult and replied: 'My father was an artisan, and by God's and my own help I have made myself into what I am now, and I thought you would respect that!' To Andersen the past *was* the past, and even in such a brutal class society as was the Danish at the time, it was generally accepted that a genius was entitled to have been born in humble circumstances.

But when the past caught up with him and became part of the present, then Andersen panicked, for it brought about a confrontation with something which he had been secretly afraid of for years and which he had tried to conjure away in one of his novels.

On 8 February 1842 Andersen wrote in his almanac: 'Dined in the Students' Union, didn't feel well in the theatre, very sad. When I came home I found a letter from my mother's daughter; I experienced that which I have described in *O.T.* Feverish. A terrible night, sensuous thoughts and despair mockingly filled my mind.'

Andersen had not seen his half-sister Karen Marie – or Karen, as he called her – since he left Odense in 1819. She was suspected of living in Copenhagen, and he may well have had nightmares at the thought of his sister being arrested either as a criminal or as a prostitute. She might have died without his knowing it, of course. And then all of a sudden Karen materialized after having found out her brother's address and written to him.

The very next morning Andersen went to see Jonas Collin, his father confessor to whom he disclosed everything. Collin, who was probably completely ignorant of the fact that Andersen had a sister, immediately asked Adolph Drewsen, his son-in-law, who was a magistrate in a police court, to obtain whatever information was available about Karen and her husband – for in her letter she must have referred to 'my husband'. The information which Drewsen was able to glean must have been fairly reassuring, for on 11 February Andersen noted in his almanac: 'Sent letter to Karen, expected her husband to call.' According to the almanac 'the husband' arrived on the following day; his name was Kaufmann, he 'looked honest and decent' and told Andersen about his poverty, whereupon he was given four rixdollars; 'he was very happy, so was I,' Andersen writes. A month later Kaufmann turned up again, and this time Andersen gave him two rixdollars. Six months later the almanac has the laconic entry: 'Given Karen's husband 1 rixdollar.' On 30 September 1842: 'Visit by Karen this morning. She looked quite well-dressed and young, I gave her 1 rixdollar.' On 25 November: 'Karen's husband 4 Mark.' There is then no further mention of either Karen or Kaufmann until 30 October 1843, when the almanac records: 'My sister announced herself at the porter's lodge' (of the Copenhagen hotel where Andersen was then staying). Whether Andersen saw her or not is not known. And this is the last known reference by Andersen to his half-sister.

When H. G. Olrik searched the official registers of Copenhagen for information about Andersen's sister he found that in 1840 Karen Marie Andersen (as she then called herself) shared a room in one of the slums of Copenhagen with a man called Peter Kaufmann, described as an unmarried labourer of twenty-nine; her profession is given as a washerwoman, and she is described as a spinster of thirty-two, though she must then have been at least forty. From the official registers it can also be seen that she died in November 1846, leaving no offspring, and was buried in a pauper's grave in Copenhagen. Not even her common-law husband was present at the funeral.

There is no reason to believe that Andersen had any contact whatsoever with either Karen or Peter Kaufmann after 1843, and he was probably ignorant of her death, for his almanac contains no reference to it.

'My mother's daughter' – that was how Andersen referred to his sister Karen. Otherwise he was lavish in his use of the word 'sister' when referring to his women friends. He liked to regard Jonas Collin's children as his brothers and sisters, and in his letters to Henriette Wulff and Henriette Hanck he almost invariably signed himself 'Broderen' (The Brother), just as they referred to themselves as his sisters (Henriette Wulff often signed herself 'Sorella'). But Andersen was reluctant to use the word 'sister' about the one person who could rightfully call herself so. The reason for this is obvious: to him Karen represented a threat, not necessarily of financial blackmail but of being confronted with a past he thought he had left behind him, a past which he had to some extent deliberately falsified by describing it in rosier and more idyllic colours than it really was. 'The swamp plant' had moved to a different soil; Karen still represented – and lived in – the swamp.

At the end of January 1843 Andersen left Denmark again, this time with Paris as his ultimate destination. Once again he spent a fortnight as Count Rantzau's guest at Breitenburg Castle, where he was able to work on a new dramatic poem, 'Ahasuerus'. He then continued to Brussels, where he went to see the Rubens collection at the art gallery; but he did not like what he saw. 'I don't like Rubens,' he wrote in his diary; 'I find those fat, blond women with coarse faces and bleached dresses very boring.'

In March he arrived in Paris – ten years after his first visit there – and he stayed for two months. Xavier Marmier's account of his life had to some extent paved the way for him and certainly made it much easier for him to establish contact with French writers. While at the opera a few days after his arrival he was asked about his nationality by the gentleman sitting next to him; when Andersen told him that he was Danish his neighbour said that he had read Marmier's account of Scandinavian literature and knew the names of two of the greatest Scandinavian writers, Tegnér and Andersen.

Andersen had the further advantage that Marmier, who spoke Danish reasonably well, was very happy to act as his cicerone and eager to introduce him to his literary and artistic friends in Paris. As soon as they had met, he took Andersen to the editorial office of the Revue de deux mondes, introduced him to his colleagues there and promised to arrange for him to meet Victor Hugo, Lamartine and others.

The first time that Andersen went to visit Victor Hugo only Madame Hugo was at home; but Hugo had sent Andersen a free ticket for his new play, Les Burgraves, at the Théâtre Français. The next time Andersen called, Hugo was at home and asked Andersen to have lunch with him. Hugo looked to Andersen much older and more worn-out than when he had seen him ten years previously. Three weeks later he visited him again and saw all his children and his wife, whom he found very beautiful. 'But there's nothing upstairs!' David, the sculptor, told Andersen, referring to Madame Hugo; David d'Angers was another of the many French celebrities whom Marmier had arranged for Andersen to meet. In his diary Andersen describes David as 'a simple, straightforward man, like a Danish peasant, dressed in a blue tunic and a Greek cap.'

Marmier also introduced him to Alexandre Dumas père. In his diary Andersen described their first meeting:

Went to Alexandre Dumas in Rue Richelieu, Hôtel de Paris; he received me with open arms, wore a blue-striped shirt and loose-hanging trousers. His bed was in the same room and unmade, the table full of papers. We sat by the fire; he was extremely cordial and natural. He told me that the King of Sweden, who had been a general with his father, had invited him to Stockholm; he wanted to go there and would then visit Copenhagen and Saint Petersburg. He offered to take me tomorrow at 8.30 to the Théâtre Français and introduce me to Rachel.

Rachel (her full name was Elizabeth Felix Rachel), the great French tragédienne, was then the rage not only of Paris but of the whole of Europe. Though she was only twenty-two, everybody knew her name, even in Denmark. Her most famous part was the title role in Racine's *Phèdre*, and this was the part she was playing at the Théâtre Français when Andersen was in Paris.

Dumas kept his promise and Andersen's diary tells us what happened:

At 8.30 I went to A. Dumas, I met him in the street with his son [Alexandre Dumas fils], who is 18, he is 36 himself. First we went to the Palais Royal where he had an appointment to see Déjazet [the popular French actress Pauline Déjazet], then to the [Théâtre] Français. I had to wait outside until he had found out whether Rachel was on stage or not. A man called me in, I was well dressed and my hair combed. By means of a screen a little room had been made at what we call 'the Royal side' [i.e., left of the stage] behind the wings; here were three stools; dressed as Phèdre Rachel received us kindly. She is beautiful and has a most interesting face; not one of her portraits looks like her. Her voice is very deep but beautiful; she asked us to sit down. I told her that in my country she was well known and popular and that her portrait was in every house; she refused to believe it and told me that if she ever came to Copenhagen she would regard me as someone she knew. I replied that she would find so many friends there that she would not want to see me. While walking up the stairs with Dumas I had said, 'You will laugh at me, but my heart is beating like that of a child because I'm going to see Rachel!' This he told her, and she exclaimed, 'I'm sure artists should be able to understand one another.' – Dumas spoke to her in a very lively way, she laughed and looked very bright, then stretched out her hand to say good-bye and stood, as Phèdre, in front of the jubilant audience. I wanted to stay, but D. said, 'Now is just the time when the actresses at Saint Martin's are wearing their short skirts, so let's go there!' Arm in arm we wandered down the Vivienne and along the entire boulevard; I kept talking the most horrible French.

A few days later Andersen sat among the audience in the Théâtre Français watching, on this occasion, a complete performance of *Phèdre*, and he was delighted and moved to see Rachel playing the part. Somewhat later he saw her again in a French adaptation of Schiller's *Maria Stuart*, in which she played Mary, Queen of Scots. He wrote in his diary:

Rachel was perfectly lovely, an entirely convincing Maria Stuart; the scene between her and Elizabeth was shattering, her 'Vous est – Elizabeth, je suis votre Reine!' superb. What a natural serenity and suffering there was in the final act! The audience shouted with enthusiasm, and I cried, 'Vive Rachel!' She looked happy this evening when she took the curtain calls, yet at the same time subdued.

Shortly afterwards Andersen received an invitation from Rachel to an evening party at her apartment in Paris. This was one of the highlights of his visit; he described it afterwards in a letter to Henriette Wulff:

Last night I was invited by Rachel to one of her special soirées. There was a splendour, a wealth in those rooms – scarlet walls, carpets of the same colour, costly curtains and tasteful furniture. I and an elderly gentleman were the first two to arrive; she asked me to sit next to her on the sofa, just in front of the fireplace; she was dressed in black and extremely graceful. I asked her to speak German, and she replied, 'Well, if you didn't speak French I would, but you express yourself better in my language than I do in a foreign tongue; your pronunciation is good – with a little more training it will be very good' – and so I had to speak French. There were costly bookcases with literature of all nations translated into French, even Swedish writers, but not a single Danish one. Shakespeare, Goethe, Racine and Corneille stood on a little table by themselves, with the busts of the two latter; I found Grillparzer's Sappho there in German; there were lovely flowers. While we were sitting there, one gentleman after the other arrived, Scribe, Gautier and – I forget all the names. She was the only lady among us, lively and lovely, she poured out tea herself, and we talked about poetry and art, and it was midnight before I managed to sneak away.

Andersen also visited Dumas again; his diary contains the following entry:

At 4.30 I went to Alexandre Dumas, he was lying writing in his bed, asked to be excused for a moment while writing, muttering some words in a half-loud voice. 'Voilà!' he cried and jumped out of bed. 'Now I've finished Act III.' It was a prose play he was writing for the Théâtre Français.

Shortly after Andersen's arrival Heine had been to his hotel and left his visiting card, and a few days later Andersen called on him at his house and was received most cordially. In his diary Andersen writes:

He told me that he had almost forgotten his German, that he had French joys and French sorrows, and a French wife. To him Scandinavia seemed to be the mystical country in which the treasure of poetry was buried; if he wasn't as old as he was he would begin to learn Danish. He was particularly interested in our Nisser [hob-goblins] and trolls; that was the reason why he had called his latest book Atta Troll ('Atta' means 'Father'). He found that only lyrical poetry was alive in Germany, mentioned Eichendorff, Uhland, Grün.

Heine had read *The Improvisatore* and found it 'plastic', he said. 'Sie sind ein wahrer Dichter!' he told Andersen and asked him to visit him frequently.

Andersen did in fact see Heine twice more during this visit. On the second occasion he told Heine three of his own tales, and they talked about Danish literature. 'You're a *raconteur*,' Heine said, adding, 'So was Goethe, but I'm not.' The third visit also seems to have been very cordial; Heine reported that he had retold Andersen's 'The Steadfast Tin Soldier' to his wife, who was delighted with it.

Andersen was particularly interested in meeting Lamartine, whose *Souvenirs d'un voyage en orient* (1835) he had read in Danish translation before embarking on his own Oriental journey. It had impressed him very much at the time but after his own visit to Turkey he was much more critical of it.

The person who established the contact was again Xavier Marmier, who told Lamartine that Hans Christian Andersen was in Paris, and as a result Andersen received a formal invitation to visit Lamartine at his house on 1 May. Andersen describes the event in his diary:

Many liveried footmen received us, we went through large rooms into one adorned with splendid paintings, including one of Lamartine in life-size. He received us very kindly; there were several Members of the Chamber of Deputies; Madame Lamartine, who is not beautiful, looks very intelligent; I spoke a good deal. Lamartine asked me to give him in German what I had written about Constantinople, then one of his friends would translate it for him. He spoke about Thorvaldsen; I informed him about the geography of Stockholm, and he thought he might go there sometime. He knew our king and queen from Italy and praised them much, especially her beauty, asked to be remembered to them.

Andersen also visited Alfred de Vigny, even twice, and on the second occasion Vigny presented him with an edition of all his own poetic and dramatic works. Later the same day Vigny unexpectedly turned up at Andersen's hotel to say good-bye. When he had left Andersen's room he shouted from the staircase: 'Come back to Paris soon, and do not forget me!'

Andersen was also invited to *soirées* by members of the French aristocracy. At one *soirée* he met Honoré de Balzac, who (according to Andersen's diary) 'paid me some compliments'. He describes Balzac as 'a little broad-shouldered lump of a man' ('en lille bredskuldret Knold'). To Ingeborg Drewsen's daughter, Jonna, Andersen wrote from Paris:

Just imagine that in a large salon at Countess [Pfaffins's] she dragged me over into her velvet sofa and asked me to sit down by her satin side – for she was dressed in the blackest of black with jewels – and here she held my hand and pulled Balzac, the author, by his hand, so that he too came to sit next to her, and then she exclaimed, 'How fortunate I am, I'm ashamed to be sitting here between two of the greatest men of our time!' 'La baronne!' I said with a reproving look and told her – all in French – how unimportant I was.

Andersen was fully aware that his French was very bad, but he was proud of being able to 'vault' ('voltigere'), as he called it, through a conversation.[16] In the letter to Jonna Drewsen, Andersen also wrote: 'You know that I have even spoken to Rachel, she who speaks the French tongue best of all here; but I was undaunted. My reasoning was this: she can hear good French spoken every day, and she herself is unsurpassed; but my French is original, and she must realize the trouble I take to arrange words in order to reveal my thoughts. Occasionally I do come to a sudden halt in the conversation, but then I say: "Voilà, c'est tout!", and then I let the other person talk. You all know me so well at home; but you do not know me when I'm abroad; the views of the Collins on languages are too severe and not those accepted by the world.'

There cannot have been many foreign writers – if indeed any at all – who managed to meet, in the course of two months in Paris, Victor Hugo, Dumas *père et fils*, Lamartine, Vigny, Balzac, Scribe, Gautier and Heine – not to mention celebrities like Rachel and David d'Angers. Andersen's extraordinary talent for meeting and talking to interesting people cannot be put down to snobbishness alone, for if, in spite of language difficulties, he had not been able to communicate and make a favourable impression, he would never have been able to establish all those contacts. Compared with what happened forty years later when prominent Scandinavian authors like Bjørnson, Jonas Lie and Strindberg were able to live in Paris for years without having the slightest contact with contemporary French writers, Andersen's talent for establishing personal relationships becomes even more striking. Andersen, 'le bon, aimable poète danois', as Alexandre Dumas called him, had a talent for making friends abroad unparalleled by any other Scandinavian author of his time – even among people who were not familiar with his best works.

Enjoying such recognition abroad, Andersen began to regard his own countrymen with even greater suspicion and bitterness than before, and sometimes even with hatred. He built up a simplified picture of recognition and admiration abroad and envy and unjustified criticism at home, often forgetting that the fact that his novels and fairy tales had made him popular in Europe was no valid reason for his countrymen to feel obliged to applaud the first performance of one of his mediocre plays in Copenhagen. There *was* some unjustified criticism in Denmark, but when contrasting his reception abroad with that at home he was not always comparing like with like.

Like a child Andersen was bitterly disappointed when he did not receive any letters or greetings from home on his thirty-eighth birthday, which he celebrated in Paris. In his diary he entered a bitter, 'No one remembered my birthday', on 2 April 1843. And when, a few days later, he received a brief note from Jonas Collin with no mention of his birthday, he wrote angrily in his diary: 'Only a brief note from Collin. Am mad with rage! No attention from those at home!' On the same day he wrote to Jonas Collin:

I was childish enough to think that 2 April would have brought back the memory of me, but this has not been the case. I have been diligent in writing to the Family, and if anyone thinks that this affords me sufficient amusement, then he is certainly wrong, for I write letters mainly in order to get letters in return. Edvard might have sent me one, for even if I am not fortunate enough to belong to the friends he takes comfort in expressing himself to when he has a deep sorrow, he might all the same, when this sorrow is relieved, remember me by writing a few words. I will be frank and admit how much it has grieved me to see how little interest they take in me at home, and by home I mean the Collin family, for I know the situation too well to imagine that the Danes should take any interest in me.

Andersen's words about 'Edvard's sorrow' refer to the fact that his eldest daughter had recently died, and though Andersen had written a letter in which he had expressed his sympathy he had had no reply. Andersen wrote to Gottlieb Collin, Edvard's brother, saying that he himself was going through 'one of those unhappy periods' from which he had suffered so often during his first journey to Italy. 'It is a kind of cold air stream coming from the Home, which makes my mind sick and poisons my blood,' he wrote, adding: 'But then I suppose this is my way of being homesick.'

Jonas Collin comforted him in his next letter: 'You are always remembered here in Amaliegaden with love, though it may not always be expressed in words.'

When Andersen did finally get a letter from Edvard it made things even worse. In his diary for 1 May 1843 he wrote: 'At home I found a letter from Edvard, as cold as a law book, so that I could think of nothing but his behaviour. How strange that I cannot get accustomed to his way of writing letters. In place of friendship he has offered me willingness to render services.'

A few days previously Andersen's fury had exploded at being told that the stage version of his *Agnete* had been booed in Copenhagen after the first performance, and thinking of his triumphs in the social and literary *salons* of Paris Andersen flew into such a rage against Denmark and the Danes generally that he wrote to Henriette Wulff:

I wish my eyes may never again see the home which can only see my shortcomings but fails to realize what great gifts God has given me! – I hate those who hate me, I curse those who curse me! From Denmark as always before the cold air streams come which petrify me abroad! They spit on me, they trample me into the mud, and yet I am a Digter of a kind God did not give them many of – and in my dying hour I shall ask God never to give any such to that nation again. Oh, what a poison has come into my blood at these hours! – When I was young I could weep, now I can't, I can only be proud – hate – detest – give my soul to evil powers in order to find a moment's relief! – Here, in this large foreign city, the best known and the noblest among the spirits of Europe receive me with kindness and love, meet me as a kindred soul, and at home the boys are spitting at the best creation of my heart! Indeed, even if I have to be judged after my death as I am being judged while I'm alive, I still say: The Danes can be evil, cold, satanic! A people well suited for those damp, mouldy-green islands from which Tycho Brahe was sent into exile, where Leonora Christina was imprisoned, where Ambrosius Stub was treated as the squires' fool, and where yet many others like them will be maltreated until the name of the people becomes a legend. – Still, I'm probably expressing myself in a way characteristic of a hissed poet; if this letter of mine were published, the whole of Copenhagen would roar with laughter. – I wish I had never seen that place, I wish the eternal God will never again let anybody with a nature like mine be born there; I hate the home, just as it hates and spits on me. – Please pray for me to God that I may find a quick death, that I may never see the place where I'm made to suffer, where I'm a stranger, a stranger like nowhere abroad.

Andersen concluded:

I'm ill this evening! My home has sent me a fever from its wet and cold woods, which the Danes stare at, believing that they love them, but – I do not believe in love in the Northern countries, only in evil and falsehood – I myself feel it in my blood, and only thus can I feel where I belong.

Andersen was afraid that Henriette Wulff might tear up this letter (which she did not do), so he copied it verbatim into his diary.

The man who later wrote his famous love poem to Denmark, beginning, 'In Denmark I was born,' and ending with the words, 'I love you, Denmark, my native land,' was absolutely sincere in his hatred of his native land and of his countrymen when he wrote this letter in the spring of 1843. And it was certainly not the last time in Andersen's life that success abroad was directly linked with bitterness at the apparent or real lack of recognition at home.

In May he left Paris and travelled via Nancy and Strasbourg back to Germany. There he also made some literary friendships. The poet Ferdinand

Freiligrath received him with enthusiasm in St Goar, for it so happened that it was their common interest in Andersen's *Only a Fiddler* that had originally brought Freiligrath and his wife together. He met the old writer Ernst Moritz Arndt and the young poet Emanuel Geibel, and everywhere in Germany there were ladies who 'loved' or 'adored' *Only a Fiddler*, or 'called it their Bible'.

Andersen returned to Copenhagen in June, but only stayed for a few days, before spending most of the summer as the guest of members of the Danish aristocracy on Funen and Zealand.

While staying on Funen he happened to meet a family, Mr and Mrs Bøving and their children. Mrs Bøving was the former Miss Riborg Voigt. The meeting is briefly mentioned in his almanac (he was not keeping a diary at the time), the only comment being the following added in brackets: 'it is 13 years'. It is not referred to in any letter. But, as Hans Brix was the first to point out, Andersen's comments on his meeting with Riborg are to be found in the sarcastic little story he wrote in the summer of 1843, shortly after that meeting, 'The Top and the Ball'. Here, in a facetious way, Andersen has retold his own love story: the enamoured top represents himself, and the ball, being 'what you might call half-engaged to a swallow' and turning down the top's proposal, represents Riborg Voigt. The mere fact that the top cannot have her makes him love the ball more than ever. The ball vanishes, and after a while 'it became nothing more than an old love-affair.' When finally, after several years, the top sees the ball again he hardly recognizes her and never mentions his old love. The moral of the story is expressed in the words: 'Love is, of course, bound to fade away, when your sweetheart has spent five years growing sodden in the gutter; you can't be expected to know her again if you meet her in a dustbin.'

This was Andersen's subtle way of declaring his old love for Riborg Voigt to be null and void.

Two months after the meeting he met another woman with whom he fell more deeply in love than he had ever done before. She was Jenny Lind, a girl of nearly twenty-three, a Swedish singer who was already celebrated and popular in her own country and who was to become within a few years the most famous and admired female singer in Europe, universally known as 'The Swedish Nightingale'.

Andersen had met Jenny Lind briefly two years before in Copenhagen, but that meeting had made no impression on either of them. In the autumn of 1843 she came to Copenhagen again, and Andersen met her at the house of one of his friends, August Bournonville, the Danish ballet master, who knew Jenny Lind from Stockholm and admired her greatly as a singer. At that time she had never sung in public outside Sweden, and Bournonville tried to persuade her to appear in a leading part in an opera at Copenhagen's Royal Theatre; for this purpose he wanted to enlist Andersen's help, so that he too could bring pressure to bear on her. She did in the end agree to play the part of Alice in Meyerbeer's *Robert of Normandy* on 10 and 13 September, and she also gave a charity concert.

The following entries in Andersen's almanac for September 1843 will give an outline of events as seen through his eyes:

3 September *In low spirits! Dinner at Bournonville's. Miss Lind from Stockholm sang for me.*
9 September *Evening with Jenny Lind at Bournonville's.*
10 September *Jenny Lind's first performance as Alice; she had curtain calls. In the evening with her at Bournonville's, they drank her toast and mine. In love.*
11 September *Sent Jenny a poem.*
12 September *This evening at Bournonville's with Jenny Lind; gave her a briefcase.*
13 September *Jenny Lind second time in* Robert; *she got a bouquet and a poem from me. Sad because she is leaving on Saturday.*
14 September *Her journey postponed. Am spending every day with her. Sent her my poems, been to Thorvaldsen's exhibition with her.*
16 September *Jenny Lind's concert, in the evening at Bournonville's. Jenny and I spoke confidently.*
17 September *Dinner at Oehlenschläger's. In the evening Jenny L. arrived, I hardly spoke to her; jealous of Günther* [a Swedish tenor]. *We drove back by omnibus, and I saw her home.*
18 September *Visited her. Read the others' poems, thought of proposing. – Had a swim. She is going to sing before the king.*
19 September *Jenny Lind's diamonds, presented by the king. Sent her my portrait, wrote a song. This evening at Nielsen's, where 300 students gave her a serenade. I love her, came home at 1.30 at night, wrote her a letter.*
20 September *At the Customs House this morning at 4.30, said good-bye to Jenny, handed her a letter which she will understand. I love!*

Before Henriette Wulff went abroad on a long journey Andersen must have told her of his love for Jenny Lind. In his farewell letter to Henriette, on 18 October, Andersen wrote: 'I still didn't get a letter from Jenny Lind yesterday. She is being idolized and garlanded every evening in Stockholm, one banquet follows another.'

On 31 October Andersen's almanac records: 'Letter from Jenny Lind this morning.' The contents of the letter are not known, but it seems clear that she cannot have regarded his letter as an actual proposal. To Henriette Wulff Andersen wrote that the two most important events after her departure in October were the publication of his new volume of *Eventyr* – 'and the fact that I got a letter from Jenny L.' He went on: 'Jenny's letter was very long and extremely cordial and kind, so completely the way I wished it be be. She is a great and lovely soul; may God see to it that her future husband makes her happy. I imagine it will be G.[17] – I am not really in a position to form an opinion about it.'

Fredrika Bremer, the Swedish novelist, with whom Andersen had corresponded for several years, was an intimate friend of Jenny Lind's, and in November she wrote to Andersen from Stockholm to say that she and Jenny had been talking about him and praising him a few days previously, for they both counted themselves among his most sincere admirers, irrespective of whether he wrote in prose or in verse. Fredrika Bremer then went on: 'But from the little letter Mlle Lind gave me from you I see that it is useless to talk to you about anyone except her.' She told him that Jenny Lind had long been the darling of the Swedish public, and then continued:

Flowers pour down at her feet, poems too, wooers likewise (though not in such quantities), and besides she charms women as much as men by her modest, natural, pleasant manners. Hers is a versatile, richly endowed nature – may God preserve her! I have always been partial to her, and like everybody else here enthralled by her wonderful gift as a singer and an actress. If you want to see Jenny Lind's eyes shine and her entire face and personality enveloped by the beauty of joy and inspiration, then speak to her about her art, about its beauty and innocence, about its beneficial influence on human souls. But if you want to see the most profound and most attractive aspect of her, then speak to her about the doctrines of religion, about the grace and will of God, about the equal worth and rights of each person in front of him, about his manifestation in Christ, about the destiny of all people – then you will see tears of joy and emotion on her young face with its childlike expression, and her eyes will shine devoutly and genuinely, then – then she is beautiful!

Quoting Fredrika Bremer's characterization of Jenny Lind, Andersen wrote to Henriette Wulff: 'These are Miss Bremer's words. Do you understand now that all my thoughts are concerned with such a pearl? And yet, she won't be mine – cannot be mine, but she must live in my soul as a good and kind spirit who – and this I know – does appreciate me, does like me – perhaps more than I deserve!'

To Ingemann Andersen wrote: 'She is the loveliest *child* I have met. In her private life she seems to me to be an ennobled Cendrillon.' And he made the following comment: 'Jenny Lind, I must add, is not good-looking at first glance; but speak to her – and every word Fredrika Bremer has said is true. However, I have spoken too much about her already. Please do not misunderstand me: she is engaged to be married!'

The last statement was not quite true, of course, but Andersen seemed to think that she was in fact secretly engaged to Günther.

On 11 October 1843 Andersen noted in his almanac: 'Began the Chinese tale.' And on the following day he noted: 'Finished the Chinese tale.' What he meant by 'the Chinese tale' was the story entitled 'The Nightingale', one of his most famous tales, a new and far more subtle version of a theme he had first used in 'The Swineherd', and there can be no doubt that it was his meeting with Jenny Lind which inspired him to write this story.

When Jenny Lind sang in Copenhagen in the autumn of 1843 she was still an unknown artist outside her native Sweden, and those who followed the fashion preferred to attend a more traditional Italian opera at the Court Theatre. It was this that Andersen translated into the conflict between the nightingale (Jenny Lind) and the artificial bird (the Italian troupe). In the story the nightingale sings before the emperor as in real life Jenny Lind sang before the King of Denmark. He presented her with diamonds; in the fairy tale the Chinese emperor presents the nightingale with a gold slipper to wear round her neck. Andersen saw Jenny Lind as a kind of musical parallel to himself: the divine natural talent, the born genius, the artist fully capable of using the great gifts given to her (him) by God. The nightingale is Jenny Lind, and the nightingale is Andersen himself. Thus the meeting with Jenny Lind sparked off one of Andersen's finest and most characteristic tales.

'The Top and the Ball' – Andersen's humorous epitaph to his love for Riborg Voigt – and 'The Nightingale' – his sincere homage to his new love, Jenny Lind – were both incorporated together with two other stories, 'The Ugly Duckling' and 'The Angel', in the first part of a volume entitled *Nye Eventyr* (New Fairy Tales), published in November 1843. Here, for the first time, the words 'told for children' had been deliberately deleted from the title-page, for Andersen now wanted to indicate that his tales – or at least most of them – were meant to be read at two different levels; by children, who would like 'the story as such', the 'plot', and what Andersen called 'the trappings', and by grown-ups, who would be able to appreciate the underlying ideas, the 'philosophy' of the tales. He explained this in a letter to Ingemann:

I believe – and it would give me great pleasure if I was right – that I have now found out how to write fairy tales. The first ones I wrote were, as you know, mostly old ones I had heard as a child, and which I then usually retold and recreated in my own way. The ones that were my own creations, such as 'The Little Mermaid', 'The Storks', 'The Daisy', were the most popular, however, and that has given me inspiration. Now I tell stories out of my own breast, catch an idea for the grown-ups – and then tell the story to the little ones while remembering all the time that Father and Mother often listen, and you must also give them something for their minds.

Andersen's four new tales were a great success. One month after their publication he wrote to Henriette Wulff: 'These tales have been accepted with unanimous applause; no other books of mine have had such a success here at home, every paper praises them, everybody reads them – and not after having borrowed them from the neighbour's neighbour, no, they are actually bought! I am appreciated as the foremost fairy-tale teller – in short, this time I have good reason to be very satisfied with the public.'

These were indeed unusual tones from Andersen.

A week later he again wrote to Henriette Wulff: 'Today Reitzel informed me that the new *Eventyr*, of which 850 had been printed, had all been sold, and that therefore we had better print another 850, considering that it is not yet Christmas! Isn't it marvellous? The book has sold like hot cakes! All papers praise it, everybody reads it! None of my books seems to be appreciated the way these fairy tales do!'

8 With kings, princes and dukes

1844-7

DURING the next four years Andersen again travelled much, and these were the years when he found himself really recognized in Europe and beyond, and famous to an extent he had never dreamed. These were also the years when, to his great delight, he found himself sought after by kings and queens, princes and princesses, dukes and duchesses, and, of course, by the nobility surrounding their courts.

Thus the highlight of his two-month visit to Germany in the summer of 1844 was his stay in Weimar. Almost immediately after he had arrived he was invited to spend a whole week as the guest of Freiherr von Beaulieu-Marconnay, Lord Chamberlain to the Grand Duke of Weimar, to whose court he was invited on several occasions. After having had tea and dinner with the grand duke and duchess the day after his arrival, Andersen went to Ettersburg, the country seat of their son Carl Alexander, Hereditary Grand Duke of Weimar, a young man of twenty-six, and his consort, a Dutch princess. In his diary for 26 June 1844 Andersen wrote: 'The young duke was extremely kind. I could have chosen him as a friend if he weren't a duke.' And later in the same entry: 'I really love the young duke, he is the first prince towards whom I have felt truly drawn; I wish he weren't a prince, or else that I was one.' Andersen read some of his own tales to the prince and 'was admired', as he notes in his diary.

Two days later he was again invited to dine with the grand duke and duchess at Castle Belvedere. 'The grand duchess told me how fond her son was of me and asked me to come again to Weimar,' Andersen noted in his diary. Later the same day at Ettersburg the invitation was repeated: 'The hereditary duke wanted me to stay longer in Weimar, pressed my hand long and firmly, said he was my friend and that he hoped sometime in the future to be able to prove it. His consort also asked me to come to Weimar again and not to forget them.'

After visiting Goethe's and Schiller's tombs he noted in his diary: 'I stood between the two of them, said the Lord's Prayer, prayed to God to let me be a *Digter* worthy of them, otherwise his will be done in bad as well as in good things.'

At the beginning of August Andersen was back in Denmark, and later, at the invitation of King Christian VIII and his queen, he went to the North Frisian island of Föhr (then part of the Kingdom of Denmark), where the royal couple were spending some time at a spa. Andersen stayed on Föhr as their guest for twelve days; his impressions of Föhr and the so-called Hallig islands, which he also visited, were later incorporated in his novel *The Two*

Baronesses (1848). Andersen dined daily with the king and queen, and he also read some of his tales aloud to them.

Wrongly believing 5 September to be the twenty-fifth anniversary of his first arrival in Copenhagen (the correct date being 6 September), Andersen celebrated this jubilee on Föhr; his diary for the day begins with the words: 'Thanked God for the 25 years!' Later in the same entry he wrote:

Spent the evening with the king, 5 September. The king came over to me, congratulating me on what I had overcome and achieved; later he came back again and asked me about my first appearance, spoke about my fame in Germany; I told him a few characteristic examples. He laughed, asked me if I had a fixed income, I told him Frederik VI had given me 400 rixdollars and that His Majesty had given me permission to keep this income, for which I was grateful. 'That's only a small sum,' he said. 'But then I don't need very much,' I said. He enquired about my works, how much they gave me, I said 12 rixdollars per sheet, that wasn't much, we spoke about living; I felt that here was an opportunity of asking for more but it was against my feelings. Then he said, 'If ever I can be of any assistance to further your literary activities, please come to me!' I thanked him and said that at the moment I didn't want to ask for anything. Rantzau, with whom I went home, said that the king had put into my mouth a request for something, but otherwise he praised my feelings, promised, if the opportunity arose, to speak on my behalf. I was a little dissatisfied with myself but put my trust in God.

From Föhr Andersen went straight to the island of Als, where he had been invited to stay at Augustenborg Castle as the guest of the duke and duchess. On the day after his arrival he had the triumph of being driven in the ducal carriage to the Bishop's Palace, the Bishop of Als being none other than the former Dean Tetens of Odense, who had confirmed Andersen in 1819. 'What a strange twist of fortune, to let me first visit the house of the man who spoke harshly to me when I came to see him as a poor boy, as the guest of a duke,' Andersen wrote in his diary.

He spent a fortnight at Augustenborg Castle, and towards the end of his stay the Prince of Nör, Governor of Schleswig-Holstein, arrived. In *Mit Livs Eventyr* Andersen writes: 'At Augustenborg I then saw nothing but kind and happy people, a harmonious family life, found everything completely Danish and thought that a spirit of peace was prevailing in this lovely place. That was in the autumn of 1844. – How soon did I see everything in a different way!' The last sentence refers to the Schleswig-Holstein revolt in 1848 against Denmark, in which both the Duke of Augustenborg and the Prince of Nör were to play prominent parts. Andersen's diaries make it clear, however, that he *did* even then feel a certain amount of tension and anti-Danish feeling, coming especially from the Prince of Nör.

From Graasten he once again continued to Germany, this time travelling more or less from one court to another. He was often invited to dine with the Grand Duke and Duchess of Oldenburg and their young son, and shortly before he left Oldenburg the grand duke presented him with a fine ring, which someone immediately informed him was worth more than 200 Prussian Thaler.

In Berlin Andersen dined with the King and Queen of Prussia, and was placed at the royal table next to the famous German scientist Alexander von Humboldt. Twice he was invited by the Princess of Prussia who asked him to read some of his tales aloud to her, and he spent one day with the king and queen at Potsdam, where again he read some of his tales. King Friedrich Wilhelm IV gave him his first decoration, the Knighthood of the Red Eagle.

Before leaving Denmark in 1845 Andersen had hoped to receive a decoration from the King of Denmark; on 31 October his diary laconically records: 'Audience with the queen, with the king, did not get it.' The same day he wrote to Ørsted: 'That which you expected me to have received and which would have given me a *very* great pleasure, I did not get. I suppose it has been forgotten, and – perhaps I shouldn't say so – this made me sad; for *abroad* this would have been a visible sign of my king's gracious attitude towards me; I had hoped for it on this journey.' Now he had a German decoration but no Danish one, and in one of his letters to Jonas Collin about obtaining the King of Denmark's permission to wear the German decoration at home Andersen wrote: 'If a tiny Knighthood of the Dannebrog were to accompany it [i.e. the permission], I wouldn't mind; you can tell the king one cannot walk on one leg. For heaven's sake, you do realize that this last part is a joke!' Andersen was in fact decorated with the Order of the Dannebrog in September 1846 and wrote to Jonas Collin that he 'was surprised and happy'.

After Berlin, where among other blue-blooded persons Andersen associated with Prince Radziwill, Prince Hermann von Pückler-Muskau and Countess von Bismarck-Bohlen, he went on to his beloved Weimar, where he was again cordially received by his bosom friend, the Hereditary Grand Duke of Weimar. The following extracts from Andersen's Weimar diaries in January and February 1846 will give an impression of the atmosphere in which he lived:

8 January *At the post office Beaulieu's servant was waiting for me. Beaulieu embraced me, asked me to come to a ball at General Beulewitz's, where I met many acquaintances and the entire ducal family. The hereditary grand duke rushed towards me, pressed my hands and said, 'I cannot receive you here the way I would have liked to at home, oh! my friend, I have been longing for you!' His consort also received me graciously. I met [Amalie von] Gross and [   ]. The grand duchess summoned me to her, my legs were so tired and I so dizzy that I was nearly fainting; she asked me what was the matter with me, and I said it was my chest, I couldn't very well tell her that my boots were squeezing me; she called the Lord Chamberlain Beaulieu and told him to send for a doctor; I told him what was the matter and said it would be better to send for a shoemaker. The grand duke very gracious, I sat at his table – went home at 11.30.*

9 January *At 10 I went to the hered. grand duke, in those splendid rooms. He came towards me, pressed me to his bosom, kissed me several times, thanked me for my love for him; arm in arm we walked to his room, sat talking for a long time until he was called to the Council of State, then he walked, arm in arm with me, to the furthermost door.*

10 January *Visits. After table walked with Beaulieu to Ober-Weimar and had coffee, then went to the hered. grand duke. I sat 'in my seat', as he called it, on the sofa; he said we must always remain friends, and that sometime I should come and stay with him for ever in Weimar. I told him I loved my native land. 'But we Germans appreciate you more than the Danes do. – All right, then alternate between us. Give me your hand!' He held it so firmly in his, told me that he loved me and pressed his cheek to mine.*

12 January *Invited to the grand duke's table, sat on his left side. . . . At 7.30 in the evening to the hered. grand duke; the grand duchess was there and later the grand duke arrived. I read 'The Fir Tree' and 'The Snow Queen'. At the table I sat on the right side of the hered. grand duke, who pressed my hand under the table. He told me that when his consort had been in labour she had told him that she wanted to be the steadfast tin soldier. The grand duchess spoke very graciously and kindly to me. Before I left, the grand duke took me into his little greenhouse, was very kind and good. At dinner-time I wore a three-cornered hat and a rapier.*

13 January *Invited to an English performance of* The Merchant of Venice *but couldn't go as I was going to the grand duchess. To her, the grand duke and a little circle of people I read 'The Top and the Ball', 'The Ugly Duckling' and 'The Daisy'. Sat at the grand duke's table; the hered. duke pressed my hand, asked me to regard W. as my second home, hoped that we might remain friends.*

17 January *Visited the hered. grand duke, who took me to his little son, Carl August, and did his utmost to make the boy laugh and be happy. 'He knows you're his father's friend,' he said. 'That's why he is so easy to get on with.' The hered. grand duke left; his young consort came in, took the little boy on her back and galloped, 'hop!' around the room, calling him 'Humpty Dumpty'; I had him on my arm and danced with him, we played together.*

22 January *At the grand duke's table, was carried there in a sedan, it is the first time in my life I have been carried.*

2 February *The Grand Duke of Weimar's birthday. Was in my very best court dress, with rapier and three-cornered hat for drawing-room. Later at a grand banquet, a multitude of uniforms, all the ladies with long trains, those of the duchesses were carried by page boys.*

7 February *Went to the hered. grand duke at 8 o'clock in the morning, he received me in his shirt, with only a dressing-gown over it: 'I can do that, we know one another.' He pressed me to his bosom, we kissed one another. 'Think of this hour,' he said, 'as being yesterday. We are friends for life.' We both wept.*

All this pleased Andersen: hobnobbing with royalty, embracing, hugging, kissing, holding hands, weeping. He loved it.

After Weimar his triumphal tour continued. In Dresden he was invited to meet King Friedrich August II of Saxony and his queen, who gave Andersen a letter of introduction to her twin sister, the Grand Duchess Sophie of Austria. In Prague he had introductions to Archduke Stephan, Governor of Bohemia, and to Count Thun-Hohenstein. In Vienna the Grand Duchess Sophie added the specific request to her invitation that Andersen should bring along some of his own tales, and chosen in such a way that they would also be suitable for her son (later Emperor Franz Joseph) to hear; the grand duchess's other sister, the

Dowager Empress Caroline was also there, and among others present, Andersen notes in his diary, were Count Bombello, Prince Wasa (son of the deposed Swedish King Gustavus IV Adolphus) and his consort, the Duke of Hessen-Darmstadt, an old archduke whose name Andersen did not remember, and a number of young princes, including Franz Joseph. After tea Andersen read five of his own tales. A few days later he received as a present from the grand duchess 'a tasteful tie-pin', which he regarded as a visible 'sign of her graciousness'.

But in the midst of all his triumphs Andersen suffered a great humiliation in Berlin in the summer of 1844 when he called on the Grimm brothers, the two famous German collectors of fairy tales with whom his own name has so often been wrongly bracketed. Andersen had no introduction to them and did not think he would need one, but when he called at their house and introduced himself to Jakob Grimm, the latter had no idea who he was, had never even heard his name. Greatly embarrassed Andersen left, less convinced of his universal fame than before.

A fortnight later, however, Jakob Grimm arrived in Copenhagen and went straight to Andersen's apartment. 'Now I know who you are,' he said apologetically, having meanwhile read some of Andersen's tales, and from then on they were friends. During the Christmas holidays 1845–6 Andersen often met both Jakob and Wilhelm Grimm in Berlin and got on very well with them.

Another person whom Andersen saw again in Germany in the winter of 1845–6 was Jenny Lind.

In March 1844 Jenny Lind wrote to Andersen from Stockholm to say that Bournonville had told her he was 'shedding tears' because of her long silence. This she took to be a joke, she wrote, but nevertheless asked her 'brother' not to be angry with her and to give her some evidence that she had not lost his friendship and goodwill. She praised his 'divinely beautiful' tales, among which she gave pride of place to 'The Ugly Duckling'. She signed herself 'your affectionate sister Jenny'.

Andersen was still in love with her, and Henriette Wulff, in whom he had confided, wrote to him from Portugal: 'Go to Sweden, break a lance, and you are sure to be victorious.' But he did not have the courage to do so.

In the autumn of 1845 Jenny Lind came to Copenhagen again, this time to give three concerts and to sing the leading parts in Bellini's *Norma* and Donizetti's *La Fille du Régiment*. During her stay in Copenhagen Andersen saw her regularly and noted in his almanac: 'Jenny is kind and loving towards me; I'm happy and hopeful – although I know – !' On 21 October there was a farewell party for her to which Andersen was invited as one of her guests. In a speech at that party Bournonville declared that all Danes wanted to be Jenny Lind's brothers. 'That would be far too many,' she said; 'I would prefer to choose one of them to be my brother, representing the others. Will you be my brother, Andersen?' This presumably was her gentle way of telling him that she was not going to be his wife.

A couple of months later Andersen and Jenny met in Berlin. Again, to get a reliable account of what happened it is safer to go to Andersen's diaries rather than to his autobiography.

Knowing that Jenny Lind was in Berlin, where her name was on everybody's lips, Andersen wrote from Oldenburg to let her know that he would soon be arriving. He did in fact arrive in Berlin before Christmas 1845, and the following extracts from his diaries show us what happened:

19 December *Arrived in Berlin at 1.15, went to the British Hotel, from where I immediately sent a waiter to Jenny Lind to say that I had arrived and would she get a ticket for me? She replied that if one was to be had I would get it, but no ticket came. . . . I went to the Opera, tickets for the pit and the gallery were available, I went to the pit, there was a low-down group of people, a drunken Frenchman; I stood by the door, heard Jenny, had really intended to be angry with her, but she won me over completely. She sings German in the same way as I read my tales, with the native language shining through, but, as they say about me, that gives it an added interest. The theatre was gloriously splendid, but I didn't really see it; I was there on Jenny's account, I heard her as in a dream. I do not love her the way I ought to, I feel.*
21 December *Drove to Jenny. 'She won't see anybody,' the porter said. 'Yes, she will see me!' 'Give me your card!', and then I didn't have one. 'Tell me your name!' – Then she came out to meet me; she was more blossoming than when she was in Copenhagen. We sat on the sofa and talked about the Collin family.*
23 December *Not in good spirits, feel somewhat lonely. – So far Jenny hasn't sent me a ticket; Miss Frohmann gave me one last night from the Princess of Prussia. . . . Jenny sang so beautifully that I wasn't angry with her. – No, no! She can't have forgotten me!'*
24 December *Have heard nothing from Jenny. I feel hurt and sad. She is not like a sister to me in Berlin. If she had wanted me to be a stranger here, she might have told me so, and I would have been so. – She did once fill my heart – I do not love her any more! In Berlin she has carved out my sick flesh with a cold knife. I wonder what thoughts are filling her mind since she pays so little attention to me, I who came to Berlin mainly for her sake, I who might have spent a much happier Christmas Eve. – I lived for her in Copenhagen – what do I get in return for all I gave, and to someone whom the world calls the noblest and the best of persons! – Now it is Christmas Eve! How happy the home where the husband has a hearth! Now the Christmas tree is lit, his wife is standing with the smallest child on her arm, it stretches out its hands towards the many candles and jumps with joy on its mother's arm, the other children shouting with joy and looking to see what presents they will get, and they are surrounded by a circle of friends. – The stranger is abroad, his Christmas trees are the stars, pictures of new towns, new faces – he flies from place to place – underneath God's Christmas tree I lift my head and say: Father, what are you going to give me? – and maybe I shall get a coffin.*

In *Mit Livs Eventyr* Andersen tells the story of his 'wasted Christmas Eve' when he was so certain to spend it with Jenny Lind that he had turned down all other invitations. His diary reveals, however, that at eight he did in fact go out to a private Christmas Eve party, returning to his hotel at eleven o'clock.

25 December *My thoughts are hidden in a veil but their flight goes towards Jenny! – What have I done to her? – Is it because she is afraid for her reputation that she pays so little attention to me? 'I do not hate you, for I have never loved you,' she once told me, I didn't understand then, I do now. . . . Letter from Jenny, she is very kind.*

26 December *Visited Jenny, who had a Christmas tree, presented me with a bar of soap in the shape of a piece of cheese, eau-de-Cologne, was quite wonderful, patted me, called me a child. We drove together to Madame Birch-Pfeiffer, who she said was like a mother to her. . . . Jenny said I was such a good man, and her brother.*

27 December *Letter from Jenny, dinner at home.*

30 December *At 2 o'clock still no ticket from Jenny, if none this time again, I shall be angry. – At this moment a ticket came from Jenny:* Parquet Rechts 161. . . . *In the second act Jenny was movingly plastic, her voice didn't quite move me in this music, she had curtain calls.*

31 December *Dinner at home. Went to Jenny at 6, where a Christmas tree was lit for my sake. Jenny sang a few songs, we talked humorously, she asked me about 'The New Maternity Ward' and said that she both thought and didn't think I was the author of it, for I was a child, and the play was* böshaft. *– As we were eating ice cream a note sounded as if coming from the piano, only more forceful. 'What was that?' we both said. But there were no vibrations in the piano, it couldn't have come from there. 'What note was it?' I asked. 'It was C!' 'My God, Collin!' I exclaimed, and a fear which forced tears into my eyes came over me, I told Jenny the name, saying that I had always been scared of visions and therefore wished to hear notes only from those dear to me when they died. – Jenny was frightened also; I was in a sad mood. – Jenny was going to a ball at the British Minister's, Lord Westmorland, I helped to choose her ribbons.*

5 January 1846 *Went out to Jenny who was busy and irritable, I, too, was worn out, have taken leave, we shall meet in Weimar.*

Andersen had already spent a fortnight in Weimar when Jenny Lind arrived. The following extracts from his Weimar diaries are concerned with her:

22 January *Jenny came last night. Visited her, she was pleased to see me and gave me her portrait.*

23 January *Visited Jenny Lind and heard her sing with Miss Achte, the latter was not successful. . . . Evening concert at court, I with a rapier and three-cornered hat; there was great splendour and beautifully lit halls. Jenny Lind sat completely alone by a window, looking down at her lap, like an animal waiting to be slaughtered. I stood at the front, next to the hered. grand duke who had pulled me forward. During the Mendelssohn Lieder Jenny's eyes fell on me, and I think she kept looking in that direction. I was presented to the Duke of Gotha, who is musical and writes poetry, he is the brother of Prince Albert of England. Jenny looked at me when I was presented to him, first I greeted her. He then presented me to his consort and asked me to visit him in Coburg or Gotha. Spoke a little to Jenny. Everybody enthusiastic. The hered. grand duchess said, 'I'm so happy, I wish I could jump about with her!' The grand duchess and everybody said they had spoken to Jenny about me.*

24 January *Didn't sleep much all night, lay bathed in sweat. With Beaulieu to Jenny,*

who had a headache. 'She wasn't very gracious,' he said when we left, I didn't like that. Walked with Jenny in the park for an hour and a half, she told me her affairs weren't too well in Sweden, that she might settle in Altona, she is very fond of Mendelssohn-Bartholdy. . . . In the theatre, invited by the hered. grand duke. Jenny Lind (Norma, *first time), enthusiastic applause.*

26 January The hered. grand duke took me to Countess Redern, where Jenny was. She, the hered. grand duke and consort, the hostess, Countess Beust and I sat at the table together, Jenny sang six songs and a hymn which moved all of us deeply. 'I cannot say anything to her, she fills me completely,' the young duchess said, she embraced Jenny, kissed her, Jenny burst into tears. . . . Went to the theatre, had taken Beaulieu's place which was better than mine; this annoyed me. He was late in coming, I was nervous. Jenny appeared in La Sonnambula, *she was marvellous.*

27 January Dined at Baron Maltitz's with Beaulieu and Jenny; for the occasion Maltitz had written a fine poem. Jenny was given a tray with a picture of Goethe's house, she was moved. In the evening a large party at Kammerherr Plötz's, all the ducal families. I read three Pictures [from *Picture Book without Pictures*], *Jenny wept over Pulcinella. She had to sing, I was in a bad mood, said so, was unkind; towards midnight we drove home. I was ill. Beaulieu told me I was falling in love with Jenny; I told him it wouldn't happen. He told me his own love story, I thought of mine and wept.*

28 January Frost and sunshine. With Beaulieu to Jenny. We went to the library, saw Schiller's skull, accompanied Jenny to the theatre. Called on Countess Redern, the footman didn't tell me somebody was there; I was received, and quite secretly the hered. grand duke and duchess were there with Jenny Lind. They immediately thought I knew, but I had no suspicion. The hered. grand duke drank a glass with me, embraced me, his consort kissed Jenny, and he returned to take her hand which he kissed. Dinner at [   ] Herder's grandson. In the evening at Jenny Lind's concert, again tickets from the hered. grand duke. Jenny changed her mind about going to Erfurth, she'll go to Leipzig tomorrow morning and from there to Berlin. Went with Beaulieu to Jenny, her gate was full of people. . . . A serenade was given in honour of Jenny outside, they played tunes from Norma *and* La Sonnambula. *'Dank, herzlichsten Dank, Ihr gute Weimaraner!' we made her say. She stood by the open window. I was affected by it. Afterwards, when everybody had left, the four of us sat round the tea table. Beaulieu asked for the paper on which he had helped her to write a song this morning. She was good and kind. 'I wonder when we shall meet again,' she said; 'but our relationship will be one for life, I hope!' – I had cramp in my throat, Beaulieu kissed me. When we left she said, 'Thank you for being so kind to Andersen!' – A lovely girl. At home we talked much about her; I was suffering; B. told me to weep freely, kissed me lovingly.*

29 January In the evening to a ball at Maltitz's. The hered. grand duke talked to me about Jenny, who filled him completely. He wishes her to be his wife's companion and live with them.

30 January The evening at the hered. grand duke's. He had written to me asking me to come half an hour early so that we could talk about Jenny. I came at 7.30, sat with him on the sofa. He was quite moved, asked me always to write about her, mention no names, only 'our friend'. – He pressed my hand in his.

Andersen's German diaries reveal all the ambiguities in his relationship with Jenny Lind, namely, that he was alternately in love and angry with her, sulking like a spoilt child; that he both wanted to be her 'brother' and play the part of a *preux chevalier*, with three-cornered hat and rapier; and that in a sense he was at one and the same time in love with both Jenny Lind and with the hereditary grand duke, well knowing that he could never attach himself fully to either of them.

After his visits to Prague and Vienna in March 1846 he continued via Trieste to Rome, from where he wrote on 2 April to Louise Lind, *née* Collin: 'I have a sister in Jenny, a faithful soul, *nothing more*; do you understand? She is not likely to marry if I have understood everything correctly; to some extent I am aware of her decision but am not entitled to talk about it. As far as I am concerned I have realized that I am able to resign myself to fate; I build no castles in Spain but accept what God has ordained for me. I feel a peace of mind as never before. – I wonder if I might be happier as a husband and whether I might be able to make another person happy.' And on the same day he wrote to Jonas Collin: 'Today I am 41! How old, and yet, inside I'm hardly more than twenty. What a life full of happiness and sunshine I have behind me, and no doubt this will continue, my faith in God is firm. Thank you, thank you, all of you at home, for your love for me. I celebrate my birthday in Rome for the third time, how few can experience this! Oh, I'm brimming over with joy.'

He attended the Easter service at Saint Peter's and wrote to H. C. Ørsted: 'I was angry with several women in the church who talked incessantly and laughed during the ceremonies, and I was a real policeman and told them to remember that they were in church and that it was Easter; they looked at me very astonished and hardly believed me to be a Protestant. The manners of each religion are sacred to me, and I am in as solemn a mood in the synagogues of Jews and the mosques of Turks as I am in our Christian churches.'

He tried to persuade the Ørsteds to visit Italy: 'Come here in two years time, then all the railways will be finished and you and your wife can fly from Copenhagen to Naples in seven days; that's nothing. How rich life is made by inventions! In one year you'll see and experience what people used to spend a lifetime seeing and experiencing. I think that our time is the most poetic one can imagine; Reason produces one flower after the other, and after all these do belong to poetry, for Truth is part of its triad. By saying so I'm thinking of what you wrote some time ago in my album: "Reason in Reason is Truth; Reason in Will is Goodness; Reason in Imagination is Beauty".'

After a month in Rome Andersen went south to Naples. In May the heat was so oppressive that he found it almost intolerable. 'The sun is pouring a bath of fire over one, it is as if one's marrow were being dried up, and one becomes quite dizzy; anxiously one looks for shade,' he wrote in his diary on 13 May. In June it was even worse. His diary for 8 June begins: 'The heat is pouring down, I hardly dare venture outside.' Directly linked with this are the last words in his entry for 9 June: 'In the evening began writing the story of my Shadow.' Thus the burning sunshine of Naples may be looked on as the inspiration for Andersen's tale 'The Shadow', which begins: 'In the hot countries, my word! how the sun scorches you.' The learned man, 'who had come straight from a cold climate to a hot one', soon realizes that during the daytime 'he and all sensible people had to stay in their houses with doors and shutters closed. It looked as though the whole house was asleep or nobody at home. To make things worse, the narrow street with the tall houses where he was staying had been built in such a way that from morning till evening it lay in the full blaze of the sun – it was really more than one could stand.' Detail after detail from the Naples diaries – the incessant noises in the street and the eternal scales coming from the opposite neighbour's house – are incorporated into this story, another example of the close links between Andersen's tales and his own experiences.

On board the boat from Naples to Marseilles he met the Marquis of Douglas; 'the only thing he knew of Danish literature was *The Improvisatore*, that was a famous work, he said; I told him I was the author, and he made a deep bow and shook me by the hand,' Andersen records in his diary.

In Marseilles he met the Norwegian violinist Ole Bull, who had just returned from America and told Andersen that in America he had thousands of admirers, his novels – and in particular *Only a Fiddler* – having been mass-produced in cheap editions.

It had been Andersen's original intention to continue his journey into Spain, but when he arrived at Vernet in the Pyrenees, immediately north of the Spanish frontier, he felt too exhausted and ill to continue into a new country, and, via France, Switzerland and Germany, he returned to Denmark. While in Germany he once again visited Weimar. His meeting with the hereditary grand duke and their mutual expressions of friendship were as exalted and hectic as before. His diary on 20 August records:

In the evening the hereditary grand duke walked arm in arm with me across the court-yard of the castle to my room, kissed me lovingly, asked me always to love him though he was just an ordinary person, asked me to stay with him this winter. – Unhappy me, who has the feeling in all this that this great love cannot possibly last. Fell asleep with the melancholy, happy feeling that I was the guest of this strange prince at his castle and loved by him. The footmen address me: gnädiger Herr! It is like a fairy tale.

During his stay in Germany in 1845 Andersen had signed a contract with Carl B. Lorck, a Danish-born Leipzig publisher, to have an edition of his *Collected Works* published in German, and this meant that for the first time he would get a fee for something published outside Denmark, all previous editions having been pirated. Andersen's *Collected Works* was to be introduced by an autobiography especially commissioned for this edition; he wrote it (in Danish) during his long journey 1845–6, and it was published in two small volumes in January–February 1847 as *Das Märchen meines Lebens ohne Dichtung*; an English edition, entitled *The True Story of My Life*, was published in London in the summer of 1847. Strangely enough, the original Danish version was not published until 1942, when H. Topsøe-Jensen edited an annotated version of it.

In Denmark the years 1844–8 saw the publication of some new plays, including two romantic dramas, *Dreams of the King* (1844) and *The Blossom of Happiness* (1847), and a libretto for *Little Kirsten* (1847), the most frequently performed Danish opera, for which J. P. E. Hartmann composed the music. A popular comedy, *The New Maternity Ward*, which Andersen had submitted anonymously, was performed at the Royal Theatre in 1845; he only acknowledged the authorship when it was incorporated in his Danish *Collected Works* in 1854.

Far more important, however, was the regular continuation of *Nye Eventyr*. Part II was published in 1845. It contained 'The Fir Tree' – a sad tale about something with which Andersen was only too familiar, the inability to enjoy the moment of happiness until it is too late – and 'The Snow Queen', that inimitable masterpiece about which he wrote to Ingemann in December 1844: 'It has been sheer joy for me to put on paper my most recent fairy tale, "The Snow Queen"; it permeated my mind in such a way that it came out dancing over the paper.' Part III of *Nye Eventyr* was also published in 1845; it contained five new tales, including 'The Elf Hill', 'The Red Shoes' and 'The Shepherdess and the Chimney-Sweep'. In 1847 the first part of a second volume of *Nye Eventyr* appeared, including 'The Darning Needle' and 'The Shadow'. Other well-known tales, such as 'The Bell' and 'The Little Match Girl', were published elsewhere and only later incorporated with the fairy tales and stories.

Gradually Andersen himself was beginning to believe that perhaps their value was not all that transitory. In December 1845 he wrote to H. C. Ørsted: 'I wonder what people will say about them in twenty years time! I don't think they will have been forgotten.'

An episode must be mentioned, which occurred in 1845 and made a very painful impression on Andersen.

In that year a new novel by Carsten Hauch, *The Castle on the Rhine*, was published in Copenhagen. In spite of Hauch's attack on him fifteen years previously Andersen had come to regard him as a friend and a writer whom he greatly admired, and in 1843 he had written to Ingemann to say how much he looked forward to Hauch's new novel. This was at a time when he had no idea, of course, that one of the characters in the novel was going to be taken as an extraordinarily malicious caricature of himself. As soon as the book was published, however, this character, Eginhard, the vain poet who ends by becoming completely mad, was identified with Andersen by both readers and critics, even publicly, and people asked why Hauch had caricatured him in this nasty way. Before reading the novel Andersen, who was convinced that Hauch was his friend, wrote a letter to Ingemann, in which he said that he had heard that Hauch was going to write an essay on his work for a literary journal, and this pleased him particularly since it would prove to the public that Hauch was kindly disposed towards him. He then continued:

I have been annoyed with those silly people who are so naughty to me that when reading a description of an egotistical poet who dies in the lunatic asylum from sheer vanity, they think, and express the opinion, that in this the author should have had me in mind. You probably know that in his latest novel Hauch is accused of having portrayed several persons, including myself; indeed, Den Frisindede *has even mentioned me as being the person from whose life Hauch has taken the material, by various associations of ideas, for one feature in this mad poet. I have frequently been asked by people in Copenhagen: 'What have you done to Hauch? This is indeed infamous!' etc., and I have replied that Hauch had never had myself in mind, that he has a noble and great character, that his feelings towards me are those of friendship and kindness.*

Three weeks later, however, after Andersen had had an opportunity of reading Hauch's novel, he again wrote to Ingemann:

I wrote to you that I must be angry with people who immediately said it was me as soon as they read about an egotistical, affected poet. Now I must judge people differently after having seen this character. Yes, indeed, they are quite right in saying: 'That is Andersen!' Here all my weaknesses are gathered together! I hope and believe that I have lived through that period; but everything that this poet says and does I could have said and done. I felt uncannily moved by this crude picture showing me in my miserable state.

He was still convinced, he added, that Hauch had failed to realize that by reading about Eginhard everybody would immediately think of Andersen, and in his letter he again spoke of Hauch's 'noble and great character'. What made the most horrifying impression on him, he said, was the description of the way in which the young poet ended by becoming completely mad, and he added: 'My own grandfather was mad, my father became mad shortly before he died. So you will understand how the mental dissolution of the unfortunate poet in Hauch's novel affects me – his dissolution is a picture of *me*.'

Andersen was right: Eginhard was, and could only be interpreted as, a malicious caricature. And it was extraordinarily generous of him to suggest that Hauch had not realized the full implications of what he had done. Ingemann tried to discuss this matter with Hauch, who would not openly admit having had Andersen in mind when he wrote about the vain poet Eginhard, though he did admit that 'one or two' of Andersen's features might have been in his mind. It was as an act of atonement, as it were, to prove his goodwill towards Andersen, that Hauch decided to write an appreciation of Andersen's work, a benevolent essay with which Andersen himself, however, was not very satisfied.

At home Andersen was still struggling to gain the admiration of the Collin family, and it worried him that J. L. Heiberg continued to be critical of his plays. He wanted to be praised by Heiberg, he wrote to Edvard Collin, 'not for the sake of my own happiness but for the sake of your father's'. He added, 'I shall not be really happy in this world, as a writer, until your father is able to say: I am proud of him!' Fatherly love and kindness Jonas Collin was prepared to give Andersen, but admiration, no!

Unfortunately the Collins were not nearly so impressed with the way Andersen was received by dukes and princes as he was himself. When, after his first visit to Weimar, he wrote to Edvard Collin describing the reception given to him by the Grand Duke and Duchess of Weimar and their son, Edvard wrote back: 'What a hell of a fuss they make of you, but it pleases me tremendously, both because, quite understandably, you are pleased with it, and also because it will annoy the others, also quite understandably. Try and see if you can't manage to bring home a decoration, that would be great fun.' This flippant tone about something he himself took very seriously cannot have pleased Andersen.

While spending Christmas 1845 in Berlin Andersen wrote a letter intended as a greeting for Jonas Collin's birthday. I quote from that letter the following paragraph:

You know that my greatest vanity, or call it rather joy, consists in making you realize that I am worthy of you. All the kind appreciation I get makes me think of you. I am truly popular, truly appreciated abroad, I am famous – all right, you're smiling. But the cream of the nations fly towards me, I find myself accepted in all families, the greatest compliments are paid to me by princes and by the most gifted of men. You should see the way people in so-called High Society gather round me. Oh, no one at home thinks of this among the many who entirely ignore me and who might be happy to enjoy even a drop of the homage paid to me. My writings must have greater value than the Danes will allow for. Heiberg has been translated too, but no one speaks of his work, and it would have been strange if the Danes were the only ones to be able to make judgements in this world. You must know, you my beloved Father must understand that you did not misjudge me when you accepted me as your son, when you helped and protected me.

But the fact that Andersen was popular among German dukes did not impress Jonas Collin, and after Andersen had given a detailed account of the goings-on in Weimar Collin wrote back a letter ending: 'And with this you must be content for the nonce. I cannot tell you about a life with dukes and duchesses, and I do not crawl about on the floor with their children. – So you'll say, "Thank you very much!", and I'll say, "You're welcome!"'

Ingeborg Drewsen was equally unimpressed; she wrote to Andersen in July 1846: 'God! how boring it must have been to be together with so many famous men as you have been. Fortunately, since the famous traveller Kohl was here I haven't seen any, for I suppose one cannot call the King of Sweden famous, and moreover I haven't seen him.'

In May 1845, however, something happened which made Andersen realize how much he was regarded a member of the Collin family. One Sunday night a messenger came to his lodgings in Copenhagen with a note which read: 'My dear Andersen, – My wife is very ill. All the children are here. Yours, Collin.' Andersen hurried to the death-bed of Jonas Collin's wife, who died a few days later.

What it meant to Andersen to have been summoned to 'the Home of Homes' by Jonas Collin on this occasion may be seen from a letter he wrote a few weeks later:

My thoughts are, and since my departure have been, so vividly in the Home; I have realized how firmly I have grown into the family, felt that in your circle I am a son, something which has made me proud in the good sense of the word. The fact that on that Sunday night you called me home together with the other children, that in one of the most serious hours I was placed among yours, has filled me with happiness and appreciation if I had not already had a thousand proofs of it. I feel strangely moved by this, I wish I could express my feeling in words, show it, show that I love you, love you with the soul of a son, O God! let me keep you long, let all of us live with you long; if you depart before me I shall be shaken, I shall be in despair.

But when Andersen again went on his triumphal tours abroad the thought kept on nagging him that the Collins still did not seem to understand how famous he had become in Europe, and from Dresden he wrote to Edvard Collin in February 1846: 'I think of your father and believe that I have given him gratification, and that thought is my supreme happiness. And yet – ? He does not realize it, he does not see it like that. Even to those closest to me at home I am only – Andersen, the harmless person with a certain amount of talent, someone who thinks very highly of himself, and Denmark has writers of a different magnitude. . . . No one at home is proud of me, I seem to be the rejected corner-stone.' Andersen's letter then continues:

It is of some importance, is it not, that I am being received everywhere by princes and by the most important men with cordial feelings and friendship? Well, you are not aware of it, I suppose – but the fact that all newspapers from one town to another write about me, that does count for something after all, even if one is only prepared to look at it from the materialistic point of view. At Oldenburg, as you know, the grand duke gave me a very costly ring in remembrance of him, in Berlin the king immediately summoned me to his table, an honour which, according to the newspapers, befalls few German writers, and I was awarded the Order of the Red Eagle. At Weimar I was accepted at court, and the young prince gave me his entire love, his friendship, and an invitation that I could stay with him for ever. In Leipzig I have signed a contract with a publisher for a very decent fee for the German edition of my Works – who at home is able to do better than that? I myself am astonished, am grateful to God; when I travel in Germany I am accepted like a prince, whereas at home I am treated like a beggar. Abroad I am overwhelmed with honour and glory, and not a single ray of sunshine reaches me from home, not a single piece of news to show me that after all my home is there. One of your father's letters was lively and good, the other one just told me what has been mentioned several times before: that I was leading an empty life and that 'it cannot be beneficial for my soul', and was I not going to write something soon? I had a feeling as if I had wanted to throw my arms round somebody's neck when he turned his back to me. I know that no one is kinder to me in Denmark than your father, but that's just it, my dear friend! – To me Denmark is in the House of Collin!

'I have been spoilt abroad, which isn't good,' he added. 'At this moment I have the thought: how fortunate if the Lord would close my eyes far away from Denmark.'

To this Edvard Collin replied:

My dear Andersen, – I take up the pen once again, and even if you do not admire me for it I admire myself for it, for I am always afraid of beginning to write long letters; but this time I could not help it after the sad letter I received from you yesterday. Nothing would be easier for me to fill my letter with, in case I was prepared to join in your complaints, but frankly, I can't. This is the situation: You are popular in Germany, in Weimar you are being spoilt, you are being kissed and hugged by all the distinguished people there. We who are your friends here at home and who happen not to like the idea of kissing one another, we do not melt away in sentimental joy over this, but we are sincerely pleased with that part of the story which is the essential one, namely that you are having a success, that you are acquiring friends, who for the time being I shall assume to be true friends, and that altogether you have been happy on this journey of yours. If you take this to be the true state of affairs which ought to remain unchanged from eternity to eternity, amen! – and compare it with coffee time in Amaliegaden, where Ingeborg teases you and Theodor tickles you and calls you pauvre pomme de terre, then, with your exquisite imagination, you immediately invent a story to the effect that you are despised in Denmark and that you despise Denmark – both statements being untrue, for, really, you and Denmark get on very well together and would get on even better if there wasn't a theatre in Denmark – hinc illæ lacrymæ! You always return to the subject of this damned theatre, and this annoys me. Is that theatre then Denmark? And aren't you anything but a playwright? Is it as such that you are being fêted in Germany? Is it not as a writer of fairy tales? And do people in Denmark not love your fairy tales? Perhaps more honestly so than in Germany! But your last letter was written in a bad mood after you had suddenly found yourself alone in Dresden after all the fuss and commotion. . . . First you are being embraced by the Weimar court for having read fairy tales, and now you are sitting alone in a hotel room. The same here: yesterday in the Casino Square the pile drivers shouted 'Hurrah!' for me to make me give them Schnapps, and today I am sitting at home in my old velvet jacket with a tummy ache. We have to put up with the ups and downs of life.

Having read Edvard Collin's letter Andersen must have realized how justified some of his cooling remarks were, for in a subsequent letter he admitted that his previous letter 'was somewhat "*irritabile genus*"', but, good gracious, why must you always have jubilation and bliss from me?'

Reminiscences of the old bitterness about the *De* or *Du* address crept up again in the correspondence. In April 1846 Andersen wrote from Rome to Edvard Collin: 'Well, when I have been made an *Etatsraad* (Councillor of State) and have a son, he shall refuse to say "*Du*" to your son Jonas if you are still no more than a *Justitsraad* (Councillor of Justice).' To which Edvard replied: 'What excellent nonsense in your letter about the old *Du* story, we enjoyed that. You fool, was it pride on my part? I can be very proud of being Number 1 among your friends, but I still do not want to be on *Du* terms with you.'

When Andersen wrote 'The Shadow' he introduced into it in a subtle way the question of *De* versus *Du*, so that only Edvard Collin would get the message.

Towards the end of this story, when the shadow has become master and the learned man his shadow, the latter one day suggests to the shadow: 'Seeing that we now travel together as equals like this and that we also grew up from childhood together, oughtn't we to pledge ourselves to address one another as "*Du*"? It would be so much more sociable.' To which the shadow, now being the real master, replied: 'It all sounds very frank, and I'm sure that you mean well; I too mean well and will be just as frank. As a learned man, you know of course how queer nature is. Some people can't bear the feel of grey paper; it upsets them. Others go all goosey if you scrape a nail against a pane of glass. That's just how I feel when I hear you saying "*Du*" to me. It's as though I were being thrust back into my first humble position with you. Of course, it's not pride – it's only what I feel. So although I can't allow you to say "*Du*" to me, I am quite willing to meet you half-way and say "*Du*" to you.'

But not long after Andersen had written 'The Shadow' he was deeply moved when Edvard Collin volunteered to go through the entire manuscript of his autobiography, which Andersen sent to him chapter by chapter from abroad. And not only did Edvard vet it for grammatical errors and misspellings, but he took it upon himself to make a fair copy of the entire manuscript in a more legible handwriting for the German translator. This was far more than Andersen had asked, and when he heard what Edvard Collin had volunteered to do he wrote: 'You don't know how this has moved me, made me ashamed, in fact I don't know the word for it, that you are copying out my biography! . . . I shall never forget this proof of your brotherly soul, it is an embrace, it is a kiss – it is an acceptance of *Du* terms – you know what I mean. Thank you!'

9 Two visits to Britain

1847 and 1857

IN THE winter of 1846–7 Andersen began to think seriously about visiting England and Scotland, encouraged by the favourable reception in Britain of his novels, *The Improvisatore, Only a Fiddler!* and *O.T.* (all published in 1845), and of *A Poet's Bazaar* (published in 1846). In 1846 his fairy tales and stories also began to appear in English; five volumes, by three different translators, were published in 1846, and in 1847 four more volumes appeared. Nearly all the British literary journals welcomed Andersen's works, and rumours of this reached him in Denmark. In July 1845 his first English translator, Mary Howitt, could write: 'Your name is now an honoured one in England.' One of the British journals in which Andersen was particularly eulogized was the *Literary Gazette*, whose editor, William Jerdan, wrote to Andersen in November 1846 to suggest that he should come to England, where he would be given a very warm reception. In his reply Andersen wrote that he had long wanted to see Britain, 'whose literature has so strangely enriched my imagination and filled my heart'. Having mentioned his childish and immature interest in Shakespeare he went on:

Later in life no author has filled me more than Walter Scott; when on my first arrival in Copenhagen I walked the streets, poor and desolate and often without money for a meal, I gave the few pence I had to get a novel by Scott from the lending library, and that made me forget coldness and hunger, I was rich and happy. How dear do I not hold Bulwer, how fervently do I not wish to press Boz's hand; when I read his books I often think: that have I myself experienced, that could I portray! . . . As the wind whistles in his bell ropes, so have I often heard it on a cold, wet autumn day, and the cricket's chirp I know well from the warm corner in my parents' poor room.

There is plenty of evidence to prove that in the course of two years Andersen acquired a popularity in Britain unrivalled by any other foreign author. Contemporary reviews and articles make it quite clear that he was universally regarded as a great, exciting, newly discovered author – 'the Dane' – a writer whose popularity rapidly exceeded that of both Madame de Staël and Fredrika Bremer, the two foreign authors who, at the beginning of the 1840s, had aroused the most interest in Britain. There is another kind of evidence too. Robert Browning and Elizabeth Barrett discussed Andersen's *Improvisatore* in their love letters; in April 1845 Elizabeth Barret wrote, 'he is a poet in his soul,' and, about the novel, 'it is a book full of beauty and had a great charm to me'. Robert Browning was vexed, 'that a man of sands and dogroses and white rock and green seawaves just under, should come to Italy where my heart lives, and discover the sights and sounds . . . certainly discover them'; and in

THE

IMPROVISATORE:

OR,

LIFE IN ITALY.

FROM THE DANISH

OF

HANS CHRISTIAN ANDERSEN.

TRANSLATED BY

MARY HOWITT.

IN TWO VOLUMES.

VOL. I.

LONDON:

RICHARD BENTLEY, NEW BURLINGTON STREET.

1845.

Title-page of *The Improvisatore*, the
first work by Andersen to be
translated into English (1845).

January 1847 Thackeray wrote to W. E. Aytoun: 'And Hans Christian Andersen, have you read him? I am wild about him, having only just discovered that delightful fanciful creature.'

Dickens, too, knew some of Andersen's work before the summer of 1847; he had certainly read *The Improvisatore, A Poet's Bazaar* and some of the tales. 'My father thought very highly of his literary work,' wrote Dickens' son about Andersen in his memoirs. And in March 1847 William Jerdan wrote to Andersen: 'It was only ten days ago that I had the opportunity to tell my friend Dickens how warmly you spoke of him, and he was exceedingly flattered by your good opinion. He has now returned to reside in London; and no one will be more desirous to give you a warm welcome than he will be.'

Before going to England Andersen wanted at least an elementary knowledge of the language, and in the winter of 1846-7 he had regular lessons. In March 1847 he wrote to the Duchess of Augustenborg: 'I am now learning some English and am planning to visit London in June.'

At the beginning of June 1847 Andersen left Denmark, and went first to Holland via Germany – a triumphal tour of nine days to Amsterdam, Leiden, the Hague and Rotterdam. He found himself even more popular there than in Germany and was fêted and celebrated by all the leading Dutch men of letters. In an Amsterdam bookshop window the portraits of two foreign authors were displayed, Bulwer Lytton's and Andersen's, and the bookseller, who recognized the latter, came out to shake hands with him. In the Hague a banquet was arranged in his honour by the editor of *De Tijd*, whose latest issue carried Andersen's portrait on its front page.

On 22 June Andersen left Rotterdam by steamer for London, where he arrived the following morning. In *Mit Livs Eventyr* he describes his arrival:

In the morning when I got up on deck I could just see the English coast; round the mouth of the Thames lay thousands of fishing-boats looking like a vast brood of chickens, like finely shredded paper, or a crowded market-place, or a camp full of tents. Indeed, the Thames does bear witness that Britain rules the waves. From here great armies of countless ships issue forth in her service. Like despatch riders came the steamers, one after another, every minute, their funnel-hats swathed in veils of black smoke, each with a red flower of sparks glowing at the top. Swelling like swans, great sailing ships glided past; pleasure yachts appeared with rich young men on board.

This is how he describes his first impression of London itself:

At the Customs House, where we landed, I took a cab and drove on and on; there seemed to be no end to this city. The congestion got worse and worse, vehicles of every kind in two lines of traffic each way; omnibuses were loaded inside and out; there were large box-like vehicles for displaying posters with the news of the day, there were men carrying huge placards on poles raised above the heads of the crowd, on which you could read about something or other to be bought or seen. All was movement, as if half London was trying to get to one side of the city and the other half to the other. Where the streets cross there is a little island in the middle with large stones round it. People would rush to this island from the pavement through one row of traffic, and wait in safety until there was opportunity to slip through the carriages to the opposite pavement. London, the greatest of all cities! I felt that straight away, and as the days went by I got to know it. Here is all that is Paris and more, here is the pulsing life of Naples without its clamour. Everything rushes past busily, but not noisily. Omnibuses, four thousand they say there are, drays, carts, cabs and elegant carriages race and rumble and jog along, as if there was some important event taking place at the opposite end of the city which at all cost they must reach. A never-ending whirlpool!

'London is the city of cities, excepting Rome; those two cities have made the greatest impression on me, London being the busy day, Rome the great silent night.' He was so happy with this observation, first noted in his diary, that he used it in letter after letter to his friends at home.

He stayed at the Sablonière Hotel, Leicester Square, and the first person he called on was Count Reventlow, the Danish Minister; the next was Carl Alexander, the Hereditary Grand Duke of Weimar, who had just arrived in London and was staying at Marlborough House. Here Andersen was received in the usual cordial way, but the duke was full of complaints about British etiquette, which made it impossible for him to associate with authors. 'Dickens has written for *Punch*, so one mayn't speak to him,' he said, according to Andersen's diary, adding, 'This is the country of freedom where one dies of etiquette.'

But Andersen's fame, which had preceded him, combined with the skilful diplomacy of the Danish Minister, opened doors to him that were normally closed to most British writers. Within a few days of his arrival he was invited to a grand evening party at the house of the Foreign Secretary, Lord Palmerston, and, two days before, his portrait had been displayed all over London on the front page of *Howitt's Journal*, introducing a 'Memoir of Hans Christian Andersen' by Mary Howitt. Andersen, who sent a copy to Mr and Mrs Edvard Collin, wrote to Henriette Collin: 'I am truly famous in a way neither I nor Denmark were aware of; whether I deserve it is another matter, but it is lovely, joyful, the Lord is wonderfully kind to me, how strange that he, too, can have his favourites – unless this happiness is a disquieting advance payment.' He told her about the homage paid him in Holland, and went on to say that on his arrival in London one of the first things he saw was Jenny Lind's portrait and next to it his own, the latter on the front page of *Howitt's Journal*.

Mary Howitt's article about Andersen began:

At the moment when Hans Christian Andersen is in this country, we believe that we cannot present to our readers a more acceptable gift than an excellent portrait and memoir of this extraordinary man. Whether regarded as the human being asserting in his own person the true nobility of mind and moral worth, or the man of genius whose works alone have raised him from the lowest poverty and obscurity, to be an honoured guest with kings and queens, Hans Christian Andersen is one of the most remarkable and interesting men of his day.

My dearest Friend, – You will have seen the little letter I wrote to your Jette, you will also have seen what it says in the journal where my portrait is that I am 'one of the most remarkable and interesting men of his day', and yet you were too proud to agree to say

'Du' to me – phew! – I might almost be vain enough to say once again: Edvard, let us be on Du terms, and you would reply as I have let my Shadow reply. Well, I suppose you have realized that the malice is directed against you. You want to play the part of Diogenes when I am Alexander! You see that I am what Ingeborg would call 'a modest fool'. But then I have been in High Society – dear me! Last night I had my début, and in the highest circles too, among the most exquisite people, so Count Reventlow and the Duke of Weimar told me. I went to Lord Palmerston's; the Hereditary Grand Duke of Weimar was kind and cordial; I spoke to the Duke of Cambridge, the Duchess of Sutherland – indeed, God knows all the names; but would you believe it, they nearly all of them knew my works, in the end I was surrounded by aristocratic ladies who talked about 'The Top and the Ball', 'The Ugly Duckling' – in the end I was quite dizzy – but not with pride.

Lord Palmerston's party was only the beginning. To his amazement Andersen discovered that he was looked upon as the literary lion of the season, and so sought after by a British aristocracy which took little interest in their own writers that he required an unreasonable amount of time and strength to dine, sup and dance at the houses of all those peers vying with one another to show off this remarkable new discovery. Andersen had to turn down many invitations but did go to luncheons, teas, dinners or late-night parties at the houses of Lady Sydney Morgan (who had hurriedly read Andersen's work before he visited her), Lord and Lady Poulett, Lady Duff-Gordon (whose translation of 'The Little Mermaid' had appeared in *Bentley's Miscellany*), Lord Castlereagh, Lord and Lady Stanley, Lord Palmerston (a second time), Sir Anthony de Rothschild, Count von Bunsen (the German ambassador), Lord Willoughby d'Eresby, and of course Count Reventlow, at whose house he was a frequent guest.

Andersen was quite overwhelmed at finding himself so well known and so popular in England, and as in Paris in 1843 so in London in 1847: the amount of praise and homage bestowed upon him abroad made him angry and bitter at the thought of not being properly recognized at home. What sparked off his fury this time was the fact that he had seen at the Danish Legation that the Danish newspapers had not said a word about the wonderful reception he had had in Holland, and on 8 July he wrote to Edvard Collin:

At this moment, probably, I am at the pinnacle of my success. From now on it must go downhill; more recognition than I have received here in this metropolis I cannot hope for. Hambro showed me a letter from his son, who is in Scotland, and in the letter he wrote: 'Look after Andersen, he is better known here than even Thorvaldsen', and it is a fact: I am a famous man. The aristocracy here, so discouraging to their own poets, have welcomed me as one of their circle. Today and during the next fourteen days I have been invited out every day, dinner at 8–11, and parties from half past eleven till late at night. It is more than I can cope with, I am sinking, am being inundated with invitations, with requests for my autograph. It is all like a dream, and in the pure pleasure that it gives me, pleasure that your father and Denmark can be proud of me, I am happy. Your father shares this pleasure – but to Denmark, to Copenhagen – I am nothing, there is not one jot of interest or sympathy. My visit to Holland has been honourable to the Danes; what was done to me there has never been done to any Dane before; but Danish newspapers which I have seen today do not mention it at all, refuse to mention it – I feel hurt, I regard this as an insult. At home they have spat on me while Europe has honoured me, and now that I am being honoured they refuse even to mention it, though they write about every twopenny-halfpenny theatre scandal at home. I am quite ill and feverish today after having seen how I am counted for nothing in my native country, which I could – God forgive my thoughts!

'Please, no moral lecture on this letter!' Andersen concluded. When Edvard Collin replied, it was a business letter, the only personal part being the words: 'All well at home. – Concerning your idolization in England I will not speak. It makes me just as giddy as it does you.'

The Hambro to whom Andersen referred in the letter just quoted was Joseph Hambro, an old Danish banker, who had left Denmark in 1840 to live in England, where he and his son, C. J. Hambro (later Baron Hambro) had founded their own banking firm (now Hambro's Bank). Joseph Hambro became Andersen's trusted friend and adviser in London, and with great hospitality he often invited his famous countryman to stay with him in Kilburn, when he needed rest and relaxation.

Even before he arrived in London Andersen knew that Jenny Lind would be there. She had arrived in April, and her first performance took place in Her Majesty's Theatre as Alice in *Roberto il Diavolo*. That was the beginning of a Jenny-Lind-Fever which lasted for many months. The enthusiasm of the public was boundless, and her name was on everybody's lips. She also appeared as Amina in *La Sonnambula*, as Maria in *Figlio del Reggimento*, and in the title role of *Norma*. Broadsheets about 'The Jenny-Lind-Mania' were sold in the streets, and pubs, cigars, hats, melons, cakes and flies for trout-fishing were named after her.

The very day after his arrival Andersen received a letter of welcome from Jenny Lind, who lived in Clairville Cottage, Old Brompton, and the next day he called on her and was invited to dine with her whenever he liked. During his stay in London he visited her six times in all, and at her invitation went to hear her first in *La Sonnambula* (when Queen Victoria, Prince Albert and the Hereditary Grand Duke of Weimar were also present) and later in Verdi's *I Masnadieri*, an opera based on Schiller's *Die Räuber*. She chided Andersen for being so obsessed with what was being written about himself.

Shortly before leaving London for Scotland Andersen wrote in his diary: 'Did not pay Jenny Lind a farewell visit, though I could very well have done so. What an enigma I am to myself! Wrote her a letter of farewell.' Andersen did not see Jenny Lind again until 1854, when they met in Vienna. She was then married to the pianist Otto Goldschmidt.

One of the Englishmen whom Andersen came to regard as a personal friend was William Jerdan. While Andersen was in London Jerdan reviewed *The True Story of My Life* in the *Literary Gazette*; the review began with a profile of Andersen, from which the following is a quotation:

Long and highly admired at a distance, and his writings established with a most popular hold on the mind of England, Herr Andersen has now been three weeks amongst us, in the literary and refined society of London, converting that admiration and popularity into warm personal regard, affectionate esteem, and cherished friendship. Every one who has met him is delighted with his character, in which is united to acknowledged originality of genius and poetic imagination, a simplicity the most captivating, and a candour and truth of that rare nature which lays the individual soul, as it were, open to the view of the most heedless observer. Some one has spoken of the peril which must attend the having a window in your breast; Andersen has such a window, and, instead of exposing him to inconveniency or danger, it seems to invite no other feelings but those which do honour to our common humanity – sincere regard, entire confidence, and unworldly love.

Jerdan went on to say that 'in his sphere Hans Christian Andersen is the counterpart of Jenny Lind' and ended by calling him 'this truly excellent man, delightful poet, and original and fertile author'.

William Jerdan was particularly eager that Andersen should make contacts with English writers, and he had planned to arrange a party at which he could meet Dickens, Bulwer Lytton, Macready, Harrison Ainsworth and others, but this proved impossible. On 6 July, however, Jerdan took Andersen to meet Lady Blessington at Gore House, Kensington. She was frowned upon in most aristocratic circles since it was an open secret that she lived with Count d'Orsay, who had previously been married to her stepdaughter. ('One daren't even mention that one wished to see Lady Blessington,' the hereditary grand duke had told Andersen at their first meeting in London.)

When Andersen first met her Lady Blessington invited him to a dinner-party she would give in his honour ten days later. In a letter to Henriette Wulff Andersen afterwards described this memorable dinner-party:

The other day I went to a dinner at Lady Blessington's, she has a big house, and in almost every room there is a portrait of Napoleon; in the dining-room there is an oil painting of him, life-size and illuminated by a big lamp; Napoleon in all his glory on the wall and – do you know who was my neighbour at the table? – the Duke of Wellington's eldest son. Before we sat down to eat Lady Blessington gave me the English edition of Das Märchen meines Lebens, *requesting me to write my name in it, and as I was doing so a man came into the room, exactly like the portrait we have all seen, a man who had come to town on my account and had written, 'I must see Andersen!' When he had greeted the company I ran from the writing table over to him, we took each other by both hands, gazed in each other's eyes, laughed and rejoiced. We knew one another so well, although we were meeting for the first time – it was Charles Dickens. He comes up to the highest expectations I had had of him. In front of the house there is a charming verandah running the whole length of the house, vine-leaves and roses hang like a roof over the pillars, here are many-coloured birds, and below a garden and a green field, green as one finds it only in England. We stood there and talked for a long time – talked English, but he understood me, I him.*

On that occasion Dickens invited Andersen to come and have breakfast with him on 1 August. On 30 July, however, Dickens wrote to say that he had to cancel the invitation. For various reasons he could not move into his London house until the middle of August, when he hoped to see Andersen instead. The following day Dickens called at the Sablonière Hotel, found Andersen away, and left a parcel containing the collected edition of his works in twelve volumes; in each volume he had written the words: 'Hans Christian Andersen. From his Friend and Admirer, Charles Dickens.' Though disappointed at not having been in when Dickens called, Andersen was very pleased with this present and immediately wrote Dickens a letter of thanks.

The publisher who had first launched Andersen in England was Richard Bentley, who had also been Dickens' publisher until they parted in anger; Bentley had published Andersen's novels and *A Poet's Bazaar*, but so far none of the tales. Andersen often saw Bentley at his London office, liked him as a person and had great confidence in him. Andersen was often invited to stay with the Bentleys in their house at Sevenoaks; in August he wrote to Henriette Wulff: 'I have spent three days in the country at Mr Bentley's in Sevenoaks, Kent; he has a wonderful house, very elegant, footmen in silk stockings waiting on the guests – that's what I call a publisher!' At a dinner given by Richard Bentley in his honour Andersen replied to a toast by making the following brief speech, the only one he ever made in English: 'I can not speake Englisch, bat I hope I scal in a neuw Worck give the Sentimens of my Heart! I thank you.' – here quoted from his diary.

Andersen's relationship with Mrs Howitt, his first translator, was somewhat less happy in spite of their previous cordial correspondence. Mary Howitt seems to have been a very strong-willed and possessive woman, who felt that she had a monopoly on translating Andersen which he ought formally to recognize. Andersen visited her and her husband, William Howitt, twice in their house at Clapton; the second visit in particular was anything but a success, and if one reads Andersen's diary the reasons are obvious: it was a very hot day; he was utterly exhausted when he arrived and found himself surrounded by a great many people whom he did not know and whose conversation he could not follow; but according to Mary Howitt the failure was entirely due to Andersen's 'oversensitive and egotistical nature'. Mary Howitt pestered him with letters, sometimes patronizing, sometimes petulant. Her translation of his German autobiography, *The True Story of My Life*, was published by Longman's while he was in London; without asking Andersen's permission she had dedicated the book to Jenny Lind and had written a preface which ended: 'It is gratifying to me to be able to state that the original Author (sic) has a personal interest in this English version of his "Life", as I have arranged with my publishers to pay Mr. Andersen a certain sum on the publication of this translation, and the same on all future editions.' The 'certain sum' turned out to be ten pounds, which Andersen refused to accept because he regarded it as her way of making him feel obliged to her. Joseph Hambro warned Andersen against her, calling the pair of them a 'translation factory', and advised him not to authorize her as his translator in spite of her offers of financial reward, and rather to accept a less profitable but more reliable offer from Richard Bentley. Mary Howitt was deeply hurt, broke off all relations with Andersen and took her revenge when in 1852, in a book entitled *The*

Literature and Romance of Northern Europe, she described Andersen as 'a *petit-maître* sighing after the notice of princes'. The works by Andersen *she* had translated received praise, but 'Andersen's subsequent productions have been failures'; he was an egotist who 'always paints himself – his own mind, history and feelings'. Her paragraph on Andersen concludes:

Perhaps much of Andersen's fame in this country arose from the very fact of the almost total ignorance here of the host of really great and original writers which Denmark possessed. Andersen stood forward as a wonder from a country of whose literary affluence the British public was little cognizant, while in reality he was but an average sample of a numerous and giant race.

At Lady Duff-Gordon's dinner-party Andersen met another woman writer, Mrs Norton, whose beautiful profile made a great impression on him. Both she and Lady Duff-Gordon were among Lady Blessington's bitterest enemies; according to his diary Andersen told them that he had seen tears in Lady Blessington's eyes when she spoke of Jenny Lind as the Sleepwalker in *La Sonnambula*. 'Indeed, this is the limit!' Lady Duff-Gordon shouted. 'Lady Blessington moved over Jenny Lind's virtue! She is despicable!'

Andersen never met Bulwer Lytton; for Parliament was dissolved on 23 July (from a building in Whitehall Andersen saw the queen's carriage arriving), and Bulwer, who was a candidate in the ensuing general election, was too busy to see Andersen. An author whom Andersen did meet, however, was Disraeli; they met at Lord Palmerston's second party, but Andersen's diary only has the laconic entry: 'Spoke to Israeli, the author, who looked Jewish.'

There are two writers who, we know, met Andersen during his visit to London, William Allingham and Leigh Hunt. The twenty-three-year-old William Allingham called on Andersen at the Sablonière Hotel with the sole purpose of telling him how much he loved him; unfortunately he failed to make himself understood, and Andersen took him to be a beggar, so that Allingham had to explain by letter the purpose of his visit. In his diary William Allingham describes Andersen as 'tall and lanky, with queer long face, but friendliness and intelligence shining through'. Leigh Hunt, who met Andersen at Lord Stanley's dinner, afterwards told his friend Allingham: 'He looks like a large child, a sort of half-angel. There were many people of rank present, yet no one in the room looked more *distingué* than Andersen, the shoemaker's son.'

There are other contemporary records of Andersen. In a letter to William Jerdan Lady Blessington wrote: 'I have seldom felt so strong an interest in a person of whom I saw so little; for he interested me as being quite as good as he is clever, and of how few authors can we say this!' Miss Mitford did not meet Andersen but heard him being constantly praised by her protégé Charles Boner, who was one of Andersen's early translators. She wrote to a friend about Andersen: 'He is the lion of London this year – dukes, princes, and ministers are all disputing for an hour of his company; and Mr. Boner says he is perfectly unspoilt, as simple as a child, and with as much poetry in his every-day doings as in his prose.'

'Farewell, farewell! said the litle swallow and flew again fort from the warm countries, far far away', to Denmark, ther it had litte nest above the window of a room in wich dwelt a poet, who can tell tales; for him it sang:— Qui'v't gar'nt! all is good and beau=tiful in England!'— 'I know that,' answered the poet.—

H. P. Andersen

Homage to England, written by
Andersen in 1847. The original belongs
to the Danish Club, London.

Andersen was indeed the lion of London: he was even made an honorary member of the Athenæum Club, and he had to pose for both a painter and a sculptor; the latter, Joseph Durham, made a bust of him as a pendant to one he had previously made of Jenny Lind.

It is true to say that Andersen took great pleasure in being pampered by the representatives of the upper classes in London, but it is also true to say that this did not make him blind to class differences; he saw and experienced at first hand wealth and splendour but he also saw destitution and poverty. His diaries bear witness to this, and in *Mit Livs Eventyr* he summed up his impression of that aspect of London:

Poverty I saw personified in a young, pale and starving girl, in miserable tattered clothes, hiding in a corner of an omnibus. Destitution I saw, and yet in all its misery it did not say a word, was not allowed to do so. I remember the beggars, men and women, carrying squares of white paper on their breasts with the words 'Pity the Starving Poor!' written on them. They dare not speak, they are not allowed to beg, so they pass you like shadows. They stop in front of you and gaze with an expression of famine and misery on their pale, emaciated faces. They take up their stand outside cafés and restaurants, pick out one person among the guests, and stare and stare at him with eyes that speak of utter wretchedness. A woman will point to her sick child, and then to the piece of paper on her bosom, whe⸱ it says: 'I have not eaten for two days.' I saw many such, and yet I was told there were only few in my part, and none at all in the rich districts, which are closed against the poor pariahs.

To Andersen one of the chief attractions in Scotland was Abbotsford, Sir Walter Scott's home. At Lady Duff-Gordon's party he had met John Richardson, one of Scott's friends, who had later written to Andersen, offering to show him Abbotsford. Andersen was even more pleased when Charles Boner took him to lunch with J. G. Lockhart and Miss Lockhart, Scott's son-in-law and granddaughter, who showed him Sir Walter's portrait and diaries and later sent him Scott's autograph and a letter of introduction to the caretaker at Abbotsford.

On 10 August Andersen and Joseph Hambro left for Edinburgh, where they were met by C. J. Hambro, who took them to his country house on the outskirts of Edinburgh. Andersen felt very much at home in this Danish family.

He spent a week in Edinburgh, and it is surprising how many of the leading Scottish writers of the day he managed to meet in that short time.

Lady Stanley had given him a letter of introduction to Miss Elizabeth Rigby (later Lady Eastlake), a writer best known for her *Letters from the Baltic*. Andersen called on Miss Rigby with C. J. Hambro on the day after his arrival. 'She had recently read my biography and was particularly pleased with the childhood story,' Andersen noted in his diary. What Miss Rigby wrote in *her* diary was the following:

I was sitting alone writing, when Andersen the Danish poet, was ushered in: a long, thin, fleshless man, wriggling and bending like a lizard with a lantern-jawed, cadaverous visage. Simple and childlike, and simpletonish in his manner. We had a great deal of talk, and after so recently reading his life, he seems no stranger to me. His whole address and manner are irresistibly ludicrous.

In spite of her unfavourable impression of him Miss Rigby invited Andersen to dinner a few days later, and after that dinner her impression of him had changed considerably, as her diary bears witness:

Andersen dined with us. He had one stream of interesting talk – perhaps rather too much of himself, but to me that was novel and entertaining. . . . Altogether he left a most agreeable impression both on mind and heart, especially on the latter, for his own seemed so affectionate. No wonder he finds people kind; all stiffness is useless with him, as he is evidently a simple child himself.

Andersen also visited Lord Jeffrey, the founder of the *Edinburgh Review*. Otherwise it was mainly the writers connected with *Blackwood's Magazine* whom he met in Edinburgh, Professor John Wilson ('Christopher North'), D. M. Moir ('Delta'), and Catherine Crowe, the novelist. They all sent him letters and books afterwards.

One evening Andersen was invited to dinner by Dr James Young Simpson, professor of obstetrics at Edinburgh, now chiefly remembered for having popularized the anaesthetic virtues of ether and chloroform in 1847, the very year Andersen saw him. Professor Simpson must have been completely obsessed with his experiments, for Andersen's diary for 17 August records:

'Dinner at Dr Simpson's, where Miss Crowe and yet another authoress drank ether; I had a feeling of being with two mad people, they laughed with open, dead eyes. There is something uncanny about this; I find it wonderful for an operation, but not as a way of tempting God.'

John Wilson and the Hambros took Andersen sightseeing in Edinburgh, and he later described one incident in a letter to Henriette Wulff:

In this country too they know me and like my writings. – Before leaving Edinburgh I had a proof of this which moved me to tears. We drove up to the famous Heriot's Hospital; when we had all written our names the porter saw mine and asked if this was the famous Dane who wrote books, and when one of our party said yes, the man asked, pointing to old Mr Hambro: 'Is that the one with the venerable white hair?' – They pointed to me, and the man exclaimed in astonishment: 'So young! Otherwise such people are usually old or dead!' He then told us that he and all the poor boys who were educated here read my stories; I pressed his hand and was strangely moved and surprised to find friends here among a new generation.

On 19 August Andersen, Mr and Mrs Hambro and their children went on a five-day trip, so that their guest might have an impression of the Scottish countryside. They travelled via Stirling, Callander, Loch Katrine, Loch Lomond and Balloch to Dumbarton. To Andersen it was a great experience to see many of the localities he knew so well from Scott's poems and novels. Dumbarton, on the other hand, was an anti-climax, for when he woke up there the next morning it was to a Scottish Sunday; he describes it in his diary: 'No one in the streets, all the doors shut, almost everywhere the curtains are drawn; people are reading the Bible or getting drunk.'

When Andersen arrived in Glasgow a period of agony began. While still in London he had received a letter from Dr Meyer, Prince Albert's private secretary, who sent him, on behalf of the prince consort, an invitation to visit Queen Victoria and himself at Osborne, on the Isle of Wight. At that time Andersen was too exhausted to accept the invitation, and with Count Reventlow's help he had written a letter of apology, saying that he would shortly be going to Scotland. Another letter had then reached Andersen, informing him that the queen and Prince Albert were also going to Scotland, and this time he was invited to visit them at Ardverikie, near Loch Laggan. Again, Andersen was inclined not to accept the invitation; in Stirling he wrote in his diary: 'Decided not to go to Loch Laggan, wrote to Professor Meyer asking his advice, saying that I would expect his reply in Glasgow.' But no letter from Dr Meyer was awaiting him at Glasgow Post Office: 'In great despair and in a sickly mood I gave up the journey to Loch Laggan, wrote a letter of apology to Meyer,' he entered in his diary. The reasons for Andersen's reluctance to go were mainly financial; he had been told that there was no proper inn within miles of the royal residence, and he thought he would have to furnish himself with a valet and appear rather richer than his purse would allow.

Greatly distressed that his refusal might be regarded as an insult to the royal family Andersen went to Edinburgh, and from there he more or less fled from

Scotland, thus missing both Abbotsford, which he had so much looked
forward to seeing, and Drummond Castle, where he had been invited to stay
as the guest of Lord Willoughby. But his tribulations were not over, for on the
train south somebody told him that his visit to the queen and prince consort
had already been reported in the papers as a fact. This was not quite true. *The
Times* had had a notice about Andersen's visit to Scotland and his invitation to
Drummond Castle, and some of the Edinburgh papers had added that
Andersen 'was honoured by an invitation from Prince Albert for Osborne,
which has been graciously exchanged for Ardverikie, in Badenoch'. But no
paper had in fact reported that he had actually been there.

To make things even worse, however, he saw a notice in *Punch* about the
invitation he had received from the royal couple, with the following comment: 'If we, as a poet, wished to dine with our sovereign – which candidly we
had a good deal rather not – we should just throw off our allegiance, which we
could not very cheerfully do, and take out letters of naturalization in some
dirty little duchy on the Continent. Coming home again as the subject of some
petty little potentate, with our genius, which is not transferable, to back us, we
should no doubt get invited to Buckingham Palace at least once in the course of
a year, to say nothing of an occasional trip to Windsor or Osborne.' When
Andersen read this in the train his feelings, according to his diary, were these: 'I
was in such a state of despair that it wouldn't have mattered to me if a railway
accident had occurred – how terribly selfish.'

Unfortunately Andersen did not see a less xenophobic notice in the
Athenæum which read:

It is stated that the Danish poet Andersen – who has been amongst us for some weeks
past, and is now on a visit to Scotland – has received an invitation for Osborne House
– now transferred, in consequence of the movements of both parties, to the royal
residence in the Highlands. Royal invitations to men of literary fame are so much
matters of course in the States on the continent – where genius is rank – that they
would not be likely to strike any stranger coming amongst ourselves as anything at
all extraordinary. But while we hope the report may be true in the case of our
distinguished guest – not for his sake, but as evidence of an improving tone in high
places among ourselves – the fact which it announces is so entirely out of the order of
proceedings at the court of a modern English sovereign that, we feel, it wants
authentication.

In London Count Reventlow had to comfort Andersen, who was in tears and
was only happy when a letter arrived from Dr Meyer, who had not been in
Scotland at all but had remained on the Isle of Wight; Dr Meyer advised
Andersen against going to Loch Laggan – a very reassuring message.

From Scotland Andersen had written to his friend Jerdan to ask whether
there might be any chance of seeing Dickens again – 'my dear Dickens' – and
Jerdan had informed him that Dickens was staying with his family at Broadstairs in Kent.

On 29 August, while Andersen was staying with Richard Bentley and his
family at Sevenoaks, he sent the following note to Dickens:

Draft of the letter from Andersen to
Dickens, written on 29 August 1847.

My dear dear Dickens!
to morow I shall kome to Ramsgate, I hope you will giw yours Adresse in the Royal
Oak Hotel, where I shall remane till the next morning, when I shall go by the
stamboat to Ostende. I must see you, and thank you; that is the last flower for me in
the dear England! Your Admirer and true Friend for ever

HANS CHRISTIAN ANDERSEN

Dickens' reply came immediately. He asked Andersen to come and have supper with him and his family the next day at five o'clock at Broadstairs, adding: 'When you come back to England – which you must take an oath today to do soon – I shall hope to see you often in my own house in London, where I have a few little pictures and so forth, that I hope may interest you. But wheresoever you are, believe me that I always am Your friend and admirer, *Charles Dickens.*'

Andersen came, and he enjoyed every minute of his stay with Dickens and his family. In the evening he returned to Ramsgate, and when he went down to the quay the next morning, there stood Charles Dickens to say good-bye. 'He had walked from Broadstairs, to say good-bye to me, and was in a green Scotch dress and gaily coloured shirt, extremely smart English. He was the last person to shake my hand in England, promised, when he received a letter from me, to write how it was in England,' wrote Andersen in his diary. 'As the ship glided out of the harbour, I could see Dickens on the furthermost point. I thought he had left long ago. He waved his hat and finally raised one hand towards heaven. I wonder if he meant to say: "we shall meet again aloft".'

Andersen returned via Belgium to Germany, where he was most unhappy to see himself ridiculed in a gossip column; his triumphs in London were seen as resulting from a mixture of his own mercenary instincts and snobbishness, and the possibility of his engagement to Jenny Lind was mentioned, though it was thought that he might prefer an Englishwoman – 'there being no shortage altogether of Leonoras for the Danish Tasso' who, it was suggested, could not make up his mind which he preferred: a blue-stocking or the sentimental type. In Hamburg he saw the latest issue of the Danish journal *Corsaren*, which contained an article entitled 'Andersen, the Lion', a sarcastic account of his success in High Society in London, illustrated with four cartoons. He also learned that while he had been away Edvard Collin had sent Jerdan's eulogy in the *Literary Gazette* to the editor of *Berlingske Tidende* in the hope that he might quote from it, but the editor had replied that he would be doing Andersen a disservice and make him the laughing-stock of Denmark if he quoted from an article in which he was seriously compared with Jenny Lind. To complete the picture let me quote what Andersen wrote in *Mit Livs Eventyr*:

I arrived in Copenhagen. A few hours later I stood looking out of my window when two well-dressed gentlemen came passing by. They saw me, stopped, laughed, and one of them pointed up to me and said in such a loud voice that I could hear every word: 'Look! There's our orangoutang so famous abroad!'

This was the kind of viciousness which hurt Andersen most of all, and to him such a remark summed up the attitude of his own countrymen towards him.

A satirical cartoon of Andersen in the
Danish journal *Corsaren* on
10 September 1847.

After his return to Denmark Andersen wrote five new tales. 'The Story of a
Mother', 'The Happy Family', 'The Drop of Water', 'The Old House' and
'The Shirt Collar', and in November 1847 he told Richard Bentley that he
would like these five tales to be printed as a book in English before they ever
appeared in Danish. For this edition, which Andersen gave the title *A Christmas*

Greeting to My English Friends, he wrote a special dedication to Charles Dickens, in which he said:

I feel a desire, a longing, to transplant in England the first produce of my poetic garden, as a Christmas greeting; and I send it to you, my dear, noble Charles Dickens, who by your works had previously been dear to me, and since our meeting have taken root for ever in my heart. – Your hand was the last that pressed mine on England's coast; it was you who from her shores wafted me the last farewell. It is therefore natural that I should send to you, from Denmark, my first greeting again, as sincerely as an affectionate heart can convey it.

In January 1848 Dickens wrote to Andersen to thank him: 'A Thousand Thanks, my dear Andersen, for your kind and dearly-prized remembrance of me in your Christmas book. I am very proud of it, and feel deeply honoured by it, and cannot tell you how much I esteem so generous a mark of recollection from a man of such genius as yours.' The story Dickens liked best was 'The Old House', he said, adding: 'I read that story over and over again, with the most unspeakable delight.' He then went on: 'Come over to England again, soon! But whatever you do, don't leave off writing, for we cannot afford to lose any of your thoughts. They are too purely and simply beautiful to be kept in your own head.'

During the next ten years Andersen and Dickens did not see one another, but it has been possible to trace almost all the letters they exchanged during these years.

In September 1848 Andersen's novel *The Two Baronesses* appeared in English, two months prior to its publication in Danish, and Andersen had arranged for a copy to be sent as a present to Dickens. As he received no reply he wrote to Dickens in April 1849, to ask whether he had in fact received the book; in a postscript he told Dickens that he was just about to leave for Stockholm and Finland.

Confirming that he had in fact received the book Dickens replied on 4 June 1849:

My Dear and admired Andersen, I send this hasty note across the water to you, to thank you for the delight your kind letter has given me, and assure you that you live, always fresh, in my remembrance. My wife and children entreat me to give their loves to you, and we all want to know when you are going to make us happier and better by writing a new book. We feel jealous of Stockholm and jealous of Finland, and we say to one another that you ought to be at home and nowhere else (unless in England where we should receive you most heartily) with a pen in your hand and a goodly pile of paper before you.

Andersen received the letter during his stay in Sweden, but a whole year went by before he replied. 'You are so vividly in my thoughts that I often think I live in the same house with you, and therefore put off writing,' he wrote in his letter, in which he particularly thanked Dickens for *David Copperfield*, which he had read with great enthusiasm. 'I long incredibly to see and speak with you,' he wrote.

to England again, soon! But whatever you do, don't leave off writing, for we cannot afford to lose any of your thoughts. They are too truly and simply beautiful to be left in your own head.

We have long since come back from that sea-shore where I said adieu to you, and are in our own house again. Mrs Dickens says I am to give you her love. So says her sister. So say all my children. And as we are all in the same mind, I beg you to receive me into the bargain, as the love of your true and admiring friend

Charles Dickens

Hans Christian Andersen.

The last page of a letter from Charles
Dickens to Hans Christian Andersen,
written at the beginning of January
1848.

'A funeral procession past my windows in Rome on 28 December 1833'. Sketch by Andersen.

Hans Christian Andersen in Rome, January 1834. Painting by Albert Küchler.

In 1840 Andersen travelled by railway for the first time. He wrote to Edvard Collin on 10 November 1840: 'For the first time in my life I have travelled by steam-carriage, 20 miles in about $3\frac{1}{2}$ hours, I am quite delighted, oh! If only you and all the others at home had been with me! Now I know what flying means! Now I know the flight of the migratory birds, or that of the cloud when it hurries on above the earth.' The letter reproduced on the right was written on 'Leipzig-Dresdner Eisenbahn-Papier' in 1841.

Hans Christian Andersen in Athens, 1841, with a fez on his head. Drawing by C. Hansen.

Dancing dervishes in Pera. Sketch by Andersen.

Der Bahnhof zu Dresden.

Der Bahnhof zu Leipzig.

Henriette and Edvard Collin, by
W. Marstrand, 1842. Edvard's friendship
with Andersen was often strained.
Henriette understood him better.

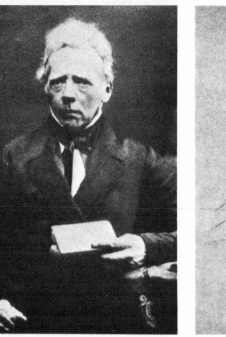

Ørsted, the discoverer of electro-
magnetism, was the first to appreciate
Andersen's genius as a writer of fairy
tales.

Søren Kierkegaard, whose first book
was a devastating criticism of Andersen's
Only a Fiddler.

Jenny Lind, 'the Swedish Nightingale'. Andersen kept this portrait in his scrapbook. By her signature Jenny Lind wrote: 'Art and religion were given to mankind to point the way to the next life.'

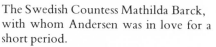

The Swedish Countess Mathilda Barck, with whom Andersen was in love for a short period.

Hans Christian Andersen, a drawing made by Ernst Meyer while Andersen was in Rome in 1841.

Carl Alexander, Hereditary Grand Duke of Weimar and from 1853 Grand Duke of Weimar.

Weimar Castle, where Andersen was a frequent and welcome guest during the years 1844–7.

Andersen emerging from the barber's shop. The caricature is by Fritz Jürgensen.

Andersen as a dandy, on his way to the Duke of Augustenborg. A caricature by Carl Hartmann made in 1845.

Andersen reading aloud to the Duke of Augustenborg and his family in 1845. Drawing by Carl Hartmann. Andersen was often invited to read his stories aloud to aristocrats and royals both at home and abroad.

Hans Christian Andersen. Portrait by
H. Olrik, 1859.

In 1853 Richard Bentley published a collection of thirty new tales by Andersen, entitled *A Poet's Day Dreams*, and this book was again dedicated to Dickens – 'as a token of kind remembrance by his Danish friend and admirer Hans Christian Andersen'.

In the summer of 1856 Andersen sent a letter to Dickens, to be delivered personally by a Danish friend, Mr Bille. But Dickens happened to be away in France at the time, and so Andersen's letter was forwarded to him there. From Boulogne he wrote a long letter to Andersen, in which he expressed his regret at not having been able to see Mr Bille, for he would have been delighted, he said, to have taken a hand that had lately been in Andersen's grasp. He then went on: 'And *you*, my friend – when are *you* coming again? Nine years (as you say) have flown away, since you were among us. In these nine years you have not faded out of the hearts of the English people, but have become even better known and more beloved, than when you saw them for the first time.' Dickens suggested that Andersen should come for another visit: 'You ought to come to me, for example, and stay in my house. We would all do our best to make you happy.' He went on to say that he was hard at work on *Little Dorrit* and that his wife and daughters would have been mortally offended if Andersen had suspected them of having forgotten him. 'They say, that if you knew them half as well as they have for years and years known Tommelise or the ugly Duck, you would know better.' Dickens ended his letter by assuring Andersen, 'that I love and esteem you more, than I could tell you on as much paper as would pave the whole road from here to Copenhagen'.

Though Andersen was delighted to receive this letter he did not reply for nine months. When eventually he did write, in March 1857, he told Dickens that he had taken up his suggestion and decided to go to England and stay with Dickens and his family – 'for if you are not in London, then I shall not come to England, my visit shall be to you only'.

This time Dickens replied at once; he implored Andersen to come and stay with him in England. The Dickens family were going to spend the summer at Gad's Hill, twenty-seven miles south of London, in Kent. 'You shall have a pleasant room there with a charming view, and shall live as quietly and wholesome as in Copenhagen itself,' Dickens wrote. If and when he wanted to go to London Andersen would always be welcome to use Dickens' London house in Tavistock Square. 'So, pray, make up your mind to come to England,' Dickens went on and continued: 'Little Dorrit at present engages me closely. I hope to finish her story by the end of this month, and that done you will find me in the summer quite a free man, playing at cricket and all manners of English open-air games.' His letter ended: 'Mind! you must not think any more of going to Switzerland. You must come to us.'

Andersen at once accepted the invitation: 'I am completely filled and thrilled with joy at the thought of being for a short time together with you, to stay in your house and belong to your circle. You do not know how I appreciate it, how in my heart I thank God, you, and your wife.' But at the same time Andersen was worried because he felt that his English was very bad, and he thought he might express himself like a true Kaspar Hauser. 'Pray do not lose patience that in English I shall express myself so heavily and awkwardly.'

At the end of May 1857 a new novel by Andersen, *To Be, or Not to Be?* was published in London and simultaneously in Copenhagen. The book was dedicated to Dickens 'by his sincere friend Hans Christian Andersen'.

At the same time Andersen left Copenhagen, and from Brussels he wrote to Dickens: 'I am longing like a child to shake your hand, see you and yours for a short happy time. . . . My visit to England is in order to see you, to be mostly with you, and I reckon that you will have me with you a week or a fortnight, and that I shall not inconvenience you too much.'

On the night of 11 June 1857 – ten years after his first visit to England – Andersen crossed the Channel from Calais to Dover – on his way to Charles Dickens.

Andersen stayed with Dickens from 11 June till 15 July, i.e. for a period of five weeks.

'My reception was very warm, Dickens took me in his arms, later his wife and children came,' Andersen wrote to Henriette Wulff from Gad's Hill. But it soon turned out that Dickens was far more busy than he thought he would be when he had written: 'You will find me in the summer quite a free man.' For immediately before Andersen arrived, Douglas Jerrold, one of Dickens' intimate friends, had died, leaving a penniless widow and children behind, and Dickens was therefore in a feverish activity all summer, arranging recitals, amateur theatricals, etc., on behalf of the Douglas Jerrold Family Fund.

All the same, Dickens and his family took Andersen on outings in the neighbourhood and also on several occasions to London, where he spent the night in the house in Tavistock Square. He was taken to see the Crystal Palace, where he heard Handel's *Messiah*, and to various London theatres; twice he saw the Italian tragedienne Adelaide Ristori, in Montanelli's *Camma* and in *Macbeth*. He also saw Charles Kean's production of *The Tempest*; it was the most lavish scenery, 'but Shakespeare disappears in the spectacle, and I came tired and empty from it, as I had only seen a magnificent panorama,' Andersen wrote to Henriette Wulff.

The Danish *chargé d'affaires* in London wanted Andersen to be presented to the queen, either at a *Levée* or at a Drawing-room, but Andersen felt that he did not have strength enough for all the ceremonies and the invitations which would follow it and preferred the quiet life with Dickens and his family.

Among his old friends from 1847 Andersen visited Baron Hambro, but William Jerdan had moved away from London, and they only exchanged

'Homage to Hans Christian Andersen' in *Punch*, 10 January 1857. During his visit to Dickens in the summer of 1857 Andersen found out that this 'genuine letter from a young lady' was written by Shirley Brooks, one of the editors of *Punch*.

HOMAGE TO HANS CHRISTIAN ANDERSEN.

A Genuine Letter from a Young Lady.

" My Dear Mr. Punch,

"we Hope you are Quite well and i wish you Many Happy returns of Chrismas and i Hope you will Excuse me riting to You but mamma Says you allways are Fond of little peeple so i Hope you will Excuse as me And charley read in the illusterated London [News] that Mr. Hans Christian andersen is Coming to spend His Hollidays in England And We shold like to see Him becase he as Made us All so Happy with is 'Betiful' storys the ugly duck the Top and the ball the snow Quen the Red shoes the Storks little ida the Constant tinsoldeir great claws and Little Claws the daring Neddle and All the rest of Them and it says in the ilustat [several attempts, a smear, and the spelling evaded by] Paper the children shold Meet him in the Crys-pallace and we shold Like to Go and tell him how much We Love him for his betiful stores do you know the tinder box and tommelise and charley liks the wild Swans best but i Hope you will Excuse bad riting and i Am

"Your affectionate
"Nelly."

" charley says i Have not put in wat 'We ment if you please Will you put In punch wat everybody is to Do to let Mr. hans Ausen know how Glad we are He is Coming."

some letters. Otherwise it was mainly the circle of Dickens' friends Andersen met, John Forster, Mark Lemon, Shirley Brooks and Wilkie Collins. At Gad's Hill he also met Miss Burdett-Coutts. Among the guests at her dinner-party in Andersen's honour was Admiral Sir Charles Napier. 'Miss Coutts must be fabulously wealthy, lodge keeper, footmen in princely livery, carpeted staircases; I was given the finest bedroom I have ever had, with a bathroom and privy, a fire in the fire-place, looking out over Piccadilly and the garden in front,' Andersen wrote to Henriette Wulff.

Andersen also visited Richard Bentley and his family, who now lived in St John's Wood, and for Andersen's sake Dickens even invited his old enemy – 'the Brigand of Burlington Street', as he had once nicknamed him – to a dinner-party at Gad's Hill, with Wilkie Collins as one of the other guests.

In London Andersen once came to a district where he was told that Jenny Lind had stayed during one of her visits to England. He wrote in his diary: 'Jenny Lind passed a summer here in one of the houses; there is one stands empty "to be let"; I imagined that to be the one. The nightingale is not in her cage; her friend, the little sparrow, chirps outside, remembers the song, remembers her – it is a sad morning.'

Andersen visited Parliament, the British Museum, Westminster Abbey – and the printing press of *The Times*, 'the place from which the queen of the newspapers goes out into the world, more than 50,000 copies. A queen flower with more than 50,000 petals, which scents and shines over the whole world, from Stockholm to Hindustan,' he wrote in his diary on 1 July.

On 4 July Andersen watched a special performance in the Gallery of Illustration in Regent Street of Wilkie Collins' *The Frozen Deep*, in which Charles Dickens played the leading part; among the other actors were Wilkie Collins himself, Mark Lemon, Miss Hogarth and some of Dickens' sons and daughters. This was followed by a one-act farce, *Two o'clock in the Morning*. Andersen wrote about it to Henriette Wulff:

I was at the performance on Saturday evening, saw Dickens in the chief part (it is a tragedy), he played perfectly, with true feeling, it was so completely different from the English-French manner of playing tragedy; it was as Wiehe at home can play. After that piece Dickens appeared as a comic actor in Two o'clock in the Morning *(with us: A Night Guest), it was priceless, he was very amusing. The other part in the play was taken by Mark Lemon (editor of* Punch*), an elderly, stout man, with a splendid, jovial face. The queen, the King of Belgium, Prince Albert and the whole of the royal family were at the performance, and otherwise no one but about 50 guests, among them I; the queen knew this.*

In most of his letters to his Danish friends Andersen was beaming with happiness. Everything was charming and harmonious, at least to begin with. He wrote to Henriette Wulff on 18 June:

The family life seems so harmonious, and a young Miss Hogarth, who has been living in this house for many years, pours tea and coffee, plays with the young Misses Dickens and seems to be a most kind and cultured lady. Dickens himself is like the best in his books: affectionate, lively, cheerful and cordial. Him I understand the best as far as speaking goes, and now – exactly a week since I came – he says that I am making surprising progress in speaking English; every hour it is better, but then I speak without fear, and even the little ones begin to understand me.

Andersen found Mrs Dickens 'so mild, so motherly, so exactly like Agnes in *David Copperfield*', and the daughters seemed to him 'pretty, natural and talented'.

But, as had been the case so often before, Andersen's happy mood did not last. He suffered from stomach trouble, toothache and fits of melancholy. And after a while he began to feel that neither Dickens' sister-in-law, Miss Georgina Hogarth, nor Dickens' children really liked him. On 22 June he wrote in his diary: 'Charles [Dickens' eldest son] was far from agreeable, and I returned in very bad humour which I could not conceal. This is the first disagreeable day in England.' But it was certainly not the last one. On 27 June Andersen wrote about a younger son, Walter Dickens, and his friend: 'Neither of them showed any interest or attention in helping me by taking a little of my luggage; they walked ahead. . . . I was heavy in the head, tired and confused, had the feeling that no one sympathized with me.' A contributing factor to his unhappiness was that the *Athenæum* contained an unfavourable review of *To Be or Not to Be?*, pronouncing the book to be 'dangerous' because it might make people doubt the dogmas of religion.

On the following day, when Dickens happened to be absent the notice in the *Athenæum* 'lay upon my heart like a nightmare', he confided to his diary and continued: 'I am not happy, cannot be so, and feel myself a stranger among strangers; if only Dickens were here!' What happened when Dickens returned is described in one of Andersen's letters to Henriette Wulff:

Dickens came home only next day. I told him of it [the Athenæum review], and he took me in his arms, pressed a kiss upon my cheek and spoke most kindly, bade me feel how immensely much God had given me, how great was my vocation – these are his words, which I repeat; he bade me, like himself, never read newspaper notices; 'they are forgotten in a week, but your book will live!' We walked up Gad's Hill, he scratched with his foot in the sand. 'That is criticism,' he said, and stroked over it with his foot: 'Gone! – But that which God has given you, that will remain!'

On 29 June Andersen entered in his diary: 'Miss Hogarth is not at all attentive, nor are the sons; there is altogether a great difference between the whole family and Dickens and his wife. Not in good spirits.' On the following day: 'The aunt [Miss Hogarth] quite decent, Dickens as always matchless. . . . Mrs Dickens tired, the daughters without thought for me, the aunt even less. Went to bed out of humour.' On 6 July, during a visit to the Bentley family, Andersen noted: 'Bentley's sons and daughters extremely kind, more sociable and sympathetic than Dickens' children.' On 12 July: 'Young Walter Dickens silly!' And on 13 July he complained about one of the other Dickens children: 'My little friend (the musical genius) appeared casual and unfriendly towards me.'

The picture is quite clear. Andersen felt happy and at ease with Charles Dickens and his wife, but he felt an unfriendly atmosphere from Dickens' sister-in-law and the children.

The question then remains: how did Dickens and his family look on Andersen? On this point some evidence is available which suggests that from their point of view the visit was an almost total failure. In fact, we can now see that their feelings towards Andersen were far less friendly than he ever suspected, even in his most pessimistic mood.

Dickens' own attitude is, in some respects, very peculiar. Against the background of his cordial and pressing invitation to Andersen to come and stay with him, some of the things Dickens wrote *about* Andersen in letters to others sound most strange. There is no mistaking the condescending tone in Dickens' letter to Miss Burdett-Coutts, written about a week before Andersen had even arrived in England: 'Hans Christian Andersen may perhaps be with us, but you won't mind *him* – especially as he speaks no language but his own Danish, and is suspected of not even knowing that.' Miss Burdett-Coutts had been present in August 1847 when Andersen visited the Dickens family at Broadstairs, so she knew perfectly well how awkwardly Andersen spoke the English language; but the surprising observation about him not even being able to speak his own native language – where did Dickens get that idea? My guess is Mary Howitt, Andersen's first translator, who had never forgiven him for not allowing her to have a monopoly of him. It is probably to her Dickens refers in another letter to Miss Coutts, written after Andersen had been at Gad's Hill for a month: 'We are suffering a good deal from Andersen. . . . I have arrived at the conviction that he cannot speak Danish; and the best of it is, that his Translatress declares he can't – is ready to make an oath of it before any magistrate.'

No one can blame Dickens for writing that they were suffering a good deal from Andersen – for even the best of Andersen's Danish friends could bear witness that at times he could well be a trial to those about him. And a few incidents during Andersen's visit to Dickens will show how demanding and self-centred he could be. Sir Henry Dickens, Charles Dickens' son, who was eight when Andersen visited his father's house, writes in his memoirs: 'On the first morning after his arrival . . . he sent for my eldest brother to shave him, to the intense indignation of the boys; and with the result that he was afterwards driven every morning to the barber's at Rochester to get the necessary shave.' Andersen's moodiness, his despair over the unfavourable criticism of his novel, all these might irritate or annoy Dickens, but they do not help to make sense of his remarks about Andersen's incapacity to speak, let alone write, his own language. What Dickens may have heard from Mary Howitt is probably an echo of the stupid criticism levelled at Andersen by C. Molbech and other Danish critics who took him to task for not writing in a sufficiently grammatical and literary style.

Andersen left England on 15 July. 'Dickens drove me as far as Maidstone; my heart was so full; I did not speak very much, and at parting I said almost nothing; tears choked my voice,' Andersen wrote in his diary.

After Andersen's departure Dickens wrote to William Jerdan:

Andersen went to Paris, to go thence to Dresden and thence home, last Wednesday morning. I took him over to Maidstone, and booked him for Folkestone. He had been here for five weeks. He had spoken of you with much regard, and, I understand or fancied, had seen you. But whenever he got to London, he got into wild entanglements of cabs and Sherry, and never seemed to get out of them again until he came back here, and cut out paper into all sorts of patterns, and gathered the strangest little nosegays in the woods. His unintelligible vocabulary was marvellous. In French or Italian, he was Peter the Wild Boy; in English the Deaf and Dumb Asylum. My eldest boy swears that the ear of man cannot recognize his German, and his translatress declares to Bentley that he can't speak Danish!

One day he came home to Tavistock Square, apparently suffering from corns that had ripened in two hours. It turned out that a cab driver had brought him from the City, by way of the new unfinished thoroughfare through Clerkenwell. Satisfied that the cabman was bent on robbery and murder, he had put his watch and money into his boots – together with a Bradshaw, a pocket-book, a pair of scissors, a penknife, a book or two, a few letters of introduction, and some other miscellaneous property.

These are all the particulars I am in condition to report. He received a good many letters, lost (I should say) a good many more, and was for the most part utterly conglomerated – with a general impression that everything was going to clear itself up TOMORROW.

It is somewhat difficult to imagine the constantly worried and anxious Andersen in the role of Mr Micawber which Dickens accords him at the end of the letter.

The memoirs of two of Dickens' children also provide some evidence of what the family thought of Andersen. Sir Henry Dickens calls him 'a lovable and yet a somewhat uncommon and strange personality', and describes him as 'decidedly disconcerting in his general manner, for he used constantly to be doing things quite unconsciously, which might almost be called "gauche": so much so that I am afraid the small boys in the family rather laughed at him behind his back; but so far as the members of the family were concerned, he was treated with the utmost consideration and courtesy.'

Mrs Kate Perugini, Dickens' daughter, summed Andersen up in harsher words: 'He was a bony bore, and stayed on and on.' And she related how, after Andersen's departure, Dickens himself could not resist the temptation of writing on a card which he stuck up over the dressing-table mirror: 'Hans Andersen slept in this room for five weeks – which seemed to the family AGES!'

It is quite safe to say, therefore, that Dickens and his family were not nearly so pleased with Andersen's visit as he was to be their guest. The reasons for this are manifold, and some of them have already been given. A contributing factor of which Andersen was completely unaware may well have been that the relationship between Dickens and his wife was not very happy at that time, even though the final reason for their separation did not appear till a month after Andersen had left Dickens' house, when Dickens met Miss Ellen Ternan. But the most important reason of all was probably the fact that Andersen stayed far too long with Dickens. In the letter he wrote to Dickens just before he arrived he spoke of staying for a week or two – and Dickens himself obviously reckoned with two weeks stay – but Andersen stayed for five. On the other hand, Dickens himself was to some extent to blame for that, for on 21 June, after Andersen had spent exactly ten days as Dickens' guest, he noted in his diary:

Yesterday Dickens begged me most charmingly not to go before I had seen the performance given for Jerrold's widow, said that he, his wife and daughters were so glad to have me with them; I was much moved; he embraced me, I kissed him on the forehead.

The performance to which Dickens referred took place on 11 July, and Andersen left four days later.

The ultimate reason for the failure is undoubtedly to be found in the fact that Andersen and Dickens were far too different for any real friendship to exist between then. Dickens could be sentimental in his books but never in private. Among his friends he was boyish and playful. Andersen's humour, which is so obvious in many of his tales, was less obvious in his relationship with others, and in a foreign language it could hardly fail to vanish. With his exceedingly emotional nature Andersen must often have appeared sentimental: to see him cry over an unfavourable notice must have seemed unmanly and undignified to a person like Dickens, who did not give a fig for reviews. Andersen loved and admired Dickens more than ever when he left England; Dickens' feelings, already considerably colder before his Danish guest arrived than his letters would indicate, had cooled even more when the guest finally departed.

One thing must be said to Dickens' credit. Andersen's diary proves that never on a single occasion did he notice even the slightest sign of irritation in his host. On the contrary – whenever Andersen felt miserable or neglected or ignored, or when he was in despair over an unkind review, Dickens alone could cheer him up. When Andersen was alone with the rest of the family, while Dickens was away, he might be miserable and feel sorry for himself. In such a mood he could write in his diary, as he did on 28 June: 'Let me learn to be friendly and kind towards strangers; the forsaken one is sent me from God that in our meeting I may seek to help him forget that it is an alien land he is in, a language foreign to me he speaks.' But as soon as Dickens returned, Andersen felt happy and at home again. In spite of all his many duties and worries Dickens was, at least outwardly, an excellent host who never for a single moment let his guest feel that he had outstayed his welcome.

On 1 August 1857 Andersen wrote a long letter to Dickens, full of profound gratitude:

My visit to England, my sojourn with you, is a highlight in my life; therefore I stayed so long; therefore it was so hard for me to say good-bye. . . . I realized every minute that you were good to me, that you were pleased to see me and were my friend. . . . I realize that it cannot have been at all easy for the whole circle to have in its midst for weeks such a one as spoke English as badly as I, one who might seem to have fallen from the clouds. Yet how little was I allowed to feel it.

Andersen ended his letter with these words: 'Forget in friendship the dark side which proximity may have shown you in me. I would so much like to live in good remembrance by one whom I love as a friend and brother.'

This letter is a moving evidence of how sincere and deep were his feelings for Dickens. With a surprising perspicacity he put his finger exactly on the spot where irritation might be understandable and natural, and begged Dickens to forget all such and think only of that which might bind them together.

Andersen is known to have written a second letter before he received a reply from Dickens. Dickens' letter is both friendly and chatty, but slightly patronizing and condescending. Andersen replied immediately with another long and cordial letter, from which the following is a quotation:

My heart clings so fervently to you, and I still hear, with thankfulness, the gentle and kind voice in which your dear wife told me many times that I was really welcome to you all, that you were glad to have me there. – I always feared that you might become tired of me, the stranger, who could not speak the language correctly. With such a feeling one has ears and eyes at one's fingertips, yet I felt and understood that husband and wife had, in this respect also, one soul and one thought. God bless you for it!

But to this letter from Andersen, written in September 1857, Dickens did not reply, nor did he ever reply to *any* of Andersen's subsequent letters. Andersen kept on sending his books to Dickens, and he wrote several letters, including letters of introduction for two of his Danish friends. The last of these letters, written in April 1862, was for the same Mr Bille whom Dickens had regretted not having been able to see in the summer of 1856. When Mr Bille returned from England and Andersen saw him in July 1862, according to Andersen's diary, 'Bille told me that he had sent my letter to Dickens but not even received an acknowledgement which was the usual polite custom in England, said that D. had insulted me. Was annoyed!' After this incident Andersen gave up writing to Dickens. In the extended edition of *Mit Livs Eventyr* (written 1868–9) Andersen writes about his relationship with Dickens: 'Later, letters came more seldom, in the last few years none at all. "Done with! done with!" and that's what happens to all stories!'

During a stay in Paris in January 1863 Andersen wrote in his diary:

Dickens is here, is going to give a recital of some of his works tonight and tomorrow. Am uncertain whether to call on him or not, he has insulted me by not receiving Bille, whom I recommended to him.

But in the end he decided *not* to call on Dickens, and so he never received an explanation for Dickens' silence.

Most Dickens scholars have presumed that he was fed up because Andersen pestered him with letters of introduction for his Danish friends. 'Many were the strangers who arrived on the Dickens doorstep with letters of introduction signed by Hans Christian Andersen,' writes Una Pope-Hennessy in her biography of Dickens. But the number of people Andersen furnished with letters of introduction over a period of more than ten years amounted to five, and none of them 'arrived on the Dickens doorstep', for Dickens did not see one of them.

I believe the explanation is to be found elsewhere. After his return from England Andersen wrote a series of articles entitled 'A Visit to Charles Dickens in the Summer of 1857', and these articles were printed in the Copenhagen paper *Berlingske Tidende*. In Denmark they did not appear in book form until 1868, but in Germany they were included in an edition published in Leipzig in 1860 under the title *Aus Herz und Welt*. The German book was reviewed in August 1860 in *Bentley's Miscellany*, a journal previously edited by Charles Dickens, and in this review, full of titillating quotations about Dickens' harmonious and idyllic family life, Andersen was taken to task for 'the way in which he had betrayed private confidence'. It seems very likely that Dickens should have seen this review, and this may well have made him angry, especially because it came at a time immediately after his marriage had broken up. Against that background he may not have liked the idea of having his idyllic family life described to the public at a time when it was common knowledge that the 'idyll' was long since shattered. Dickens might have felt that Andersen had betrayed his confidence by exploiting a private visit as material for publication. Thanks to the manner in which *Bentley's Miscellany* hypocritically exploited Andersen's harmless little sketch, it may well have been interpreted by Dickens, whose nerves were certainly overwrought at the time, as if Andersen were publicly taking Mrs Dickens' part, and it is a well known fact that Dickens broke off relations with any previous friend who spoke up for Mrs Dickens.

Two days after Dickens' death in June 1870 Andersen wrote in his diary:

On the evening of the 9th Charles Dickens died, I read this evening in the newspaper. So we shall never see one another more on this earth, nor speak together. I shall not have any explanation from him as to why he did not answer my later letters.

10 Years of triumph and despair

1848-60

IN THE decade between Andersen's two visits to Britain events of great importance changed the whole course of Danish history. In January 1848 Christian VIII died, and with him the period of Absolutism, which had lasted since 1660, came to an end, for within a year his successor, Frederik VII, was to give Denmark a free constitution based on universal suffrage. Then a rising in Schleswig-Holstein in the early part of 1848, in which the Duke of Augustenborg and the Prince of Nör – two of Andersen's former acquaintances – played leading parts, led to a war lasting for nearly three years. The war took a bad turn for Denmark when the Duke of Augustenborg enlisted Prussia's help.

A wave of patriotism swept over Denmark and Andersen, who shared his compatriots' feelings to the full, was eager to use his influence in Britain to gain sympathy for the Danish cause; so in April, a week before the fatal battle of Schleswig where the Danish army was defeated, he wrote the following letter to William Jerdan, which the latter immediately printed in the *Literary Gazette*:

Copenhagen, April 15th, 1848.

Dear Friend, – It is but a few weeks since I wrote to you, yet within that period of history there lies a series of events, as if years had elapsed. Politics have never been my theme, – the poet has another mission; but now, when agitation goes through all lands, so that one cannot stand on any soil without feeling it at one's fingers' ends, one must speak of it.

You know how it is at this moment in Denmark. We have war! but a war that is carried on by the whole enthusiastic Danish people; a war wherein the noble and the lowly born, inspired with his just cause, voluntarily places himself in the ranks of battle. It is this enthusiasm that I must paint to you; this love of our country, which fills and elevates the whole Danish nation.

The false light in which the leading party of the Schleswig-Holsteiners have, for a series of years, through the medium of German newspapers, set us before the honest and clever German people, – the treacherous manner by which the Prince of Augustenborg got possession of the Fortress of Rendsborg, saying that the Danish King was not free, and that it was in his royal interest that he acted, – has stirred up the Danish people, who have risen as one man. All the frivolities and trifling occurrences of everday life disappear before greater, nobler traits.

Every one is in motion, but with order and unity. Contributions in money stream in from all places and all classes, to aid the cause; even the poor artisans and servants bring their tribute. It was stated that there was a want of horses for the army, and in a few days so many were sent to the capital from town and country, that the minister of war issued a notice in the journals that there was no necessity for more. In every house, and in the higher and lower girls' schools, the females prepare lint for the wounded. In the boys' schools, the upper classes are employed making cartridges; and such of those as can bear arms exercise themselves in the use of weapons. Young counts and barons enter the ranks as common soldiers; and this feeling, that all stand equal in affection for, and defence of, their country, as you can well conceive, strengthens the courage and enthusiasm of the soldiery. . . .

Up to this moment, and as we further hope, the Lord of hosts is with us. The King, with his army, goes boldly and victoriously forward. The island of Als is taken, as well as the towns Flensborg and Schleswig. They now stand on the frontiers of Holstein, and have taken above a thousand prisoners of war, most of whom have been brought to Copenhagen, greatly enraged at the Prince of Augustenborg, who, notwithstanding his promise to sacrifice life and blood with them, left on the first attack, when the Danes, with shot and bayonet, forced their way into Flensborg.

In our time the storm of change passes through all lands; but there is One above all who changes not – it is the just God. He is for Denmark, which only demands its rights; and they will and must be acknowledged, for truth is the conquering power for all people and all nations. May every nationality obtain its rights, and all that truly is good have its progress! This is and ought to be, Europe's watchword, and with this I look consolingly forward. The Germans are an honest, truth-loving people; they will get a clear view of the state of affairs here, and their exasperation will be transformed to esteem and friendship. May that hour soon arrive! and may God let the light of his countenance shine on all lands.

HANS CHRISTIAN ANDERSEN

Having read Andersen's letter in the *Literary Gazette* Richard Bentley wrote saying: 'Denmark has the heartiest good will in England; I trust she will be able to stem the torment of these German anarchists. One sickens at the continual repetition of the cowardice in high places, which might have crushed these monsters at their birth.'

But when Andersen replied from Funen on 24 May, the situation had changed dramatically. Andersen thanked Bentley for the sympathy he had expressed for the Danish cause and then went on:

These are heavy, unhappy days, a great injustice is being done to little Denmark. You know that the Prussians have penetrated into the country itself, have occupied Jutland and are daily requisitioning foodstuff, wine and tobacco, are sending out troops to take away whole herds of horses, cloth from the factories, in short, they are oppressing in the hardest possible way this poor country and are taking away the civil servants if they are unwilling to give them what they demand. And just these last few days they have levied – and that is really the limit – a forced contribution of four million rixdollars, payable before 28 May, as otherwise it is their intention to use the power and terror of war! Jutland is unable to pay this sum, not even half of it is available; so the Prussians intend to plunder and set the towns on fire. That such things can happen in our days, that such things can happen in civilized nations, that is to me as if I were dreaming a bad dream.[18] . . . Denmark is a small country, she is being overpowered, she is suffering the greatest injustice, she is bleeding to death. Britain has guaranteed us Schleswig, we have looked confidently towards Britain. Noble, high-minded Britain! Oh, that help might come! Just from there I should like to see it coming, there where my heart has grown firm by the friends I have there and by the spiritual nationality I have acquired there.

'War is a terrible monster, living on blood and burning towns,' Andersen wrote to Henriette Wulff in June of that year. To him it was particularly bitter that Germany should be the enemy of Denmark, Germany, where his works had been appreciated so early, and where he himself had found so many friends. In *Mit Livs Eventyr* he writes:

I suffered more than most in my mind as a result of this unhappy war which had been inflicted on us. I felt more than ever before how firmly I had grown to my native soil and how Danish was my heart; I could have taken my place in the ranks and gladly have given my life as an offering to victory and peace, but at the same time the thought came vividly over me how much good I had enjoyed in Germany, the great recognition which my talent had received there, and the many individuals whom I there loved and was grateful to. I suffered infinitely!

In the autumn of 1848 a new novel by Andersen, *The Two Baronesses*, was published in London, two months before its publication in Denmark. Richard Bentley had agreed to pay Andersen a fee of £200 on condition that the manuscript was sent to him in time to publish the novel in English well ahead of the Danish edition, thus preventing pirate publishers from stealing the market.

The Two Baronesses was Andersen's fourth novel, and though not a great masterpiece it is still worth reading: it is a very entertaining, well constructed and charming book, not least thanks to its lively and often grotesque humour. The novel is in three parts. Part one takes place mainly on Funen; part two moves to the Halligs, the Frisian islands which had made such a great impression on him when he stayed on the island of Föhr in 1844; part three is mainly set in Copenhagen and reflects many of his own impressions from his early years in the Danish capital.

The character of the eccentric old baroness, who is in fact the main character in the novel, was inspired by Mrs Bügel, a lady in Copenhagen who was both very eccentric and very wealthy, and to whose dinner-parties and literary *salons* Andersen was invited as a regular guest until for some reason he fell into disgrace. In the novel the baroness's father was a poor peasant, exploited and cruelly maltreated by the rich and haughty baron, who kicked her pregnant mother and gave herself, an innocent child, a lash of the whip for having tried to relieve her father's sufferings when he had been put on the 'wooden horse' as a punishment for not being able to pay his dues. When she grew up she married the baron's son and eventually, after her husband's death, became the sole owner of the estate. But she had never forgotten what she experienced in her childhood, and she hated the memory of her father-in-law and everything for which he stood.

The second baroness is a young girl also from a background of extreme poverty; but her mother died when she was born, her father vanished, and she herself was brought up as an orphan by a kind clergyman and his sister on the Hallig islands. At the age of fourteen, to save the life of her sweetheart, she follows the example of Jeanie Deans in Scott's *The Heart of Midlothian*, one of her favourite books; just as Jeanie Deans travelled all the way from Scotland to London to seek an audience of George II's queen, so Elizabeth, the heroine, steals away from home and travels alone all the way from the Hallig islands to Copenhagen in order to plead with Frederik VI on behalf of the boy whom she believes may be hanged for murder. However, she eventually marries the grandson of the old baroness and becomes a baroness herself.

The novel is set in Denmark in the 1830s and depicts people of many different social groups. The message of the novel is that true nobility is of the mind, not of the blood, or, in the words of the old baroness: 'We are all of one piece – all made from the same clod of earth; one came in a newspaper wrapping, another in gold paper, but the clod should not be proud of that. There is nobility in every class; but it lies in the mind and not in the blood, for we are also one blood, whatever they may say.'

Though the bulk of the novel was written in Denmark before and after Andersen's first visit to Britain, part of it was written in London, and his impressions of Scotland and his renewed reading of Sir Walter Scott's novels are clearly reflected in the latter half of the book. *The Two Baronesses* differs from Andersen's previous novels in being much less of a disguised auto-biography, though there are certainly many details which can be traced back to his own life story. There is also a certain amount of humour at his own expense in the portrait of the *Kammerjunker*, a man tormented by all kinds of frailties, fond of travelling, fond of talking about himself, and constantly out of luck in love affairs. Herman, the young baron, is also clearly voicing Andersen's opinions when he talks about the Danes: 'Good nature is not, at least at this time, a characteristic of the Danish nation; there is in us a tendency to deride, which is far more conspicuous. We have a keen sense of the ridiculous, with a resulting literature of comedies, but amongst the masses this sense is perverted into a desire to turn things inside out or upside down – to turn everything to ridicule.'

When Herman expresses his views as to what a novel should be like he is also speaking with Andersen's voice:

In novels and romances I would not have events alone, but characters and poetry; a novel that contains only events is read but once; the unexpected, the surprising, which was the life and soul of it, is departed, dead after perusal; on the other hand, where the human character appears forcibly and naturally drawn, where thought exists in living words, where poetry has its imperishable growth – to such a work we return again and again: that book is read and re-read, one comes from it refreshed, as from a ramble in the woods in spring.

When his old critic and enemy J. L. Heiberg thanked him for *The Two Baronesses* – 'from which one comes refreshed, as from a ramble in the woods in spring' – Andersen was, of course, overjoyed.

At the beginning of May 1849 Andersen wrote to Richard Bentley that spring had come, 'but not with better days for my dearly beloved, suffering father-land.[19] A tremendous number of enemies against a brave little nation demand-

'Farväl' ('Good-bye'). Caricature of
Andersen as a toady in Sweden in 1849
by D. von Dardel.

ing its right. Much blood is flowing, human beings are maimed, towns are
being burnt! I live in constant tension, it is impossible to tear one's thoughts
away from the terrifying events; I cannot find peace and quiet to work, every

day I have been waiting and hoping for a message of peace, for the sympathy of greater powers for my Denmark, but nothing has come.' He went on to say that during the previous year he had had plans for going to Sweden but had found it impossible to tear himself away from home at that important time; now, however, he had planned to leave 'in two or three weeks time, if only by then the bells of peace might ring happily for my dear native country'.

On 17 May Andersen did leave Copenhagen for Sweden. He spent nearly three months there, travelling first to Gothenburg and Trollhättan and then via the Göta Canal to Stockholm. He made the acquaintance of a number of Swedish writers and had an audience with King Oscar I to thank him for the Knighthood of the Northern Star which he had been awarded in February 1848. His diary records the event:

Went to the king at 10, was admitted at twelve, was infinitely bored, terribly nervous. – The Home Secretary was in there very long, they fetched maps. 'I suppose they're carving up Schleswig.' Finally I was admitted, the king was very kind, there was something almost shy about him, but he was very cordial as if we had often met before. I thanked him for the Order of the Northern Star, spoke about the similarity between Stockholm and Constantinople.

King Oscar told Andersen that he hoped to be able to bring about a peace but thought that there was in Denmark a pro-war faction; after all he had to think of the interests of two nations, he said.

Andersen spent six days in Uppsala and then returned to Stockholm, where he was invited to have dinner with the king and queen at the royal palace. After dinner he read them four of his tales – 'on hearing "The Story of a Mother" the king and queen wept,' Andersen noted in his diary.

As usual when he was abroad Andersen managed to meet most of the prominent writers and leading cultural figures of the country, and much homage was paid to him in many parts of Sweden – not only because he was Hans Christian Andersen but also because he was seen as a representative of Denmark, for which country there was much sympathy in Sweden at the time. It was one of Andersen's ambitions to visit Dalecarlia, and this he did in a horse-drawn carriage, which enabled him to travel to the Säter Valley and the neighbourhood of Lake Siljan, where he witnessed the traditional Midsummer festivities.

It was unavoidable that the war should affect the relationship between Andersen and his German friend Carl Alexander, the Hereditary Grand Duke of Weimar, and this caused Andersen much anxiety and sorrow.

In February 1848, shortly before the war broke out, he had been awarded the Order of the White Falcon by the Grand Duke of Weimar, and had cheerfully written to his friend Carl Alexander: 'I now possess a visible tie which connects me with the home that Goethe, Schiller and the great writers of German literature called theirs.'

In May 1848 he wrote again to Carl Alexander, but this time in a different vein: 'Denmark, my native country, and Germany, where there are so many whom I love, are facing one another in enmity! Your Royal Highness will be able to appreciate how all that pains me,' and later in the same letter: 'When shall we meet again, my noble friend? Perhaps never more!' To this came the reply: 'Have our feelings towards one another anything to do with the battle of political opinions? Have we become friends on account of our political views? Certainly not! The harmony of our souls, our minds, our fantasy brought us together and will also unite us in the future. Promise me, my dear friend, that the time and the opinions of the moment shall never be allowed to influence our friendship.'

When, however, the Hereditary Grand Duke of Weimar went to take an active part in the war at the head of a contingent of Weimar volunteers in Schleswig-Holstein, Andersen felt that he could not write to him any more. From Motala he wrote to Edvard Collin on 22 July 1849 to say that he had received a letter from Carl Alexander, who 'was very sad that for many months I had not written to him, thought that our friendship had nothing to do with politics, and that it would grieve him very much if he was disappointed in my feelings towards him; this I found very depressing, for he must be able to understand that I cannot write to him when I read in the papers that he goes to Schleswig-Holstein.'

Meanwhile, however, Carl Alexander had returned to Weimar, and Andersen wrote to him in August: 'I have received no answer to my last letter which I wrote to you in the spring. Afterwards I heard that a contingent of Weimar troops had marched to the north, and finally I read that your Royal Highness had yourself gone to the seat of war. I understood the circumstances, and sorrowed deeply on account of them, but could write no more. But now that the proclamations of peace are ringing in my ears I may follow the wishes of my heart and send this letter to my friend.[20] . . . My heart is entirely Danish, but my true friends in Germany I still love. But now peace! Peace! May God let peace descend on the nations!' In a postscript Andersen added: 'Your noble heart, and every noble German heart which loves the truth, will feel that Denmark is blameless and good, and has suffered an injustice.'

When the peace treaty was finally signed in Berlin in July 1850 Andersen was staying at the manor of Glorup on Funen, and from there he wrote to the hereditary grand duke:

Peace! Peace with Germany! It rings through my heart. It is really like sunshine, like a festive Sunday! Peace! Peace with Germany! I feel so happy that it will now be known that Denmark wanted no more than her rights. May no more blood flow, may the work of peace, once begun, prosper in God.

He went on to explain how in the forest solitudes of Glorup, 'I received the proclamation of peace even earlier than I had dared to hope. I was fetched in from the count's deer park by a gamekeeper; he said they had been looking for me everywhere to tell me the good news, i.e. the authentic news of peace. I hurried to the castle and saw the printed document. Oh, my noble friend, if only I could have embraced you at that moment! I had to cry for joy and return

to the forest again, where I sang German and Danish songs from an over-
flowing heart.'

It was not until the beginning of January 1851 that the Three Years War
came to a final end. During those three years Andersen had often been
depressed and thought that his progress as a *Digter* had come to an end; but
now he was happy and elated; while the troops were returning to Copenhagen
after the war he wrote in his diary: 'It's a wonderful time, the hearts of people
are meeting, people love and appreciate one another.'

Andersen was not idle as a writer during the war years in spite of frequent
attacks of depression and misgivings about himself. A typical example of these
misgivings is a letter to Mathilde Ørsted, in which he wrote: 'The feeling of
not yet having produced anything really clever – and my conviction of being
unable to do so – torments me terribly! Many people talk and write about my
vanity, my over-estimation of my own capabilities. Oh, how little we humans
know one another!'

In addition to *The Two Baronesses*, which had been completed in the summer
of 1848, he wrote a prologue for the centenary celebrations of the Royal
Theatre, Copenhagen, a libretto for an opera, a Danish adaptation of a French
farce, three fairy-tale plays, a number of poems, including his patriotic song 'In
Denmark I was born', two new tales, and a travel book, *In Sweden*. This last
was published in May 1851 in English as *Pictures of Sweden* shortly in advance
of the Danish edition, and though much shorter than *A Poet's Bazaar* it ranks
with the latter as one of Andersen's best travelogues. In *Mit Livs Eventyr*
he himself refers to it as 'my most carefully prepared book', adding that
he thinks, 'it displays better than any other of my writings those points most
characteristic in me: descriptions of natural scenery; the fantastic and romantic; humour and poetry, in so far as the latter may be given in prose'.

Though based on Andersen's travels in Sweden in 1849 *In Sweden* is no
ordinary travel description, and the chapters do not necessarily follow his own
itinerary. The book is a mixture of fact and fiction, of legends, fantasy, history
and personal experience; at times being like a series of stories and tales – in fact
some of the chapters were later incorporated into Andersen's *Eventyr og
Historier*.

In one respect the book is unique in Andersen's production: he keeps himself, his own person, very much in the background; thus he has resisted the
temptation to tell his readers about all the prominent Swedes he met, about his
visits to the king and queen, and about the homage paid to him by students and
others. The book is, as the English title implies, a series of pictures of Sweden,
coloured by Andersen's own artistic temperament, an inspired homage to a
neighbouring country with which he had fallen very much in love. No Dane
had ever written a better book about Sweden.

The final chapter of *In Sweden*, which is called 'Poetry's California', merits
special discussion. It is an epilogue to which Andersen himself attached great
importance, for in it he attempted to say with what poets and creative writers
should concern themselves in the future. The rapid advance of science and

knowledge was an unexploited mine of inspiration for writers of the present and the future, he suggested. 'Our time is the time of discoveries – poetry also has its new California.' Instead of following the old Romantic Muse who represented superstition and glorification of the past, poets would be wise to follow youth which represents science and knowledge and whose call is, 'Follow me towards life and truth.' He gave a description of a drop of marsh water, transilluminated by a ray of light, and thereby becoming 'a living world full of creatures in strange shapes, fighting and revelling – a world in a drop of water'; this, of course, is a reference to his tale, 'The Drop of Water'. He saw before him a time when the voice of knowledge itself would sound throughout the world; the age of miracles seemed to have returned:

Thin iron ties were laid over the earth, and along these the heavily laden carriages flew on wings of steam like the flight of a swallow; mountains were compelled to open themselves to the inquiring spirit of the age; plains were obliged to raise themselves. And human thoughts were borne in words, through metal wires, with the speed of lightning, to distant cities. 'Life! life!' sounded through the whole of nature. 'It is our time! Poet, you possess it! Sing of it in spirit and in truth!'

'Indeed, in knowledge and science lies Poetry's California!' he repeated. 'The sunlight of science must penetrate the *Digter*; he must perceive truth and harmony in the minute as well as in the immensely great with a clear eye: it must purify and enrich his understanding and imagination, show him new forms, which will make his word even more alive.'

There can be little doubt that the direct inspiration for the ideas of this epilogue came from a book by H. C. Ørsted, *The Spirit in Nature*, published in 1850. Having read Ørsted's book Andersen wrote to him to say how much he liked it and how much he agreed with the philosophical ideas put forward in it. Andersen also said that in his religious beliefs he preferred knowledge to blind faith: 'It does not do the Lord any harm to be seen through the intelligence he himself gave us. I refuse to go towards God blindfold; I want to have my eyes open, to see and to know, and even if I do not arrive at any other goal than the person who is content with just believing, then after all my thought has been enriched.'

During the Three Years War Andersen's only journey abroad had been to Sweden, but he had travelled fairly extensively in Denmark. When he was in Odense, he wrote in his diary for 9 June 1850: 'Towards ten o'clock I drove into my old native town, grateful towards God who has guided my progress in the world; without him I should have been sitting here as a poor artisan, being mocked by my companions. It is thirty-one years since I left this place – *he* who has guided me during that time will not let go of me in the time to come.'

Now that the war was over he could once more travel freely in Europe, and he wondered what it would be like to visit Weimar again. He did not want to be humiliated on account of his pro-Danish views, and so he wrote to his old friend Count Beaulieu-Marconnay, the court chamberlain, to inquire whether, being a Dane, he might find it unpleasant to visit Weimar at that time, in which case he would prefer to postpone his trip for another year. Count Beaulieu replied with an insolent and arrogant letter: if Andersen was so one-sided in his views that he considered Denmark right and Holstein wrong in every respect, then he had better stay away. He then added: 'If that is not the case, however, then you may be sure that people will only regard you as the popular and decent poet and friend with whom one does not discuss politics.' Edvard Collin drafted a very sharp reply for Andersen and said he hoped he would refuse the honour of being able to walk uninhibited among the great men of Weimar as 'ein lieber braver Poet, mit dem man eben nicht von Politik spricht'. Andersen did not use Collin's draft, however, but wrote a calm and dignified letter, in which he said: 'I truly confess there was something in your letter which surprised and grieved me – words which I did not think you could have written to me.' Beaulieu's letter made Andersen decide not to go to Weimar, and to Edvard Collin he wrote: 'I would prefer not to go to Germany at all.'

But Germany was, after all, the gateway to Europe, and in the middle of July 1851 Andersen went abroad again. This time taking Jonas Collin's eldest grandson, Viggo Drewsen, with him as his guest. On the whole they visited places in Germany where Andersen himself had been before, but they continued as far as Prague before returning to Denmark.

The following year Andersen went abroad again, and this time Weimar was his first destination. He arrived on 19 May, and his diary for the following day records his meeting with the hereditary grand duke, whom he had not seen for five years:

At 11.30 I went to the hered. grand duke, he was with his mother, I was taken into his room, where there was a fire in the stove. I felt nervous. He arrived, embraced me and kissed me lovingly; we spoke about the war years, and I gave an account of the good Danish cause.

To Ingeborg Drewsen Andersen wrote: 'Everywhere I have been received as a welcome old friend.' He described to her a distinguished visitor: 'The Empress of Russia has been here, but only for two days. She is very much afflicted, has to be carried upstairs and is almost blind. What a tragedy! Poor woman! To suffer, and at the same time to be in command of mighty Russia, which is as large as the surface of the moon.'

The following is a quotation from the same letter:

Last Sunday I was invited to dine with the old grand duke; his consort, who is the Emperor of Russia's sister, is an intelligent and very kind old lady; she received me very cordially. 'Many sad days have passed since we last saw one another!' she said. . . .

Today I have visited Liszt, who resides outside the town and lives with Princess Wittgenstein; their relationship is a great scandal in such a small town as Weimar, but she is well spoken of, however. They would like to be married, but since they are both Roman Catholics and she has left her husband, the pope will not allow this.

Andersen often saw Franz Liszt and the princess and got on well with them. By this time Liszt had lost all interest in Mozart, having discovered a new genius, Richard Wagner. On 3 June Andersen wrote to Ingeborg Drewsen: 'For my sake – and I'm prepared to believe it – Wagner's two most famous operas, *Tannhäuser* and *Lohengrin*, have been performed; they are not performed anywhere else, and it is Liszt who has arranged to stage them.' One day, following a visit from Liszt, Andersen wrote in his diary. 'He and the princess seem to me like spirits of fire, burning and flaming wildly; they can warm you for a moment, but one cannot get near them without being burnt up.' A few days later he read them his story 'The Nightingale'; this was Liszt's favourite tale, and the princess interpreted it as meaning that Liszt was the nightingale and Sigismund Thalberg the artificial bird.

After three weeks at Weimar Andersen went to Leipzig, where he was joined by Viggo Drewsen. The presence of kings and queens always had a magnetic effect on Andersen, and in Munich he met no less than two kings of Bavaria, the ruling monarch, King Max (Maximilian II), and his father, ex-King Ludwig I. King Max invited Andersen to dine with him, and they went on a boat trip to an island where the king had a villa. Andersen's diary describes their conversation:

I sat alone with the king on a bench. He spoke about everything God had given me, about the fates of men, and I said I would not like to be a king, it was such a great responsibility, I would be incapable of fulfilling the task; he said that God must give one power, and through him one did what one was capable of.

There were certain people in Germany Andersen did not want to see again, especially the people who had been concerned with the Schleswig-Holstein rising. But in Frankfurt he met some German friends who insisted that he should go with them to Homburg. Andersen's diary of 14 July records the following dialogue:

'What there?' I asked. 'The Duchess of Augustenborg and the princesses have asked us to take you there when you arrive.' – 'This is a joke!' – 'I'm serious, you must go, they are definitely expecting you.' 'I can't, it's impossible! I can't visit the Augustenborg family.' – 'Are you afraid of your countrymen?' – 'I hadn't thought of that. I can only say that it is against my feelings. It is impossible – even to meet them would be painful to me. Once upon a time they were kind and good to me, but there is an unhappy time in between; they have brought misfortune and unhappiness to my native land. I'm not judging them, but I couldn't bear to meet them.'

The next day his friends tried to pretend that the whole story had been a joke, but Andersen knew they were lying.

In the summer of 1853 there was a serious cholera epidemic in Copenhagen. Almost five thousand people died in less than three months. Andersen stayed away from the capital for the whole summer, afraid of catching the disease himself and very anxious about all his friends there.

In 1849 a collected edition of all the fairy tales and stories – forty-five in all – was published with illustrations by a young Danish artist, Vilhelm Pedersen, now recognized as Andersen's Danish illustrator *par excellence* and known and

loved by generations of children in Denmark and elsewhere. In 1853 publication began of a Danish edition of Andersen's *Collected Works* in twenty-two
volumes. With this in mind Andersen decided to write a new and extended
version of his memoirs, the autobiography which was to a large extent based
on *Das Märchen meines Lebens*. For the next two years he was busy writing this
book, whose eventual title was *Mit Livs Eventyr*.

During the years 1854–8 Andersen spent two months or more abroad each
year, mainly in Germany, and he was in Weimar in 1854, 1855, 1856 and 1857.
When he went to Weimar in 1854 the old grand duke had died and Carl
Alexander had succeeded to the title. Andersen wrote in his diary on 30 June
1854: 'The duke wanted me to visit the Duchess of Augustenborg at Gotha,
I said it couldn't be a pleasure to her and I knew it wouldn't be one to me; he
thought one ought not to bear a grudge and that ladies were above politics. I
didn't like the conversation, but he meant well.' On this occasion, however, he
met the Duchess Hélène of Orléans, the widow of Louis Philippe's eldest son,
and in 1855 he met the Grand Duke of Weimar at Wildbad. In 1856 Andersen
went from Weimar to the Castle of Ettersburg to see the grand duke and
duchess and wrote in his diary:

*Saw first the small princesses; 'ich kenne Sie auch!' said the smallest one and curtsied.
The grand duchess received me very kindly and welcomed me. The dowager duchess
was there and saw how the grand duke pressed me in his arms, kissing both my cheeks.
Tears came into my eyes. I thought that I, the son of the poor shoemaker and the
washerwoman, was now being kissed by the grandson of the Emperor of Russia, how
the extremes were meeting.*

Andersen's last visit to Weimar was in August 1857, after his visit to Dickens.
The grand duke had invited him to be present on 3 September, the centenary
of his grandfather's birth, when statues of Goethe and Schiller were going to
be unveiled. Andersen had first sent a polite refusal, but following another
letter from Carl Alexander, who was upset that Andersen did not accept, he
changed his mind and did go, arriving in Weimar on 1 September. There was
the usual cordial embracing and kissing of cheeks and holding of hands, and
on 3 September there were great festivities, and Andersen was invited to sit at
the ducal table for the banquet. 'It was a great moment when the two poets
Goethe and Schiller were unveiled, Schiller looks like me,' Andersen noted in
his diary the next day. There was a special concert in the theatre two days
later, for which Liszt had composed most of the music, but Andersen did not
like it; in his diary he writes: 'It was wild, unmelodious and obscure, in
between cymbals were struck; when I first heard it I thought a plate had fallen
down; it was devilish music.' On 6 September Andersen left Weimar. 'Went
to the grand duke, who begged and commanded that I should write to him
every month. Invited me to go with him to Wartburg today, but I didn't
accept.'

Andersen never saw the grand duke again. When he was in Germany in 1858
he refused to see Carl Alexander, for during the summer of 1858 the political
situation was such that he felt he could not possibly visit a German prince again.

Some letters were exchanged during the next few years, and then the correspondence ceased for seventeen years owing to the tension between Denmark and Germany before and after the war in 1864.

Andersen's journey in the summer of 1854, on which Viggo Drewsen's younger brother Einar had accompanied him, took him through Germany to Prague, Vienna, Trieste, Venice and Verona. In Vienna he met Jenny Lind-Goldschmidt again; he attended a charity concert she gave there, and the next day he and Einar Drewsen were invited to dine at her house. She had a son, 'who resembled her somewhat and had Goldschmidt's brown eyes,' Andersen noted.

In Bavaria Andersen was again received by King Maximilian; he described the meeting in a letter to Ingemann:

I was fetched in a royal carriage, I stayed at Hohenschwangau, was placed at the royal table next to the king and the queen, and with the king I was taken by carriage on an excursion of several hours into the Austrian Tyrol; no one asked me about passports, something which is always a torment to me; it was lovely there, and the king, who had read Das Märchen meines Lebens, *spoke much about my childhood, about my development, and the various people I had met. He was very sympathetic, and to me it seemed like a fairy tale that I, the poor shoemaker's son, was flying across the mountains at the side of a king.*

In August 1855 Andersen again visited the King of Bavaria; he wrote to Henriette Wulff about this visit which took place in Nuremberg:

Just as I was about to leave I happened to hear that King Max and his queen were in the town and were staying up at the castle; so I put off my journey, and as soon as their Majesties heard that I was here I was invited to the royal table and was received most cordially, most beautifully. We dined at the castle in the large banqueting hall, where the wood panelling is beautifully carved, walls and windows medieval, and right outside, down below, lay the old town in sunshine.

In his diary Andersen noted with obvious pleasure that at the royal table he was called 'Königl. dänischer Hofrath', and that he was placed next to the king.

From Wildbad, where he spent four days, Andersen wrote to Jonas Collin: 'To my great annoyance the Prince of Nör is here; today I saw him from behind. I do hope we shan't meet!' They did not.

In Switzerland he met Richard Wagner, who was then living in exile in Zurich. Andersen's diary briefly records: 'Visited Wagner, the composer, who received me very kindly. I stayed there for half an hour.'

In Wildbad Andersen also met his old friends Edvard and Henriette Collin, who were staying at the spa for health reasons. Over the years Andersen's relationship with Edvard Collin had become much less complicated, partly because Andersen had become less demanding and emotional in his friendship, partly because Edvard Collin had become less domineering and more tactful.

'Good gracious, how different we are, and yet we get on very well together,' Edvard wrote to Andersen in June 1851. A few days later Jonas Collin wrote:

I can tell you, my dear Andersen, that it is with the greatest joy I have heard Ingeborg and Edvard telling me of the affectionate correspondence you and he have had in recent days; I cannot describe to you how happy I was, first when Edvard said to me, 'I have had such a nice letter from Andersen,' and then immediately afterwards when Ingeborg said, 'Andersen writes that he has had such a nice letter from Edvard.' And I say again and again, 'How wonderful! Now I can take the side of both of them!'

To some extent Henriette Collin had taken over the personal correspondence with Andersen, while it was Edvard who conscientiously looked after the business side, was in charge of Andersen's financial affairs, renewed Andersen's lottery ticket, discussed contracts, and so on.

Henriette Collin stayed on at Wildbad after her husband had left, and in a letter from Copenhagen Edvard was able to quote what she had written home to him: 'Andersen is, of course, the main object of our conversations, and it is him I can thank for all the kindness which is being shown to me. Please tell him that, and that I regret every disrespectful word I have ever said about him. He is indeed terribly famous!' To have such words coming to him from the Collin family was like manna from heaven to Andersen.

In his letters to Henriette Collin Andersen often showed his sense of humour – even to the point of making fun of himself. In June 1856 he wrote a letter from Germany in which he explained that he had been bitten by a dog, and though the dog's teeth had not penetrated his skin he was still afraid of getting rabies. He went on to say that he had happened to meet the King and Queen of Saxony at a poultry exhibition in Dresden; they had recognized him and talked to him. He then continued: 'I think people believed me to be a foreign prince. When I left, all the footmen took off their hats. – And then a dog has the audacity to bite me, and from behind!'

In another letter Andersen wrote of the drawbacks of being famous:

There are many female writers here at Maxen, and one of them, otherwise quite excellent, is much given to assaulting me with kisses whenever I read something which moves her – but she is old, fat and warm! – The other day at the table I had such a well-intentioned embrace; when she left, another female writer whispered to me: 'If you are often rewarded as you were this evening, then I don't envy you!' – If only I knew when these assaults were coming, then I could turn away, but I'm taken by surprise!

Whatever caused the following note to be written in Copenhagen in December 1860 I have no doubt that Andersen wrote it with his tongue in his cheek:

Mrs Collin, – I'm sorry you are trying to run away from me! Now I shall leave the house, the day after tomorrow I shall go away and – soon I shall die.
Yours respectfully, H.C.

On 15 May 1857 Andersen's fifth novel, *To Be, or Not to Be?*, was published by Richard Bentley in London five days prior to its publication in Danish. As mentioned in the previous chapter, it was English reviews of that novel which caused Andersen so much distress during his visit to Dickens. When he returned to Denmark and saw the Danish reviews he found little consolation. 'As far as I am concerned the reception of my new book here at home has given me but little pleasure.'

There is no reason to change the verdict of those critics today: *To Be, or Not to Be?* is not a good book; it is an impossible mixture of a novel (with very little plot), a philosophical essay and a religious tract. Under the influence of 'modern materialists', such as Strauss and Feuerbach, Niels Bryde, the cardboard hero of the novel, loses his Christian faith, only to regain it at the end, when he becomes firmly convinced of the immortality of the soul – while not in any way abandoning his profound interest in science. To quote Andersen's own words in the final chapter: 'like a new Aladdin he had descended into the cave of science in order to find among its wonderful fruits the lamp of life, and he was holding – his mother's Bible, not its body, but its divine soul.'

In spite of his undogmatic Christianity there was one dogma which Andersen accepted wholeheartedly: the immortality of the soul. But this idea, which he managed to put across beautifully in some of his tales, such as 'The Little Mermaid', 'The Snow Queen' and 'A Story of the Sand Dunes', is nothing but an empty postulate in this novel.

Admittedly, there are some interesting and some amusing elements in the novel. The reader is left in no doubt, for instance, that the author dislikes both Grundtvig's 'Edda-Christianity' and Kierkegaard's 'stalactite cave spring of humour and cleverness', as the heroine calls it; she is also fed up with his 'crawling along the pavement of language to get to the temple of thought,' for; 'the road was so long that the green stuff she found was not freshly sprouting'.

None of the characters can be identified with Andersen himself, though as always there are recognizable elements, for instance when Niels Bryde is described as a boy, who 'had an inborn fear of dogs, it was a great distress to him that these creatures existed; if a dog as much as sniffed at him a shock went through all his limbs'.

For part of his journey in 1855 Andersen had invited Edgar Collin, another of Jonas Collin's grandchildren, to travel with him, and after having travelled alone in Germany in 1856, he decided to invite Viggo Drewsen's younger brother, Harald, to be his travelling companion in the summer of 1858. There were frequent conflicts and points of irritation when Andersen travelled with his young friends. He did not always find them considerate or grateful, but his diary reveals that he found Harald Drewsen's company even more trying than usual; Andersen found Harald boring, silent, surly and irritable, and if one adds to this Andersen's own moodiness, his anxious temperament, it is easy to see why they did not get on very well together.

Before leaving for Germany in June 1858 Andersen had said good-bye to one of his oldest, most loyal and faithful friends, Henriette Wulff, who had decided to emigrate to America. She had previously been to the Danish West Indies and to the United States with her brother Christian, who had died in South

Carolina in 1856. She had several friends in the United States and had often tried to persuade Andersen to visit the New World, with which she had fallen in love. After Andersen had left Copenhagen he wrote to her from Sorø:

It was with a heavy heart, I think far more so than you realized, that I said good-bye to you, although I am fully convinced that we shall meet again more than once in this world.

Thank you for your faithfulness towards me, in spite of the fact that we are, as you say, and as I think you are right in saying, so different in many ways. Thank you for being so indulgent with me in all my irritability.

Andersen's friendship with Henriette Wulff had begun when he was still a schoolboy and had stayed at her parents' home, and it had remained constant over the years. In a way she and Henriette Hanck (who had died in 1846) were like sisters to him, the only 'sisters' on whose friendship he could always rely. Her letters show how much she liked Andersen as a person and how sincerely she admired him as a writer (much more so than members of the Collin family), and they reveal what a great personality this little hunchbacked spinster was; in spite of her profound admiration for Andersen she did not always agree with him and was not afraid of saying so.[21]

As a typical example of their occasional difference in outlook let me mention her reaction to one particular aspect of Andersen's autobiography. Before the actual publication of *Mit Livs Eventyr* in 1855 Andersen sent the galley proofs to Henriette Wulff as they came from the printer's, eager to have her favourable comments. On the whole, her comments were favourable; but on one point she could not refrain from telling him how much she disagreed with him, a point, she wrote, 'in which you and I are as different as possible; you, incomprehensibly, are a royalist and an aristocrat, while my nature is definitely democratic and egalitarian, so that I assure you I cannot with the best will in the world make sense of your own and several other people's feelings in these matters'. She then went on:

To me it is a total denial of oneself, of one's own person, of the gifts God has graciously given us, such an incomprehensible self-humiliation that I am surprised when some-body like YOU, *Andersen – if you do recognize that God has given you special spiritual gifts – that* YOU *can consider yourself* HAPPY *and* HONOURED *to be placed – well, that is what it says – at the table of the King of Prussia or of some other high-ranking person – or to receive a decoration, of the kind worn by the greatest of scoundrels, not to men-tion a swarm of extremely insignificant people. Do you really place a title, money, aristocratic blood, success in what is nothing but outward matters,* ABOVE *genius – spirit – the gifts of the soul?*

Andersen had no answer to Henriette Wulff's highly justified question. Later in that same year, when he was again travelling in Germany Henriette Wulff wrote to him: 'Where are you now, my dear Andersen? I imagine with King Max, whom you love and honour, I know; and though I am not a lover of kings I should be extremely pleased to know of your being with someone whom you love and who (*entre nous*) I am also convinced must have a noble character – since you are fond of him; you know that my confidence in you is almost unlimited.'

On 12 July 1858 Henriette Wulff left Denmark, to go first to Germany and then by steamer from Hamburg to New York. Shortly before leaving Denmark she wrote to Andersen, who was already in Germany:

My dear, good Andersen, – I am very fond of you and like you very much whenever I think of you as you are TRULY *and* REALLY *– and that I do so very often I need not tell you; how often have I done so – but I'm not going to keep silent about it – not until I have to keep silent for ever.*

She had to spend more than a month in Germany waiting for the departure of her boat, and from Eisenach she wrote to Andersen, who was then staying with Harald Drewsen near Dresden, that they were only separated by a six-hour train journey, and suggested that he and his young friend should come and spend a few days with her. 'I almost think it is your duty in a way to come and see me once again and say good-bye to me before my long voyage and give me your brotherly blessing,' she wrote. Unfortunately Andersen was not the sort of person who found it easy to change his plans (except by 'royal command'), and he gave Henriette Wulff two reasons for his refusal: if he went to Eisenach he would have to call on the Grand Duke of Weimar, which for patriotic reasons he did not wish to do, and he had promised Harald Drewsen that they would be returning via Brunswick, Harald being particularly interested in old buildings. Henriette Wulff pointed out that the first reason was not valid any more, because the grand duke had already left the Duchy of Weimar for other parts of Germany, but she added, 'a promise to your young friend I find sufficient reason for you not to depart one single step from your way'. Later in the same letter she wrote:

Would you believe it – I often forget that you are what is called a famous man, in fact, I forget it probably too often simply because I look into my own heart and the feelings THERE *which I have always felt towards you. . . . Please forget* ALTOGETHER *my inconsiderate little plan, of which I ought never to have spoken a word, that I admit quite candidly. One ought to know one's friends, and if one does, then one ought to act accordingly – that I did not do, and the fault is mine and mine alone.*

I read your letter with my heart – this one is written with my heart, please read it that way – however, I KNOW *you will; I know your heart, it is a safe anchoring place, it will not betray the trust I have in it, of that I am fully and firmly convinced,* EVEN THOUGH *appearances might give a different picture once in a while.*

In her last letter, written ten days before she was due to sail to America, she wrote to Andersen: 'Please do not forget me entirely! With an unchanged sisterly mind I shall think of you, whom I have been fond of for so many years. God bless you and be with you!'

On 1 September Henriette Wulff left for America on board the *Austria*. On 13 September, a few days before the ship was due to arrive in New York, she caught fire and sank; of the 560 people on board only 90 were saved, Henriette Wulff was not among them.

Not until 7 October did Andersen learn of the disaster; and at that time the press did not know the names of all the people who had been saved, and though deeply moved and grieved he still hoped that Henriette Wulff might be alive; in this state of distress he wrote to B. S. Ingemann about the *Austria*:

Miss Henriette Wulff, the daughter of Admiral Wulff, was on board. You know that I have known her since my earliest youth, that I went regularly to her parents' house and had in her until the very last days a faithful, sisterly friend. You have seen her; in her small deformed body a great and strong spirit reigned. The last time she was in America her brother died from jaundice; desolate and lonely she had to make the journey home to this country; she did not feel too happy here, her heart was set on the country in the new world where her brother had his grave and she herself many friends.

On 18 October Andersen learned that Henriette Wulff was not among those who had been saved; on the evening of that day Jonas Collin wrote to him:

My dear Andersen, – At this moment Ingeborg has been here to tell me that you have just left her with a broken heart after having a few moments before received confirmation of that which there was reason to fear about the fate of the unfortunate Henriette Wulff. I have felt strongly moved by the event that happened to the Austria *and the horrifying scenes connected with it, which grievously affect many families and friends, consequently also you, who had to lose in such a sad way a true, dear and faithful friend from the days of your early youth. Be assured that in my heart I share your sorrow.*
Your fatherly friend C.

To Mrs Læssøe Andersen wrote about the burning of the *Austria*:

Day after day my imagination had been stirred by the terrifying vision of it; it frightened me to experience how vividly everything appeared before my feverish mind; for several weeks I have been unable to work. . . . She [Henriette Wulff] *was one of the few people who really and truly loved me; she appreciated me and overrated me. She had the fullness of her feelings to give, and she did give it, something which I did not return sufficiently – and this is something for which I reproach myself now. I am grieved that in Germany, on my journey last summer, I did not make the detour she wanted me to make, so that we might have met once more before she left Europe.*

Later in life Andersen received many pressing invitations to visit the United States, but the thought of Henriette Wulff's fate on board the burning *Austria* prevented him from ever accepting any of these invitations.

In the summer of 1859, for a change, Andersen did not go abroad but spent three months travelling in Jutland, where he visited the remoter parts which he had not seen before, including the west coast and the northernmost part of Denmark, the Skaw. After his return to Copenhagen he wrote a travel description entitled 'The Skaw' and a tale inspired by his visit, 'A Story of the Sand Dunes'. Referring to the latter he wrote to King Max of Bavaria:

The entire description is the result of a visit I made last summer to the most interesting and remarkable part of my country: West Jutland right up to the Skaw. Here the scenery is very unusual; from the magnificent beech woods in the eastern part, which is still the haunt of the eagle and the black stork, one reaches vast moors covered with heather and dotted with countless barrows from ancient times. The fata morgana *of the desert here displays her airy mirages; the west coast presents green meadows and gigantic sand dunes, towering with their jagged peaks like a chain of alps, a bulwark against the rolling sea. There I spent the summer, having also visited the northernmost point of the country: the Skaw, where the North Sea and the Kattegat break against one another, and where, as in the fairy tale of the enchanted forest, the church, covered with drifting sand and overgrown with sea hawthorn and wild roses, presents a peculiar spectacle, with only the spire projecting above the sand dunes. The town itself has no streets or alleys, all the houses being scattered at random among the waves of sand, with ropes stretching from one piece of wreck to another to show the way.*

Andersen's letter to King Max was really a letter of thanks for having been awarded the 'Maximilian Knighthood'. He was now being showered with royal favours, even at home. In Denmark he had been given the title of Professor in 1851, and in 1858 he had been awarded another Danish order.

From the latter 1850s Andersen became a regular visitor to the manors of Basnæs and Holsteinborg in South Zealand, and there he found peace and quiet to work. In February 1858 he wrote to Mrs Scavenius, the owner of Basnæs:

The reason why I have not written to you for a long time, indeed have stopped writing letters to my dear friends abroad, is that since I returned from Basnæs I have been as productive as I haven't been for a long time; I have now put on paper no less than seven new tales, so that a volume has already been with the printer's for some time.

These were indeed productive years for Andersen. During the years 1858–9 no less than twenty new tales were published in a volume which appeared in four instalments under the title of *Nye Eventyr og Historier*.

In 1860 Andersen went on an even longer journey abroad than in any of the previous years; he left Denmark at the end of May and only returned in November. One of the highlights of his stay in Germany was his visit to Oberammergau, where he saw the performances of the Passion Plays at the beginning of July, something of which he later gave a full description. He spent a long time in Switzerland, mainly at Brunnen, at Le Locle in the Jura mountains (where he had not been since 1833), and in Geneva.

As usual he succeeded in being received by kings and queens. In June he was invited to call on Queen Maria of Bavaria in Munich, and in October, on his return journey, he was summoned to an audience with King Max, who pressed his hand and told him how much he liked his writing. On 2 November, just as he was about to leave Leipzig, he was told that King Johann of Saxony would like to hear him reading some of his tales at the royal castle the following evening; so Andersen postponed his departure, and before the King and Queen of Saxony and various other members of the royal family he read four of his own tales; after supper the king gave him a diamond ring. Unfortunately his pleasure at receiving this was marred to some extent when Ingemann later told him that such a ring might have been a suitable gift for a musical virtuoso but not for a man like Andersen, who ought, at least, to have been given a decoration.

On his return to Denmark, Andersen passed through his native Odense, which he found much changed; he wrote to Henriette Collin: 'It has become a very pretty town, smartened up but infinitely boring. All the old houses have been torn down and sleek square boxes put up instead. Another storey and some big window-panes have been added to the house where I spent my childhood; where my parents' small living-room used to be, there is now a long passage. I did not know anybody. . . . I felt sad and was a stranger at home.'

In December 1860, when back in Copenhagen, he was invited to spend an evening with Prince Christian (later Christian IX) and his children. Even at home, Andersen was now recognized as the most famous of all living Danes.

ANDERSEN had been reluctant to visit Italy again as long as the war of Italian liberation was going on; he admired Garibaldi but preferred to do so at a safe distance. In April 1861, however, he did go again and while in Florence he attended the celebrations of the first anniversary of the unification of Italy; and a little later, when in Genoa, he heard the news of the death of Cavour. His main destination was Rome, which was still not a part of unified Italy, and this time he invited Jonas Collin junior, the twenty-one-year-old son of Edvard and Henriette Collin, to travel with him.

Edvard Collin, who knew that Jonas was not among the easiest of people to be with, wrote to Andersen: 'I regard it as a sacrifice in more than one respect on your part to take such a young travelling companion.' There were in fact some clashes, partly because Andersen tended, as Jonas Collin claimed, to treat him as if he were a boy of fourteen, partly because Jonas was a stubborn and somewhat irritable young man who admitted that he suffered from fits of bad temper. In May Edvard Collin wrote to Andersen: 'I keep on hoping that you will not regret having done what you did; you can rest assured that Jonas is grateful to you, although he may not be able to express it very much in words; that is hardly his line, as it certainly isn't mine.'

Reverting to the old conflict between Edvard and Andersen about *Du* and *De* there is something touching in Andersen's entry in his diary on 20 August, just before he and Jonas returned to Denmark:

In the evening I carried out what I had decided to do all the time: I suggested to him [Jonas] that he should say 'DU' to me; he was surprised but in a firm voice said YES! and thanked me. Later on, after I had gone to bed, he came in to me before lying down, took my hand, once more repeating a deeply felt 'Thank you!' so that tears came into my eyes; he pressed a kiss on my forehead and I felt very happy.

Five days later Andersen was able to report in a letter to Edvard Collin: 'I do think Jonas has come to like me, and I have become fond of him as if he were a son, if not a brother.'

During his visit to Rome in 1861 Andersen made the acquaintance of Bjørnstjerne Bjørnson, the Norwegian poet, whom he liked very much – in spite of the trick Bjørnson played on him the day he and Jonas arrived in Rome, described by Andersen in his diary:

Bjørnstjerne Bjørnson immediately came over to us and was extremely kind. 'Have you seen Uncle Peppo?' he said; 'He is very angry with you, he has heard from the English and the Germans that you have written a book in which he is mentioned and that people say he is evil, and so he loses many bajocchi.' *I was highly affected; this man, who doesn't understand me but hates me all the same, wants to hurt me. I shall be killed, was my thought; I was extremely worried, my stay here a pain, I wish I could leave immediately.*

The next day Andersen wrote in his diary: 'Slept badly, in a sweat of fear. Bjørnstjerne came, regretting what he had said, told me that of course there was nothing in it.' But Andersen believed the story to be true and refused to credit Bjørnson's denial; indeed, had it not been for Jonas he might well have left Rome immediately.

Andersen must later have expressed his warm feelings of friendship in a letter to Bjørnson to which the latter replied:

The fact that I can be fond of YOU, *so full of character, with so much behind you, with such a glorious love in your way of speaking and behaving – and – please, forgive me! – with so many weaknesses which one must take into account and to which one must pay tender regard all the time – well, that I can understand. But that you should be so fond of me, who is too hard, too temperamental for you and either too irritable or too rash, and who is anyway incapable of giving much in your company, either from the heart or from the mind, because I am being outbid, often also (please, forgive me once more!) because you keep talking all the time – well, that is something I cannot quite understand.*

Andersen's letter must have been full of some of the usual whimperings and complaints, for Bjørnson's letter continued:

Whenever I read your letter it makes me laugh, for it seems as if you are finding too much draught and are being pushed by crowds everywhere. I wonder whether, at the moment you enter heaven, you won't turn round and ask Peter to close the door against the draught – that is, unless you want to go back the minute you are in the doorway because you're being pushed by the crowds. – All right – as I was just writing to a friend yesterday: there is no other person in Denmark about whom it is possible to tell so many jokes as H. C. Andersen, and there isn't a man in Denmark since Holberg who has told so many himself.

At the home of the Danish consul in Rome Andersen met the American sculptor William Wetmore Story; he and his wife had lived in Rome since 1848 and were the close friends of Robert Browning and Elizabeth Barrett Browning, both of whom Andersen also met in 1861.

When in 1903 Henry James' book *William Wetmore Story and his Friends* was published it contained what James called 'a pleasant legend of kind distinguished visitors' to the Storys' house in Rome, 'one of them incomparably benevolent to a languid little girl who needed amusement and who was for ever to be grateful'. The 'legend' as told by Henry James is the following:

Hans Andersen, whose private interest in children and whose ability to charm them were not less marked than his public, knew well his way to the house [at 93 Piazza di Spagna], as later to Palazzo Barberini (to the neighbourhood of which the Improvisatore *was able even to add a charm); where the small people with whom he played enjoyed, under his spell, the luxury of believing that he kept and treasured – in every case and as a rule – the old tin soldiers and broken toys received by him, in acknowledgement of favours, from impulsive infant hands. Beautiful the queer image of the great benefactor moving about Europe with his accumulations of these relics. Wonderful too our echo of a certain occasion – that of a children's party, later on – when, after he had read out to his young friends ' The Ugly Duckling', Browning struck up with the 'Pied Piper'; which led to the formation of a grand march through the spacious Barberini apartment, with Story doing his best on a flute in default of bagpipes.*

Strangely enough, there is no reference to these events in any of Andersen's letters from Rome, but the publication of his diaries proves the 'legend' to be historically correct – apart from the fact that Henry James was wrong in believing that Andersen had met the Storys before May 1861, when they were already living at the Palazzo Barberini. This is what Andersen wrote in his diary on 13 May:

At two o'clock I went with Jonas to the American sculptor Story, who is very rich and lives in the Palazzo Barberini, very sumptuous; here came many Americans, English, also French, I made paper cuttings for the children, had to read IN ENGLISH the beginning of 'The Ugly Duckling', but it was too bad and I got Story to read the rest. Here was a brother of Longfellow, the poet, here was the poet Robert Browning, who in a circle of children read two of his own poems for them, one about the Piper from Hamelin; he dressed himself up and played the part of the Piper, the children following him in a crowd through the room; we played an English children's game with dancing. ... The children of the house placed a wreath of jasmins on my head, a young girl gave me some lovely roses.

On 17 May Andersen wrote in his diary: 'Visited the English poetess Mrs Browning, who kindly expressed her pleasure at seeing me; she looked very ill.' Elizabeth Barrett Browning's impression of Andersen is also on record, for on the day after his visit she wrote to a friend:

Andersen (the Dane) came to see me yesterday – kissed my hand, and seemed in a general VERVE for embracing. He is very earnest, very simple, very childlike. I like him. Pen [her twelve-year-old son] says of him, 'He is not really pretty. He is rather like his own ugly duck, but his mind has DEVELOPED into a swan.' – That wasn't bad of Pen, was it?

On 21 May Andersen wrote in his diary: 'Visited Story, each of the little boys pressed upon me one of their toys as a memento,' and on 28 May: 'Poem and letter from Browning.'

Unfortunately Andersen seems to have lost both the letter and the poem Browning sent him; it is possible, however, that the poem may have been a copy of one which Andersen's visit inspired Elizabeth Barrett Browning to write, in fact her last poem. It is entitled 'The North and the South', and takes the form of a dialogue between 'the North' and 'the South', each of them long-ing for that which the other possesses. The three last stanzas of the poem are quoted here:

'Yet oh, for the skies that are softer and higher!'
   Sighed the North to the South;
'For the flowers that blaze, and the trees that aspire,
And the insects made of a song or a fire!'
   Sighed the North to the South.

'And oh, for a seer to discern the same!'
   Sighed the South to the North;
'For a poet's tongue of baptismal flame,
To call the tree or the flower by its name!'
   Sighed the South to the North.

The North sent therefore a man of men
   As a grace to the South;
And thus to Rome came Andersen.
– 'Alas, but must you take him again?'
   Said the South to the North.

On 21 May Mrs Browning sent a copy of the poem to Thackeray, in his capacity as editor of the *Cornhill Magazine*, and in an accompanying letter she wrote: 'Hans Christian Andersen is here, charming us all, and not least the children. So I wrote these verses.'

A month later Elizabeth Barrett Browning died.

On his way back from Italy Andersen received a letter from Adolph Drewsen about the declining health of old Jonas Collin: 'When you left this city, my dear Andersen, you were prepared for the possibility that you might not see again him whom with so much right you can call your father; this will now be so, as far as human calculations are to be relied on.'

In letter after letter Edvard and Henriette Collin kept Andersen and Jonas informed about the gradual decline of the old man's health. His death occurred after Andersen had arrived in Denmark but before he reached Copenhagen. A letter from Edvard gave the news, and from Sorø Andersen wrote back: 'The news of his death did not overwhelm me as it would have done previously, but in the course of yesterday, even last night and today, it has filled my thoughts, I have a desire to be with you, to speak to you.'

In fact, for a time the death of Jonas Collin brought Andersen closer to Edvard Collin, as indicated by a draft letter, written just before Christmas 1861, in which Andersen writes: 'My dear, faithful friend, – Thank you for the past year! With all its serious implications for both of us I have, I think, gained by having so to speak moved closer to you; you have been so cordial, so faithful towards me, your wife so extremely kind.'

In 1861 the first instalment of a new series of *Nye Eventyr og Historier* was published, containing among others the tales 'Twelve by the Mail-Coach',

'The Beetle', 'Dad's Always Right', 'The Snow Man' and 'The Muse of the New Century'.

Andersen wrote 'The Snail and the Rosebush' on his Italian journey. Its direct inspiration can be traced back to a discussion with Jonas, who claimed that his self-centred cousin Viggo Drewsen ranked far above such a person as Bjørnson; according to Jonas, 'Viggo Drewsen was concerned with his own development and didn't concern himself with other people; this made me write the story of the Snail and the Rosebush,' wrote Andersen. Ten days later, when he read the story aloud, 'Jonas found great malice against Viggo, who – even if he were never to show any results to the world, even if he were to lie naked in the street like Lazarus – would rank as an *excellent* human being.'

While staying in Switzerland Andersen began writing a long tale which he first called 'The Mountain Hunter', then 'The Eagle's Nest', and finally 'The Ice Maiden'. Another tale, 'The Psyche', was conceived and written in Rome and then rewritten on his return to Copenhagen. These were published as a second instalment of his *Nye Historier og Eventyr* in November 1861.

King Frederik VII was fond of hearing Andersen reading his own tales and treated him almost like an old friend. On 27 January 1861 Andersen's diary records:

At 8 p.m. at the king's, read my new fairy tales. The king himself put sugar and water in front of me and three times offered me his hand, which I kissed; he was very open and cordial. 'But how can you think out all these things?' he said; 'How does it all come to you? Have you got it all inside your head?' 'I have nothing when I'm abroad, but when I arrive on my native soil, then it all pours forth.'

In September Andersen was invited by King Frederik to dine with the Italian minister; the diary records: 'The king nodded down towards me at the table and welcomed me home [from Italy]. I thanked him for kindly wishing to see me. "Of course, you know, old boy, that I wanted you to come along," he said.'

After attending a banquet at the royal palace in October 1861 Andersen took home as a kind of souvenir the petals of a red stock which had decorated the royal table, and his diary reveals that for days afterwards he was obsessed with the crazy idea that he had committed a base and unforgivable crime by taking away this decoration. He writes in his diary: 'I have a feeling as if I had committed a felony and would end in despair, would be dragged down into the mire, be mocked and despised! I cannot lift myself out of this madness except for short moments, then I sink into it again.' His diary affords several examples of such ideas which he knew perfectly well to be dotty.

A few lines further down in the same entry he shows that he was far from being mad and that his sense was of a far higher order than so-called 'common sense'. In a conversation about other subjects the director of Copenhagen's Royal Theatre had told him that he had sinned against nature by letting animals speak in his tales. 'Well, Your Excellency, I replied, that is quite true, but then Your Excellency does not understand the language of animals; they must speak the way I let them speak.' He added the scornful observation that this had been said 'by one of the men of intelligence, it was the Head of the Theatre who made such a remark'.

In February 1862 Andersen received a gold box with the king's initials inlaid in precious stones on it and with the gift came the following letter:

My good Andersen, – It is a pleasure to me to send you my thanks for the happiness you gave me by reading aloud some of your pretty tales the other evening, and I can only say that I congratulate my country and her king on possessing a Digter *such as yourself. Yours benevolently,*
FREDERIK R

A few days later Andersen was invited to a ball given by Prince Christian (later Christian ix) and felt as unhappy as at the Naval Cadet Ball in 1825 when he wore the wrong kind of suit: 'I alone wore black gloves, felt terribly embarrassed by it.'

In 1862 Andersen unexpectedly received a substantial sum of money from his Danish publisher for a new edition of his *Collected Tales* and so decided to go to Spain, a country he had never visited before, and again he invited Jonas Collin junior to go with him as his travelling companion.

They left Denmark in July, spent a whole month with Jonas' parents and sister in Switzerland and arrived in Barcelona at the beginning of September. After ten days there they went by boat and coach to Valencia, whence they continued via Alicante, Murcia and Cartagena to Málaga, where Andersen felt happier and more at home than in any of the previous towns. He was profoundly shocked, however, when he attended a bull-fight. 'That is a brutal, abominable popular entertainment,' he wrote, fully convinced that it would soon be prohibited by the government. He and Jonas continued by coach to Granada, where they spent two weeks, witnessing among other things the festivities in connection with Queen Isabel ii's visit to Granada. After another week in Málaga they went by boat to Gibraltar and then crossed over to Morocco, where Andersen had been invited to stay as the guest of Sir John Drummond Hay, the British Consul General in Tangier, and his Danish-born wife. This was one of the highlights of his journey, and he was invited to have tea with the Pasha of Tangier, a somewhat mixed pleasure for Andersen, who never drank tea anyway and disliked the sweet mint tea served on this occasion; when pressed to drink a third cup he had the ingenuity to say to the pasha that it was against his religious principles to have more than two cups of tea.

From Tangier the journey continued by boat to Cádiz, then by train to Seville, Córdoba, and via Santa Cruz to Madrid. In Madrid Andersen met two of the better known Spanish writers of the day, Ángel de Saavedra, Duque de Rivas, and Juan Eugenio Hartzenbusch. He did not particularly like Madrid, and wrote to Henriette Collin:

Today we went to a bull-fight, I hope for the last time, but Jonas very much wanted to go; we saw the intestines hanging out of the bodies of the poor horses, saw blood spurting from the bull's horns, heard the crowds cheering and the music sounding with

Ved Husets Muur stod en Hæk af Geranier,
Der sad hun paa Trappens Marmorsteen,
Saa ung, saa deilig, hun solgte Kastanier,
Sad med Blomst i Haaret og bare Been,
Hun saae med to Livsens Øine paa Een,
Var man ei en Ismand, strax blev man en Spanier.
(Ill. Tid. Nr. 184 P. 219.)

H. C. Andersen i Malaga.

Danish cartoon of Andersen in Spain (1863).

trumpets and castanets. Salons and theatres are all that Madrid has to offer; these do not compensate for its being so expensive, nor more especially for its bad climate.

In December Andersen and Jonas went on to Paris. But that city had lost its fascination for Andersen, and it was mainly for Jonas' sake that he stayed there for two months. He was pleased, however, to meet Bjørnson again. He was the prime organizer of a party given in Andersen's honour by a group of Scandinavians in Paris; Andersen wrote to Edvard Collin: 'Bjørnson made a wonderful speech for me, to which I could only reply that while he was speaking it had seemed to me as if I was lying in my coffin, on which occasion the speaker always emphasizes all the good points and sees everything in the most flattering light.'

At the end of March 1863 Andersen and Jonas were back in Denmark after a journey which had often strained their relationship. Andersen himself had suffered from his usual fits of nervousness, had been over-anxious and easily upset, and Jonas had been arrogant, selfish and extremely stubborn. In Granada there had been a painful scene after dinner one evening during which Jonas had reminded Andersen of all the kindnesses his grandfather had shown him; shortly after they had left Spain Andersen wrote in his diary about Jonas: 'He is selfish, a Tartuffe, not at all a nice travelling companion.'

Andersen's visit to Spain had not been an unqualified success; he did not know the language and did not know anyone in Spain, and people in Spain had never heard of him. The first Spanish translation of his tales was published four years after his death, and so he was treated like any other ordinary tourist; on more than one occasion people even laughed at him because of his unusual appearance, as the following extracts from his Granada diary show:

9 October *I saw a couple of young soldiers and also some ladies on the balcony notice my long figure and laugh; how fortunate that Jonas wasn't there. I felt humiliated and embarrassed, went into a side street.*
11 October *Walked about in the streets to see the usual sights, was laughed at for my long figure.*

After his return to Denmark Andersen completed a new travel book, *In Spain*, published in 1863 as part of his *Collected Works*. Translations of this book were published in Germany and England in 1864 and in America in 1870.

In Spain has not the same fascination as some of Andersen's other travel books, though it contains many interesting passages; his opportunities for personal contacts were limited, and much of his information is second-hand, based on other travel books on Spain. He himself had changed: when he was young he travelled from an insatiable desire to see and experience things, now that he was older he travelled because he felt lonely and often bored at home. At the age of fifty-eight Andersen was beginning to feel that he was getting old; this is reflected in some of the entries in his diary in the autumn of 1863:

13 September *Dined at the Collins'. Eating and drinking I observe as that which unites us, binds us together. The youthful spirit and the freshness of youth are over.*

16 September *I am not satisfied with myself. I cannot exist in my loneliness, am tired of life.*
5 October *Felt old, downhill, melancholy.*

In November 1863 the unsophisticated, jovial Frederik VII died, and Andersen, who had first met him in Odense when they were both children, felt a sense of personal loss, though he soon found himself accepted as a welcome guest at the palace of King Christian IX, a more dignified and reserved king, whose sons and daughters, however – Crown Prince Frederik (later Frederik VIII of Denmark), George (later George I of Greece), Alexandra (later Queen Alexandra of Great Britain) and Dagmar (later Empress of Russia) – were all brought up on Andersen's tales and loved him both as a writer and as a person.

Christian IX inherited the throne at a time when Denmark's prospects were very gloomy; a new war with Germany over Schleswig-Holstein seemed imminent. In his continuation of *Mit Livs Eventyr* Andersen describes his own feelings at that time:

I still believed in the deliverance by God, but my heart was often full of anxiety, yet never have I more fervently felt how firmly I clung to my native land. I did not forget how much affection, recognition and friendship I had met with in Germany, how many dear friends I had there, but now a drawn sword had been placed between us. I do not forget kindnesses shown to me, nor do I forget friends, but my country is like my mother to me: she holds and always will hold first place.

In December 1863 Denmark had evacuated her troops, and Prussia, in alliance with Austria, occupied Holstein. On 1 February 1864 the Prussian-Austrian army crossed the Eider, and within a few months the Danish army was totally defeated. In the autumn of 1864 Denmark had to sign a peace treaty which forced her to surrender the duchies of Schleswig, Holstein and Lauenburg to Germany.

Describing the situation when the German troops were forcing their way into Jutland and when an invasion of Funen was expected any day, Andersen writes in his memoirs:

I lost for the moment my hold on God and felt myself as wretched as a man can be. Days followed in which I cared for nobody, and I believed nobody cared for me. I had no relief in speaking to anyone; there was no point in it. Then there was one person, however, who approached me with kind understanding and a loving heart, Edvard Collin's excellent wife; she spoke compassionate words and bade me give thought to my work.

What Andersen wrote about losing his hold on God at that time is borne out by his diary of the summer of 1864. On 30 June he wrote: 'Godless and therefore unhappy'; and on 1 July: 'God has let go of us, we cannot reach him; like a prisoner I am waiting for my death sentence. . . . God has let go of me and of us! – How desolate I feel, no friends, lonely within myself, and the days to come will be even worse, until it ends – in the grave!'

Even after the war was over his depression continued, as the following extracts from his diaries show:

9 September *I have no future any more, nothing to look forward to, no ideas, I am washed out!*

31 October *I'm irritable and melancholy, angry with very many people. Only unhappiness, distress, violation, oblivion and death await me.*

20 November *Low spirits, the tumour in my hand will lead to an operation, I think, and I shall die from it. It is time for me to die anyway, and while thinking so I do not seem to have enjoyed life, not to have accepted the gifts God gave me. My good fortune is over now; the war has separated me from many friends whom I shall never be able to meet again, and here at home I must just wait to be buried.*

In the spring of 1864 Andersen made the acquaintance of Bulwer Lytton's son, Edward Robert Lytton (later Earl of Lytton), better known by his pen-name 'Owen Meredith', who was then First Secretary to the British Legation in Copenhagen. They met on 14 April when Robert Lytton invited Andersen to dine at his house, and it was only then that Andersen heard about Elizabeth Barrett Browning's poem, as can be seen from his diary of that date:

I had to speak English, Lytton speaks German very well, but in the mood of my heart I could not speak that language, found it unpatriotic, and so I said in my bad English: 'At the moment there is in that language too much sound of cannon and of the cries of enemies; I should prefer to speak bad English.' He showed me the Last Poems *by Elizabeth Barrett Browning, who lived much in Italy and died in Florence recently. I spoke to her when I was in Rome last. Her* LAST *poem is called 'The North and the South' and is very flattering to me. Lytton Bulwer made a good impression on me.*

For quite some time Andersen had felt unable to write any new tales; the war with Germany and the bitterness caused by its outcome seemed to have dried up his inspiration completely. But during one of his visits to the manor of Basnæs in 1865 he suddenly felt in the mood to write again. The first tale he called 'The Will-o'-the-Wisps are in Town', and it begins:

There was a man who used to know a great many new fairy tales; but now they had run out, he said. The Fairy Tale who used to come and visit him of her own accord no longer came knocking at his door; and why didn't she come any more? It's true that for a very long time the man hadn't thought of her, hadn't really expected her to come and knock; and it is unlikely that she would have come anyway, for outside there was war and inside there was the misery and sorrow that war brings with it.

'The man' was of course Andersen himself, and once inspiration returned to him tale after tale 'knocked at his door'; in November 1865 he was able to publish a new instalment of *Nye Eventyr og Historier*, containing seven new tales.

At the beginning of 1865 Andersen had received an invitation to go to Portugal, one of the few European countries he had not so far visited. The invitation came from two Portuguese businessmen, the brothers Jorge and José Torlades O'Neill, who had lived in Denmark for four years as children, staying with the Wulffs.

Andersen was very excited by the invitation and decided to accept it and go to Lisbon in September. But as so often before, his feelings were ambivalent, as the following extract from a letter to Edvard Collin shows:

I have quite vividly imagined to myself several times that I had already left by now, that I was in Lisbon, and this has been so vividly in my mind that I have suddenly felt a longing for those nearest and dearest to me, a fear that I might never see them again, a clinging to my home, and also a horrible fear of being taken ill abroad, worst of all on the journey from Madrid to Lisbon. I am in two minds, like Hercules at the parting of the ways.

When Andersen finally made up his mind to go, news of an outbreak of cholera in Spain put him off. When there were no more cases of cholera in Spain he heard rumours of cholera in Paris and once again postponed his journey.

In January 1866 he wrote to Edvard Collin that it might have been better if he had never been invited to visit Portugal, for then he would never have thought of doing it; 'but this invitation made me itch to go, and I should gladly have left if disease had not been travelling through the countries. My mind has not been at rest ever since the invitation came, and I don't think it will be until I have completed that journey.'

Andersen eventually left Denmark on 31 January 1866 and stayed away for seven months. He first went to Holland, where he spent five weeks in Amsterdam before going on to Leiden and the Hague. He had a brilliant reception everywhere, and all the leading Dutch writers paid him homage. Passing through Antwerp and Brussels he continued to Paris, where he watched horse racing at Vincennes with the Danish crown prince. In Paris he also visited Rossini, the composer, who received him kindly but 'had a somewhat slumping appearance and wasn't quite clean'. Rossini later invited him to attend a concert, but Andersen was unable to accept. He also received an invitation from George Sand, who waited all day for him to come, but he had received the invitation too late to be able to go.

On 13 April he left Paris for Bordeaux, whence he had intended to continue to Lisbon by boat. But when he found that there was a chance of seeing Ristori, the great Italian tragedienne, whom he had previously seen in London as Lady Macbeth, playing the part of Medea, he decided to stay a few days more, which meant missing the boat and going to Lisbon via Madrid. 'Coming from Spain into Portugal was like coming from the Middle Ages into the present time,' he noted in his diary.

Andersen was given a warm reception by his old friends and stayed first with Jorge O'Neill and his family at their country house outside Lisbon, and then with José O'Neill and his family at Setúbal, also visiting Aveiro, Coimbra, Cintra and Lisbon. He was invited to the home of the blind poet Antonio Feliciano de Castilho, whose Danish-born wife acted as their interpreter, and was received by King Fernando, the father of the reigning King Luis I. He went on expeditions into the countryside, riding on a donkey, to the monastery of Brancanes and to Monte Luis and Monte Arrábida, and in Setúbal he witnessed the Feast of S. António and saw a Portuguese bull-fight, which he found far less cruel than the Spanish equivalent. He went on a boat trip and just missed seeing the stalactite grotto-chapel in the Arrábida, though his account of this grotto is apparently still used by every Portuguese tourist guide and brochure. In Coimbra he was impressed by the sight of students in their medieval costumes which reminded him of Faustus and Theophrastus. Cintra, which Byron had called 'the new Paradise', fascinated him; in his travel account, *A Visit to Portugal*, published after his return to Denmark as part of his *Collected Works*, he writes of Cintra:

It is said that everyone finds a part of his own fatherland in Cintra. I found Denmark there, and I thought too to rediscover many dear places from other fair lands – the green fields of Kent, the huge wild rocks of Brocken; I could fancy myself by the shores of Lake Geneva and in the birch woods of Leksand.

In Cintra Andersen met Robert Lytton again, now posted to the British Legation in Lisbon. This is how Andersen describes his visit to Lytton in his diary:

Lytton read aloud 'The Butterfly' and 'The Snail and the Rose Tree', kissed my hand. He did the same in the hall at my departure, embraced me and kissed me and told me that he was very fond of me and that in Copenhagen he had never dreamt that we might meet here.

Lytton's description of the meeting is also available, for he wrote from Cintra to a friend:

Andersen, the Danish poet (the 'ugly duckling') has been here, and quite in his element. One day, when he dined with us, I read aloud after dinner to my wife and the Brackenburys one of his little stories: and he was so well pleased with my doing this, that he jumped up and kissed me, as Mrs. Disraeli would say, 'all over'. He is a perfect faun, half child, half God.

That kissing took place is beyond doubt, but there seems to be some disagreement about who kissed whom.

With great fear and trepidation Andersen decided to go from Lisbon to Bordeaux by boat, and the entry he wrote in his diary on board the steamer reveals his nervous state of mind:

I thought of Jette Wulff in the burning ship, I lay at night counting the hours, thought of the moment when a disaster might happen, whether we might collide with another vessel, whether we might sink, perhaps this would happen within the next ten minutes, I felt a fear of death and considered it likely that we should never reach Bordeaux.

He did reach Bordeaux safely, however, and returned to Denmark via France and Germany.

After his return from Portugal Andersen spent the first three weeks as the guest of some friends in a villa called 'Rolighed' ('Quietude') just outside Copenhagen, and during the last nine years of his life 'Rolighed' became to him almost a second home, in the same way as Jonas Collin's house had been his first home in Copenhagen, his 'Home of Homes'.

'Rolighed' was owned by Moritz G. Melchior, a wealthy businessman of

Jewish descent; his wife, Dorothea Melchior, was the sister of Martin R. Henriques, a Copenhagen stockbroker whom Andersen had first met at August Bournonville's house, and during the last decade of his life the Melchiors and the Henriques were among Andersen's closest and most generous friends. There are more than a hundred letters extant from the correspondence between Andersen and the Henriques family 1860–75, and a similar number of letters exchanged between Andersen and the Melchiors (mainly Mrs Melchior) over the same period. During the years 1867–75 Andersen spent long periods every year as a welcome guest at 'Rolighed', and he also often stayed with the Henriques family at 'Petershøi', their country house. These two families were entirely selfless in their love and admiration for Andersen, and showed immense consideration and kindness. They made Andersen feel at home and gave him the security he needed so badly. In one of his earliest letters to Mrs Henriques, Andersen wrote:

How happy you are! After all, a home, a real home, is the greatest of blessings. I shall never get it on this earth, and that is why I am so restless, feel a desire to be on the move all the time, which, however – if I have to open my heart truly – does not satisfy me completely.

Both the Henriques and the Melchiors were eager to give the elderly homeless Andersen a home. To begin with he spent more time with the Henriques family; later on he spent much more time with the Melchiors at 'Rolighed'. But there was never any kind of jealousy between the two clans. Andersen's relationship with the Collins had always been fraught with difficulties and complications; with the Henriques and Melchior families he experienced the blessing of uncomplicated friendship.

In Copenhagen he still circulated among his various friends for dinner according to a more or less regular routine. Thus in the mid-sixties, he usually dined with Edvard and Henriette Collin on Mondays, with Ingeborg and Adolph Drewsen on Tuesdays, with H. C. Ørsted's widow and daughter on Wednesdays, with the Melchiors on Thursdays, with Mrs Ida Koch, Henriette Wulff's sister, on Fridays, with a Mrs Neergaard (until her death in 1866) on Saturdays, and with Mr and Mrs Henriques on Sundays.

Andersen's diary for the year 1867 opens with the words: 'Began with the rich man's worry about money: fear of losing what one owns.' Financially he was quite well off. A business letter from Edvard Collin the following day informed him that his total fortune now amounted to 12,506 rixdollars.

Andersen was beginning to feel old, and in the autumn of 1866 Henriette Collin more or less forced him to buy his own bed for the first time: 'Now I am going to have a house, even a bed, my own *bed*; it terrifies me! I am being weighed down by furniture, bed and rocking chair, not to mention books and paintings.' He also wrote to J. P. E. Hartmann, the composer: 'I have had to invest one hundred rixdollars in a bed, and it is going to be my death-bed, for if it does not last that long, then it isn't worth the money. I wish I were only twenty, then I'd take my inkpot on my back, two shirts and a pair of socks, put a quill at my side and go into the wide world. Now I am, as Mrs Collin writes so beautifully, "an elderly man", so I must think of my bed, my death-bed.' On 8 January 1867 he wrote to Henriette Collin: 'I think Death is going to snatch me away this year; if only I knew, I should fly out immediately into the wide world in order to breathe properly before my breath is removed altogether from this sack of worms.'

Andersen did in fact 'fly out into the wide world' again, for as soon as the World Exhibition opened in Paris in the spring of 1867 he went there to see what he called 'the fairy-tale sight of our time'. Later in the same year he decided to go to Paris yet again in order to pay a second visit to the exhibition, for Paris had inspired him to begin writing a new fairy tale called 'The Wood Nymph', and Melchior had secretly given him a sum of money sufficient to enable him to travel with a young friend. This time Paris seems to have rejuvenated him; he wrote in his diary on 5 September: 'It is a beautiful evening, we are in Paris, I am young, 62 seconds in the great year of Eternity.'

Following his return to Denmark an incident occurred which deserves mention because it counterbalances the stories of his selfishness and vanity. Some letters written by Carsten Hauch as a young man had been published without his knowledge and consent, including some in which Hauch had been derogatory about Andersen. Andersen read the printed letters, and wrote in his diary on 14 November: 'There is one from Hauch about my *Journey on Foot* and me which is almost defamatory to me: I am called a toady and described as entirely pitiable, my personality is exposed. My first impression was: Thank God that it wasn't I who wrote this; this must really be painful to Hauch who has called himself my friend and admirer in recent years.' Andersen drafted a very nice and consoling letter to show Hauch that he bore no ill will towards him, and he went to see him personally to comfort him. In his diary he records: 'I told him this meant nothing to me now and that no one would think that I was a heartless person, and that my first impression after reading the letters was: Thank God it wasn't me, I'm sure poor Hauch is very sad!' Hauch was moved and pressed Andersen to his breast.

On 6 December 1867 the town of Odense honoured its most famous son by awarding him the freedom of the town. This was also seen as a suitable occasion for Odense to arrange for the prophecy by now known all over the world, that one day Odense would be illuminated in Andersen's honour, to be fulfilled, and so, after all the speeches and celebrations and the formal banquet at the town hall there was a torchlight procession which Andersen watched from the town hall – a great climax to the day, but unfortunately marred by the fact that the guest of honour was then suffering so badly from toothache that he was hardly able to enjoy his moment of triumph. He describes the occasion in his memoirs:

How happy I was, and yet – up to heavenly bliss man dare not exalt himself; I had to feel that I was only a poor child of humanity bound by earthly frailty. I suffered from a dreadful toothache which was made intolerable by the heat and by my own excitement up there; all the same I read a fairy tale to my little friends. Then the deputation came from the various corporations of the town, who with torches and waving banners came through the streets to the Town Hall. I was now going to see the prophecy fulfilled which the old woman made when as a boy I left my birthplace: Odense was going to be illuminated in my honour. I stepped over to the open window; there was a blaze of light from the torches, the open square was completely filled with people, the sound of singing came up to me, I was overcome in my soul, and also physically overcome, was unable to enjoy this climax of happiness in my life. My toothache was intolerable; the icy air which rushed in at the window made it blaze up into a terrible pain, and so instead of fully enjoying the happiness of these minutes which would never recur, I looked at the printed song to see how many stanzas were left before I could slip away from the torture which the cold air sent through my teeth. It was the pitch of suffering; when the flames of the torches piled together in a bonfire sank down, then my pain also decreased.

But a moment of triumph it was all the same, and in his last entry for the year 1867 Andersen refers to that year as having been 'the most honourable and varied to me. I was twice in Paris . . . I have been made a Councillor of State, and in Odense I have experienced a homage which is among the rarest which this world can offer anyone.' The entry ends with these words: 'My Lord God, my only God, thank you for the bygone year, I wonder what the new one can, dare, will, and must bring. I pray to you, Lord, to give me strength to accept it, please do not let go of me!'

In the autumn of 1868 Andersen first made the acquaintance of a twenty-six-year-old Danish literary critic, Georg Brandes. On 27 October he wrote in his diary: 'Had a visit from Brandes, the critic, who heard me read 'The Wood Nymph' with apparent satisfaction; he thought it was moulded together solidly, perfect in details as well as in its entirety. Expressed himself warmly.' Andersen was pleased to find himself appreciated by a young scholar and critic noted for his extraordinary brilliance.

But more was to come. In February 1869 one of Georg Brandes' teachers, Professor Rasmus Nielsen, began a series of lectures about fairy tales and folk tales, and Andersen, who attended the first of these lectures, wrote in his diary: 'It was very interesting, but I listened with a certain amount of shyness since the entire lecture was concerned with me as a writer of fairy tales, though he did not mention my name a single time.' Andersen had a feeling as if he were dead – 'and was now witnessing one of the respected professors lecturing on me in the University of Copenhagen'.

In July 1869 the first instalment of a lengthy essay by Georg Brandes on 'H. C. Andersen as a Writer of Fairy Tales' appeared in a journal called *Illustreret Tidende*. It begins with the following paragraph:

You need courage to have a talent. You must dare trust your own inspiration, you must rely on the idea of your brain being sound, you must rely on the form which comes naturally to you, even if it be a new one, having a right to exist; you must have gained the courage to face the risk of being called affected or wild before you can trust your instinct and follow it wherever it may take you or direct you. When as a young journalist many years ago Armand Carrel was reprimanded by his editor who exclaimed, pointing to a paragraph in his article: 'One doesn't write like that,' he replied: 'I do not write the way *one* writes but the way *I* write,' and this is the general formula of talent. It justifies neither slovenly work nor affectation, but confidently it expresses the right of a talent – in cases where no accepted form and no given material are able to satisfy the special demands of its nature – to select new material, establish new forms, until it finds a site for construction of such a kind that without overstraining itself it can use all its strength and express itself freely and easily. Such a site for construction H. C. Andersen found in the fairy tale.

The essay itself was a brilliant and scholarly attempt to define Andersen's unique place as an artistic creator of fairy tales, written with great sympathy and understanding; it is usually considered the first piece of serious scholarship devoted to Andersen's literary art.

When Andersen read Brandes' essay he was delighted. But he was more than a little puzzled when the following day he received this letter from Georg Brandes:

Dear Sir,

Among all writers you are the one who has been most unjust to literary criticism, having lent your support to every vulgar prejudice against it, brought it into contempt and disrepute.

To me literary criticism is a branch of learning and a passion, and, of course, like other people I imagine that everybody else must be able to see the excellence of my profession.

In the Illustreret Tidende *for tomorrow I have begun a series of articles about your fairy tales. I shall ask you not to judge them until you have finished reading them, and – if you find that I have not revenged myself on you for your many bad words about literary criticism – to be prepared to have a little faith in this aesthetic branch of learning, and not to forget the kindness you have previously shown*

your sincere and cordial critic
G. BRANDES

Andersen replied with a letter which begins:

My dear Friend, – I received your letter late last night. . . . With the cleverness and intense sensitivity of youth you have looked right into the bottom of the heart of my little spiritual children, and while reading your essay I experienced a happiness which I wish God may repay to you.

After having thanked Brandes for his letter Andersen continued:

But regarding the beginning of it I must say that I assume you to be joking and not to be serious. No one has, in days gone by, been more harshly and ruthlessly treated by what is called criticism than me; it did its utmost to annihilate and destroy me; I was silent, and I suffered. . . . Now the young generation is compensating for the crimes committed by the old generation, and you, my dear friend, are among the young men whom I trust and appreciate. I have struck out against empty, evil, pernicious criticism for its barking, and I intend to go on doing so; old debts must be paid. But when you read Mit Livs Eventyr *you will see how warmheartedly and gratefully I acknowledge and preserve in my memory every kind appreciation, every encouragement. My heart is not devoid of gratitude.*

To this Georg Brandes replied:

What I wrote about your attitude to literary criticism was certainly seriously intended, though I do not like you less for it. You have considerably damaged the position of the critic – already difficult enough in itself – in this not highly developed country; you have contributed towards spreading the view that he is inspired by envy and that he wears a belt of snakes. I am not prepared to admit that in your tales you have made any distinction between bad and good criticism. To you the critic is the RAISONNEUR, *the barren and useless detractor. . . . A literary critic is someone* WHO KNOWS HOW TO READ, *and who teaches others the art of reading. . . . I admit that you have made a distinction between* DISAPPROVING *and* KIND *judgements; but I think you have drawn the line wrongly. There is only one line, the one which separates* TRUE *judgements from* FALSE *ones,* SERIOUS *ones from* MALICIOUS *ones, and this latter distinction is often confused by the public – especially if supported by a great authority – with the former.*

However, here is my hand! I am very far from feeling any kind of resentment against you, to whom I am indebted for a true spiritual enrichment. In my humble way I have wished to contribute towards a realization of what you really mean to Denmark. If I have succeeded in this I shall be pleased.

An indication of Andersen's increasing fame and popularity was the vast number of letters he received from admirers all over the world, especially from children. As an example, the following is an undated letter from an English girl:

The Cottage, Wimbledon Common, S.W. london.

dear mister Hans Andersen a littel girl wishes you meny Happy returns of the Day and she likes youer fairy tales very much

I remain youer
ETHEL H. WEGUELIN

The following letter was simply addressed on the envelope: 'Hans Andersen, Denmark':

Ulva Cottage, Hamilton, Scotland.
1st January 1869.

Dear Hans Andersen
I DO *like your fairy tales so much that I would like to go and see you but I cannot do that so I thought I would write to you when papa comes home from Africa I will ask him to take me to see you. My favourite stories in one book are 'The Goloshes of fortune', 'The Snow queen' and some others. My papa's name is* DR. LIVINGSTONE *I am sending you my card and papa's autograph. I will say good bye to you and a happy new year I am your affectionate little friend.*

ANNA MARY LIVINGSTONE

P.S. *please write to me soon my adress is on the first-page and please send me your card.*

On 14 January 1869 Andersen noted in his diary: 'Had a letter with a photograph of a little girl in Scotland, it was a letter from the daughter of Dr Livingstone, the famous traveller. She wrote to me in her childish way and wished me a happy New Year, sent her father's autograph.' A few days later Andersen wrote a reply to Anna Mary, and over the next five years Andersen and Livingstone's daughter exchanged altogether thirteen letters. Her last letter, dated 24 September 1874 describes Livingstone's funeral in Westminster Abbey.

Andersen's talent for communicating with children comes out best and most characteristically, of course, in relation to children he knew personally. The following extracts from letters exchanged in the summer of 1867 between Andersen and Mrs Melchior contain messages to and from a little boy too young to be able to read or write, William, the Melchiors' nephew, of whom Andersen was very fond:

Andersen to Mrs Melchior, 31 July *Please tell William that a little while ago a fly came to rest on my ear; it told me that it had seen William writing a letter to me, the fly wanted to know what he was writing, but he chased it away. Is that true?*
Mrs Melchior to Andersen, 5 August *Little William, who was here yesterday, found your story about the little fly amusing but said that he didn't chase it away at all.*
Andersen to Mrs Melchior, 7 August *Please tell my friend William from me that he did in fact chase away the fly, who was supposed to have brought him greetings; the fly assures me this is so and tells me it can swear that his hand was dirty; she quite clearly noticed a splotch on his hand when he chased her away. Who shall I believe, the fly or William? By the way, please tell him that the fly is a flying princess; her father is still alive and reigns over all human noses.*
Andersen to Mrs Melchior, 12 August *Please tell William that I have sent off a sparrow with greetings; it will fly past him in the garden three times, which means, 'Hello, William!'*

It is relevant to quote from Georg Brandes' essay on Andersen a paragraph which deals specifically with Andersen as a children's classic:

How fortunate Andersen is! What author has a public like him? . . . His book of fairy tales is the only book that we have spelt our way through and that we still read today. There are some among them whose letters even now seem to us larger, whose words appear to have more value than in other books, because we first made their acquaintance letter by letter and word by word. And what a delight it must have been for Andersen to see in his dreams this swarm of children's faces by their thousands about his lamp, this throng of blooming, rosy-cheeked little curly-pates, as in the clouds of a Catholic altar piece, flaxen-haired Danish boys, sturdy English babies, black-eyed Hindu girls – rich and poor, spelling, reading, listening, in every land, in every tongue, some healthy and merry, weary from sport, some sickly and pale after one of the countless ailments visited upon the children of this earth – and to see them eagerly stretch forth this jumble of white and brown little hands after each new leaf that is ready! Such devout believers, such an attentive, such a tireless public, as no other writer has ever enjoyed.

12 The old man

1869–75

APART from his birthday Andersen had always considered the day he first arrived in Copenhagen as the most important day in his life, and, 6 September 1869 being the fiftieth anniversary of this day, his friends arranged a banquet in his honour, attended by 244 people. There were speeches and songs, and this time no toothache prevented the guest of honour from enjoying the homage paid to him.

At the end of September Andersen went abroad again, staying away for almost six months. He wrote to Henriette Collin: 'I am beginning to look forward to this journey; having happily left fifty years behind I may not have many years left to live in and even less in which to travel, so while my mind is still fresh and I can truthfully claim to be young I wish to enjoy a few months abroad.'

Unfortunately, the journey was not the success he had hoped it would be. From Toulon he wrote to Henriette Collin: 'So far this journey has not given me much joy, and I almost think the result will be that I shall settle down more at home. One thing is certain: I shall never again embark on such a major journey alone; I have never felt so lonely and oppressed in my mind as on this occasion.'

He spent Christmas at a 'Pension Suisse' in Nice, and in a letter to Edvard Collin he described what happened after the Christmas tree had been lit: 'A gentleman came forward, saying, "We are gathered here from all parts of the world, and amongst us is a man who has given all of us many happy hours. Let us thank him in our own name, and in the name of our children," whereupon a little girl came over to me with a big laurel wreath, with fluttering silk ribbons in the Danish colours; they all applauded.' Spontaneously Edvard Collin replied: 'I went over to my study immediately to write to you with tears in my eyes, for your description moved me deeply, not because your human vanity had been flattered but because God's strange ways with you were revealed therein again and again. – And how good it is to feel humble – and I know you do that – confronted with such honours; it is good to begin the year in such a way.'

Feeling too lonely to continue on his own Andersen invited Jonas Collin to join him in Nice, but he was still not happy; he wrote to Mrs Melchior: 'The whole of this journey has filled me very little, I almost feel that all I have done is to have wasted time and money.' With Jonas he visited Paris for the last time and then travelled back via Belgium and Germany and was pleased to be in Denmark again in March 1870.

While he had been away three new tales had been published, 'Chicken-

Grethe's Family' (based on the strange story of Marie Grubbe about whom Jens Peter Jacobsen later wrote his famous novel), 'What the Thistle Found Out', and the humorous 'Something to Write About'.

In 1870 he wrote what was to be his last novel, *Lucky Peer*, an amusing and well-written variation of one of his favourite themes: the child born in poverty but destined by his artistic genius to win greatness and fame contrasted with the child born with a silver spoon in his mouth, who ends with nothing but his riches to boast of. Peer, whose parents live in the attic, was born on the same day as Felix, the son of the well-to-do merchant who occupies the main part of the house. In this book Andersen again uses the Aladdin theme, so well expressed in Adam Oehlenschläger's play, a romantic theme which he had already used in his first novel, *The Improvisatore*, and also in his first story, 'The Tinder Box'. It would be wrong, however, to identify the title character with Andersen, though it is obvious that much of what Peer experiences is very similar to what Andersen experienced in his early years. The descriptions of Peer's life as a youthful ballet dancer and singer are clearly drawn from Andersen's own experiences in the Royal Theatre, and the schoolmaster Herr Gabriel and his wife, at whose house Peer boards for a while, bear an obvious resemblance to Dr and Mrs Meisling,[22] though they are depicted less maliciously than were Mr and Mrs Knepus in *Only a Fiddler*. The social satire is also less forceful than in some of his earlier novels because of the generally cheerful and good-humoured character of *Lucky Peer*, though it is true that the following extract, in which the singing master chides Peer for allowing himself to be exploited in aristocratic circles, carries an obvious message, with a certain amount of self-criticism in it:

'How young you are, my friend,' he said, 'that you should be pleased to associate with those people. They may be all right in a way, but they look down upon us commoners. To some of them it is nothing more than a matter of vanity, an amusement, and to others it is a kind of certificate of culture that they invite into their circle artists and others who rank as the heroes of the moment; the way they are accepted in the *salons* is like flowers in a vase: they serve as decorations and are later discarded.'

'How bitterly and unreasonably you speak,' said Peer. 'You do not know these people, and do not wish to know them.'

'True!' said the singing master. 'I do not belong among them. And neither do you! And they all know and remember that. They applaud and regard you as they applaud and regard the race horse expected to win the race. They'll drop you the moment you are out of fashion. Don't you understand? You aren't sufficiently proud. You are vain, and you show it by seeking the company of these titled people.'

Peer, the musical genius, dies from a heart attack at his moment of triumph, after receiving the applause for the opera *Aladdin*, which he composed and in which he himself sang the title role. But it is not a tragic death – he was 'the fortunate among millions'.

On the day Andersen completed the draft manuscript the Franco-Prussian War broke out. The horrors of that war tormented Andersen's sensitive mind during the ensuing months. On 14 August he wrote to Mrs Henriques: 'I am completely overwhelmed by all the fighting and the shedding of blood. If, in your quiet, peaceful home, I hadn't been able to finish my latest story about Lucky Peer, well, then it would probably never have been finished.'

His diary reveals his feelings at the time:

15 October *The war in France overwhelms me, I am suffering from* idées fixes *which make me mad; the terrors of France are constantly showing themselves before me as if I had to live through them myself: I see myself pierced by bayonets, the city is burning, friends are dying, or I dream of being thrown into prison.*

17 October *My mind is overwhelmed as I keep on thinking of the terrors suffered by the French people, think of the mortal sufferings experienced by the German soldiers. O Lord! how can a royal heart bear such things? I remember how simply and cordially he* [Wilhelm I of Prussia] *and his queen once said to me: 'If I am really sad I read Andersen's tales and then feel myself comforted and refreshed'.*

31 October *Satan whispers evil things into my ear. The war is going to kill me.*

31 December *Blood-filled, horrible year 1870.*

One of the many persons to whom Andersen read some chapters from his latest novel was Henrik Ibsen, who was in Copenhagen in the autumn of 1870; according to Andersen Ibsen found what he heard 'very poetic'.

Andersen and Ibsen had in fact met eighteen years previously; this fact emerges from a letter Ibsen wrote in May 1852 from Copenhagen to the board of governors at the Bergen Theatre: 'I have made the acquaintance of H. C. Andersen; he strongly advises me to make an excursion from Dresden to Vienna in order to see the Burg Theatre; he may go there at the same time and will then be willing to help me.'[23] Nothing came of this plan, and in 1870 Andersen had presumably forgotten all about the young Norwegian he met in 1852 when the latter was completely unknown as a playwright. Now everybody in Denmark knew Ibsen's name, and when Andersen heard that Henrik Ibsen was among the guests at a dinner-party given by some of his friends, he was hurt and annoyed at not having been invited 'to see this Norwegian poet who does not like the Norwegians'. A fortnight later, however, while staying with the Melchior family Andersen wrote to Henriette Collin:

Ibsen, the poet, dined here at 'Rolighed' the other day and was very charming, unassuming and likable.[24] *I really did take a liking to him, but certainly not to* Peer Gynt, *which I have now read; it appears to me to be so crazy that it goes beyond what is permissible. What is the meaning of it all? Furthermore, the verses aren't good, and in several places there is something far too cynical about it, e.g., at the Mountain Troll's feast.*

Mrs Collin's advice was: 'Leave *Peer Gynt* alone and read *Brand* and *The Pretenders* instead.'

Andersen's international fame had not brought him much money, for there was then no international copyright agreement, and publishers were free to publish translations without paying any fees or royalties. Most publishers outside Denmark did not even bother to send him complimentary copies of the translations of his works. He only received fees for translations when he arranged to let a certain publisher have his manuscript well in advance of its publication in Danish; otherwise the risk of rival editions was too great. In Germany Andersen had such an arrangement with the Danish-born Leipzig publisher C. B. Lorck, from whom he received 300 Thaler for an edition in thirty-eight volumes of his *Gesammelte Werke* (1847-8), 27 Frederikdores for *Ahasuerus* and 200 rixdollars for *In Sweden*. In England his special contracts with Richard Bentley produced a sum total of £345.

In 1866 Andersen was approached by Mrs Margaret Gatty, the author of *Parables from Nature*, who admitted in her letter that her stories were 'instigated by the perusal of some of your wonderful fancies'.[25] On behalf of herself and her London publishers, Bell & Daldy, she asked permission for some of Andersen's later tales to appear in *Aunt Judy's Magazine*, which she edited; this they did, but the only financial reward Andersen received was a fee of £10 when the stories were included in a volume published by Bell & Daldy in 1869 under the title *Later Tales*.

In America Andersen had been a best-selling author for thirty years before he received a penny. He had no contact whatsoever with American publishers and very little with individual Americans; his main contacts in the States were Longfellow, who sent him greetings, poems and photographs, and Marcus Spring, an American businessman, socialist and philanthropist, who with his wife, Rebecca Spring, kept on trying to persuade Andersen to visit their country.

In the late 1860s, however, Andersen began to correspond with an American author of children's books called Horace Scudder, who edited the *Riverside Monthly Magazine for Young People*. In 1861 Scudder had written an article about Andersen's tales in the *National Quarterly Review*, and during the years 1862-8 he had written four letters to Andersen without receiving a reply. Being an ardent admirer of Andersen, he did not give up, and in the end he not only succeeded in establishing a regular correspondence with Andersen but also in securing him as a regular contributor to his *Riverside Magazine*, where ten of Andersen's later tales were published in 1868, 1869 and 1870, prior to their publication in Danish.

During the years 1871-3 Scudder arranged for the publication of *Lucky Peer* (in instalments) and three new tales in *Scribner's Monthly*, and in cooperation with the publishing firm of Hurd and Houghton he also arranged for an extended version of *Mit Livs Eventyr* to be published in New York; it was for this edition Andersen wrote an appendix covering the years 1855-67. Furthermore, Scudder was instrumental in producing a so-called 'Author's Edition' of Andersen's *Collected Writings* in ten volumes, published in New York 1870-1. In fact, over the years Scudder sent Andersen the largest amount of money he ever received from any foreign country, fees totalling £450.

In spite of the fact that they never met, the correspondence between Andersen and Scudder developed into much more than a mere exchange of business letters;[26] for Scudder regarded himself as a humble disciple of the great master. Andersen's letters were usually very cordial, though he was somewhat annoyed with Scudder for printing in the *Riverside Magazine* a letter from an anonymous Dane which gave a completely distorted view of Andersen and his relations with Danish children; it was stated, for instance, that in Copenhagen Andersen was always referred to as 'Little Hans' and that whenever he appeared in the streets he was immediately followed by a huge crowd of children who pulled his coat tails and asked him to tell them fairy tales, which 'Little Hans' was usually sufficiently kind and good-natured to do. In protest against all this nonsense (which anticipated the way Andersen was depicted in the Danny Kaye film) Andersen wrote:

This dear compatriot, whose intentions towards me are evidently the best, can hardly have known me or even have had a good look at me. It would never occur to a Danish child in the street to pull my coat tails and thus fall upon me. The little folk would give me a mild and friendly greeting, nod at me from a window, or the parents would take them out on the street to me and tell me something or other – how much the child thought of me, or rather of 'Andersen's Fairy Tales'. When I was a child my parents called me Hans Christian.[27] *Since that time I have never been called that except by Americans and Englishmen when they used it along with the name* ANDERSEN. *Even the appellation of 'Hans', which is repeated a number of times, sounds funny, and it will raise a smile with those who read it here at home, as it is not the custom and is never used here.*

In January 1871 Andersen wrote to Horace Scudder: 'In the spring I shall probably take a trip up to Norway.' But when spring came he was still in Denmark, and he wrote to Henriette Collin from South Zealand: 'God knows how far I shall travel this summer. If you see the stork in flight the first time it means that you will be going on a journey; yesterday I saw it, but it was not flying, it was strutting along – does that mean that I, too, shall only be strutting away a little?'

On 8 June Bjørnson wrote from Norway: 'My dear, wonderful Andersen, – You must come up here this year. I shall see to it that you will come to love us as we have loved you for a long time. Please do come!' And on 1 July Andersen wrote to Henriette Collin: 'I have had another letter from Bjørnson asking me to come up to Norway, but he does not want me to come until August, and then "the young trolls will keep their feet off the table and stand to attention to greet me".' (This is a reference to Andersen's satire on Norwegian uncouthness in his tale 'The Elf Hill'.)

Andersen did eventually go to Norway at the end of July and spent a happy month there. From Norway he wrote to Adolph Drewsen: 'Bjørnson is unsurpassed in being kind and considerate, he is completely filled with the thought that I should feel at home and happy, as indeed with gratitude I do.' On 18 August there was a banquet in Andersen's honour, with Jørgen Moe, the well-known collector of Norwegian folk tales, as the main speaker. In a letter to Horace Scudder after his return home Andersen described his visit to Norway in these words: 'Every day was like a celebration, everywhere I met cordial and sympathetic friends, and the landscape itself, with its mountains, forests, and foaming streams was picturesque and lovely. I long to go there again.'

Two days after his return from Norway Andersen drove out to 'Petershøi', and there, according to his diary, he met 'a young English lady who used to have my fairy tales under her pillow as a child and believed me to be an angel'. During the next fortnight there are various references in his diary to this young lady, whose name was Annie Wood.

Two years later Miss Wood recorded her impressions of Andersen in an article entitled 'A Few Weeks with Hans Andersen', printed in *Temple Bar*, February 1875. Having first described her own excitement at meeting Andersen she writes:

I stood alone on the step of the verandah, gazing at him, my heart so beating from excitement, I was glad no one, in their eagerness to speak to him, had time to notice me. At last, then, I was in the presence of the man whose writings had been the joy of my early life, dearer to me than aught else in the world! I stood still, scanning his features after a while, and wondering unconsciously why such a wonderful genius need be so very plain in appearance. Presently I felt, rather than saw, his look wander from his friends to my solitary figure on the step, and as he moved forward I heard him say in a frank simple way, 'Ah, here is a new face – she does not know me.'

Madame H[enriques] turned, and smiling to me as I intuitively drew near, answered gaily, 'This is our dear English guest, who has been so longing to see you, dear Andersen, that she has thought of nothing else for days, I know.' 'Good,' he replied, holding out his hand, and as I put mine into his with a thrill of delight, nay, almost of reverence, he said in his broken English:

'Ah, you would know me? you love me all the time? I will gif you one portrait of Andersen the poet. Have you read my stories?' he added, suddenly changing to German, which he speaks better than English.

'They were the sunshine of my childhood,' I answered warmly, all my shyness disappearing before the man's simple, childlike manner. 'I loved them better than any other, I slept with them under my pillow from the time I was six years old and could read.'

'Oh! that is good,' he replied, rubbing his hands, as is his wont when pleased. 'Come, you and I will talk a little; I will give you my portrait; we will be friends, dear friends – shall we? You are so glad to know me? Every one likes me, Andersen. But now I must talk to all these good people, and if you don't understand the Danish, I will translate for you, come.' He turned from me, and with the same simple manner in which he had thus spoken of himself to me, he took a seat, and asked the company if they would not like to hear all about his adventures since he had been away.

After having described how Andersen produced from his pocket a letter from Livingstone's little daughter and told her how much it warmed his heart 'when the children tell me they love me', Annie Wood gives a description of her general impressions of Andersen as she remembered him from those autumn weeks in 1871:

His is a simple nature, easy to read in his every-day relations with his fellows. I was charmed with him as a companion. Living in the same house with him, in the free unrestrained intercourse of the country, I spent many a delightful hour by his side, drinking in the wondrous fancies of his brain and listening to his quaint talk, which seemed to come from some far-away world into which he alone, of all I had ever met, had gained admittance. In the cool of the afternoon he liked to walk in the fields with any of our party who were so inclined. For the first quarter of an hour he would not talk much, but shamble along, poking his stick into every hole and corner, or touching with it every odd thing that lay in his path. Then something would attract his attention – a bit of glass, a faded flower, or a half-eaten insect – no matter what it was, he would stoop and pick it up, touch it tenderly, bend over it caressingly, and then, in a kind of low, half regretful tone, he would begin and tell the story of its life, its joys, its sorrows, and the sad destiny which brought it to the spot where he had found it, till I would stand listening in hushed awe, looking at the thing in his hand, and then at the dreamy face speaking so earnestly, and wonder if the man had really a soul and body belonging to this same earth that all the rest of us dwelt in so prosaically, or if he would presently vanish into the spirit realm from whence he gathered his fanciful ideas, and be no longer by our side.

He seemed to me to live in a world peculiarly his own, all his ideas, thoughts, and actions differing from those around him, and his fanciful interpretations of the everyday incidents of life often made me smile, and made me envy the dear old man the power he had of drawing pleasure to himself and giving amusement to others, from many of the small vexations which are apt to occur in the best regulated and most orderly households.

On 28 October 1871 Horace Scudder wrote to Andersen:

Now let me hope that your Norway trip has left you in such good spirits and with such zest for travelling that you will listen seriously to a proposition which your publishers here desire to make. So many people would be made happy by a visit from Andersen to America that we most earnestly hope you may be induced to come over NOW *and spend at least six or eight months. Your publishers will most gladly charge themselves with the expenses of your passage to and from America and will entertain you in their own homes in Cambridge and New York just as long as you will do them the honor to visit them: nor can we doubt that wherever you travelled in America you would find doors fly open at your approach.*

In his diary Andersen mentions having received this invitation and adds: 'I should like to accept but have a premonition of the torments of the sea voyage and fear not having the stamina to go through all this. I should prefer to die in Denmark.' To Scudder he wrote that his letter was not an easy one to answer: 'I have a great desire to visit America and my friends there, but [I have] a dread of the great ocean on which my very dear friend, Miss Wulff, lost her life on a burning ship, the *Austria*.' It was obvious, however, that he was tempted: 'I have an infinite desire and longing to see the great country to the West, and the many there who are so friendly and good to me.'

A few months later a friend of Andersen's who had just returned from America told him that he had met Longfellow, who had asked him to pass on the message that if he would read aloud three of his tales in America – something which might be rehearsed thoroughly in advance to overcome the language problems – then he would be certain of making a fortune; in fact, he would be able to make as much money as Dickens had done on his American tour.

Quite apart from Andersen's fear of suffering the same fate as Henriette Wulff if he attempted to cross the Atlantic, the two invitations came too late. Andersen was now too old to undertake such a journey.

In March 1872 a volume containing thirteen new tales by Andersen was published, eight of them having been previously published in America. Among the better known of these late tales are 'Luck May Lie in a Pin', 'The Most Incredible Thing', 'The Great Sea-Serpent' (about the telegraph cable connecting America with Europe) and the satirical 'The Gardener and the Squire'.

Shortly afterwards Andersen went abroad again, with William Bloch, a young Danish writer to whom Andersen had taken a liking. It was the usual continental tour, through Germany (where Andersen and his friend visited Ibsen in Dresden) to Prague and Vienna, but then extended with a visit to Venice.

In the summer of 1872 Andersen was back home, but not very happy, as can be seen from these extracts from his diary:

16 June *I feel morbidly depressed.*
23 June *I am wasting my time, have no ideas for literary activity. Depressed about it.*
30 June *Give me something to do, it is miserable to be so lazy.*
1 July *Not satisfied with myself. My youthful spirit is evaporating. Nothing to look forward to. I'm irritable, dissatisfied and lazy.*

It was not long, however, before he again found inspiration to write 'Auntie Toothache', 'The Flea and the Professor' and 'The Gate Key'.

On 22 July 1872, when Andersen was staying with the Melchiors at 'Rolighed', he had a visit from 'an Englishman from the British Museum, an admirer of mine, I gave him my photograph, and he stayed for supper'. The Englishman was the twenty-three-year-old Edmund Gosse, who later described his visit to the Melchiors' house in his book *Two Visits to Denmark* (1911):

Suddenly, however, as we were seated in the living-room, there appeared in the doorway a very tall, elderly gentleman, dressed in a complete suit of brown, and in a curly wig of the same shade of snuff-colour. I was almost painfully struck, at the first moment, by the grotesque ugliness of his face and hands, and by his enormously long and swinging arms; but the impression passed away as soon as he began to speak. His eyes, although they were small, had great sweetness and vivacity of expression, while gentleness and ingenuousness breathed from everything he said. He had been prepared to expect a young English visitor, and he immediately took my hand in his two big ones, patting and pressing it. Though my hands have no delicacy to boast of, yet in those of Hans Andersen they seemed like pebbles in a running brook, as E[lizabeth] B[arrett] B[rowning] might say.

The face of Hans Andersen was a peasant's face, and a long lifetime of sensibility and culture had not removed from it the stamp of the soil. But it was astonishing how quickly this first impression subsided, while a sense of his great inward distinction took its place. He had but to speak, almost but to smile, and the man of genius stood revealed. I experienced the feeling which I have been told that many children felt in his company. All sense of shyness and reserve fell away, and I was painfully and eagerly, but with almost unprecedented success, endeavouring to express my feelings in Danish.

After taking Gosse over the house and showing him the view of the Sound from his balcony, Andersen read him a story he had just completed, 'The Cripple'. This is how Gosse describes it:

He read in a low voice, which presently sank almost to a hoarse whisper; he read slowly, out of mercy to my imperfect apprehension, and as he read he sat beside me, with his amazingly long and bony hand – a great brown hand, almost like that of a man of the woods – grasping my shoulder. As he read, the colour of everything, the twinkling sails, the sea, the opposing Swedish coast, the burnished sky above, kindled with sunset. It seemed as if Nature herself was flushing with ecstasy at the sound of Andersen's voice.

Gosse was fortunate in having made Andersen's acquaintance on a day when he was in a relatively happy mood, for his diary for the ensuing months shows that he was often very depressed:

12 September *In a dark and unhappy mood, thinking of death. . . . Dr Bloch told me about the lunatic asylum in Aarhus and the mad people there, about the first symptoms of madness; I had a feeling of fear that he might see the same symptons in me.*
28 September *Melancholy mood,* tedium vitae *and a strange fear of becoming insane.*
6 October *Nervous, ill-tempered and – godless; consequently I am in despair.*

In November 1872 Andersen's last four tales were published, 'Old Johanna's Tale' (based on childhood reminiscences), 'The Gate Key', 'The Cripple' and 'Auntie Toothache'.

About the same time he was taken seriously ill, and the symptoms of his illness make it almost certain that this was the beginning of the cancer which eventually killed him. He was bed-ridden for months and soon became a very weak and frail old man. 'I shall hardly survive this winter, I shall probably have a setback and die,' he wrote in his diary on 9 February 1873. During his illness he was greatly encouraged by the fact that both the king and the crown prince as well as other members of the royal family often came to visit him.

In spite of his weakness he insisted on going abroad again in the spring of 1873, his companion this time being Nikolaj Bøgh, a young Danish writer; for two and a half months they travelled in Germany and Switzerland. This was to be Andersen's last journey abroad.

From Switzerland he wrote to Edvard Collin on 22 May:

I have many friends, indeed some who are so vividly kind and sympathetic to me as if I belonged among their close relatives, for instance the Melchiors; but you, my dear friend, are the earliest of my friends, right back from the time you helped me with my Latin composition, when you seemed to me to be a little too much of a mentor, until these last few years when everything was resolved. . . . On every occasion your many wonderful qualities stand out, and I am not the only one to see you in this light. You are infinitely dear to me, and I shall pray to God for you to survive me, for I cannot think of losing you. What I am writing here flows from my heart, you will understand me. It is wonderful to have friends in this world, friends such as I have.

The trivial matter of a totally inaccurate article about him, published in the *Chicago Times*, overshadowed part of Andersen's stay in Switzerland: 'It put me into the darkest possible mood, I slept badly, sweated and felt a feverish fear of an accident.' On the Lake of Lucerne he 'had a strange fear coming over me, wasn't interested in living any more, was afraid of dying, thought that the next tremor of the soul would make me insane'.

Back in Denmark he was again often very unhappy. On 3 September he wrote to Henriette Collin:

I am more depressed than any one imagines, I have spent endlessly long days recently, I am not looking forward to anything, have no future any more, the days are washing over me, and I am really only waiting for the curtain to fall. How very ungrateful, you will say. Well, I know everything there is to say.

On 1 November he wrote in his diary:

Am extremely desolate and suffering, wrote a letter about it to Edvard Collin. I shall never be well again, and death is slow in coming. I want to die, and at the same time I fear it.

The letter to Edvard Collin included the following paragraph:

Now it is thirteen months since I was taken ill; I know they say I'm improving, but I don't believe it to be true. It is becoming obvious to me that I shall not get well, but only God knows how long I shall have to stick it out. I feel terribly lonely, and my thoughts are becoming more and more morbid. Please come and see me soon. You are one of the few friends who can encourage me whether I speak sense or not.

Edvard Collin responded immediately, for later the same day Andersen continued his diary:

At dusk, immediately after supper, Edvard Collin came to see me. I told him about all the strange ideas which tormented me, and he immediately accepted this and told me of corresponding examples in himself, how – just like me – he would get out of bed at night to attend to fire and light though he knew perfectly well that he had put out everything before going to bed. I was so encouraged by his sympathy and his whole manner of speaking that my mind was completely at ease and I felt as if reborn.

On 15 December he wrote to Henriette Collin:

I see no progress, no future; if this is the way old age is coming then it is terrible.

His health improved slightly at the beginning of 1874, though he was still weak and suffered occasional pains; his changing mood could still be influenced by the most trivial matters, and he would easily burst into tears. Being no longer able to do any kind of creative writing he found a certain amount of comfort in devoting himself to decorating a large screen with a remarkable collage of pictures cut out from illustrated magazines, photographs, etc.; for days he could be completely absorbed in this work.

On 2 April 1874, his sixty-ninth birthday, Andersen wrote in his diary:

Today happens to be Thursday in Easter week as it was on the day of the Battle of Copenhagen [2 April 1802]. I was in a very serious mood on this morning of my sixty-ninth birthday and did not feel well at all. When I went to the window I saw the ship outside with its flags hanging out, but the Danish flag was at half mast; this was a symbol of death, not of happiness; it depressed me and I took it as a bad omen though I fought against this superstition.

The king's birthday present was to award Andersen the title of *Konferensraad*. The Melchiors gave a dinner-party for him, and his entry for the day ends: 'I was in a quiet, happy mood all evening.'

A few weeks later he noted:

Received a telegram from the Grand Duke of Weimar; he wanted to know about the state of my health. This moved me deeply: we had not corresponded since the last German war against Denmark. I have often been sad that all connections between us had been severed, and I could not make up my mind whether I oughtn't to write to him sometime. Now he is so sympathetic and kind that he is the one to make the first approach. I wrote immediately a telegram and also a letter, which I asked Mr Collin to render into better German.

Andersen, who had not seen his former friend the grand duke since 1857, wrote in his letter: 'During the many great, now almost historical, events I did not write; year followed upon year, and I did not know if I dared again renew a correspondence which at one time made me very happy. Now I feel that I dare and that I can.'

In the spring of 1874 Edmund Gosse came to Denmark on a second visit, anxious to meet Andersen again. Since 1872 he had exchanged letters with Andersen and had been very eager to translate the latest tales and have them published in Britain as a separate volume, but in a letter dated 18 March 1873 he explained why his efforts had been in vain:

No one here in London will risk the publication of a translation of your last stories. Perhaps this will surprise you as much as it did me, but the reason of it lies in the extreme popularity of your works amongst us. Unless a very cheap and common edition were brought out, – and this would not be worth your while or mine, – the publishers fear that the translation would at once be pirated by other publishing-houses, and they themselves would lose their profits. Added to this is the difficulty of an already-existing translation in America. You know there is no copyright-treaty between England and Denmark, or between England and America, so your works are thereby open to a double danger.

On 20 January 1874 Andersen had written to Gosse:

My literary activities have been at rest for a long time. I was taken ill one year and four months ago, and I am still suffering; my health is improving though very slowly, my liver has been badly affected, I am still short of breath and have pains in my legs; it is only with great difficulty that I am able to climb stairs; I cannot as before visit my friends, they must come to me, but in this they are very faithful. My doctor thinks that in the spring I may recover in health and strength, and then I want to travel. I very much long to visit England and my friends there, but I am afraid this will be too exhausting for me; I think I must go to the mountains in the south.

Shortly after his arrival Gosse went to visit Andersen in his apartment in Nyhavn. He had written in advance to ask if Andersen could see him and had received a little piece of paper, tremulously scribbled over, to say that he was welcome. When he arrived, however, Andersen's landlady at first refused to admit him: '"Impossible!" she said, "the Konferenceraad (Privy Councillor, for he was thus addressed) could see no one. He was very tired, very weak".' Gosse's account then continues:

Perceiving my great disappointment and anxiety, and learning that Andersen had summoned me himself, she finally withdrew to see her master, and returned, visibly displeased, to announce that the Konferenceraad insisted upon my coming in, but, as she privately added, 'You must not stay more than two minutes; he is very ill.' As I entered the bright, pretty sitting-room, Hans Christian Andersen was coming in from an opposite door. He leaned against a chair, and could not proceed. I was infinitely shocked to see how extremely he had changed since I had found him so blithe and communicative, only two years before. He was wearing a close-fitting, snuff-coloured coat, down to his heels, such a burnt-sienna coat as I remember to have seen Lord Beaconsfield wear as he went walking slowly up Whitehall, on Mr Corry's arm, in the later 'sixties. This garment, besides being very old-fashioned, accentuated the extreme thinness of Andersen's tall figure, which was wasted, as people say, to a shadow. He was so afflicted by asthma that he could not utter a word, and between sorrow, embarrassment and helplessness, I wished myself miles away.

The door at which he had entered remained open, and I supposed it to lead to his bedroom. I implored him to return to it, and allow me to come at a more favourable moment. But, while he leaned heavily on my wrist, and stumbled back, I discovered that it was not a bedroom, but a library, in which he was easily persuaded to sink upon a very comfortable sofa. He now found his voice, and would by no means suffer me to go. I must take a chair at his side, and he held my hand affectionately in his. He explained, with great sweetness, that this was not the beginning, but the end of a malady. He had suffered ever since the New Year from a most painful illness, as indeed I knew; but, although he was very weak, he declared that he was almost well. I had, till now, hardly perceived a third person in the room, a good-looking young fellow, to whom Andersen now presented me. 'This is Nikolaj Bøgh. You read so much Danish, that I daresay you know his poems. He is like a son to me; God bless him!' He went on to say that Bøgh had never left him since his last severest attack of illness, and that he hoped he never would. 'I should have died without him!' and still holding me by one hand, he affectionately pressed that of his young friend with the other.

A few days later Andersen wrote inviting Gosse to call on him again, and this is how Gosse describes his third and final visit to Andersen:

Georg Brandes was my companion to the door of the house in Nyhavn, but he left me there, not because he was not welcome to the aged writer, but because we both believed that the excitement of a double visit might be harmful to Andersen. The latter had, indeed, suffered from another relapse, but I found him in his sitting-room dressed to go out and, even to my great surprise, posed before the camera of a photographer. I waited in the background until this performance was concluded; it had tired him very much, and I only stopped a few minutes longer. He was affectionate and pathetic; he spoke of the great illustrated edition of his *Fairy Tales* which was then in preparation for the following Christmas, and promised to send me one of the earliest copies – 'if I live till then, ah! dear, – if only I live till then!' His servants were bustling around us, in the midst of packing up for a visit he was paying to Count Danneskjold-Samsøe; it was thought that the air of the city was bad for him, and he was being hurried away to the country. He was sad, but not agitated; he said farewell with much tenderness; his last words were 'Remember me in your dear and distant country, for you may never see me again!'

Two days after Gosse's visit Andersen left Copenhagen, to go not to Count Danneskjold-Samsøe as Gosse thought, but to Count Holstein of Holsteinborg in South Zealand, where he stayed for nearly a month. After that he spent a fortnight with the Melchiors at 'Rolighed', and then went to the manor of Bregentved as the guest of Count and Countess Moltke.

From Bregentved he wrote to Mrs Melchior:

No fairy tales occur to me any more. It is as if I had filled out the entire circle with fairy-tale radii close to one another. If I walk in the garden among the roses – well, what stories they and the snails have told me! If I see the broad leaf of the water-lily, then Thumbelina has already ended her journey on it. If I listen to the wind, then it has told me the story about Valdemar Daae and has nothing better to tell me. In the wood, underneath the old oak trees, I am reminded that the Old Oak Tree has told me its last dream a long time ago. Thus I do not get any new, fresh impulses, and that is sad.

While staying at Bregentved Andersen received a letter from a little girl in America. Enclosed with the letter was a dollar bill and a clipping from an American paper with an invitation to the children of America to pay off their debt to Andersen and secure for the old man a comfortable old age. According to the article Andersen was supposed to have said that he had never received a single dollar from America. Commenting on this in his diary Andersen wrote: 'this annoyed me, since in recent years I have regularly received small sums of money through Horace Scudder. It made me nervous, I could not fall asleep and had a bad night.'

This letter was the beginning of a saga, which caused Andersen a great deal of worry and concern. He had never made any statement of the kind attributed to him, though strangely enough, in a moment of annoyance, he had written in his private diary on 16 October 1873: 'Again a letter of admiration from America came in the post. It would be better if they made a collection over there and sent me a sum of money in my meagre old age.' But now that his ill-considered wish was beginning to come true it made him very unhappy, and he immediately wrote to his friend Mr Bille, the editor of *Dagbladet*, to ask his advice on how to stop this collection. He was reluctant to keep the dollar bill, and equally reluctant to return it to the well-meaning child who had sent it, unhappy to be thought of and represented as an old pauper in need of charity, and worried in case Horace Scudder and his other American friends might believe that he had pretended never to have received any money from America. Bille advised him to wait and see what happened to the American collection, known as 'The Children's Debt'. 'His counsel quieted me somewhat, but I am still not, as I should be, in good humour,' wrote Andersen.

While Andersen was staying at 'Rolighed', Moritz Melchior told him that the American minister had arrived and had some money for him from America. Andersen's reaction can be seen from his diary:

I shuddered. The sum he brought was 200 Danish rixdollars from children in Washington. I found the sum small, but kept it for the time being, and asked him in the meantime to write to the senders and tell them that I was not poor, that I received 1000 rixdollars annually from the state, and that lately I had been receiving a modest sum half-yearly from my publisher in New York. I became nervously wrought up and slept poorly.

A fortnight later he received a clipping from a New York paper which told of two little girls who had given their 'tribute' to 'the old story-teller Hans Christian Andersen', and on the following day more clippings arrived, which made Andersen fly into a rage; but when the articles had been translated to him he was moved at realizing the feelings behind the gift.

In the end he decided to send a message to his readers in America, by writing a letter to the editor of the *Philadelphia Evening News*, from whom he had received some of the contributions. After stating that he had been informed that a popular subscription had been started in several places in the States he went on:

The thought that has motivated this expression touches me deeply. I have always felt it my pleasure and good fortune that my stories have found readers so far from my homeland and from the narrow confines of its language, and that they have been spread over the whole world. And of all that Providence has done for me, I have been grateful for nothing more than this, that it has permitted me to influence such countless numbers of young souls, and to bring something noble and good, as I hope, to so many child-like hearts. This moves me deeply, and I value sincerely the expression of devotion and gratitude towards me. I value it all the more, as it comes to me after a long siege of illness and under *presumed* difficult economic conditions.

He then went on to 'clear up a possible misunderstanding'. He was still weak and would soon be seventy; 'but I am not in need'. Denmark would not 'permit its creative writers to suffer want'. From the Danish government he received annually 'an honourable recompense', and also 'an income from my work as an author'. Though it was true that he had received practically 'no remuneration for the numerous translations of my works into foreign languages', he did occasionally receive some fees – 'as for example from the so-called "Author's Edition" in America'. He therefore asked his friends in

America not to think of him as a poor old abandoned author who is worrying about his daily bread and is obliged to neglect his ailing body'. He was moved that in America so many children should be 'breaking their little banks open to share what they have saved with their old author, who they think is in dire need', but he must insist 'that I cannot accept any gift that is sent me by an individual'. If this happened, 'instead of a feeling of pride and gratitude, I would be exposed to humiliation'.[28]

Andersen's calm and dignified letter did not put an end to his worry over the American 'Children's Debt'. In October he was told that the gift of a carriage was being considered, and later a fellow-countryman living in America came and told him that he had suggested that the money might be spent on erecting a statue of Andersen in a public park somewhere in America. But Andersen was furious with this man for making suggestions without first consulting him.

The end of the story was something of an anti-climax: Andersen received a sum of 200 dollars and a sumptuous work in two volumes entitled *Picturesque America*.

Unfortunately, a Danish nationwide attempt to honour Andersen also brought him worry and unhappiness.

Towards the end of 1874 he was told that a special committee had planned to collect money from all over the country towards erecting a statue in 'Kongens Have', Copenhagen's central park, on his seventieth birthday. Mrs Melchior gave him a copy of the appeal, and he was very pleased with the wording of it. 'I sat for a long time until late in the evening thinking of the wonderful way in which God had guided and helped me along in this world.'

The first disappointment came when his old friend August Bournonville criticized the whole idea; Andersen had many friends, Bournonville said, but also many enemies, and the latter might well be outspoken in their criticism of erecting a statue to a person who was still alive. 'I think there is a lot of truth in what he said; it began to make an unpleasant impression on me, and my good spirits of this morning sank to zero.' Mrs Melchior's reaction was that Bournonville must be either mad or envious.

Another difficulty arose in February 1875 when Andersen was approached by another committee with a request for his permission for them to launch an appeal towards a 'Hans Christian Andersen Orphanage', which he gladly did. But then Melchior and Bille were displeased and told him that he ought not to have agreed before the target towards the statue had been reached. 'This depressed me,' Andersen wrote; 'I thought it might give the impression that I would rather see my statue than an orphanage. I sat at home all evening in a sad mood.'

Worse was to come. The money for the statue was collected (he was informed of it on his seventieth birthday), and among others the sculptor August Saabye was asked to submit a sketch. When Andersen saw the sketch he was furious; he wrote in his diary on 29 May: 'Visit by Saabye, whose sketch for my statue I cannot stand, for it reminds me of old Socrates and young Alcibiades. I couldn't tell him that but refused to pose or speak to him altogether today. I was more and more enraged.' What Andersen specifically objected to was that Saabye's idea was to represent Andersen reading aloud to a child, and Andersen objected to what he called 'the tall boy who is lying right up against my crutch'. He wrote to Jonas Collin:

Saabye came to see me again last night. My blood was boiling, and I spoke clearly and unambiguously, saying that none of the sculptors knew me, that nothing in their attempts indicated that they had seen or realized the characteristic thing about me that I could never read aloud if anyone was sitting behind me or leaning up towards me, and even less so if I had children sitting on my lap or on my back, or young Copenhagen boys lying leaning up against me, and that it was only a manner of speaking when I was referred to as 'the children's writer', my aim being to be a writer for all ages, and so children could not represent me; naïvety was only part of the fairy tale, humour on the other hand was its salt, and my written language was based on the folk language, that was my Danishness.

In the final version of Saabye's statue in 'Kongens Have' there are no children; Andersen is sitting with a book in his hand, reading aloud to an invisible audience.

One of the few pleasures left for Andersen in his old age was to be invited time and again to meet members of the royal family. On one occasion after he had visited the queen mother at Sorgenfri Castle he went on to Bernstorff Castle, where he was received by the king and the entire royal family. 'Princess Alexandra looked young and happy, she had brought with her two sons and three daughters, good-looking children, they played with the clever little Prince Christian, and they all knew "the old story-teller"', he wrote to Henriette Collin afterwards.

Andersen's seventieth birthday, 2 April 1875, was celebrated not only nationally but also internationally.

The day before his birthday the royal carriage was sent to fetch him to Amalienborg Castle where the king bestowed upon him yet another decoration and spoke of the happiness he had brought to all the countries of the world.

The birthday itself, to which Andersen had looked forward with a certain trepidation, began with a reception and ended with an early dinner-party at the Melchiors' house, followed by a visit to the Royal Theatre, where two of Andersen's plays were being performed. 'What a wonderful, magnificent day,' Andersen commented in his diary; 'and yet, how pitiable is my frail body in carrying all these blessings from God. I could not sleep when I went to bed, was overwhelmed with thoughts and gratitude.'

Among the many birthday presents was a special polyglot volume, for which the learned philologist Vilhelm Thomsen had been responsible, *The Story of a Mother. In fifteen languages.*

None of the tributes pleased Andersen more than a leading article in the London *Daily News*, in which he was referred to as 'the poet, who perhaps touches a wider circle of admirers than any other living man of letters'.

Andersen, the article went on, 'is dear to the children of every European country, and has established his fame in the hearts of future generations'. The leader-writer went on to say that after the world-wide importance of the *Eddas* and the sagas other European countries had taken the lead in the world of literature, and then continued:

Hence a Danish poet like *Andersen* finds it no easy matter to pass the wall of ice which severs the genius of the North from that of England and France, as *Brynhild* was guarded from her lovers by the fence of fire. Only the fame of *Ibsen* is vaguely rumoured, only *Thorvaldsen* is widely known in plastic art. But *Hans Andersen*, the son of the cobbler in Odense, is a household word, and the creations of his fancy have passed into the great Pantheon where *Shakespeare*'s people, and *Homer*'s and *Scott*'s, enjoy a life less perishable than that of mortal men. . . .

It has been given to *Hans Andersen* to fashion beings, it may almost be said, of a new kind, to breathe life into the toys of childhood, and the forms of antique super-stition. The tin soldier, the ugly duckling, the mermaid, the little match girl, are no less real and living in their way than *Othello*, or *Mr. Pickwick*, or *Helen of Troy*. It seems a very humble field in which to work, this of nursery legend and childish fancy. Yet the Danish poet alone, of all who have laboured in it, has succeeded in recovering, and reproducing, the kind of imagination which constructed the old fairy tales.

In his diary of 10 April Andersen mentions this eulogy with joy and pride; he was probably particularly happy to read one of the concluding sentences: 'It is only a writer who can write for men that is fit to write for children.'

Andersen only lived another four months after his seventieth birthday; here are some characteristic extracts from his diaries for the next two months:

16 April *Letter from a man in Boston, I can't understand it and am therefore nervous. The Melchiors, with whom I dined, explained that he wished to obtain information concerning which of the various English and American translations was most successful. How am I to know?*

19 April *Dined alone with the Collins; Jonas saw me home. Today has been quite like summer, and I have felt much better.*

22 April *A fine article about me in yesterday's* Dagbladet *about the way in which almost all the Paris newspapers had spoken of my seventieth birthday with great sympathy.*

24 April *Received the* London Illustrated News *with my portrait in it.* Über Land und Meer *has a bad portrait of me; a kind article, but lies upon lies about me and my development.*

26 April *Dined at the Collins'. Spoke much to Louise Drewsen about the old days and the oppression I suffered in the Collin house, especially with old Collin. – A letter from the Duke of Weimar; I make out from it that a decoration from him is on its way to me.*

2 May *The Weimar Order of the Commander is waiting for me at the Customs House.*

4 May *A constant stream of letters asking for 'autographs'; they come from America, Germany and England.*

7 May *Letter to the Grand Duke of Weimar.*

8 May *Letters from all over about autographs. It is a mania; I shall not reply.*
15 May *It is terrible to be surrounded by fools. The things I must suffer!*

After a detailed description of a very bad day on 22 May, when he was very ill and helpless, Andersen concluded his entry: 'Now Jonas came, helped me to put on warm, dry clothes; I lay back in bed very feeble. Jonas spent the night here, staying in the front room.'

On 12 June Andersen was moved out to 'Rolighed', where the Melchiors had hired a special man-servant to look after him. Two days after his arrival he wrote in his diary: 'They must indeed be tired of me out here, I am too much of a nuisance. – Today my spirits are very low. O Lord! Lord! What is going to happen to me, pitiable sick person that I am!'

June 19 was the last day on which Andersen was able to write in his diary himself; during the next few weeks he dictated all his entries to various members of the Melchior family. Towards the end of July his mind was clearly disturbed at times, and after 27 July he was not even able to dictate; from then on Mrs Melchior continued the diary on her own.

On 2 August she wrote: 'A few days ago he asked me if I would promise to cut open an artery when he died. . . . Jokingly I told him that he could do as he had done previously, viz. write the words "I am not really dead" and put it in front of him on the table. – A slight smile passed over his sunken features. All day he has been repeating, "I do not understand anything. Am I better today? How strange it all is!"'

Mrs Melchior's last entry, dated 4 August 1875, ends with the words: 'Now the light has been extinguished. What a happy death! At 11.05 our dear friend breathed his last sigh.'

13 What was he like?

HAVING read some of Andersen's posthumously published letters Georg Brandes described him in a letter to Bjørnson as 'a mind completely and entirely filled by himself and without a single spiritual interest'. However harsh these words may seem they are not entirely unjustified. Throughout his life the one thing which interested Hans Christian Andersen most was: Hans Christian Andersen. All his life he had a desperate craving for affection and praise, and his famous vanity was to a large extent a childlike inability to conceal his pleasure at winning recognition and fame. His diaries and letters abound with stories of strangers abroad who, when learning that he was a Dane, asked him whether he knew Hans Christian Andersen, and each time he was equally delighted to report their reaction when he revealed his identity. Edvard Collin describes how one day Andersen, seeing a man he knew on the other side of a street in Copenhagen, crossed over and said, 'Now I'm being read in Spain, well, good-bye!'

Much of Andersen's best fiction is also basically about himself, not only the novels but also the fairy tales and stories. He is the soldier in 'The Tinder Box'; he is the sensitive princess who can feel one pea through twenty mattresses and twenty featherbeds; he is the student in 'Little Ida's Flowers'; he is the little mermaid, the outsider who came from the depths and was never really accepted in the new world into which he moved; he is the little boy who could see that the emperor had nothing on; he is the ugly duckling transformed into a beautiful swan; he is the fir tree incapable of enjoying the moment and always hoping for something better to come; he is the poet in 'The Naughty Boy'; he is the gardener in 'The Gardener and the Squire', etc., etc. Andersen has, as Hans Brix once said, written more self-portraits than Rembrandt ever painted. His critics called it being obsessed with himself; he called it being subjective, and wrote in his diary: 'It can never be wrong for a *Digter* to be subjective, for that in itself is a sign of the amount of poetry he has inside himself.' His quarrel with some of his early Danish critics, especially Molbech, was that they wanted him to write the way *they* wrote; he wrote in his diary on 27 March 1834: 'Let me follow my own nature. Why must I trot according to fashion? If my gait is slouching, well, then it is the natural way for me to walk. If he [Molbech] doesn't find nuts on my tree but apples, then it doesn't necessarily mean that my tree is no good.'

Throughout his life Andersen was an outsider, and one of the keys to the understanding of his nature is his loneliness. The restless old bachelor, who never managed to have a home of his own, lived in hotel rooms, in other people's guest rooms or, at best, in a couple of furnished rooms in Copenhagen. And there is plenty of evidence that he would have liked to have had a home of his own; on Christmas Day 1865 he wrote to Martin R. Henriques from one of the Danish manors where he was then staying: 'It is a happy and wonderful thing to have a home as you do. One understands that best when one has no home oneself and is a lonely migratory bird who must be grateful to find shelter under a hospitable roof.'

For many years Jonas Collin's house was Andersen's 'Home of Homes', though his feelings towards the Collin family were extremely mixed, and much of his vanity is linked with a never satisfied desire to be properly appreciated by them and to feel that they were grateful for the reflection cast by his glory on 'the House of Collin'; but, as Edvard Collin says in his book, 'The House of Collin' did not feel things that way. He admits that 'there was an element of self-sufficiency in our family life; in that little world of ours we stuck to the tone which expressed the character of the house'.

It was in many ways a very closed world. The Collins had their own special vocabulary and their own special sayings which they used amongst themselves, though they were not always understood, or for that matter intended to be understood, by the outside world. They cultivated a kind of linguistic free-masonry, and some Collin phrases found their way into Andersen's prose. He himself contributed to their family argot in several ways. One day he came rushing in to tell the Collins that an important battle had raged at Magenta; shortly afterwards somebody else brought the same information whereupon Andersen hurriedly interrupted him, saying: 'It's I who know that!' From then on the words 'It's I who know that!' became a stock phrase in the Collin family. They also said '. . . n'est pas?', this being a famous example of Andersen's French.

In his book on Andersen and the Collin family Edvard Collin writes that at first Andersen was 'happy among us, happy to see himself treated like a son of the house, but not without sadness for not being one', and he adds that Andersen's sadness was owing to the fact 'that he did not find his works sufficiently appreciated *by us*; and that sadness was bound to increase as he was gradually being recognized by others'. According to Edvard Collin Andersen's basic sentiment was spleen. 'Under this term I include all the other characteristics that people have found in him: vanity, impatience, suspicious-ness, irritability, etc.', he adds and quotes a note he found among Andersen's papers, dating from about 1848: 'I have heard it said about the English that they suffer from spleen; about this disease I only know that it is a peculiarity and at the same time a *tristesse* which often makes them take their own lives; I myself suffer from something similar.'

When Edvard Collin had concluded his main account of Andersen he invited his niece, Jonna Stampe, *née* Drewsen, to add her comments, for he knew her to be the member of the family who had been particularly biased in favour of Andersen. She did not conceal her criticism of the Collins' attitude to Andersen and even wrote: 'Andersen's earliest contemporaries were too narrow-minded to appreciate him properly.' This criticism was later echoed by her daughter, Rigmor Stampe, who wrote: 'However kind they were to him, these nice people, he was all the same a stranger among them, not flesh of their flesh, nor spirit of their spirit.'

In November 1839 Andersen wrote to Louise Collin:

I have already for a long time had to regard Edvard as a stranger; that is what he is – and remains! I have always looked up to your father as to someone infallible – he has pushed me away harshly – if only I could see my own errors then I would change my ways, but I can't! And yet I suppose he is right when judging the way a stern god may judge. I feel my own impotence, feel how useless I am in this world, how empty all my efforts are – and yet one dare not die.

From Oldenburg he wrote to Jonna Drewsen in September 1844:

Now I shall soon be back at Amaliegaden [where the Collins lived] . . . if only you would all be pleased with me, if only I should find in your circle tolerably reasonable treatment – but I suppose it'll be all right, goodness knows I have no great expectations. If only they would be human, but I know the way things are: in Europe I am a Digter, at home quite a decent person with talent of a sort, but terribly vain, and there I can only be placed in the seventh line AFTER the great ones – well, that's the way it is, and then one has got to put up with it! I shall be held up to ridicule a little when I get home, just so that I can feel that I'M ONE OF THEM and that they are quite something!

The love/hate relationship between Andersen and Edvard Collin has been dealt with at great length in the previous chapters of this book, and it will suffice here to add a few more quotations to illustrate the complexity of their friendship. In his book Edvard Collin makes the comment that he was never 'mawkish' in his relationship with Andersen; but what Andersen really hated most of all was being lectured to by Edvard and receiving a cold business-like letter in answer to a warm, friendly letter. When, as happened occasionally, Edvard sent him a few kind words Andersen's heart would melt immediately. From Dresden he wrote to Henriette Collin in October 1860:

As far as your husband is concerned, all his letters on this journey have been so wonderful, so cordial, written just as a friend writing to a friend, so that I am truly grateful to him for it. Even though once upon a time, when I was young, he wrote some letters to me the tone and expression of which cut deep wounds into my then slightly too soft mind, he has now more than compensated for it – please embrace him on my behalf! That is one of the advantages of growing old that one begins to understand and appreciate one's faithful friends from the early days.

Predictably, the pendulum would swing back again, as the following extracts from Andersen's diaries show:

7 April 1864 Edvard somewhat narrow-mindedly represents the time of Frederik VI, he is a bureaucrat; towards me he is kinder, more polite than in the old days, but there are still relics of old judgements in him.
27 December 1864 Had a letter from Edvard, dry, business-like, it annoys me as do almost all his bureaucratic, imperative letters.

30 November 1865 *Dined at E. Collin's. At long last his putting himself above me is
beginning to disappear; he almost seems to accept me as an independent person.*
7 January 1866 *Slept badly, on an under-mattress which was too short, and was
thinking all the time of the hotel in which the Collins want me to live. I have a slavishly
ingrown feeling of having to obey the Collin family – it really is too bad!*

In August 1867 he wrote in his diary: 'Still felt the old dependency on the
Collins, wondered what they would say.' Five months later relations had
improved once again, for in January 1868 he wrote: 'I have the feeling that
Edvard has been moving warmly towards me, in his words and in his behaviour; he respects me and behaves completely differently from the way he
used to.'

At last Andersen was beginning to be accepted in his own right in the Collin
family.

Socially Andersen was also an outsider, as he was always very much aware.
His slavish admiration for royalty, his obsequiousness towards princes and
dukes, was surely linked with the fact that he was the son of a poor shoemaker
and a washerwoman and that he was born in the age of absolutism when kings
were still regarded as superhuman. Royalty was above criticism as far as
Andersen was concerned, but he always liked to pretend that he admired their
souls more than their crowns; the nightingale is speaking with Andersen's
voice when it says of the Emperor of China: 'I love your heart better than your
crown . . . and yet there's a breath of something holy about the crown.'

Andersen's attitude to members of the aristocracy was far more ambivalent.
It is true that he liked being treated as a welcome guest by members of the
Danish aristocracy but it is also true to say that it was often they who took pride
in showing off Andersen, rather than the other way round. It is not too much
to say that there was in Andersen an inborn positive dislike of aristocrats of the
blood; they were associated in his mind with haughtiness, selfishness and
stupidity. This attitude to blue-blooded aristocrats is clearly reflected in many
of his prose works. While staying as the guest of Count Moltke at the manor of
Glorup in June 1850, Andersen commented in his diary on the behaviour of
some of the other guests: 'It is terrible to hear the emptiness of the aristocratic
world, hear them laying down the law decisively and unhesitatingly about
everything, ignorantly, stupidly.' He was both surprised and annoyed when,
in May 1854, he met a German *Geheimerath* in Dresden who 'seemed to be
very interested in aristocracy, and when he heard my "Swineherd" he was
astonished at the terrible satire as he called it'. In March 1867 he reported that a
certain Danish countess had told him that several people were amazed 'that I
who moved in the circles of the highest aristocracy should have written such
a story as "The Porter's Son"'.

In some posthumously printed aphorisms Andersen writes: 'There is no
other true nobility than that of the mind, and in times to come princes will
choose their great men from it. In Denmark nobility means Tordenskjold,
Bartholin, Griffenfeld, Tycho Brahe, Ørsted, Thorvaldsen. . . . Most of those

of noble birth are no more than the shield-bearers of the nobility of the mind; they are nothing but the show-dish, entirely insipid.'

After Andersen's death Nikolaj Bøgh found among his papers a draft entitled 'Which Guild is the most famous?' from which the following is an extract:

I maintain that the Shoemakers' Guild is the most famous, for I am the son of a shoemaker. By all means, let the other guilds, the carpenters', the blacksmiths', the tailors', the braziers', the watchmakers' – indeed, all the many indispensable artisans skilful at their respective trades, send their spokesmen, prove their fame to be greater than that of the shoemakers. Phidias and Ahasuerus, Hans Sachs, the shoemaker! . . . An eagle is part of royal coats-of-arms; the shoemakers have such a one too, even with two heads, and nobody has ever made any complaint about it. In London, that great metropolis, they have begun publishing a Shoemakers' Journal in our time. No aristocratic family has been written about as much as the Wandering Jew, a shoemaker. He lives in legends and songs and is immortal. From Nuremberg, at the time of the Master Singers, the name of Hans Sachs, the shoemaker, shines forth. Our age has given each trade its own right, each man is free to speak his mind, the word nobility applies to anything that is clever, whether coming from behind the plough, from the workshop, or from science and art. It has been said, it has been written. But now let us confine ourselves to the workshop, that of the shoemaker. I who write these lines was born down there.

Andersen was well aware of the irony that he, who really despised 'the nobility of the blood' and believed in 'the nobility of the mind' should be so pleased to spend so much time with the Danish aristocratic families in their beautiful manors and castles. His dilemma was the dilemma of the goblin in 'The Goblin at the Grocer's', who came to realize that his heart lay with the poor student in the attic and that this was where he really belonged. But then he had second thoughts about moving up there: 'I can't give up the grocer altogether, because of the cream and the butter;' and the story ends philosophically: 'That was quite like a human being. We, too, have to go to the grocer for the cream and the butter.'

Andersen went to his aristocratic friends 'for the cream and the butter', but his heart was not with them. And yet he had lost contact with the social class from which he came, and a sudden confrontation with social outcasts was liable to frighten him. He wrote in his diary on 26 June 1850: 'A nasty vagabond stood near the spring, I had a feeling that he might know who I was and might tell me something unpleasant, as if I were a pariah moved up into a higher caste.'

It would have been possible – and completely truthful – to have ended the previous chapter with a paragraph saying that after Andersen's death a leather purse was found hanging round his neck, inside which was a letter from Riborg Voigt; Jonas Collin, who found it, burned the letter unread. The leather purse can still be seen as an exhibit in the Hans Christian Andersen Museum in Odense.

But such an ending would have placed undue emphasis on this incident and might well have been interpreted as a proof of Andersen's lifelong devotion to the girl he first fell in love with and never forgot. This might indeed have been what Andersen, as he lay dying, intended to tell the world, but I do not think this story should be taken too seriously. The leather purse was undoubtedly the one he carried his money in when travelling abroad, on a string round his neck, as a safeguard against pickpockets and robbers,[29] and the implication that he kept Riborg's letter there all the time can be rejected, I think. The letter itself must have been the one the text of which has been quoted in this book on page 77, the brief and quite unromantic little note copied out verbatim by Andersen in *Levnedsbogen*, for he wrote: 'All I have from her are a few words.' I suspect that in his old age, while tidying up his letters, Andersen came across this letter, which brought back to him an almost forgotten past, and that he then decided to keep this memory of his youth on account of its sentimental value.

Evidence has already been given to show that Andersen was in fact relieved that he never married Riborg Voigt. Similarly, he was relieved that he had never married Louise Collin. At her silver wedding in 1865 he made a speech at the dinner, and so did her brother-in-law, Adolph Drewsen; but the latter, according to Andersen's diary, made a not very felicitous reference to the fact that Andersen had not been present at Louise Collin's wedding to Mr Lind, having left the country in a hurry immediately beforehand. Reporting this Andersen writes: 'Love, unrequited love, was what people had to think of, . . . now, here at home, I thank God that I did not become Louise's husband, then quite a different kind of poetic activity, God knows which one, would have been mine.'

In spite of his longing for a home of his own Andersen probably realized that he would have found it difficult to settle down to the life of a married man.

It has been suggested on more than one occasion that he was really a homosexual, and that his love for Riborg Voigt, Louise Collin, Jenny Lind, etc. was mere pretence, a kind of window-dressing to disguise the true facts about his nature at a time when homosexuality was regarded with horror and disgust by most people. In his important psychiatric study of Andersen Professor Hjalmar Helweg mentions an article entitled 'H. C. Andersen. Beweis seiner Homosexualität' by a certain Albert Hansen in *Jahrbuch für sexuelle Zwischenstufen* (1901), and he also draws attention to the fact that in Magnus Hirschfeld's book *Die Homosexualität* Andersen is mentioned as one of the famous homosexuals. Helweg, however, rejects the theory; he says of Andersen:

By nature he was heterosexual, but the feeling of inferiority deeply rooted in his nature made heterosexual relationships – whether legitimate or illegitimate – impossible to him. Physically he remained an incurable masturbator, and spiritually he sought and found refuge in glowing friendships which might occasionally have an erotic character. If under favourable circumstances he had met a homosexual young man whom he liked it is not easy to say what this might have led to. Maybe he would then in practice have become a homosexual, but it is safe to assume that Andersen would not have found any repose in such a relationship. Whether he would have found it if in time he had been married to a kind and good woman seems uncertain as well – but at least there were periods during which he suffered acutely from the lack of a home and a woman's love.

Hjalmar Helweg brings in another argument which seems to me to carry much weight:

Finally, one thing makes it unlikely that Andersen should have entered gradually into homosexual relationships. Edvard Collin was an intelligent man, who knew Andersen thoroughly. If there had been even the slightest suspicion that Andersen was homosexual it is quite unthinkable that Collin – especially at a time when homosexuality was generally regarded as a despicable vice and *only* as a despicable vice – would have allowed his young son to travel round Europe as Andersen's sole companion. Andersen lived so close to the Collins that they could not have escaped being suspicious if he had really been homosexual and followed his nature in practice. And such a suspicion did not exist.

There is plenty of evidence in Andersen's diaries that he was physically attracted to the opposite sex; but equally, the candid character of his diaries makes it almost certain that he never had a sexual relationship with another person, male or female.

The following extracts from Andersen's diaries in Naples in 1834 may be quoted as an example:

19 February *At dusk I was surrounded by pimps who wanted to recommend* bella donna; *I can feel that the climate is having an effect on my blood, I felt a violent sensual passion but resisted.*

21 February *I was not left in peace to see Vesuvius by pimps, a boy of ten or twelve followed me through the whole length of the street telling me about a* donna molta bella excellenta; *it made me very sensual and passionate, but I resisted the temptation all the same. If I get home without having lost my innocence I shall never lose it.*

23 February *Tremendous feeling of sensual desire and internal battle. If it is a sin to satisfy this mighty desire, then let me fight it; I am still innocent, but my blood is burning, in my dreams everything inside me is boiling. I think the South is demanding its due! I'm half ill. – Happy he who is married, who is engaged to be married! Oh! If only I was tied with strong ties. But I want to, I do want to fight against this weakness.*

26 February (after having been offered a girl of thirteen who 'had only this month given herself over to the flesh'): *God! Lead me towards that which is best and most sensible. I do not regard this satisfaction as a sin, but I find it abhorrent and dangerous with such persons, and an unforgivable sin against an innocent being.*

28 February *I'm sure experienced people will laugh at my innocence, but it isn't really innocence, it is an abhorrence of this thing for which I have such a dislike.*

I believe that Andersen was scared of sex and also of its possible consequences. While staying at Le Locle in Switzerland in August 1833 he wrote in his diary:

I visited an Asyle pour les enfants malheureuses, *founded by Marianne Calame. There were some very fine faces among the children; perhaps their father is now wallowing in wealth, or perhaps some young traveller just enjoyed an hour of*

*dalliance among the mountains, and now the unfortunate children who were born as
a result must suffer. They sang movingly a song for us, which brought tears to my eyes;
in my heart I promised God never to seduce anybody and bring such an unhappy
creature into the world.*

In Italy some of Andersen's compatriots planned to deprive him of his virginity
by taking him along to a brothel, but they failed.

The diaries make it clear that in refraining from entering into any illicit
sexual relationships he was, so to speak, 'behaving as a good boy' to the Collin
family, and so he was extremely upset when later on members of that family
teased him for 'not behaving like all other young men' when he was abroad.
He wrote in his diary in Copenhagen on 11 December 1837: 'When I was
abroad it was only in order not to hurt their feelings, and it is out of regard for
them here at home that I have never followed my passions, and yet this is not
appreciated; I left them in a rage, felt a change in my behaviour; I want to be
like other men, I thought.' But alas! his fears still prevented him from being
'like other men'. The fact that his sexual desire was directed towards women
rather than towards men is also borne out by an entry such as the following,
written at the manor of Bregentved in July 1842: 'Sensually disposed, a passion
in my blood of an almost animal-like kind, a wild desire for a woman to kiss
and embrace, exactly as when I was in the south.'

There were undoubtedly some feminine elements in Andersen, and there
were times when his feelings for Edvard Collin and the young Hereditary
Duke of Weimar and Harald Scharff, a young Danish ballet dancer, appeared
to be feelings of love more than of friendship, though Andersen's use of the
word 'love' should not necessarily always be taken at face value. He was probably aware of this tendency in himself, and he was hurt and annoyed when a
German author asked him if he had never loved, and said that 'one didn't find
that in my books, there love came flying down like a fairy, and I myself was a
kind of halfman'.

When Andersen was in Portugal he was completely taken aback when his
friend Jorge O'Neill suggested in the most straightforward language that it
was time for him to 'kneppe' (fuck), and that this could easily be arranged in
Lisbon. He suggested that Andersen was suffering from an unsatisfied sexual
desire and maintained that one should not neglect one's duties to one's body.
But Andersen refused the offer of being taken to a prostitute.

In so far as the evidence of the diaries can be relied on, the nearest Andersen
came to 'sinning' was in Paris in 1866, 1867 and 1868, when on a few occasions
he went to a brothel, with his young Danish travelling companions, to look
at some naked girls. His comments on one occasion were: 'I left the place
completely innocent but had talked for quite a while with the poor child for
whom I felt sorry and who was surprised that I wanted no more than to talk
to her.' In 1868, when he was in Paris with Einar Drewsen, they both went to
a brothel, 'where I was only talking to Fernanda, the little Turkish girl, while
E. amused himself. She was the loveliest of them, we spoke about Constantinople, her native city, about the illuminations there on Mahommed's birth-

day; she was very insistent *pour faire l'amour*, but I told her I had only come to talk, nothing more. "Come again soon," she said, "but not tomorrow, for that's my day off." Poor woman!'

There is something profoundly innocent about the elderly Andersen carrying on polite conversations with naked prostitutes in French brothels. He was too scared to go beyond that. And he was furious when Theodor Collin, who disapproved of sexual abstinence, suggested that he 'paid secret visits to women'. – 'How wrongly they judge me!' he commented in his diary.

It is perhaps not surprising that in his old age this confirmed bachelor should have become increasingly prudish. This is seen, for instance, in his attitude to Georg Brandes' famous lectures on 'Main currents in nineteenth-century European literature'. Andersen did not attend the lectures but read some of the published volumes afterwards, and while reading the volume entitled *The Romantic School in Germany* he wrote in his diary on 1 August 1874: 'Am reading Brandes' book. He himself does not say anything demoralizing, but by means of quotations he manages to sow poison from other books; he is in favour of free love, of the abolition of marriage, and these are lectures given mainly to young girls.' Three days later he wrote: 'Have finished Brandes' book; in it there is a German poem [a quotation from Novalis' *Heinrich von Ofterdingen*], it lies in the book like a flower, a lecherous flower. A young girl who is on heat and longs to be embraced by *ein süsser Knabe* is angry with her mother for not being allowed to reveal to him the beauties with which nature has endowed her.'

It is ironic that to many of his Victorian translatresses Andersen was far too daring in referring to erotic matters in his tales, and they published bowdlerized versions considered to be more suitable for British children.

One of the reasons, but as already pointed out by no means the only reason why Andersen never married, may have been his unusual and to many of his contemporaries apparently unattractive appearance. He himself was always very conscious of the fact that his appearance was against him. Like his own ugly duckling he was 'different'. He was so tall, for instance, that in his student days he was known in Copenhagen as '*lange Andersen*'; Chamisso in 1831 called him '*der baumlange Däne*'. But what worried him most of all was that he was considered ugly. From Florence he wrote on 9 April 1834 to his friend Christian Voigt:

I often think: if only I were handsome OR rich and had a little office of some kind, then I would get married, I would work, eat and finally lie down in the churchyard – what a pleasant life that would be; but since I am ugly and will always remain poor nobody will want to marry me, for that is what the girls look for, don't you know, and they are quite right. So I shall have to stand alone all my life as a poor thistle and be spat at because it happened to fall to my lot to have thorns.[30]

Andersen was often photographed but rarely satisfied with the results. In Dresden in 1854 he wrote in his diary: 'Was driven over to be photographed, posed three times, looked like a peeled nutcracker.' When in October 1864 he posed for H. V. Bissen, the Danish sculptor, the latter told him that the Lord had taken time to make his head more special than that of most others. Abroad he was sometimes laughed at by people who did not know him; during a visit to Gothenburg in July 1871 Andersen noted that 'there were some simple people who seemed to be staring at me, didn't find me to their taste, laughed as I was laughed at in Granada. I was ill at ease though these people in Sweden looked like boiled potatoes.'

William Bloch, Andersen's young travelling companion in 1872, described the appearance of the old Andersen as he remembered him:

He was tall and thin, strange and bizarre in his movements and his carriage. His arms and legs were long and thin out of all proportion, his hands were broad and flat, and his feet of such gigantic dimensions that it seemed reasonable that no one would ever have thought of stealing his goloshes. His nose was in the so-called Roman style, but so disproportionately large that it seemed to dominate his whole face. After one had left him it was definitely his nose one remembered most clearly, whereas his eyes, which were small and pale and well hidden in their sockets behind a couple of huge eyelids half covering them, did not leave any impression. They were kind and friendly, but the fascinating interplay of light and shadow, the ever changing, expressive vividness that makes people's eyes a mirror of everything that goes on inside them, of that they had nothing. On the other hand there was both soul and beauty in his tall, open forehead and round his unusually well-shaped mouth.

Andersen suffered from a number of nervous disorders and mental disturbances, some of which may be common enough in many people, but in his case some were so marked that at times he was hardly in control of himself. By most of his contemporaries they were not thought of as mental disturbances but as 'oddities' peculiar to Andersen.

Among Andersen's friends it was well known that he suffered from various idiosyncrasies, one of them being that he refused ever to eat pork for fear of trichinae. Once, after having eaten a meal the main course of which he thought to be veal, when he found that it had been pork his anxious comment in his diary was that he was now afraid he had trichinae. He was also firmly convinced that the Danish fruit soup known as *Sødsuppe* upset him, and it was a constant source of irritation to him that the Ørsted family were in the habit of serving this particular dish when he went to visit them.

Once, when on a visit to Germany, he thought that the coffee served at breakfast had a strange taste, and having reported this fact in his diary he continued: 'What is wrong with me, a nasty taste and fire in my blood. The coffee-pot was not as it should have been, the waiter says, I've probably been poisoned.' On another occasion he reported: 'At breakfast I took some bitter drops, afterwards I had what I hope is an *idée fixe* that I had drunk tar ointment, having accidentally changed the bottles, this worried me.'

Sometimes his fears were not linked to any hypothetical cause, as when he wrote in his diary on 6 February 1868: 'Feel wobbly at the knees. I think I am suffering from spinal consumption, once in a while I feel an internal shock which almost makes me fall over.'

Having recorded on 31 May 1870 that he had either got a splinter in his foot or scratched himself on a pin he commented: 'Perhaps my death will come as a result of such a tiny cause; it must come soon.'

During a visit to 'Petershøi' in 1871 he noted in his diary: 'Got a thorn into the longest finger on my right hand, which caused me pain the whole day since we only managed to get parts of it extracted with a needle.' This incident happened during Miss Annie Wood's visit, and she can take up the story:

One morning, when I had known him about a fortnight, in gathering some gooseberries, he ran a thorn from the bush into his finger. I have no doubt the pain was disagreeable, but it seemed more than he could bear. He would let no one touch his hand for hours to extract the thorn, and it was only by the united influence of the whole household, that at last he was persuaded to bathe the swollen finger in hot water to subdue the swelling and ease the pain. Then came the terrible necessity, for terrible it was to him, of extracting with a needle the unlucky thorn. Each one proffered their services, but in vain – he would not have it touched. He could not eat his dinner, and began to be feverish and really ill. Distressed to see him suffering so acutely from such a slight cause, I entreated to be allowed to act as a doctor to the tortured finger, and ease the pain by taking it out. To one of his nervous and sensitive nature, the consent to such an undertaking was no slight thing to grant; but worn out with the local annoyance, and also, I fancy, not liking to show such sensitive weakness to a comparative stranger and a foreigner, he gave a feeble nod of assent, which I there and then acted upon, and almost before he knew it, I lifted the little black thorn from its lurking-place, and lo! the terrible operation was over, and the throbbing pain at an end.

When Andersen and William Bloch were in Innsbruck in the spring of 1872, Andersen fell out of his bed one night and hurt his knee. There are innumerable references to this accident in Andersen's letters home during the next few weeks, and William Bloch wrote in his own diary in Munich on 22 May: 'It goes without saying that the fall he had the other night has stirred A's imagination strongly: he has been very afraid of getting hydrarthrosis of his knee, cancer, the rose, etc., and he also asked me, "Do you think this may lead to a *concussion?*"'

The following description of what happened during their visit to Vienna in 1872 is also taken from William Bloch's diary:

Andersen was choking and had to leave the table, accompanied by our host and hostess, and everything was very quiet while Andersen was heard coughing and spitting in the other room. Against the protest of the hostess he maintained that there had been a pin in the meat; he had swallowed it and could clearly feel it sitting inside him. That evening and the following day he was very worried about the consequences. His anxiety was so pronounced that it had completely removed his fear that a little spot above one of his eyebrows might grow into a large excrescence which would cover the eye, which again had made him forget that he might possibly rupture himself because I had touched his stomach slightly with my walking stick, which again made him abandon the thought of having hydrarthrosis of the knee, something he was much concerned about when he arrived in Vienna.

The fact that Andersen was occasionally aware of being a hypochondriac may be seen from an entry in his diary on 18 October 1861: 'I am frequently nervous, suffer from fear and weight on the chest, believe that I shall collapse, go mad or have an apoplectic fit, and yet I don't do anything to prevent it, eat and drink as much as I like.'

Among Andersen's other nervous sufferings was a pronounced agoraphobia, which was liable to make him tremble even when walking across some large city square and heavily leaning on somebody's arm.

He also suffered from what he himself called 'Pas-Angst' ('Passport Fear'), an irrational fear that his passport was wrongly worded, or had been wrongly endorsed, with some terrible consequences for him. His diaries are full of entries such as the following, written in Constantinople on 4 May 1841: 'Worried in case my passport was not quite right. Oh! how good I am at tormenting myself!' When, in Prague in 1851, he discovered that Viggo Drewsen, his companion, had forgotten to put his signature to his passport, Andersen was convinced that this would result in grave difficulties for both of them, and he added: 'I was in that self-tormenting mood which almost kills me.'

Like so many other nervously disposed people Andersen suffered from *folie de doute*. An evening at the theatre could be ruined at the thought that he might have forgotten to put out the light in his apartment or lock the front door. After he had posted letters he might be afraid that he had put the letters in the wrong envelopes, or that he had got the name wrong; thus, after he had sent a copy of *In Spain* as a present to King George of Greece, he was worried that he might have written 'Otto' instead of 'George'; 'this became an *idée fixe* with me,' he wrote in his diary.

Trifles, such as whether he had paid too much or too little for a tram ticket or for some stamps at a local post office, could worry him for days. Once in Franfurt a waiter gave him a Prussian bank-note which he later found had not been legal tender for the last fifteen years. When he made this discovery he wrote a letter to an acquaintance in Frankfurt, in which he told him how he had come to possess this invalid *Thaler-Schein*, delivered the letter to the post office – and then regretted having done so, since it might lead to the Frankfurt waiter being dismissed, and so went back to the post office and reclaimed the letter.

The following entry, dated Copenhagen, 25 January 1866, is typical of the way Andersen (quoting his own words) 'knew how to plague himself to the most exquisite degree': 'Did not get my winter coat from the tailor's by 9 o'clock, so he gave me another new one to wear until mine was ready later in the day. When I went into the street it occurred to me that it might belong to somebody else, and supposing he came and said, "You're wearing my coat!" It seemed to me that people were staring at me.'

In a letter of 5 June 1869 Andersen wrote to Henriette Collin about his own tendency to let his imagination run riot: 'I have plenty of imagination, indeed to some extent I make my living from it, but sometimes it does inconvenience me, especially when I think that it isn't in command, and it then turns out to be very much in command.'

When travelling abroad he could be driven mad by irrational fears. On the voyage from Cartagena to Málaga he was suddenly torn by fear because in the darkness he had not seen young Jonas Collin on deck. 'I imagined him fallen overboard, the screw underneath the ship made a terrible noise as if it were going to break something, I wondered whether in the dark we might not get too near land and run aground, and in the end it all became so vivid in my mind that the perspiration stood out on my forehead.'

Among Andersen's constant fears was that of being the victim of a fire and consequently he always carried a rope in his trunk, so that in case of fire he could tie the rope to a window-bar and climb down.

Another of his fears was that of being buried alive; that he might be assumed to be dead when he was in fact only apparently dead; this fear became an obsession, and occasionally he would put a notice on his bedside table with the words 'Jeg er skindød' ('I am not really dead'). He insisted that his friends must promise to cut an artery before the lid was put on the coffin, so that there would be no chance of his waking up in the coffin after having been buried.

Some of his fears were so irrational as to be almost insane. Immediately before the great occasion in 1867 when he was given the freedom of Odense, he wrote that he had 'a strange crazy fear that someone is going to murder me, or that in Odense someone intends to ruin the celebrations for me; I feel very worried'. And when one day he was told that a Jutland farmer had been to see him in Copenhagen he noted in his diary: 'I had the idée fixe that he wanted to murder me.' The following day he wrote: 'The man came well before nine, a Jutland farmer called Gjerlev, with quite a decent face; by reading my works he had arrived at the conviction that I was a kind person, willing to help people. (So I wasn't killed on this occasion.)' All the farmer wanted from Andersen was help to gain an audience with the queen mother.

Andersen was aware of the dangers of his unstable mind; on 8 September 1855 he wrote to Edvard Collin: 'I am like water, everything moves me, I suppose it is part of my poetic nature, and it often brings me joy and happiness, but very often it is also a torment.'

In his book about Andersen and the Collin family Edvard Collin speaks of the mixture of irritability and sensibility which accompanied Andersen faithfully throughout his life, or at least from the time he began coming regularly to the Collins' house. Andersen's irritability, which was probably linked to his fits of depression, is very frequently in evidence in his diaries, right from his younger years when it might manifest itself as a general annoyance with his surroundings, and a desire to 'box everybody's ears', up to the time of his travels abroad with some young person, when the words 'sygelig afficeret' ('morbidly affected') constantly creep in, for instance on his journey abroad with Einar Drewsen in 1854:

1 June E. sulky and not the way I wanted him to be, I was morbidly affected.
15 June [Einar] again sullen and stiff. I asked him to be kind and gentle towards me, I was a sick person. He remained unchanged, then I became furious, told him several examples of the lack of attention he had shown towards me, he was angry, it made me cry, and in order to restore the balance I had to please him again.

His diaries show that during his last few years he might occasionally lose control of himself and be completely unreasonable in his behaviour towards Miss Hallager, his landlady in Nyhavn, whose tardiness was a constant source of irritation to him. At times he would shout at her, distort her words and tell her that she was killing him.

He was often genuinely afraid that he might become insane, as both his father and his grandfather had been. As early as 1841 one finds in his diary the words: 'Afraid of becoming mad', and that fear recurred frequently and in his old age became almost an obsession. Obviously, this fear was linked with his frequent fits of depression; he wrote from Dresden to Edvard Collin on 26 October 1860: 'Once in a while I am overwhelmed with a demoniacal *tedium vitae*, I felt this a couple of times in Geneva; it was as if I had to jump into the Rhone, and I hurried away, felt the devilish element inside me and prayed in anguish to the Lord, who has overwhelmed me with his grace and much happiness, something I do not deserve at all.'

The fear of ending his life as a madman very much increased in his old age, as can be seen from the following extracts from his diaries:

14 March 1869 *In bad spirits; occasionally I am on the point of going mad.*
5 November 1870 *I have a feeling that I may become mad.*
1 March 1871 *Last night I again had some of my insane fantasies.*
2 March 1871 *God has given me imagination for my activity as a* Digter *but not to make me qualify as a candidate for the madhouse! What are these crazy notions which so often haunt me?*
16 September 1874 *Again on the point of insanity.*

One day in March 1871 Andersen was told that a parcel had arrived for him from Leipzig. Not knowing what the contents were he confided to his diary: 'In accordance with my mood I suddenly had the idea that it was something evil, sent to me by enemies, and my imagination conjured up a variety of malicious ideas. I felt quite ill.' On the following day he wrote: 'Lay in a feverish sweat this morning, felt nervous and fearful of the misfortune which seemed to be intended for me.' The next day the parcel arrived; it turned out to be a box containing a reading desk decorated with a special Hans Christian Andersen motif, a present from a German bookseller. Relieved, and ashamed at the same time, Andersen wrote in his diary: 'That was all, and as usual I had allowed my imagination to run riot about misfortune and evil intentions.'

On the following day another incident stirred his imagination; he had been to the theatre, and 'as I left I happened to push very lightly, almost only touch with my walking stick, a man, so lightly indeed that I did not apologize, but when I came out into the street my imagination got the better of me, once again I had a crazy notion; I feel that I am on my way to the madhouse.'

One of the *real* afflictions from which this *malade imaginaire* suffered was toothache; it began when he was quite young, and it continued until he had lost all his teeth – and even then his false teeth caused him much pain.

He wrote in his diary on 18 May 1831: 'My teeth cause me tremendous pain; the nerves are really fine keys on which the indiscernible pressure of the

Hans Christian Andersen photographed
in his apartment in Nyhavn,
Copenhagen, in May 1874. Andersen
loved being photographed and would
even pose when he was very old and
frail.

Photograph of Andersen, presented to Edmund W. Gosse. The inscription on the back of the photograph reads: 'Min unge Ven Hr Gosse et glædeligt Nytaar! hjerteligst H. C. Andersen. Nytaarsaften 1872.' (My young friend Mr Gosse a happy New Year! most cordially, H. C. Andersen. New Year's Eve 1872.) The original photograph belongs to the author of this book.

Edmund W. Gosse, the English critic, photographed in Copenhagen in May 1874.

Georg Brandes, the Danish critic, photographed *circa* 1869.

Andersen reading aloud to some young
ladies at the manor of Frijsenborg in
1865.

'The Home of Homes'. In 1838 Jonas
Collin moved from Bredgade to
Amaliegade, and Andersen visited the
new home regularly until Jonas Collin's
death in 1861. The house is still standing.

Painting of Henriette Wulff by Adam Müller. She was Andersen's sisterly friend and was later described by Dr A. G. Drachmann as being 'extremely deformed (hunch-backed) and, apart from her eyes, in no way beautiful.'

A photograph of Andersen taken in Munich, 1860.

Left The panel representing Britain in the screen which Andersen made as an old man. The Thames, Parliament, Queen Victoria etc. form a background for Shakespeare, Byron, Scott, Dickens and Tennyson. The destitution he knew from Dickens' novels and saw in 1847 has also found a place in this remarkable montage.

Above Collage by Andersen, 'made *c.* 70 years before the days of cubism,' as Kjeld Heltoft points out. It was made for a daughter of Louise Lind (*née* Collin) and pays tribute to three Danish writers, Thomas Kingo, Ludvig Holberg and B. S. Ingemann – and to a mutual friend: *'Christine from Christinelund, She is as sweet as she is round!'*

Andersen's statue by August Saabye in
'Kongens Have', Copenhagen.

Andersen's diploma as Freeman of the
City of Odense, 1869.

air plays, and so there is a concert in the teeth, now *piano*, now *crescendo*, all tunes of pain caused by changes of climate.' On 1 April 1864 he wrote: 'I have become an old man, I have false teeth which give me pain. I am not at all well, am approaching the grave and final departure.' Three years later a terrible toothache ruined the day for him when Odense celebrated its famous son, and one of his last stories is the brilliant 'Auntie Toothache', with its horrifying visit by 'Madame Toothache herself, her infernal Satanic Frightfulness':

'Dear, dear, so you're a poet, are you?' she said. 'Very well. I'll compose tortures for you in every metre. I'll give you iron and steel in your body, new fibres in all your nerves.'

I felt as if a red-hot gimlet was piercing my cheekbone; I writhed and squirmed.

'A capital toothache!' she said. 'Quite an organ to play on. Concert on the Jew's harp – magnificent – with trumpets and kettle-drums, piccolos, and a trombone in the wisdom-tooth. Great poet – great music!'

And she struck up – no doubt about that – and her appearance was frightful, even though you could hardly see more of her than her hand, that shadowy ice-cold hand with the long skinny fingers. Each of them was an instrument of torture. Thumb and first finger had forceps and screw, the second finger ended as a sharp-pointed awl, the ring finger was a gimlet and the little finger squirted mosquito poison.

'I'll teach you metrics!' she said. 'A big poet must have a big toothache, a little poet a little toothache.'

'Please let me be little,' I begged. 'Don't let me be anything! I'm no poet, I only have fits of writing, like fits of toothache. Do go away!'

Andersen had a ticket in the Danish state lottery, which he kept renewing year after year, for to him this was a kind of talisman, a symbol of whether the goddess of good fortune was on his side or not. During the 1850s and 1860s he kept on writing to Edvard Collin from abroad: 'Please let me know that I have won in the lottery.' And when the lottery was drawn without his number coming out he was bitterly disappointed. The 20th April 1856 must have been a sad day, for the entire entry in his diary reads: 'Did not win in the lottery; received no letters.' To him a near miss was better than nothing; he wrote on 10 July 1860: 'I didn't win in the lottery, but the number I had chosen – 17 – was near the winning one: 18.' Time after time his diary contains a resentful: 'Did not win in the lottery,' sometimes with comments such as: 'The lottery has been drawn for three days, but once again my numbers haven't come out; I'm not going to get any riches from there.' At times his lack of luck made him quite angry; once he wrote to Mrs Melchior: 'If Mrs "Lottery", who has now for years been a bag of lies, were to present me with a suitable sum this time I could make plans for going abroad; but I have no faith in that woman.' On 13 September 1872 he wrote in his diary: 'It really is too annoying, I didn't win in the lottery this time either. Be cursed!' The following day: 'I haven't won anything at all in the lottery. Feel very bitter. My lucky star has deserted me.'

When eventually in November 1873 Andersen did win 500 rixdollars on his lottery ticket he hardly made any comment once he knew he had won.

Unlike his father, who was an atheist, Andersen was a deeply religious person, whose religious beliefs may be summed up by saying that he believed in the

existence of a god, in the importance of behaving decently, and in the immortality of the soul. This famous triad of God, Virtue and Immortality,
which is the basis of theological rationalism, was also the basis of Andersen's
religious belief.

He firmly believed in some kind of divine providence and was so convinced
that God had definite plans for him that at times he would even argue with
God; in his schooldays he once wrote in his diary: 'It wasn't fair of the Lord
to let me be so unlucky in Latin', and in moments of joy he felt a desire to
'press God to my heart'.

Andersen's religion was a primitive and undogmatic one, in which he saw
Christ as the great teacher and model to mankind, and Nature as God's
universal church. He very rarely went to church, and the contrasting religious
philosophies of Grundtvig and Kierkegaard, his two great contemporaries,
left him cold. One of his favourite quotations from the Bible was, 'Except ye
become as little children, ye shall not enter the kingdom of heaven'; this, of
course, is the ultimate message of 'The Snow Queen'.

Once, when staying at Holsteinborg, Andersen read two of his tales to a
dying invalid, and in taking leave of her he said: 'We'll meet again.' 'Yes,' she
replied, 'up there.' 'Perhaps,' Andersen said, 'and if you get there before me,
then please remember me to my friends, I have several of them up there.'
'You have indeed,' she said.

Occasionally Andersen was taken to task by people with strong feelings
about religious dogma. With Ingeborg Drewsen, for instance, he quarrelled
about the resurrection of the body – 'she believes in it, I don't'. After Andersen
had read Søren Kierkegaard's *The Concept of Fear* he became involved in a
theological discussion with young Jonas Collin, who told him categorically
that 'God and Christianity are two different things'. Andersen's diary continues: 'I said that God was the almighty one, he was the sole power. – "That
isn't Christianity: the Jews also believe in a god, but not in Christ!" – So here I
was told unambiguously of the expulsion of God from Christianity by the
new god Christ.'

At the manor of Basnæs Andersen had several arguments with Lady
Scavenius and others about religious matters; thus on 14 July 1870 he recorded
in his diary: 'I told them that the teaching came from God and that it was a
blessed thing, but that conditions of birth and family, however interesting they
might be, were not essential to me. Then the storm broke out and they said
that the teaching had no significance if one did not take into account his birth
and his death. The last addition was necessary to confirm his firm conviction
of truth, etc. – If I did not believe in the Father, the Son and the Holy Ghost,
then I wasn't a Christian. I replied that I believed in them as concepts, not as
persons, not as bodily creations – they almost gave me up.'

One evening in October 1871 when Andersen happened to express his
views on God and Christ, on the Virgin Mary, and so forth, a lady, who was a
firm supporter of Grundtvigian ideas, exclaimed: 'Dear me! Then you must
be a Jew!' When Andersen told her of his love of, gratitude towards, and
admiration for Christ as a human being who was entitled to ask others to

follow his example, the poor lady burst into tears and rushed out of the room. 'There was quite a scene,' Andersen writes. 'I was unhappy if I had "offended" someone who had never so far thought about matters of faith, and later in the evening I tried to clear everything up and pacify her, in which I seemed to succeed. I said, "A father gives each of his two daughters a costly ring; one of them is firmly convinced that it is genuine and it would never occur to her to doubt it, she is happy in her blind faith; the other one wants to know and so goes to an expert with the ring and by having it examined learns that it is in fact genuine. In this latter way I have become convinced that what Christ teaches does in fact come from God."'

At times Andersen felt so close to God that it was natural for him to conclude an entry in his diary with the words: 'Thank you for this day, dear God!' At other times he was filled with doubt and worry. Here are some characteristic extracts from his diaries in 1860:

3 September *It is to me as if my spirits are weighed down by a nightmare – whence does it come, why is it there? I am strangely miserable. But I dare not ask you, God, to help me, for I don't deserve it – why must I always be so privileged? No one knows his destiny from one hour to the next.*

4 September *The wish to die suddenly very often comes to me.*

5 September *My mind won't lift! Please, God! make me happy!*

27 October *I'm drifting like a bird in the gale, a bird that cannot fly and yet cannot quite fall either. O Lord! My God! have mercy on me!*

28 October *I am a sinner, a frail, vain person – I have been given far too many precious gifts, now I must also suffer adversity, and then I complain like a spoilt child. Who listens to me? No one! No one!*

14 November *It's no use praying, God won't change the course of events. In good days I cling to him, in bad days I do not support myself on his unchangeable will. I know that like a child I must ask for his forgiveness because I am being punished, please forgive me then, but I don't want to ask the impossible. I know that in the course of time I shall succumb. Rather be oneself in abandonment than to be longing in the flames, hoping for a blessed existence which we are not going to achieve. . . . Went to bed as usual in a bad mood, godless.*

20 November *Up at half past eight, lovely sunshine. Please, God! let it shine in clarity into my mind in Christianity and God!*

17 December *The good which I intend to do I don't do. And the evil things I do not intend to do I do. I have no future to look forward to.*

Andersen wrote in his diary on 10 July 1864: 'Anguish and sorrow take me out on to deep waters – shall I be lifted up there, or shall I sink? Religion is my light, my salvation, my faith. Do I believe that God and Jesus are one, as the believers want them to be, then the Virgin Mary must be the chosen one among humans, then in our humble way it is so near at hand to pray to her to plead with God on our behalf. What thoughts I have! God, my Lord! make thy light shine in me and have mercy on me, I am about to let go of you to whom I should hold on with the faith of a child.' And on 2 May 1866: 'How strange – in anguish and suffering I am unable to pray to God, I believe in a destiny, a necessity, but in

joyful and happy days God is very near to me, then I have prayers and gratitude, then there are humble thanks of bliss in my soul and my thoughts.'

Having just been informed of Carsten Hauch's death Andersen wrote in his
diary on 5 March 1872: 'Is he now dust and ashes, dead, extinguished, put out
like a flame which does not exist any more? O God, my Lord! Can you let us
disappear completely? I have a fear of that, and I have become too clever – and
unhappy.'

The question has frequently been raised as to whether Andersen was fond of
children or not. I think the answer is fairly simple: he liked the children with
whom he had a personal relationship, but he was not the kind of joyous and
playful entertainer immediately attracting children from far and near that
posterity has sometimes made him out to be. Like most other adults Andersen
could be irritated and annoyed by spoilt and badly behaved children, but
usually he found it easy to get on with them because he was so much of a child
himself.

Edvard Collin has this to say on the subject:

In a number of houses where he looked in almost every day there were small
children whom he got to know. He told them stories, which he partly made up on the
spur of the moment, partly borrowed from well-known fairy tales; but whether the
tale was his own or was reproduced from someone else's the manner of telling it was
entirely his own, and so vivid that the children were delighted. He, too, enjoyed
giving his humour full play; the tale went on all the time, with gestures to match the
situation. Even the driest sentence was given life. He didn't say, 'The children got into
the carriage and then drove away.' No, he said, 'They got into the carriage – "good-
bye, Dad! good-bye, Mum!" – the whip cracked smack! smack! and away they went,
come on! gee-up!' People who later heard him giving a reading of his tales will
be able to form only a faint idea of the extraordinary vivacity with which he told
them to children.

Rigmor Stampe, who was Ingeborg Drewsen's granddaughter (and thus the
great-granddaughter of Jonas Collin) offers the following personal testimony
in her book on Andersen:

I cannot remember that we were ever anything but completely at ease in our relations
with Andersen – whereas there were at that time in our various family circles other
old uncles and aunts who caused us young people to feel a true dislike for them
because of their caresses and their over-sentimental behaviour. Andersen, on the other
hand, was always tactful and unobtrusive and was never repellent.

He was also kind and good to us children. He took us to the theatre, brought us
presents from abroad, indeed, for one of his favourites he had a present every day for
a long time. And then he told his fairy tales to the children in many different homes;
later on, he sent them the small printed editions as they were published.

Anyone who has read the story entitled 'Heartbreak' cannot doubt Andersen's
basic sympathy for children. In the fenced-in part of the back yard a special
exhibition has been arranged for all the children living in the street, the charge
for admission being a trouser-button – 'that was something every boy would
have and could also pay for the little girls with'. So all the children from the

street and the back lane came along, paid their buttons and saw the pug's grave.

But outside the tan-yard, right against the gate, was a ragged little girl, standing so gravely there, with the prettiest curls and delightfully clear blue eyes. She didn't say a word, and she didn't cry, but every time the gate opened she looked as far in as she could. She hadn't a button – she knew that – and so she was left standing sadly outside, standing there till the others had all had their look at the grave and had gone away. Then at last she sat down, held her little brown hands before her face and burst into tears; she alone had not seen the dog's grave. That was heartbreak, as bitter for her as it may sometimes be for one who is grown up.

Because of his emotional nature, his streak of sentimentality, and his proneness to tears, it is sometimes assumed that Andersen lacked a sense of humour. Nothing could be farther from the truth. Anyone who has read his tales in the original will know that it is one of their greatest assets; unfortunately (as will be shown later) some of the Victorian translators and translatresses managed to remove much of the humour, thus giving undue emphasis to the sentimental element.

It was not only in his tales and his novels that Andersen was able to express his humour; there is plenty of evidence that he also did so in everyday life. On this subject Edvard Collin writes:

In his speech and conversation, whenever irony came in and his humour had full outlet, he could be extraordinarily amusing. I have never known anyone who was able in such a way to pick out some individual feature, unimportant in itself though it might be, and let his humour work on it, without undue regard to correctness. Almost every day he had a funny story to tell about something or other which he had experienced, and it is not surprising that once, after such an anecdote, Captain Wulff tore his own hair while shouting: 'It's a lie, it's a bloody lie, such things never happen to any of us,' – a scene which Andersen rendered very amusingly.

Here is another comment from Edvard Collin's book:

Andersen's sense of humour and fun might get the better of his egocentricity to such an extent that when he saw himself being placed in a funny light be might find it amusing (though only in our private circle). This was especially obvious with [Ingeborg Drewsen], for instance when she caught him in a little white lie. But also when he told her about an actual event in which his name was not mentioned but with which he could be linked by an association of ideas; whenever he told her something like that in the most innocent tone of voice and she then replied, 'I know perfectly well why you're telling me that, but you aren't going to fool a seven-year-old fox cub,' – then he would scream with delight at having been caught out.

Even on the most solemn occasions, as when he was being publicly eulogized, he might suddenly catch sight of a funny twist – witness the following from his diary of 19 June 1846, where he is reporting van der Vliet's speech at a banquet in his honour: 'King Christian VIII and Friedrich Wilhelm of Prussia had given me decorations; when these were placed on my coffin (at this point the fat waiter grinned) he hoped that God would give me the crown of honour for the beautiful fairy tale of my life.'

Andersen's main talent was, needless to say, his literary talent. But he had others as well. He had a good singing voice, loved singing and was easily persuaded to sing Danish songs in a circle of friends abroad.

He also had a talent for reading his own tales aloud, whether privately or publicly. On 29 April 1863 the Danish author Henrik Scharling heard Dickens reading his *Christmas Carol* and an episode from *The Pickwick Papers* in London. In his diary he commented: 'He often rendered the dialogues magnificently, but in matters of pure narration or description H. C. Andersen is far superior to him.'[31]

Though without any kind of formal education Andersen also had an artistic talent, to which his many pencil and pen sketches bear witness. These were mainly made during his many journeys abroad and were intended for his own use as a kind of visual record of things or scenery he had seen and wanted to be able to recapture later on. If the camera had been invented we might never have had Andersen's unpretentious sketches and drawings, the charm of which lies in the fact that they are the works of an amateur, the word being interpreted in its original sense of someone who pursues a form of art from a natural love for it and not for gain. If Andersen had been taught all the academic and formal rules of composition and perspective, etc., his sketches might well have lost their natural simplicity and also the intensity and spontaneity which make them so attractive; they would probably have been more 'correct' from a technical point of view, but they might also have just been nice picture postcards rather than personal artistic expressions.

One of the earliest landscape drawings must be one he made during his first journey abroad; it is of the German castle of Regenstein. In his book about his journey to the Hartz Mountains, which he published in 1831, Andersen writes of Regenstein Castle: 'This impressed me so much, was so inspiring that before I realized it the pencil was moving in my hand, making a sketch of the enormous visual impression in my diary; I became an artist without ever having received an hour's instruction.'

Many of his sketches were made in 1833–4, during his stay in Le Locle in Switzerland and his first journey to Italy. From Rome he wrote to his friend Ludvig Müller: 'Whenever I see something beautiful I cannot help thinking, "How shall I manage to describe this to the dear ones at home?" And then my pencil runs over the paper, and my imagination says, "Now I have the skeleton, now I shall be able to illuminate and develop it from there".' He wrote to Edvard Collin from Naples: 'In Mola di Gaeta we saw Cicero's baths, of which I made a sketch, for I have become quite a draughtsman and the artists in Rome all encourage me on account of my good perception; in any case my many sketches (already more than a hundred) are a treasure to me which will give me much pleasure at home. If only I had learnt drawing!' Less than a month later he wrote to Henriette Wulff: 'Now I have very nearly 200 sketches.'

In 1866 Andersen wrote in a letter to Henriette Collin: 'You know that I have never learnt to draw, neither have I trained myself in it, and yet I often feel a desire to sketch on paper what I think I cannot render in words. I once showed some of my sketches from Italy to H. C. Ørsted, who was not an artist, admittedly, and he thought that if I had not become a writer I should have become a painter.'

As an artist Andersen was not naïve but naïvistic, as Kjeld Heltoft rightly points out in his excellent book *H. C. Andersens Billedkunst*, which deals with all aspects of Andersen's visual art. Heltoft tells us that a total of 70 pencil sketches and 250 pen drawings by Andersen have survived.

Another of Andersen's special talents was making quite sophisticated and often very amusing paper cuttings, and of these more than 1500 have been preserved. Sir Henry Dickens, who was eight when Andersen visited Gad's Hill in 1857, writes in his memoirs: 'He had one beautiful accomplishment, which was the cutting out in paper, with an ordinary pair of scissors, of lovely little figures of sprites and elves, gnomes, fairies and animals of all kinds, which might well have stepped out of the pages of his books. These figures turned out to be quite delightful in their refinement and delicacy in design and touch.' Rigmor Stampe writes of these cuttings:

They were very important to the children of the family. While Andersen was talking he would fold a piece of paper, let the scissors run in and out in curves, then unfold the paper, and there the figures were. They were, so to speak, little fairy tales, not illustrations for his written tales but expressions of the same imagination. One fully recognizes Andersen in them. They were not like other people's paper cuttings, but they often had a similarity to one another: here as in his writings he was essentially concerned with a limited series of motifs which he went on repeating. There were castles, swans, goblins, angels, cupids and other imaginary characters, many hearts, a dead man hanging in a gallows, a 'chamberlain with his key hanging on his back', a windmill in the shape of a man – the wings being his arms and legs – and many others.

One might add that storks, graceful female ballet dancers and pierrots were among his favourite motifs in his paper cuttings – but also horrible demons, and naked witches with four or more breasts.

In 1926 the eldest of Count Holstein's daughters recorded her memories of Andersen cutting out paper figures at Holsteinborg: 'When I was a child I was happy whenever he cut out little interconnected dolls of white paper, which I could place on the table and move forwards by blowing at them. He cut out many silhouettes, some of which Mamma later glued on to lamp-shades. He always cut out with a pair of enormously big scissors – and to me it was incomprehensible how with his big hands and the enormous scissors he could cut out such pretty and fine things.'

For the six-year-old son of a singing master at the Royal Theatre Andersen filled a whole book of sixty pages with a variety of illustrations and captions, and there are thirteen other exercise books made by Andersen for the children of his friends, all of them full of illustrative material, which today we would call 'montages' or 'collages'. This was also the technique he used in his old age for decorating the eight panels of a big screen, each panel being devoted to a particular theme: two of them to Denmark, one to Sweden and Norway, one to Germany and Austria, one to Britain, one to France, one to the Far East, and one to Childhood. But in the case of this screen it is the composition of each panel which is original; none of the pictorial material is Andersen's own; it is a true collage of photographs, illustrations and reproductions from a variety of sources. Seen as a whole the screen reveals much about Andersen's concept of the world, both present and past. Into each panel, against a background of local architecture and scenery, he put pictures of his heroes and – as a counter-balance – scenes of social realism or sarcasm. Thus on one panel a picture of a fool has been placed next to his own portrait, and underneath all the Danish writers and poets is a motley crowd of cats and dogs, hens, parrots, owls, pigs, a fox, a toad, and a prisoner chained by a fairy. Prominent among Andersen's British heroes are Shakespeare, Byron, Scott, Dickens and Tennyson; but in the same panel poverty and destitution are also represented as he knew them from Dickens' novels and from his own visit to London in 1847. Goethe, Beethoven, Mozart, Heine and Schiller are all represented in the German/Austrian panel; but underneath the picture of a German granny reading fairy tales to a sick child is that of a fox lying in wait to catch a hen. In March 1874 he wrote to Lady Holstein about the screen: 'I have tried to put into each panel a poetic idea or an historical account, and they say it is all like a big, multi-coloured fairy tale.'

In an important passage in his book on Andersen Edvard Collin writes:

I should like to refer to what was really essential in Andersen and concerns his character – the character which is so frankly revealed in his letters to our family, in which the world and its verdict are disregarded. I have looked into the depths of his soul, and I have not allowed myself to be put off by the excesses of his imagination by having referred to them. I know that he was *good*. This simple testimony will not be misunderstood by those who really knew him.

Edvard Collin was not the sort of person who used emotional terms lightly, and coming from him the testimony carries special weight.

But Andersen is far too complex a character to be summed up in a few adjectives; he is a man of deep and apparently irreconcilable contrasts.

The same contrasts are to be found in his writings. Anybody who tries to analyse the philosophy of his tales will find that there is in them a deep dualism. 'The Bell' and 'The Shadow', for instance, have themes which are basically very similar, and yet they express two contrasting philosophies. 'The Bell' is an optimistic story about the triumph of goodness, about the victory of genius, the story of how two young boys, both of them representing 'nobility of mind' – one of them coming from a poor background (Andersen himself), the other a young prince (Ørsted? Thorvaldsen? the Duke of Weimar?) – ulti-mately find their way to the mystic bell beyond the forest, the bell which represents what Ørsted called 'the Spirit of Nature', while all the others, ordinary people, stop at the cheap imitation bells. 'The Shadow' is a pessimistic story about the triumph of empty imitation and the defeat of genius, a story in which the learned man, the scholar, he who fought for truth and beauty, is beheaded, while the shadow, the parasite, steals his fame and is rewarded by marrying the princess.

The same dualism is to be found in Andersen himself; he was full of deep inner conflicts which often made life difficult for him. Sometimes one aspect was more visible to the outside world than the other: everybody could see his vanity, but only those who knew him well were aware of his humility. The contrasts in this complex person are legion: he was a Christian rejecting the main dogmas of Christianity; he was a generous miser; he was a social snob who invariably stood up for the underdog; he was more intense both in his hatred and in his love of his native land than any other writer of his time; he was scared stiff of all the dangers connected with travelling, and yet no other contemporary European writer travelled more than he did; in his auto-biographies (and many of his letters) there is a constant undertone of profound gratitude for the wonderful way his life had developed, and yet a year before he died he wrote in his diary: 'Internally I do not at all feel kind, grateful or patient.'

At a dinner given in 1948 in honour of Jean Hersholt, Andersen's American translator and a collector of Anderseniana, Dr Topsøe-Jensen expressed the complexity of Andersen's character in these words:

It was not the way that his life ran that was so fantastic. In America especially, where so many poor lads have had a terribly hard time of it and yet become famous, the story of the shoemaker's son will not appear so unusual. No, what is unique in Hans Christian Andersen is his personality. Among those no longer living there are few whom we know so thoroughly as we do him, few natures so richly endowed, few that seem to embrace such unparalleled contradictions. A creature of inspiration with natural primitive gifts, he was at the same time a patiently persevering artist, a man familiar with every detail of his craft, who filed and polished his work until it acquired the character of looking easily inspired; who for years on end could save up ideas and fancies, so that they might be fitted in at the right moment as though they were the fruit of a sudden impulse. At one and the same time, child and philosopher; unrestrained in joy and sorrow, and yet with the sure tact of a diplomat in difficult situations; vain and humble; wrapped up in himself to an extraordinary degree, and yet most ready to help others; a man of emotion and feeling, and for all that possessed of a wonderfully impish humour. By nature pessimistic and melancholy, but a convinced optimist in cultural matters; Danish to the core – and yet understood by the whole world.

It is obvious that in spite of his egotism, his irritability and his various eccentricities Andersen must have had a charismatic personality, a talent for attracting unusual people, of catching their interest and establishing contact with them. Even when a boy in Odense he was different from other children, and his talent for making other people interested in him was part of his 'being different'. In Copenhagen the same pattern repeated itself when, against all odds, the failed young singer, dancer, actor and playwright somehow caught the interest of benefactors without whose help he could never have survived. And again and again the same thing happened to the mature man and to the famous writer, whose personal contacts with the leading cultural figures of Europe were second to none.

His life story is not the rosy fairy tale he liked to pretend it was. Nor is it as tragic as he sometimes tried to convince himself. But it is a strange and fascinating story about that strange and remarkable outsider, Hans Christian Andersen, whose language of communication proved to be more universally intelligible than that of any other writer.

The Emperor walked under his high canopy in the midst of the Procession.

Part two: The Tales

1 The range of Andersen's tales

TODAY Andersen's fame rests entirely on his fairy tales and stories. They have been translated into well over a hundred languages and are still being published and republished in millions of copies all over the world; but it is important to realize that when people speak of *Andersen's Fairy Tales* they are not necessarily speaking of the same tales.

The total number of tales published in Denmark during Andersen's lifetime under the title *Eventyr og Historier* is 156; but although they have all been translated,[1] many are unfamiliar in Denmark, and even fewer are well known abroad.

In the English-speaking world the early tales, those published between 1835 and 1850, are the ones best known. Judging by present-day editions the following thirty appear to be the most popular (the year of publication in Denmark being given in brackets): 'The Tinder Box', 'Little Claus and Big Claus', 'The Princess on the Pea',[2] 'Little Ida's Flowers', 'Thumbelina',[3] 'The Travelling Companion' (1835); 'The Little Mermaid', 'The Emperor's New Clothes' (1837); 'The Steadfast Tin Soldier',[4] 'The Wild Swans' (1838); 'The Garden of Eden', 'The Flying Trunk', 'The Storks' (1839); 'Willie Winkie' (Ole Lukøje),[5] 'The Swineherd', 'The Buckwheat' (1841); 'The Nightingale', 'The Top and the Ball',[6] 'The Ugly Duckling' (1843); 'The Fir Tree',[7] 'The Snow Queen' (1844); 'The Darning Needle', 'The Elf Hill',[8] 'The Red Shoes', 'The Shepherdess and the Chimney-Sweep', 'The Little Match Girl' (1845); 'The Shadow' (1847); 'The Old House', 'The Happy Family' and 'The Shirt Collar' (1848).

If I were asked to select the sixty tales which I considered most characteristic and representative, I would probably include most of these thirty, but I would certainly not regard them as adequately representative of the many different aspects of Andersen's genius.[9]

Andersen was a creative writer, not just a collector of folk tales. It is therefore wrong to bracket him, as is often done, with the brothers Jakob and Wilhelm Grimm, or with Asbjørnsen and Moe, the two Norwegian collectors of folk tales.

Nevertheless, a few of his tales, especially some of the early ones, were based on traditional Danish folk tales which he had heard as a child in Odense.[10] Two months before the publication of his first four tales he wrote to Ingemann: 'I have given a few of the fairy tales I myself used to enjoy as a child and which I believe aren't well known. I have written them completely as I would have told them to a child.'

The inspiration for 'The Tinder Box', which is clearly in this category, appears to have come from two interdependent sources: partly from a Danish folk tale sometimes called 'The Spirit of the Candle', which again is based on the story of 'Aladdin and the Wonderful Lamp' in the *Arabian Nights*, and partly from Adam Oehlenschläger's famous Romantic play *Aladdin* (1805), a work greatly admired by Andersen, who liked to identify himself with Aladdin as Oehlenschläger saw him: the genius predestined to move along the road from poverty to greatness and fame. In writing the opening story in his first volume of fairy tales Andersen must have had in mind both the crude plot of the folk tale he had heard as a child, and the philosophy of Oehlenschläger's poetic masterpiece; but it was a matter of great importance to him not to appear to be imitating the latter. As Hans Brix puts it: 'In his first tale, "The Tinder Box", he deliberately chooses the Aladdin story in its popular form. The very fact that it is exactly the same theme [as Oehlenschläger's] forced him to be entirely original: not a single detail must bear any resemblance. It is a true contest with Oehlenschläger.'

The three dogs appear to be Andersen's own invention – in the folk tale an 'iron man' (or a 'steel man') appears whenever the hero lights the candle, and the treasures in the cave are guarded by a sleeping troll. But the most important innovation was the style in which the tale was told, a narrative style, which was entirely Andersen's own, simple and straightforward, devoid of all the literary conventions of the time:

Down the country-road a soldier came marching. Left, right! Left, right! He had his knapsack on his back and a sword at his side, for he had been at the war, and now he was on his way home. But then he met an old witch on the road. Oh! she was ugly – her lower lip hung right down on her chest. 'Good evening, soldier,' she said. 'What a nice sword you've got, and what a big knapsack! You're a proper soldier! Now I'll show you how to get as much money as you want.' – 'Thank you very much, old witch!' said the soldier.

Little Claus, the hero of 'Little Claus and Big Claus', is another Aladdin character, certainly not a moral hero, but a cunning David who cannot help beating Goliath in the end. Andersen's story was taken from a Danish folk tale called 'Big Brother and Little Brother', recorded in several parts of the country. There are many similarities to the folk tale, but it is also obvious that Andersen has made a number of deliberate changes. Thus in the folk tale Big Brother actually kills Little Brother's grandmother (believing that it is Little Brother he is killing), but Andersen has seen to it that Little Claus's grandmother was already dead when Big Claus 'gave her a great clump on the forehead'. 'The unfaithful wife', a stock character in adult folk tales and *fabliaux*, did not seem to Andersen to belong to a nursery tale, and so he explains why the farmer's wife had to hide the parish clerk in the chest when her husband returned unexpectedly, by saying: 'the farmer had the strange failing that he never could bear the sight of a parish clerk' – an explanation completely satisfactory to a child.

The nearest known equivalent for 'The Princess on the Pea' is a Swedish tale (related to Tieck's 'Puss in Boots') about a poor girl who goes out into the world accompanied by a cat (in some versions a dog), which advises her to present herself at the royal castle as a princess. Being suspicious the queen puts the alleged princess's sensitivity to the test by secretly placing some small objects (a bean, peas, a piece of straw) under her mattress; but on each occasion the cat (or dog) warns the girl so that next morning she can pretend to have slept very badly, thus proving her delicacy and sensitivity. In the Swedish version, therefore, the heroine wins by cheating, whereas in Andersen's version the heroine proves herself to be a real princess by actually being hypersensitive.

'The Travelling Companion' is based on a Danish folk tale called 'The Dead Man's Help', which contains all the basic features of Andersen's tale. As early as 1829 Andersen had used folk material for a story he called 'The Ghost', and it is interesting to compare it with 'The Travelling Companion'. In 'The Ghost' the language is precious and abounds with hackneyed literary clichés; in 'The Travelling Companion' this has been superseded by a much more directly spoken language – it is possible that Andersen tried out the story on children and found that it did not work in its first form.

In 'The Wild Swans' Andersen again followed a traditional folk tale fairly closely, and in this case he had access to a printed version published in Matthias Winther's *Folkeeventyr* (1823) (the same theme also occurs in Grimm's 'Die sechs Schwäne'). In a letter dated 5 October 1838 Andersen wrote: 'Please read Matthias Winther's fairy tale of 'The Wild Swans' and tell me whether my rewriting of it is good or bad.' Unlike the folk tale Andersen refrains from inflicting cruel punishment on the villains, who are, in his version, the evil stepmother (a witch) and the archbishop (a kind of Grand Inquisitor). He has superimposed a religious element: at the end Elise is depicted as a saint, saved in the nick of time from being burnt at the stake, and while her eldest brother explains her innocence, 'a perfume as of a million roses spread around, because every faggot from the stake had taken root and put out branches, and a high sweet-smelling hedge stood there with crimson roses. Right at the top was a single flower of the purest white, glittering like a star.'

In an explanatory note to 'The Swineherd' Andersen says that the tale on which it was based contained features, 'which could not decently be retold in the manner in which they were told to me as a child'. The folk tale in question, 'The Proud Maid', is the story of an arrogant girl who rejects her princely suitor, but ends by accepting him when he appears in the guise of a beggar whose possessions she happens to covet. In order to get hold of them she agrees to allow him to spend a night, first in her bed-chamber, and later in her bed. The tale is known internationally in a number of versions, but the part which Shakespeare used in *The Taming of the Shrew* has been omitted by Andersen, who discarded the happy ending. In 'The Swineherd' the haughty princess, who scorns genuine beauty (the rose and the nightingale), but is prepared to degrade herself by kissing the stranger for the sake of his trivial mechanical gadgets, is eventually banished from her father's kingdom, and the prince, who has come to despise her, rejects her.

Andersen specifically refers to 'The Garden of Eden' as being 'one of the many tales I heard related as a child'; he only wished it had been much longer, he says. The tale on which the first part is based is called 'The Isle of Bliss' and can be traced back to a story by Countess d'Aulnoy (1650–1705). It is about a prince, who loses his way and suddenly finds himself at the home of the four winds and their mother; one of the winds carries him to the beautiful fairy on the Isle of Bliss, where he stays for three centuries without noticing the passage of time; only on his return to his earthly home does it catch up with him. Further inspiration was the dramatic poem *Lycksalighetens ö* (1824–7) by the Swedish writer P. D. A. Atterbom, and some themes in the *Arabian Nights*.

'Simple Simon' is a humorous story without any fairy-tale element; it has various ancestors in folk-tale tradition. Simple Simon (by Andersen called Klods-Hans) is a kind of de-sentimentalized male Cinderella, and his two elder brothers, who are 'so clever that – well, the fact is they were too clever by half', correspond to the ugly sisters. While they ride off to propose to the princess on a coal-black and a milk-white horse respectively, Simple Simon rides on his billy-goat. Their useless knowledge does not help them win the princess, who cannot resist Simple Simon and admires his intrepid actions. Some of the objects the hero picked up on his way to the royal castle were such as could not be mentioned in decent company; so Andersen's hero collects less objectionable items, a dead crow, an old clog with the vamp missing, and mud straight out of the ditch. They all come in useful in his conversation with the princess, during which he is never at a loss for an answer.

This is how 'Dad's Always Right' begins:

Now listen! I'm going to tell you a story I heard when I was a boy. Since then the story seems to me to have become nicer every time I've thought about it. You see, stories are like a good many people – they get nicer as they grow older, and that is so pleasant.

The story which Andersen heard as a child is sometimes called 'The Praiseworthy Wife', because it is about a woman who always looks on the best side of her husband's bad bargains. In Andersen's story the husband, a poor Funen farmer, leaves home to sell his horse at the nearby market, but before getting to market he manages to swap the horse for a cow, the cow for a sheep, the sheep for a goose, the goose for a hen, and the hen for a bag of rotten apples. Having followed the folk tale thus far, Andersen then introduces two Englishmen. Now, what everybody knew about the English was that they were tremendously rich and fond of betting; so on hearing the farmer's story the two Englishmen were immediately prepared to bet a bushel of gold that the farmer's wife will be angry when he returns and tells her about his bargains; but the farmer insists that she will give him a kiss and say: 'Dad's always right!' which is, of course, exactly what she does.

Whereas the above nine tales were based on folk tales Andersen had heard, but (apart from a single case) never read, three of his others have literary sources.

'The Naughty Boy', Andersen's story about Cupid, who shoots his arrows into the hearts of innocent people (including the poet himself), is based, as Andersen openly admits, on a poem by Anacreon.

In his commentary to the 1862 edition of *Eventyr og Historier* Andersen states that 'The Emperor's New Clothes' is of Spanish origin and mentions Prince don Juan Manuel as the author to whom he is indebted for the idea. Infante don Juan Manuel (1282–*c*.1349) is famous for his *Libro de Patronio* or *Conde Lucanor* (1328–35), a collection of fifty-one cautionary tales, based on Jewish and Arabic literature. Andersen did not know the Spanish work but had read one of the stories in a German translation entitled 'So ist der Lauf der Welt'. He took the main plot from this, while at the same time giving it a universality which the Spanish version did not have.

The Moorish king of the original has been changed into an emperor, whose empire could be nowhere and anywhere in this world, and the swindlers have been reduced from three to two. But the most important change is in the magic quality of the clothes made by the fraudulent weavers. In the Spanish story they claim that the material is invisible to any man who is not the son of his presumed father; in Andersen's story the swindlers claim that 'the clothes made from their material had the peculiarity of being invisible to anyone who wasn't fit for his post or was hopelessly stupid'. It is this which makes Andersen's story universally applicable, ridiculing the snobbery of people who pretend to understand or appreciate things they do not really understand or appreciate, in order not to be considered ignorant or stupid.

'What's this?' thought the emperor. 'I can't see anything – this is appalling! Am I stupid? Am I not fit to be emperor? This is the most terrible thing that could happen to me. . . . Oh, it's quite wonderful,' he said to them; 'it has our most gracious approval.' And he gave a satisfied nod, as he looked at the empty loom; he wasn't going to say that he couldn't see anything.

In Andersen's original manuscript the story ends with everybody admiring the emperor's new clothes, the implied moral being that people willingly allow themselves to be deceived. *Mundus vult decipi*. The final paragraph ran as follows:

'I must put on that suit whenever I walk in a procession or appear before a gathering of people,' said the emperor, and the whole town talked about his wonderful new clothes.

Having sent the manuscript to the printer's Andersen had misgivings about this ending, and a few days later – on 25 May 1837 – he wrote to Edvard Collin, who was responsible for the proof-reading:

The story 'The Emperor's New Clothes' ends with the following paragraph: 'I must put on that suit, etc.' I want this to be deleted completely and the following inserted instead, as it will give everything a more satirical appearance:

'But he hasn't got anything on!' said a little child.

'Goodness gracious, do you hear what the little innocent says?' cried the father; and the child's remark was whispered from one to the other.

'He hasn't got anything on! There's a little child saying he hasn't got anything on!'
'Well, but he hasn't got anything on!' the people all shouted at last. And the
emperor felt most uncomfortable, for it seemed to him that the people were right. But
somehow he thought to himself: 'I must go through with it now, procession and all.'
And he drew himself up still more proudly, while his chamberlain walked after him
carrying the train that wasn't there.

It was this ending – probably added after Andersen had read the original version to a child – which gave Andersen's masterpiece its final touch.

Finally, it should be mentioned that the *Rahmenerzählung* or 'narrative
frame' of 'The Flying Trunk' has been taken, with a few modifications and a
complete change of style, from a story about Malek and Princess Shirine in
A Thousand and One Days (1711–12) by Pétit de la Croix, which had been
translated into Danish. The story within the story, however, is very much
Andersen's own.

The remaining 144 tales are entirely his own invention, though this does
not, of course, mean that he did not use themes or features from other sources.[11]

Andersen called his tales *Eventyr og Historier*, thus making a deliberate distinction between *Eventyr* (fairy tales, French *contes de fées*, German *Märchen*) and
Historier (stories), the former with, the latter without a supernatural element
in them. Thus 'The Little Mermaid' is a fairy tale, 'The Emperor's New
Clothes' a story. But the dividing line is not always quite clear, nor is Andersen
always consistent; in spite of its title 'The Story of a Mother', for instance, is
not a 'story' but a 'fairy tale'; 'The Snow Queen' has the sub-title 'A Fairy
Tale in Seven Stories'. He first used the term *Historier* in 1852; until then he
had consistently used the term *Eventyr*. In *Mit Livs Eventyr* he explains that he
had gradually come to regard the word *Historier* as better covering his tales in
their full range and nature: 'Popular language puts the simple tale and the most
daring imaginative description together under this common designation; the
nursery tale, the fable and the narrative are referred to by the child as well as
by the peasant, among all common or garden people, by the short term:
stories.'

In the following discussion of Andersen's tales (a word I use to include both
'fairy tales' and 'stories') I propose to divide them into seven groups: (1) fairy
tales proper, in which the supernatural element is a dominating one, (2) tales
mainly enacted in the natural world but containing an important element of
magic, (3) tales in which the main characters belong to the animal world,
(4) tales in which the main characters are trees or plants, (5) tales in which
inanimate objects have become animated, (6) 'realistic' tales set in a fantasy
world, and (7) realistic stories, anecdotes or *fabliaux* set in a real world.

Fairy tales proper

In his book *H. C. Andersens Eventyrverden* Bo Grønbech describes the geography of Andersen's poetic universe in these words:

Our own geography has no validity. Immediately outside the typically Danish town
in which Gerda grew up she arrives at 'the river'; during her wandering into the

world she soon reaches a non-localized kingdom of the well-known fairy-tale type, and from there she goes to Lapland, whence she is again able to continue her wandering on foot to Spitzbergen. Travelling towards the East from human dwellings one reaches the Garden of Eden or to the splendid castle of the Sage. If one goes far enough through the wood one may end up at Death's hot-house. The mermaids and mermen live at the bottom of the sea, and the uncanny brewery of the marsh-woman is situated under the ground, as is the forecourt of hell. Heaven is the kingdom of God and the angels and not a cold and empty space.

In 'The Little Mermaid' the human world only exists in so far as it relates to the dreams, the longings and the love of the little mermaid, and the only human being who has a clear identity is the prince. The main emphasis is on the 'sea people', especially the sea king, his mother and his six daughters. Living at the bottom of the sea as they do, their existence mirrors human existence: the sea king is a widower, looked after by his mother, who wears her status symbol, 'twelve oysters on her tail, while the rest of the nobility had to put up with only six'. The sea king's palace corresponds in splendour to a royal palace on dry land: 'It's walls are made of coral, and the long pointed windows of the clearest amber; but the roof is made of cockleshells that open and shut with the current.' Here little fishes fly in and out like swallows in a human dwelling, and outside the palace there is a lovely garden 'with trees of deep blue and fiery red'.

Just as the human world has its witches, so the world of the mermaids has its witch, living 'on the far side of the roaring whirlpools', and to get to her you have to pass over hot bubbling mud and go through a wood, whose trees and bushes are half animals, half plants. The sea witch sits in her house, built of the bones of shipwrecked humans, 'letting a toad feed out of her mouth, just as we might let a little canary come and peck sugar. She called the horrible fat water-snakes her little chicks and allowed them to sprawl about her great spongy bosom'.

Goodness and unselfish love also exist at the bottom of the sea, personified in the little mermaid who ultimately rejects the temptation to save her own life by stabbing the prince, whom she loves, with the knife, for which her sisters had paid the price of their beautiful hair. The main difference between the mermaid and the prince is that the latter has an immortal soul. By transforming the little mermaid in her dying moment into one of 'the daughters of the air', Andersen indicates that she may acquire an immortal soul in three hundred years time.

'The Snow Queen' has no clear dividing line between the natural and the supernatural world. The Snow Queen is first introduced as a fictional, fairy-tale character, but she materializes and takes Kay away to her kingdom of cold reason, because the splinter from the devil's glass had made him ripe for it. In his last, scared moment, before the Snow Queen's kisses make him forget everything, he wants to say the Lord's Prayer but can only remember the multiplication table.

Gerda preserves all the qualities of innocence and warmth which Kay has lost, and though she can be delayed in her search for Kay (by the old woman with the sun hat, by the mistaken identity of the prince, by the wild and spoilt little robber girl) nothing can prevent her from carrying on until she finds him. Having been carried by the reindeer to Lapland, Gerda continues to the Finmark, where she sees the Finn woman, who is so clever that she can tie up all the winds in the world with a thread of cotton and make a drink so potent that it would give Gerda the strength of twelve men; but that still won't be enough, the Finn woman says to the reindeer, explaining:

'I can't give her greater power than she has already. Don't you see how great it is? Don't you see how man and beast feel obliged to serve her, and how far she has come in the world in her bare feet? She mustn't learn of her power from us; it lies in her heart, in her being a dear innocent child. If she can't reach the Snow Queen and get rid of the glass from little Kay, then there's nothing we can do to help.'

In the end Gerda reaches the Snow Queen's palace. The walls are built of drifting snow, while the windows and doors are cutting winds. In the middle of the unending snow hall is a frozen lake called the Glass of Reason, where Kay is trying to make up the word ETERNITY out of flat pieces of ice. 'If you can find me that pattern, then you shall be your own master, and I'll make you a present of the whole world and a pair of new skates,' the Snow Queen had told him. Gerda's tears of joy when she finds Kay thaw out the lump of ice in his heart and dissolve the little bit of glass there, and Kay's own tears cause the splinter to trickle out of his eye. Such is their happiness that even the pieces of ice dance with delight and settle down to form the very word Kay had been unable to form.

While 'The Snow Queen' has a pure entertainment value for small children and a deeper symbolic significance for their elders, 'The Story of a Mother' may be called a purely allegorical fairy tale, or a poetic myth, with an appeal almost entirely for adults. Only the first paragraph describing the mother sitting by the bed of her dying child takes place in a recognizable world; from then on the allegory takes over. Disguised as an old man Death enters, and while the mother dozes off for a minute he vanishes with her child, and the clock stops – time ceases to exist. Then the desperate mother begins her search, which is entirely unlike Gerda's.

Out in the snow she meets Night, 'a woman in long black clothes', who requires her to sing all the songs she used to sing to her child as the price for telling her which way Death went with the child. Later, at a crossroads, a bramble bush 'with neither leaf nor blossom, for it was midwinter and the twigs were all frosted over', wants to be warmed at her breast before telling her which road to take. The thorns pierce her flesh, but 'the bramble shot out fresh green leaves and blossoms in the cold winter's night – such was the warmth from a sorrowing mother's heart'. At a lake she must weep out her eyes before being carried across 'to the great greenhouse where Death lives and looks after flowers and trees', and here the old woman who looks after the graves and the greenhouse reveals that 'every human being has his tree of life or his flower, each one according to his nature'; the old woman's price for her help is the mother's long black hair, in exchange for her own white hair.

Among millions the mother recognizes the heart-beat of her own child, 'a little blue crocus that stood there weakly and drooping'. Then Death arrives.

'How were you able to find your way?' asked Death. 'How could you get here more quickly than I did?'
'I am a mother,' she said.

In despair she threatens to pull up all the flowers unless Death gives her back her child; but then she realizes that she would make other mothers unhappy. Death gives her back her two eyes which he has fished out of the lake and shows her the future of two children, one whose life will be happy and one whose life will be miserable, and tells her that one of the two is her child. Terrified the mother asks Death to take away her child: '"Forget about my tears – my pleading – all that I have said and done!" And Death went away with her child into the unknown land.'

I have dealt at some length with these three tales because I consider them the three greatest of Andersen's fairy tales.[12]

'The Elf Hill', one of Andersen's most amusing fairy tales, takes place entirely in a world of supernatural beings, the occasion being the Elf King's party in honour of some prominent guests, the Norwegian Dovre Troll and his two ill-mannered sons. Only very select guests are to be invited, not even ghosts will be admitted, says the Elf King's housekeeper, enumerating the guests:

The merman and his daughters must first be invited, though I dare say they are not very keen on coming ashore; still I'll see that each of them gets a wet boulder or something better to sit on, so I rather fancy they won't say no this time. All old trolls of the first class with tails must be asked, and the river-sprite and the goblins; and then I don't see how we can leave out the grave-pig, the death-horse and the church-lamb. It's true that they really rank among the clergy, who don't belong to our people, but those are just their duties; they are nearly related to us, and they pay us regular calls.

The food is exquisite and suited to the occasion:

The kitchen was crammed with frogs on the spit, snake-skins stuffed with little children's fingers and salads of toadstool seeds, moist mouse-noses and hemlock, beer from the marsh-woman's brewery, sparkling saltpeter wine from the burial vault – all very substantial. Rusty nails and bits of stained-glass window were for nibbling in the sweet course.

The natural world only comes into the story through the comments of the lizards and the earthworm. After sunrise, when the banquet is over, one lizard says to another:

'Oh, I *did* enjoy the old Norwegian Troll!'
'I prefer the boys,' said the earthworm, but then of course he couldn't see, poor creature.

Another fairy tale full of humour is 'Willie Winkie', whose title character describes himself as an ancient heathen – 'the Romans and Greeks call me the

Dream God'. The fairy tale consists of seven stories which Willie Winkie tells a little boy called Hjalmar in his dreams during a whole week.

Nothing is impossible to Willie Winkie. He can turn flowers into trees, put Hjalmar's bad writing in the copybook through a drill, make the furniture talk and take Hjalmar on an excursion into the landscape picture on the wall. One night Hjalmar is out at sea, the next night at the wedding of two mice, for which he becomes so tiny that he can borrow a tin soldier's uniform and be transported to the party in his mother's thimble. Another night Hjalmar is taken to the wedding of his sister's two dolls, Herman and Bertha. The ceremony is performed by Willie Winkie, dressed in Hjalmar's granny's black petticoat, and they all sing a song, written by the pencil. On Saturday Willie Winkie explains that he must see to it that everything is ready for Sunday; for instance, all the stars must be taken down and given a thorough polish, with each star and the corresponding hole being numbered, so that they can find their right places again. At this point the portrait of Hjalmar's great-grandfather protests that Willie Winkie is muddling the boy with wrong ideas: 'A star is a globe, the same as the earth; that's just the beauty of it.' So next evening Willie Winkie takes the precaution of turning the portrait to the wall before continuing his stories.

In 'The Goblin at the Grocer's' the main character is the Danish *nisse*, a kind of benevolent hobgoblin, whose loyalty is divided between the grocer and the student, i.e., between material and poetic values; he wisely decides to share himself between the two.

Unlike most of the other fairy tales 'The Marsh King's Daughter' can be determined both in time and place. The time is the end of the Viking Age, the place partly North Jutland, partly Egypt. The commentators are a couple of storks who spend the summer in one place, the winter in the other. The title character is the daughter of the evil Danish Marsh King and an Egyptian princess; like another Thumbelina, she was found on the leaf of a water-lily, and the Viking's wife became her foster-mother. But because of the different character of her parents she is a beautiful girl with a wild and evil spirit during the day, and a toad with a kind though sad nature during the night – the Beauty and the Beast combined in one person. Eventually goodness conquers evil in her, and, finally united with her real mother, she flies back to Egypt, where she saves the life of the pharaoh. The ending is yet another version of the ancient legend about someone being allowed to spend three minutes in heaven – to find out on returning to earth that three hundred years have passed.

The time and place of 'The Ice Maiden' can also be stated exactly; the place is Switzerland (with various locations given) and the time the middle of the nineteenth century (Rudy's death by drowning took place in 1856). Behind the love story of Rudy and the Miller's daughter is the underlying theme of the Ice Maiden, the Queen of the Glaciers, a dedicated enemy of man, who is constantly trying to give those who venture into her territory the kiss of death.

The Ice Maiden is Fate; what she is determined to get, she will eventually get. She lives at the bottom of the glacier, in a torrent of melted ice and snow; it is her laughter people hear when an avalanche is falling. 'If I move my palaces the roar is more deafening than the rolling thunder,' she says. This is how Andersen describes her:

She, the slayer, the crusher, is partly the mighty ruler of the rivers, partly a child of the air. Thus it is that she can soar to the loftiest haunts of the chamois, to the towering summits of the snow-covered hills, where the boldest mountaineer had to cut footrests for himself in the ice; she sails on a light pine twig over the foaming river below and leaps lightly from one rock to another, with her long, snow-white hair fluttering about her, and her blue-green robe glittering like the water in the deep Swiss lakes.

Tales with an element of magic

This group of tales can hardly be described as fairy tales, for they include no supernatural beings. Their characteristic feature is that, at some crucial point in the tale, natural laws are broken.

'The Shadow', one of Andersen's most important tales, may serve as an example. The only violation of the laws of nature is that a man one day finds himself without a shadow; gradually, however, a new shadow grows out from his feet; 'the roots must still have been there'. The vanished shadow, which has become an independent being, turns up after several years, prosperous and well-dressed, at his former master's house and later invites his less prosperous master to a spa, where he pretends that the master is his shadow. By using the wisdom of the learned man (his former master) the shadow wins the heart of a beautiful princess, and when the former master refuses to act as the shadow's shadow he is executed on their wedding-day.

'The Shadow' begins in 'the hot countries', then moves back to a northern country and finally to an anonymous spa and to the anonymous kingdom of the princess. We are told that the learned man writes books about 'what is true and good and beautiful in the world' and in describing his reaction to having lost his shadow Andersen makes an oblique reference to Chamisso's *Peter Schlemihl*:

He was very annoyed, not so much because the shadow had disappeared, but because he knew there was a story, well known to everybody at home in the cold countries, about a man without a shadow; and if he went back now and told them his own story, they would be sure to say that he was just an imitator, and that was the last thing he wanted.

When the shadow first presents himself again to his former master he tells him about the time he vanished in the south. The learned man had been fascinated by a strange house opposite in which music was heard but from which no human being ever emerged, except on one occasion when he had a brief vision of a young girl coming out on to the balcony – only to vanish again. It was into that house the shadow went, and in that house Poetry herself lived. 'I was there for three weeks,' says the shadow, 'and it meant as much as living for three thousand years and reading all that man has imagined and written down.' But pressed to explain what he experienced there, the shadow keeps on repeating: 'I have seen everything and I know everything.'

The knowledge the shadow has acquired over the years turns out to be of a special kind:

'I saw what none are supposed to know – but what all are dying to know – trouble in the house next door. . . . If I had edited a newspaper, it would have had plenty of readers! But I used to write direct to the person in question, and there was panic wherever I went. They were terribly afraid of me – and, oh! so fond of me. The professors made me a professor, the tailors gave me new clothes; I was well provided for. The master of the mint made me coins, and the women said I was handsome. And that's how I became the man I am.'

While the shadow prospers, the learned man is in despair because no one bothers about the things he writes about, the true, the good and the beautiful.

What first impresses the princess when she meets the shadow is that he is able to tell her much about her own country she did not know, for 'he had peeped in at the windows on every floor and seen all sorts of things through them'. When she wants to test his wisdom the shadow tells her that her questions are so elementary that even his shadow – as he pretends the learned man to be – can answer them. 'He has now been with me so many years, listening to me all the time – I should imagine he can.' Impressed with the learned man's conversation the princess reflects: 'What a man this must be when his mere shadow is as wise as that.'

As a contrast to this pessimistic story about the victory of the parasite, about people preferring the shadow to the substance, there is 'The Bell', which also belongs to this category; for though the bell and its sounds are described in tangible, realistic terms, as an object which people try to locate and identify, always in vain, it is not a bell in any realistic sense; it is a romantic philosophy, a way of life, and a way of looking at life.

There are for instance certain times when some people can hear this mystic bell:

It was as though the sound came from a church in the very depths of the silent, fragrant wood; and people looked in that direction and became quite solemn.

In their search for the bell grown-ups are either distracted by cheap imitation bells, or are preoccupied with elaborate theories about the origin of its sounds. Then young people take over; boys and girls coming from the solemnity of Confirmation Sunday feel drawn to the ringing of the unknown bell; but they too drop out from the search one by one, distracted by a variety of other things. In the end only two boys are left, a prince and a pauper. The prince goes to the left, the poor boy to the right, and their search becomes more and more difficult and hazardous. At sunset the prince finds himself facing the open sea, the sinking sun like a great shining altar:

Nature was a great holy cathedral, in which trees and hovering clouds were its columns, flowers and grass its altar-cloth of woven velvet, and the vault of heaven its mighty dome.

Here the poor boy meets the prince, for the road each of them has taken has led to the same goal:

They ran to meet each other, taking each other by the hand there in the great cathedral of nature and poetry. And above them sounded the sacred invisible bell, while blessed spirits hovered about it in joyful praise to God.

The magic elements in 'Something to Write About' are the spectacles and the ear-trumpet belonging to the wise woman, whom the young man, who wants to become a poet by Easter, consults. His trouble is that he cannot think of anything to write about, for it seems to him that every good idea has been used long before he came into the world. When the wise woman lends him her spectacles and her ear-trumpet he can see and hear all the prosaic everyday things telling their poetic tales, but when she takes back her glasses and her trumpet, he can no longer see or hear a thing.

'Very well, then you can't be a writer by Easter,' said the wise woman.
'No? But when can I?'
'Neither by Easter nor by Whitsuntide. You'll never learn to hit on anything.'

So the only thing left for him to do is to become a literary critic.

The trunk in 'The Flying Trunk' was of a very special kind – as soon as the lock was pressed the trunk could fly. In 'The Swineherd' the gadgets invented by the disguised prince defy the laws of nature: the pot which has the peculiarity that if one holds one's finger in its steam, one can at once smell what is being cooked on every fire in the town, and the rattle which, when swung round, plays 'all the waltzes and jigs and polkas that anybody had ever heard of'.

'Everything in its Right Place' is a completely realistic story up to the point when the young tutor begins to play the flute he has cut out of a historic old willow tree, which symbolized the brutal way in which the old aristocracy had oppressed the poor. The flute suddenly transforms the whole social order in such a way that everybody finds his place in the social scale, not according to his title, rank or fortune, but according to his true human value.

Tales in which animals are the main characters

Andersen's use of animals as characters differs essentially from that of Aesop, La Fontaine and Lessing. His animal tales are not anecdotal and hardly ever teach a moral lesson; unlike the classical fables they certainly do not serve a rationalistic philosophy. Andersen's animals have a psychological make-up which is very much like that of certain humans, and their conversation and general behaviour mirrors that of human beings. Among his favourite animal characters are the inhabitants of the farmyard – cocks and hens, ducks and drakes, geese, ganders and turkeys, and they are usually selfish and narrow-minded. Other favourites are storks, usually with a broader outlook, being birds of the world. A variety of other creatures – cats and dogs, rats and mice, fishes, birds, snails, insects – play prominent parts in Andersen's tales.

The best example of these stories is 'The Ugly Duckling', which begins with 'the stork on his long red legs, chattering away in Egyptian, for he had learnt that language from his mother', and then moves on to the manor-house park, where a tame duck is sitting on her nest. Coming out of the eggs one by one the little ducklings are amazed at how big the world is; but their mother tells them that what they see is not the whole world: 'Why, it goes a long way past the other side of the garden, right into the parson's field; but I've never been as far as that.' The ugly duckling, whose egg broke later than the others, does not conform to the rules of the farmyard but commits the unforgivable sin of being different:

'Ugh! What a sight that duckling is! We can't possibly put up with him' – and one duck immediately flew at him and bit him in the neck.
'Leave him alone,' said the mother. 'He's doing no one harm.'
'Yes, but he's so gawky and peculiar,' said the one that had pecked him, 'so he'll have to be squashed.'

Pecked and jostled and teased by all the other inhabitants of the farmyard, even by his own brothers and sisters, the duckling runs away to the great marsh where the wild ducks live. 'What a scarecrow you are!' they say, 'but that won't matter to us, as long as you don't marry into our family.' The wild geese, on the other hand, being young and perky have a Bohemian attitude to life.

'Look here, my lad!' they began. 'You are so ugly that we quite like you. Will you come with us and migrate? Not far off, in another marsh, are some very nice young wild-geese, none of them married, who can quack beautifully. Here's a chance for you to make a hit, ugly as you are.'

During the big shoot the ganders are killed, but even the retrievers won't touch the duckling.

Then, towards evening he comes to a poor little farm cottage – 'it was so broken-down that it hardly knew which way to fall, and so it remained standing'. Inside the house lives an old woman with her cat and her hen.

The cat, whom she called Sonny, could arch its back and purr; it could even give out sparks if you stroked its fur the wrong way. The hen had such short little legs that it was called Chickabiddy Shortlegs; it was a very good layer, and the woman loved it like her own child.

The house has its own social order and its strict conventions:

Now, the cat was master in the house and the hen was mistress, and they always used to say 'We and the world', because they fancied that they made up half the world – what's more, much the superior half of it. The duckling thought there might be two opinions about that, but the hen wouldn't hear of it.
'Can you lay eggs?' she asked.
'No.'
'Well, then, hold your tongue, will you!'
And the cat asked: 'Can you arch your back or purr or give out sparks?'
'No.'
'Well, then, your opinion's not wanted, when sensible people are talking.'

The duckling goes through all kinds of hardship until finally in the spring he sees some beautiful swans; bowing his head he expects to be killed by them – but then he sees a reflection of himself in the water, 'no longer a clumsy greyish bird, ugly and unattractive – no, he was himself a swan!' The moral of the tale, which has become proverbial, is that inborn qualities are more important than upbringing: 'It doesn't matter about being born in a duckyard, as long as you are hatched from a swan's egg.'

'Thumbelina' is full of animals, some of them nasty, others likable. On her way through life Thumbelina is first kidnapped by an ugly, slimy toad, who wants her son to marry her, then liberated by the fishes and the butterfly, and eventually caught by a cockchafer, whose family all find her ugly:

'Why, she's only got two legs,' they said. 'What a pitiable sight!' 'She hasn't any feelers,' they went on. 'She's so pinched in at the waist – ugh! she might almost be a human. Isn't she ugly!' exclaimed all the cockchafers.

'It's Perfectly True!' begins in a hen-house, where a hen preening herself causes a little feather to come out and flutter down. The news of this event, whispered from hen to hen, is passed on to the owls and picked up by the pigeons until finally it returns to the very hen-house where it originally took place. The story by this time is that 'five hens have all plucked out their feathers to show which of them had got thinnest for love of the cock. Then they pecked at each other till the blood came and they all fell down dead, to the shame and disgrace of their family and the serious loss of their owner'.

'The Happy Family' is about two old snails living among the burdock leaves in the park of an old manor-house; they are convinced that the forest of burdocks has been planted entirely for their benefit:

They had never been outside it, though they realized that something else existed in the world called *The Manor*, where you got boiled and then turned black and were laid out on a silver dish; but what happened after that nobody knew. They couldn't anyhow imagine what it felt like to be boiled and to lie on a silver dish, but it must be delightful and very much the correct thing. Neither the cockchafer nor the toad nor the earthworm, when questioned, could reply; none of them had ever been boiled or laid on a silver dish.

The main characters in 'The High Jumpers' are the flea, the grasshopper and the skipjack (a toy made from a wishbone), who compete to see which of them can jump the highest. The flea has perfect manners; 'he had of course gentle blood in his veins and was accustomed to mix only with mankind, and that does make such a difference'. The grasshopper is wearing his native green uniform and boasts of his old family in Egypt and of his ability to sing. When the skipjack wins by jumping into the princess's lap, the flea goes abroad on foreign service, 'where he is said to have been killed', and the grasshopper goes and sits in a ditch, pondering on the way of the world.

Concerning the idea behind 'The Beetle' Andersen explained in 1862:

In an issue of *Household Words* Charles Dickens had collected a number of Arabian proverbs and idioms; among them he emphasized this one: 'When the Emperor's horse was shod with gold shoes the beetle also put out his leg.' We suggest, Dickens says in a note, that Hans Christian Andersen should write a tale about this subject. I wanted to do so, but no tale came forth. Only nine years later, during a visit to the

Danish manor of Basnæs, where I happened to read Dickens' words again, did the tale of 'The Beetle' suddenly spring forth.

Deeply humiliated that the blacksmith refuses to give him gold shoes when the emperor's horse has got them, the beetle leaves the stable and on his way through the garden meets a variety of other creatures – some ladybirds, a caterpillar, two frogs, a couple of earwig families and some of his own relations. Self-important and arrogant as he is, the beetle despises the others for being different and therefore inferior. After having gone through various tribulations – being picked up by zoologists, caught by two children, who send him out sailing, tethered to the mast in an old broken clog – the beetle finally ends his journey by returning to the emperor's stable, where he finds himself sitting on the emperor's horse. And now he begins to understand: 'Why was the horse given gold shoes? He asked me that as well, the blacksmith did. Now I realize. It was because of me that the horse was given gold shoes.'

There is a paragraph at the beginning of 'The Ice Maiden' which is worth quoting. Rudy, who is still a small boy, has been learning a great deal from his conversations with Ajola, a dog, and a tom cat, who first taught him to climb:

'Come up here on the roof,' the cat had said to him quite clearly, 'for when you're still a child and cannot yet talk you have no difficulty in understanding the language of hens and ducks, cats and dogs; they speak as plainly to children as their parents do if only the children are small enough; then even grandfather's walking-stick can neigh and become a horse with a head, legs and a mane. Some children lose this gift later than others, and then the grown-ups say that they are slow in developing and that they remain children for too long. Grown-ups say a lot of silly things.'

Andersen remained a child the whole of his life in that he never lost this understanding.

Tales in which trees and plants are the main characters

I shall choose 'The Fir Tree' and 'Little Ida's Flowers' as examples of this category.[13]

We follow the fate of the fir tree from its childhood in the wood to its death as a withered and discarded Christmas tree. In all its life it had never had a happy moment, for either it was looking forward to something better than the present, or it was thinking nostalgically of the past.

When it was small it was in a hurry to grow big, hated being called 'a dear little tree', and never felt able to enjoy the warmth of the sun or the sweetness of the air. It was envious of the big fir trees which were felled to make masts for splendid ships, and its impatience increased when it saw its friends being taken away before Christmas and heard the sparrows describing the glory and splendour in store for them as Christmas trees. But when its own turn came and it was the first to be felled, it had no thoughts of happiness, being 'so sad at parting from its home, from the place where it had grown up'.

The fir tree is taken into a house and decorated for the great event.

'Tonight,' they all said, 'tonight it's going to sparkle – you see!'
'Oh, if only tonight were here!' thought the tree. 'If only the candles were already

lit! What happens then, I wonder? Do trees come from the woods to look at me? Will the sparrows fly to the window-panes? Shall I take root here and keep my decorations winter and summer?'

From sheer longing the tree gets barkache, 'and barkache is just as bad for a tree as headache is for the rest of us'. When the great moment comes and the candles are lit, the fir tree is so tense that it is unable to enjoy the moment but looks forward to a repetition the next night. Instead it is put up in the attic, where it entertains the mice with nostalgic memories of its early youth and retells the story of Humpty-Dumpty it heard on Christmas Eve. The rats, however, are less easy to please than the mice:

'Is that the only story you know?' asked the rats.
'Only that one,' replied the tree. 'I heard it on the happiest evening of my life, but I never realized then how happy I was.'
'It's a fearfully dull story. Don't you know any about pork and tallow candles? One about the larder?'
'No,' said the tree.
'Well, then, thank you for nothing,' answered the rats and went home again.

In the end the tree is taken out into the yard, all withered and yellow, and is trampled on by the children.

And the tree looked at the fresh beauty of the flowers in the garden and then at itself, and it wished it had stayed in that dark corner up in the attic. It thought of the fresh days of its youth in the wood, of that merry Christmas Eve, and of the little mice who had listened with such delight to the story of Humpty-Dumpty.
'All over!' said the poor tree, 'if only I had been happy while I could. All over!'

In 'Little Ida's Flowers' it is the student, 'who knew the most lovely stories and could cut out such amusing pictures', who tells Ida that when the flowers hang their heads and look quite withered it is because they have been at a dance on the previous night. 'When it's dark and we are all asleep,' he explains, 'they go hopping round quite gaily; almost every night in the year they have a dance.' He also tells her how the flowers communicate with each other by signs: 'Surely you've noticed them when it's a bit windy – how the flowers keep nodding and fluttering their green leaves; that means as much to them as if they talked.' This annoys the grumpy old councillor. 'Fancy filling a child's head with such rubbish,' he says. 'All stuff and nonsense!'
    One night Ida wakes up in the middle of the night, hears music coming from the next room, and when she peeps in, this is what she sees:

All the hyacinths and tulips were standing on the floor in two long rows; there wasn't one left in the window, where the pots stood empty. Down on the floor all the flowers were dancing round so nicely together, actually doing the Grand Chain, and holding each other by their long green leaves as they swung round. But over at the piano sat a tall yellow lily, which little Ida was sure she had seen last summer; for she remembered the student saying: 'Isn't it like Miss Lena!' Everybody had laughed at him, but now Ida, too, thought that the long yellow flower really was like Miss

Lena. It had just the same way of sitting at the piano, and of turning its sallow oval face first to one side and then to the other, while it nodded time to the pretty music.

The climax of the evening is when suddenly the drawing-room door opens and a whole throng of beautiful flowers comes in:

Two lovely roses, wearing little crowns of gold, led the way; they were the king and queen. Next came the most charming stocks and carnations, bowing in every direction. There was a band playing, too – great poppies and peonies blowing away on pea-shells till they were purple in the face, and harebells and little white snow-drops tinkling away as if they had real bells. It was such funny music. After that came a lot of other flowers, and they all danced together – the blue violets and the red daisies, the ox-eyes and the lilies-of-the-valley. And it was pretty to see how the flowers all kissed each other. At last they said good-night to one another, and little Ida also crept away to bed, where she dreamt of all she had seen.

Tales in which inanimate things become animated

Andersen's ability to give life to inanimate objects was one of the most striking innovations of the nursery tale. The following is a quotation from *Chambers's Journal*, 13 October 1855:

In many a nursery, the warlike 'tin-soldier' (now invariably a Russian, as he used to be a Frenchman), the top, the ball, and even Nurse's darning-needle, have all become so many deathless heroes of romance, through the magic touch of this gentle Scandinavian enchanter.

In an essay entitled 'Hamlet and the Danes'[14] G. K. Chesterton writes about Andersen:

His treatment of inanimate things as animate was not a cold and awkward allegory: it was a true sense of a dumb divinity in things that are. Through him a child did feel that the chair he sat on was something like a wooden horse. Through him children and the happier kind of men did feel themselves covered by a roof as by folded wings of some vast domestic fowl; and feel common doors like great mouths that opened to utter welcome. In the story of 'The Fir Tree' he transplanted to England a living bush that can still blossom into candles. And in his tale of 'The Tin Soldier' he uttered the true defence of romantic militarism against the prigs who would forbid it even as a toy for the nursery. He suggested, in the true tradition of the folk tales, that the dignity of the fighter is not in his largeness but rather in his smallness, in his still loyalty and heroic helplessness in the hands of larger and lower things.

The first tale in which Andersen gave life to inanimate objects was in fact 'The Steadfast Tin Soldier', again about someone who is different – unlike all the other tin soldiers he only has one leg. Whatever happens to him he always behaves with the decorum of a man in uniform. He falls in love with the little dancer cut out of paper, but does not betray his feelings, and when the search goes on for him in the street after he has fallen out of the window, he is still following the rules:

If only the tin soldier had called out 'Here I am!' they would have found him easily enough; but he didn't think it would be right to shout out, as he was in uniform.

Arthur Rackham's illustration
to 'The Steadfast Tin Soldier' (London 1932).

He keeps a stiff upper lip even when faced with terrible dangers, as when the paper boat into which two street-boys have put him drifts from the gutter in under a broad culvert, where a water-rat asks for his passport and pursues him in raging fury. In the open sea he is swallowed by a large fish but is still shouldering arms while lying at full length inside the fish. The fish is caught, cut open, and out comes the tin soldier – back in the same house as before:

There they were – the same children, the same toys on the table, the same beautiful castle with the pretty little dancer who still stood on one leg and kept the other one high in the air – she, too, had been steadfast. This touched the tin soldier, who could have wept tears of tin, only that would hardly have done!

Only in death is the tin soldier united with the dancer, in the glowing stove:

The tin soldier was melted down to a lump and, when the maid cleared out the ashes next morning, she found him in the shape of a little tin heart; but all that was left of the dancer was her spangle, and that was burnt as black as coal.

Another famous example of this category[15] is 'The Darning Needle', about which tale Andersen wrote the following explanatory note in 1862:

In the summer of 1846, during a fairly long visit to Nysø together with Thorvaldsen, who enjoyed 'The Top and the Ball' and 'The Ugly Duckling', he said one day: 'Well, why don't you write us a new amusing tale? You're capable of writing even about a darning needle!' – and then I wrote 'The Darning Needle'.

This explanation is amusing but cannot be quite true, for Thorvaldsen died in March 1844, and 'The Darning Needle' was written at the manor of Bregentved in 1845 and published in 1846. The germ of it is to be found in 'Willie Winkie' (1841), in which Hjalmar asks Willie Winkie to tell him 'the story about the darning needle who was so stuck-up that she fancied she was a sewing needle' – almost verbatim the opening of 'The Darning Needle': 'There was once a darning needle who was really so fine that she fancied she was a sewing needle.'

In spite of having warned the fingers (the only human element in the story) to handle her carefully the darning needle breaks when being forced to try to mend the cook's slippers. Put together with a drop of sealing-wax she is stuck in the front of a scarf.

'Look, now I'm a brooch,' said the darning needle. 'I was certain I should make my way in time. One who *is* something will always go far.' And she laughed inside her, for you can never tell from the outside whether a darning needle is laughing.

She talks to her neighbour, a pin, with a mixture of flattery and condescension, and holding herself up proudly she falls into the washtub and gets lost:

'I'm too fine for this world,' she said as she sat in the gutter. 'Still, my conscience is clear, and that's always a comfort.' And the darning needle held herself straight and kept up her spirits.

In the gutter all sorts of things go floating over her – sticks, straws, bits of newspaper, and she is appalled at their egocentricity:

'Look at the way they go sailing along,' said the darning needle. 'Little do they realize what is at the bottom of it all. *I* am at the bottom – here I sit. . . . Look, there goes a stick that thinks of nothing but "stick", and that's what he is. There goes a straw – see how he twists and turns! Don't think so much about yourself, or you'll bump into the kerb. . . . There goes a bit of newspaper – the news in it is all forgotten, and yet it still spreads itself. . . . I stay patient and quiet. I know what I am, and I shan't change.'

The title character in 'The Shirt Collar' is a kind of male counterpart to the darning needle. The story begins:

There was once a swell gentleman whose entire kit consisted of a bootjack and a comb – though he had the neatest shirt collar you ever saw, and it's about this collar that our story is to be.

Being old enough to think about getting married the collar first proposes to a garter he meets in the wash, but though he flatters her by calling her 'a girdle,

a kind of understrap', she won't have anything to do with him. Next he proposes to a hot iron going over him:

'Madam,' said the collar, 'dear widow lady, I'm getting so hot, I shall soon be quite
another person; I'm losing all my creases. Ugh! You're burning a hole in me – oh!
will you marry me?'
'You rag!' said the iron, going disdainfully over the collar; for she fancied she was a
steam-engine meant to draw trucks on the railway.

Being a bit frayed at the edges the collar has to be cut by the pair of scissors,
to whom he next proposes, calling her a great *ballerina*. But the scissors give
him such a jag that he has to be thrown away. Lastly the collar proposes to the
comb – only to find that she is already engaged to the bootjack.

'Engaged,' sighed the collar. Now there was no one left to propose to, and so he came
to despise the whole idea.

At last the collar finds himself in a bag at the paper-mill, together with a lot of
other rags, to whom he brags about his past, turning all his defeats into con-
quests. His punishment is that he is made into paper, into that very bit of paper
on which the story is printed.

   One of Andersen's most sophisticated stories about inanimate objects has no
title, for it is a story within a story: it is the tale told by the owner of the flying
trunk to the King and Queen of Turkey to prove to them that he is worthy of
marrying their daughter. It is a very amusing domestic conversation-piece
which takes place in the kitchen. In order of appearance the characters are: a
bundle of matches, the saucepan, the tinder box, the earthenware jar, the
plates, the broom, the bucket, the tongs, the tea urn, an old quill pen, the tea
kettle, and the market basket. The personality of each of the characters comes
out in their contributions to the conversation, and they are all extremely
human. This gem of a story is Andersen at his malicious best.

   In an essay about Andersen in *Books and Authors*, 1922, Robert Lynd wrote:

Andersen's genius as a narrator, as a grotesque inventor of incident and comic detail,
saves his gospel from commonness. He may write a parable about a darning-needle
alive, like a dog or a schoolboy. He endows everything he sees – china shepherdesses,
tin soldiers, mice and flowers – with the similitude of life, action and conversation.
He can make the inhabitants of one's mantelpiece capable of epic adventures, and has
greater sense of possibilities in a pair of tongs or a door-knocker than most of us have
in men and women. He is the creator of a thousand fancies.

Realistic tales set in a fantasy world

As the best example of this category I shall discuss 'The Nightingale', universally considered to be one of Andersen's masterpieces.[16]

   Although this tale is set in China, it soon becomes clear that it is a fictitious
and fantastic China. With the exception of the nightingale and Death towards
the end of the tale, all the characters are very human, for better or worse.[17]

   'The Nightingale' is basically the story of nature versus artificiality, and this
conflict is illustrated not only by the contrast between the real nightingale and

the mechanical bird, but also by the contrast between the ordinary Chinese people (represented by the fishermen and the poor kitchen-maid) on one hand, and by the Chinese imperial palace, its courtiers and civil servants, on the other. The difference is to be found even in the palace gardens; in the remote parts, where the inhabitants of the palace never go, there are deep lakes and glorious woods going right down to the sea; in the garden immediately out-side the palace only rare and precious flowers, with silver bells attached in order to draw attention to them. Above these differences sits the Chinese emperor himself, almost a prisoner of his surroundings, but with an apprecia-tion of real values when he has a chance to see or hear them.

The remoteness of China allowed Andersen to invent a world full of *chinoiserie* and stiff, formal rules. The palace itself is made of porcelain, and on special occasions it is polished so that the china walls and floors glitter in the lights of thousands and thousands of gold lamps. The emperor sits in a gold chair when reading, and we are told that his gentleman-in-waiting 'was so grand that, whenever anyone of lower rank than himself ventures to speak to him or ask a question, he only answers "P!" – and that means nothing at all'. The punishment for a courtier who falls into disgrace is that he shall be punched in the stomach after supper, and the reward for the kitchen-maid for finding the nightingale is that she shall have a regular situation in the kitchen and be allowed to watch the emperor eat his dinner. The courtiers' ignorance of the natural world is such that when they hear a cow mooing or frogs croaking they believe these sounds to be the nightingale's song. When they first see the nightingale they are disappointed because she looks so ordinary. 'I expect she's off colour through having so many distinguished visitors,' the gentleman-in-waiting says.

A golden perch is provided for the nightingale, and the reward for her beautiful singing is the offer of a gold slipper to wear round her neck. The social order inside the palace is described: the court ladies show their approval by gurgling whenever anyone speaks to them; and at the bottom of the scale: 'Even the lackeys and lady's maids expressed their approval; and that's saying a good deal, for they are the most difficult of all to satisfy.'

Into this kind of artificiality the nightingale is supposed to fit:

She was now to remain at court and have her own cage, with leave to go out for two walks in the daytime and one at night. She was given twelve attendants, who each held on tightly to a silk ribbon fastened round her leg. There was absolutely no fun in a walk like that.

The arrival of the artificial nightingale, covered all over with diamonds, rubies and sapphires, results in complete chaos, for the two birds cannot sing together. The Master of the Emperor's Music declares that it is not the fault of the artificial bird: 'It keeps perfect time and follows my methods exactly.' The real nightingale flies away and is regarded as being ungrateful and banished from the Chinese empire. The Master of Music explains why the artificial bird is preferable to the real one:

'You see, ladies and gentlemen and, above all, Your Imperial Majesty, with the real nightingale there's no telling what's going to happen. But with the artificial bird everything is fixed beforehand. Such-and-such will be heard and no other. One can account for it all: one can open it up and show the cylinders, how they go round, and the way in which one thing follows from another!'

The artificial bird is promoted to be Chief Imperial Bedside Minstrel of the First Class on the Left, and the Master of Music writes a work in twenty-five volumes about it. 'It was very long and learned, full of the most difficult Chinese words, and everyone pretended they had read and understood it, or else of course they would have been thought stupid and got punched in the stomach.'

Then one evening the mechanism inside the bird goes wrong, the bearings being almost worn out, and from then on it is only allowed to sing once a year.

Five years later, as the emperor lies dying, longing for music to take his thoughts away from death, he appeals to the artificial bird, but in vain, and it is the real nightingale singing in the tree outside who wrestles with Death in an effort to save the emperor's life:

She had heard of her emperor's distress and had therefore come to sing him consolation and hope; and as she sang, the shapes grew fainter and fainter, the blood in the emperor's weak limbs ran faster and faster, and Death himself listened and said, 'Go on, little nightingale, go on!'

The nightingale goes on, and for each song she sings Death gives up one of the treasures he had taken from the emperor until, longing for his garden, Death floats like a cold white mist out of the window.

Realistic stories set in a recognizable world

As a good example of this category I have chosen a story which is relatively little known internationally, 'The Gardener and the Squire'.[18]

It is set in an old Danish manor house owned by a rich nobleman and his wife. To keep the large garden they employ a clever gardener, Mr Larsen, and it is a pleasure to see how nice and tidy he keeps it. Two big half-dead trees swarming with rooks and crows, who have built their nests in them, are an eyesore to the gardener, who wants to get rid of them; but to the squire and his wife both the trees and the birds represent the romantic past, and they will not hear of Larsen's suggestion that the old trees should be cut down to make way for something better:

'My dear Larsen, haven't you enough room already? With your flower-garden, glass-houses and kitchen garden?'
Yes, he had all these, and he tended and looked after them with great attention and skill. His master and mistress admitted this, but they were afraid they had to tell him that at other people's houses they often ate fruit or saw flowers which were better than anything in their own garden. The gardener was sorry to hear this, for he did his best that the best should be done. He was good at heart and good at his job.

One day the squire tells Mr Larsen that in the house of some distinguished friends they had had some excellent fruit and suggests that Larsen should cultivate this particular species. When it emerges that in fact the fruit came from their own orchard, they refuse to believe it until Mr Larsen produces a written statement from the fruiterer.

'How very odd!' said the squire.

And now every day at the manor huge bowls of these magnificent apples and pears from their own garden appeared on the table. Bushels and barrels of the fruit were sent to friends in and out of the town, and even abroad, bringing no end of pleasure. Still, they had to admit that of course there had been two unusually good summers for fruit trees; these had done well all over the country.

After the squire and his wife have dined at court they send for the gardener and tell him to get some melon seeds from their majesties' greenhouse, for they had such delicious melons at court. Again it turns out that the melons came from Larsen's greenhouse, and again he can produce a statement to that effect.

This was indeed a surprise for the squire, and he made no secret of the incident, but showed people the certificate and even had melon seeds sent out far and wide just as previously the cuttings had been.

Then news came back that the seeds were striking and setting admirably and the plant was called after the squire's manor, so that in this way its name could now be read in English, German and French. That was something never dreamed of before. 'I do hope the gardener won't begin to think too much of himself,' said the squire.

Mr Larsen's ambition, however, is to establish himself as one of the leading gardeners in the country, and he does produce some first-rate gardening.

But, all the same, he often heard it said that his very first fruit, the apples and the pears, were really his best; all that came after was much inferior. The melons were no doubt extremely good, but they were of course something quite different. His strawberries might be called excellent, and yet no better than those to be found on other estates; and when one year the radishes were a failure, it was only the unfortunate radishes that they talked about and not a word about anything else that turned out well.

It was almost as though the squire felt relieved to be able to say, 'Well, Larsen, rather a poor year, eh?' They quite enjoyed saying, 'Rather a poor year.'

When Mr Larsen brings in beautifully arranged flowers he is told: 'You have taste, Larsen. That's a gift, not of your own, but of God.'

One day he brings in a big crystal bowl with a leaf of a water-lily and on top of this a brilliant blue flower, which the squire and his wife take to be an Indian water-lily. It is admired by everybody who sees it, including a princess. But the squire and his wife are appalled when they find out that the blue flower came from the kitchen garden, being the blossom of an artichoke.

'You should have told us that straight away,' said the squire. 'We couldn't help thinking it was a rare foreign flower. You've made us look ridiculous in the eyes of the young princess.'

But when they apologize to the princess and assure her that Mr Larsen has been told off, she says: 'How unfair! Why, he has opened our eyes to a splendid flower we had never noticed; he has shown us beauty where we never dreamed of looking.' So Mr Larsen may again bring a fresh artichoke blossom.

'It's really quite handsome,' the squire said; 'altogether remarkable.'
And the gardener was praised.
'That's what Larsen enjoys,' said the squire. 'He's a spoilt child.'

An autumn gale blows down the two half-dead trees, and in their place Mr
Larsen makes a most unusual and varied extension of the garden and puts up a
flagstaff flying the Danish flag and nearby a pole, round which the hops twine
their clusters in the summer and autumn and in winter a sheaf of oats is hung to
feed the birds.

'Our good Larsen is getting sentimental in his old age,' said the squire. 'But he's
faithful and devoted to us.'
With the New Year there appeared in one of the capital's illustrated papers a picture
of the old manor house, showing the flagstaff and the sheaf of oats for the birds at
Christmas, and emphasis was laid on the happy idea of keeping up a time-honoured
custom in this way – an idea so very characteristic of the old place.
'They beat the big drum for every mortal thing that Larsen does,' said the squire.
'He's a lucky man. I suppose we ought almost to be proud of having him.'
But they weren't in the least proud of it. They felt that they were the master and
mistress and could give Larsen a month's notice if they liked, but they didn't do that.
They were kind people, and there are so many kind people of that sort. What a good
thing that is for all the Larsens!

I have tried in this chapter to show the wide range of Andersen's *Eventyr og
Historier*. The grouping into seven identifiable categories is my own, and,
admittedly, only one among several possible ways of looking at them.
Another useful way might be to divide them into two groups: tales with a
special appeal to children and tales with a special appeal to adults. The best of
them, however, would fall into both categories: children will understand them
in their way, and adults in theirs.
    In 1861 Bjørnstjerne Bjørnson wrote in a letter to Jonas Collin junior:

It is quite wrong to speak of what Andersen is writing now as 'fairy tales'. That was
the name of his very first what you might call little bits of things, that could be put
into a nutshell and then taken out again to span the world. Moreover, the form in
which these tales were cast was quite perfect, concerned as it was solely with the very
core of his subject. But now that Andersen has, often unjustly, been hustled out of the
domain of the novel, of the drama and of philosophic narrative, the result has merely
been that these thwarted suckers have thrust their own way out through the rock at
some other point, and that he now has – God help us! – the novel, the drama and his
philosophy all turning up in the fairy tale! That this is no longer a fairy tale, is
obvious. It is something that is Andersenian, that is anyhow not generally dispensed
by a literary pharmacist. . . . It is something that has no limits above or below, and so
none in its shape – which, therefore, only a perfect genius can keep in hand. . . . But
that freedom from all restraint – that assumption that all form and a whole world of
tragic, comic, lyric and epic speculation, all singing, preaching, jesting, the animate
and the inanimate, merge together as though in paradise – all this makes one tremble
for the appearance of his next work. What secret is he going to solve? What journey
must we make? And will it succeed or fail?

2 'The whole world and a pair of new skates'

A COMPLETE analysis of Andersen's language and style is only possible, of course, in the language in which he wrote, Danish; but certain characteristic features can also be found in good translations.

Unfortunately, most of the nineteenth-century English translations are very unsatisfactory, and this is particularly true of some of those made during the years 1846–8, when 'Hans Andersen' became a household word both in Great Britain and America. If Comte de Buffon's famous dictum, 'Le style est l'homme même', were applied to those translations it would be more valid for the translator than for the author.

Admittedly, Andersen is not easy to translate. His language is full of colloquialisms, special Danish idioms, untranslatable puns and an atmosphere of intimacy between writer and reader, which is strengthened by the frequent use of such Danish adverbs as *saa, da, vel, nok, jo,* many of which defy translation. As R. P. Keigwin, in my opinion the best of the English translators, put it in his preface to the centenary edition of the first four tales, published by Cambridge University Press in 1935:

He sprinkled his narrative with every kind of conversational touch – crisp, lively openings, to catch the listener's attention at a swoop; frequent asides or parentheses; little bits of Copenhagen slang; much grammatical licence; and, above all, a free use of particles – those nods and nudges of speech, with which Danish (like Greek) is so richly endowed. So completely did Andersen maintain the conversational tone in his *Tales* that you are quite shocked when you occasionally come across some really literary turn.

It is necessary to say something about the early translations, because millions of readers have based and are still basing their opinion of Andersen on them; many of these translations are still being reprinted even today (though often without any mention of the translator's name), partly because age has made them sacrosanct, and partly because publishers do not have to pay royalties on them.

It is not generally realized that some of Andersen's early translators did not know Danish at all but translated from the German versions, some of them very mediocre. Others, who were able to boast on the title-page that their version was 'translated from the original Danish', had such a limited knowledge of the language that they made the most appalling mistakes.

As an example of a translator who committed elementary errors, let me mention Mary Howitt, who was responsible for the first printed English version; she knew German, and via Swedish (which she knew imperfectly) she had acquired an elementary reading knowledge of Danish. Here are some examples of her innumerable blunders: she translates *Sommerfugle* (butterflies) as 'summer birds', *den bløde Jord* (the soft ground) as 'the bloody earth', and *listede* (crept) as 'listened'. The sentence *I kan gjerne lee med!* (You may as well join in the laugh) she renders as 'I cannot help laughing', and *det hjelper dog, man siger sin Mening* (it does some good, after all, to express one's opinion) as 'that is better: one sees his meaning!' She writes of a song that it was 'written in pencil', when the whole point is that it was 'written by the pencil', and by misunderstanding the Danish word *Tallerknerne* (the plates) she writes 'All the talkers shook for pleasure', where the real meaning is 'All the plates rattled with joy'. She is capable of making a translation which conveys the exact opposite of what is meant, e.g., where a correct translation would be, 'Down in the street the officials were being flogged,' Mary Howitt puts, 'Down in the street the royal officers were beating people.'

Mary Howitt is fond of archaic phrases: 'If thou wilt sail with me, little Yalmar, thou canst reach foreign countries,' and by retaining the Danish word order her English is often very clumsy: 'Thou shalt have thanks, thou old grandfather,' or 'Yes, that thou mayst believe!'

Furthermore, she bowdlerizes Andersen. This is how he begins 'Thumbelina':

There was once a woman who wanted to have a wee child of her own, but she had no idea where she was to get it from. So she went off to an old witch and said to her, 'I would so dearly like to have a little child. Do please tell me where I can find one.' 'Oh, that!' said the witch. 'Nothing easier. Take this barley-corn – mind you, it's not the kind that grows out in the fields or that the fowls are fed with. Put it in a flower-pot, and see what happens!'

This is how it comes out in Mary Howitt's translation:

Once upon a time, a beggar woman went to the house of a poor peasant, and asked for something to eat. The peasant's wife gave her some bread and milk. When she had eaten it, she took a barley-corn out of her pocket, and said – 'This will I give to thee; set it in a flower-pot, and see what will come out of it.'

She was obviously afraid that Andersen's opening might arouse children's interest in where babies came from. In 'The Garden of Eden' she removes any suggestion of sensuousness. 'The loveliest girls, slender and graceful, clad in billowy gauze that revealed the beauty of their limbs, swayed in the dance' is reduced to: 'The most beautiful maidens floated in the dance'. Then at the end she adds a long final moralizing paragraph of her own.

Some other translators were even worse in their tendency to 'improve' Andersen. Charles Boner, whose translations were all made from the German, may be mentioned as an example of a translator who suffered chronically from literary ambition. Unlike Andersen he despised everyday speech; instead of 'the sweetheart' he would write 'the affianced one', instead of 'people', 'mortals', and instead of 'see', 'behold'. Boner liked inserting adjectives which are not in the Danish text; where Andersen writes 'the knife',

Boner writes 'the fatal knife' or 'the murderous instrument'; where Andersen writes 'the little mermaid', Boner writes 'the dainty little mermaid'. No effort is spared to make Andersen's straightforward dialogue read like a book; instead of letting the ball say to the top: 'But I promise never to forget you,' Boner makes the ball say: 'But this I assure you, forget you is what I shall never do.' Andersen's 'None of them was so full of longing as the youngest' is much too simple for Boner, who writes: 'But none of the sisters felt so lively a longing for this day of infantile restraint as the youngest'; and instead of writing, 'And then at last she was fifteen', Boner writes, 'At length the much-desired fifteenth year was attained'.

Even worse than Mary Howitt and Charles Boner is Caroline Peachey, whose English translations of Andersen's tales are more frequently reprinted than those of any other English translator. R. Nisbet Bain, Andersen's first English biographer, wrote in 1895 of her version, entitled *Danish Fairy Legends and Tales*:

Other translators may misunderstand, and therefore misinterpret, their Andersen. Miss Peachey presumes to embellish and even bowdlerize him. In 'The Tinder Box', the dog that had the gold is expanded into 'the monstrous guardian of the golden treasure'. The soldier, who, by the way, put up not at an inn but at a *hotel*, is so modest that he 'kneels down and kisses the princess's *hand*' – quite a new departure. We all remember that the queen in the same story is described as a wise woman who 'could do something more than ride in a coach'. Miss Peachey is careful to add, 'and look very grand and condescending'. Four adjectives suffice Andersen for describing the little match girl's grandmother: Miss Peachey requires three sentences.

Caroline Peachey's language is dull and flat where Andersen's is lively and colourful. In 'The Ugly Duckling' Andersen writes: 'The raven who perched on the fence kept squawking "ow! ow!" – he felt so cold. The very thought of it gave you the shivers. Yes, the poor duckling was certainly having a bad time.' Caroline Peachey reduces this to: 'and the raven sat on the edge and croaked – the poor duckling was certainly not very comfortable!' She does not understand Andersen's sense of humour and entirely fails to reproduce it. In 'The Little Mermaid' Andersen writes: 'At last she could keep it to herself no longer, but told one of her sisters; and immediately all the rest got to know, but nobody else – except a few other mermaids who didn't breathe a word to any but their nearest friends.' This, in Caroline Peachey's version, reads: 'At last, being unable to conceal her sorrow any longer, she revealed the secret to one of her sisters, who told it to the other princesses, and they to some of their friends.'

Both Charles Boner and Caroline Peachey took over a German translator's 'improvement' on 'The Princess on the Pea' so that instead of putting *one* pea under the twenty mattresses and twenty featherbeds the queen puts *three* peas. (One can almost hear the sceptical translator arguing, 'Surely, she cannot feel *one* pea through all those layers!') Since they could not very well call the story 'The Princess on the three Peas', they then had to alter the title to 'The Real Princess'.

Owing to the constant reprinting of her translations Caroline Peachey has done more damage to Andersen's image in the English-speaking world than anyone else. She may have been the worst of Andersen's English translators but there are several runners-up; fortunately most of their translations are now forgotten.

Madame de Châtelain was another early translator, who managed to do exactly the opposite of what Andersen did – she used expressions which are utterly incomprehensible to children, such as 'patrimony', 'promiscuously' and 'metamorphosed'. Instead of writing, 'John just couldn't stop telling about how nice the princess had been to him, and how lovely she was', she writes: 'Johannes could not cease expatiating on the gracious reception he had met with from the princess, and on her extreme beauty.'

Alfred Wehnert wrote in the preface to his translation of *Andersen's Tales for Children*: 'There is no need of an excuse for offering a new translation of his tales, so justly esteemed are they for their freshness of tone, and the simple purity they breathe.' Unfortunately, Alfred Wehnert succeeded in ruining the very freshness of tone he extolls.

Wehnert had no hesitation whatever in adding substantially to Andersen's text; in fact, some of his versions are twice as long as Andersen's. Here is an example taken at random from 'The Nightingale':

Five years had now gone by, and presently the whole country was filled with sorrow, for really in their hearts they were all fond of their emperor; but now he was ill and not likely to live, it was said.

And this is Alfred Wehnert:

Five years had now passed over, when the whole land was unexpectedly thrown into the deepest distress, by the startling news that the old Emperor was so seriously ill that his death might momentarily be expected, for all were sincerely attached to their magnanimous monarch, by whose decease they would in fact gain nothing, but might be much worse off under his successors.

Later editions of Andersen's tales were a mixture of Caroline Peachey's and Alfred Wehnert's translations, and the results have done much damage to Andersen's prestige as a writer.

Discounting adaptors and translators of single tales there have been about thirty English and American translators of collections of the *Fairy Tales and Stories* between 1846 and 1974, and in my opinion by far the best and most loyal are R. P. Keigwin, Paul Leyssac, Reginald Spink, L. W. Kingsland, and Jean Hersholt. Of these the first four are 'English' translations, the last one 'American'.

I have omitted from this account a discussion of the innumerable editions of Andersen's tales in which it is stated that they are 'based on', 'adapted from', 'founded on', 'arranged from', 'retold after' or 'suggested by' some tale or tales by Andersen – who often has to put up with the further ignominy of having his name mis-spelt as 'Anderson'. All one can say is that in all such cases the reader is at least warned that what he is getting is not the genuine article. I have also disregarded the many individual stories which have been 'dramatized by', 'versified by', 'retold in rhyme by', 'edited for little folk by', 'told to the children by' or 'arranged for little readers by' people who thought they were capable of improving on Andersen by pinching his ideas and ruining his style.

Some of these adaptations and rewritings are utterly grotesque. In 1944 an edition of 'The Little Match Girl' was published in New York, with the following note printed on the dust-jacket: 'Children will read with delight this new version of the famous old Hans Christian Andersen tale. For in it the little match girl on that long ago Christmas Eve does not perish from the bitter cold, but finds warmth and cheer and a lovely home where she lives happily ever after.'

Andersen's style was entirely his own, and far removed from that of the traditional folk or fairy tale.

Grimm's *Märchen* report events impersonally: 'Once upon a time there was a soldier who had served the king faithfully for many years. Now that the war was over and the soldier had been wounded many times, he could not serve any longer.' Compare the opening lines of 'The Tinder Box': 'Down the country-road a soldier came marching. Left, right! Left, right! He had his knapsack on his back and a sword at his side, for he had been at the war, and now he was on his way home.'

Andersen wrote two versions of 'The Goloshes of Fortune'. The first begins:

In one of the houses not far from the King's New Square people had been invited to a party, a very large party, in order to obtain, as many people do, a regular subscription to the mutual invitations of others.

The second, revised version begins:

It was in Copenhagen. At one of the houses in East Street not far from the King's New Square there was a big party on; people have to have one of these now and again, because then it's over and done with and you can be invited back.

In this version he has put his personal stamp on the style, which has become light and humorous.

'People were supposed to hear the narrator in the style, and so the language must approach that of oral narration,' Andersen explains; adding that his tales 'were told for children, but the grown-up person should be allowed to listen as well.'

Told for children – yes, indeed! This is how 'The Happy Family' begins:

The biggest leaf in this country, depend upon it, is a burdock leaf. Hold it in front of your tummy, and it would do for an apron; put it over your head in the rain, and it's almost as good as an umbrella – it's a tremendous size.

There is no doubt for what category of listeners this is intended. Nor is there in the opening lines of 'The Drop of Water': 'I suppose you know what a magnifying glass is – a sort of round eye-glass that makes everything a hundred times bigger than it is.' What he is describing without using the difficult word is, of course, a microscope.

The direct appeal to the youthful listener, which is characteristic of the oral narrative, has often been preserved. 'Dad's Always Right' begins:

Of course you've been in the country, haven't you? You know what a real farmhouse looks like, with a thatch roof all grown over with moss and weeds and a stork's nest perched on the ridge – we can't do without the stork – and crooked walls and low-browed windows, only one of which will open. The oven pokes out its fat little stomach; and the elder-bush leans over the fence, where there's a little pond with a duck or some ducklings, just under the wrinkled willow tree. Yes, and then there's a dog on a chain that keeps barking at all and sundry.

'The Shepherdess and the Chimney-Sweep' also opens with a question to the listener: 'Have you ever seen a real old-fashioned cupboard, its wood quite black with age and carved all over with twirls and twisting foliage?' Or the question may be put teasingly, as in the opening lines of 'The Farmyard Cock and the Weathercock': 'There were two cocks, one on the dunghill and one on the roof-top: vainglorious both of them. But which achieved most? Give us your opinion – we'll stick to our own.'

The unforgettable colloquial opening of 'The Snow Queen' in Danish: '*See saa! nu begynde vi . . .*' is very difficult to translate adequately, and many have ruined it altogether. In the following version I have combined what I consider to be the best elements in Keigwin's and Spink's translations:

Now then, here's where we begin! When we get to the end of the story we shall know more than we do now; for it has to do with a wicked imp – one of the wickedest – Old Nick. One day he was in excellent spirits, because he had made a looking-glass which had this about it – that everything good and beautiful that was reflected in it shrank up into almost nothing, whereas everything useless and ugly stood out worse than ever.

Few writers can use truisms with such deliberately humorous intent as Andersen.[19] The opening lines of 'The Nightingale' may serve as an example: 'You know of course that in China the emperor is a Chinese and his subjects are Chinese too.'

Some openings go straight to the point, such as this one in 'Five Peas from One Pod': 'There were five peas in a pod; they were green, and so they thought the whole world must be green – and that was right enough.' (Some weeks later things have changed: 'The peas turned yellow and the pod turned yellow. "The whole world's turning yellow," they said, and they had a perfect right to say it.')

In 'A Good Temper', on the other hand, the point is not to go straight to the point:

From my father I have inherited the best possible thing – a good temper. And who was my father? Well, but that has nothing to do with temper. He was lively and vigorous and plump; his person, outwardly and inwardly, was at complete variance with his profession. And what was his profession, his place in society? Well, if it were

to be written down and printed right at the beginning of a book, then it's likely that a good many people, when they read it, would put the book aside and say, 'It strikes me as horrible; that kind of thing doesn't appeal to me at all.' And yet my father was neither horse-butcher nor hangman – on the contrary, his job often placed him ahead of the very worthiest men in the town and he was there quite properly, quite in his own right. He had to go first – before the bishop, before princes of the blood – yes, always in the foremost place, for he drove a hearse.
There, now it's out.

There is something very homely and unpretentious about Andersen's fairy-tale kings. Some of the kingdoms, like that of the prince in 'The Swineherd', are quite small, though in his case 'large enough to marry on'. After the prince has smeared his face with brown and black and pulled a cap down over his eyes, he goes over to another kingdom (which cannot be very large either), where he knocks on the door, and obviously, the emperor himself answers it:

'Good morning, Emperor!' he said. 'I wonder if you've got a job for me here at the Castle.'
'Ah, well,' said the emperor, 'there are so many come and ask that. But now, let me see – yes, I want someone to mind the pigs. We've such a lot of pigs.'

We meet the emperor again later in the story when he steps out on to his balcony and sees that something is going on over by the pigsties:

He rubbed his eyes and put on his spectacles. 'Why, it's the ladies-in-waiting, up to some game or other. Perhaps I'd better go and have a look' – and he gave a hitch to the back of his slippers, for he had trodden them down at the heel.
Phew! What a hurry he was in!
As soon as he came down into the courtyard, he crept along very quietly. And the maids-of-honour were so busy counting the kisses, for it had to be fair do's – he mustn't have too many kisses, nor yet too few – that they never noticed the emperor, who now drew himself up on tiptoe.
'What's all this?' he said, when he saw them kissing; and he slapped them over the head with his slipper, just as the young pigman was having his eighty-sixth kiss.
'Out you get!' said the emperor, for he was furious.

His love for the princess having turned to disgust the prince 'went into his kingdom, shut the door and bolted it'.
  The king in 'The Travelling Companion' is also very human, and very accessible even to a complete stranger like John:

'Come in!' cried the old king, as John knocked at the door. John opened it, and the old king came out to meet him in his dressing-gown and embroidered slippers. He was wearing his gold crown, while he held the sceptre in one hand and the gold orb in the other. 'Just a moment!' he exclaimed, and he popped the orb under his left arm so as to be able to shake hands with John. But directly he heard that John was a suitor, he began to cry so hard that he dropped both sceptre and orb on the floor and had to wipe away his tears with his dressing-gown.

After his daughter, the princess, has arrived, they all go upstairs, 'and the

Danish illustration by Andersen's first
illustrator, Vilhelm Pedersen, to
'The Swineherd' (Copenhagen 1847).

young pages served them with jam-tarts and ginger-nuts, but the old king
was so upset he couldn't eat a thing, and anyhow the ginger-nuts were too hard
for him'. The last addition removes any vestige of sentimentality from this
part of the story.

The king is not afraid of showing his feelings. Before John made his first
guess the king 'stood drying his eyes with a white handkerchief'; but after
John has made the correct guess, then: 'Bless my soul, how pleased the old king

was! He turned a somersault – you never saw such a beauty! – and everybody clapped both for him and for John, because he had guessed right at the first time of asking.'

Like king like people: 'The old king was so upset by all this sorrow and misery that he spent one whole day every year on his knees praying. . . . The old dames who went in for brandy coloured it deep black before they drank it – that was their way of mourning – and more could hardly be expected of them.'

After John has married the princess there is a happy ending for the old king too; he 'lived long and happily and allowed their little ones to ride-a-cock-horse on his knee and play with his sceptre'.

A fairy-tale princess is not bound by the usual conventions. She may announce that she is going to marry the man who in her opinion is best able to speak up for himself (this happens both in 'The Snow Queen' and in 'Simple Simon'), or her father may offer her as a prize to the winner of a competition (as in 'The High Jumpers'):

'Now the one that jumps highest shall have my daughter,' said the king; 'for it seems so shabby that these gentlemen [meaning the flea, the grasshopper and the skipjack] should have nothing to jump for.'

A Turkish princess may agree to marry a complete stranger who crawls in through the window and kisses her when she lies asleep on the sofa. 'This woke her up, and she was very frightened, until he told her he was the Turkish God who had come down to her from the sky. She liked that very much.' But she insists that he must come and have tea with the king and queen on the following Saturday and have a really fine story to tell them. 'My mother likes a story to be goody-goody and correct, but my father likes it to be funny, so that he can laugh.'

The simplicity of the royal family, however, is not matched by the people who surround them at court; here the pomp and ceremony can be really frightening:

All the ladies-in-waiting with their maids and their maids' maids, and all the gentlemen-in-waiting with their footmen and their footmen's footmen who have pages, stood lined up all round; and the nearer they stood to the door, the haughtier they looked. The footmen's footmen's page, who always wears slippers, stands so proudly in the doorway that one can hardly bear to look at him.

In contrast to the homely miniature royal court Andersen describes the evil troll's dwelling inside the mountain. In the corridor 'there were hundreds and hundreds of glowing spiders that ran up and down the wall and shone like fire', and in the great hall, built of gold and silver, red and blue flowers as large as sunflowers gleam from the walls, 'but the flowers couldn't be picked because their stalks were horrible poisonous snakes and the petals were flames that darted out of their mouths. The ceiling was entirely covered with shining glow-worms and sky-blue bats that flapped their wings in the most extra-ordinary way'. The music is provided by great black grasshoppers playing on Jews' harps, 'and the owl – for want of a drum – beat his own stomach'. The courtiers all look very handsome and distinguished, but anyone with eyes in his head soon sees through it all: 'They were nothing but broom-handles with cabbage-heads to them, that the ogre had bewitched into life and given embroidered robes. Well, it didn't anyhow make any difference; they were only used for show.'

The Norwegian Dovre King is in a different category altogether, a distinguished ruler of a troll kingdom, and a person who commands respect: 'There stood the old troll from Dovre in his crown of stiff icicles and polished fir-cones, wearing, too, bearskin and sleigh-boots.' As in the human society there are class distinctions among trolls: the ones with tails are superior to the ones without. Trolls differ from humans in that they are all left-legged and that they don't throw shadows; their customs also differ: when a troll proposes to a girl he changes boots with her, which is considered smarter than exchanging rings.

The Snow Queen's palace is in a completely different category, unlike any other royal palace; it is huge, empty, ice-cold and glittering, and it is characterized by the absence of gaiety and merriment:

Never was there any jollification, not even so much as a little dance for the bears, when the gale could play the horn and the polar bears get up on their hind legs and show off their party manners. Never a little social with mouth-slapping and paw-rapping; never the smallest tea fights for the snowy vixens; all was bare, bleak and vast in the halls of the Snow Queen.

In the world of animals, plants and inanimate objects Andersen identifies himself with his characters; their tastes, knowledge and general philosophy are all conditioned by their circumstances. Everything is seen from the point of view of the individual speaker. Thus the mice ask the fir tree: 'Do tell us about the loveliest place on earth. Have you ever been there? Have you been in the larder, where there are cheeses on the shelves and hams hanging from the ceiling – where you can dance on tallow candles and you go in thin and come out fat?'

Roses cannot be expected to have a profound knowledge of astronomy, and so they explain space as they see it: ' ". . . during the daytime the sun is very warm, and at night the sky shines even more beautifully; we can see that through the small holes in it." It was the stars they thought were holes, for the roses didn't know any better.'

The sparrows are critical of human inventions: 'They've a thing nowadays they call the Almanac. I suppose it's an invention of their own, and so everything's got to go by it; but it doesn't. When spring arrives, the year begins; that's nature's way, and that's what I go by.'

Before the autumn comes the storks give their young a potted geography of the country to which they will soon be flying. 'Egypt is where we fly to, with her three-cornered houses that go tapering to a point until they're higher than the clouds. They're called Pyramids and are older than any stork can imagine. There's a river that overflows, so that the land all turns to mud. We can walk about in the mud and eat frogs.' The mother stork explains to the young storks why it would be unwise to think of spending the winter in Denmark: '"It's so cold here that the clouds freeze to bits and then flutter down like scraps of white paper." It was snow she meant, only she didn't know how to explain it more clearly.'

The storks have not a very high opinion of the human race:

'Man is the most conceited of creatures,' said the stork. 'Listen what a clatter they make. But their rattle can't compare with ours. They plume themselves on their ready speech and on their language. A fine language, indeed, that slops over into gibberish every day's journey we go; they just can't understand each other. We can speak our language all over the world, both in Denmark and in Egypt. Men can't fly either. They get speed with a discovery they call "the railway", but they often break their necks doing that. It gives my beak the shivers when I think of it. The world can do without mankind; we don't need them. If only we may keep frogs and earth-worms!'

Nevertheless, most of Andersen's non-human characters are remarkably similar to human beings. As Georg Brandes said: 'Andersen does not depict the animal in Man but Man in the animal.'

In the following conversation between a male stork and his wife hatching her eggs, the logic is really that of an expectant mother:

'I've something really dreadful to tell you,' he said to the stork mother.
'Then don't!' she answered. 'Remember I'm sitting and it might upset me, and that would affect the eggs.'

When her husband begins his story she interrupts him: 'How long-winded you are! The eggs might catch cold. I can't bear to be kept in suspense.'

The ugly duckling's mother talks like a mother in a maternity ward: 'But just look at the others – the loveliest ducklings I've ever seen. They all take after their father – the wretch! Why doesn't he come and see me?'

The beetle, too, reacts with the logic of certain humans: 'I never ask a second time,' said the beetle, when he had already asked three times without getting an answer. Even trees have learnt tricks from humans: 'The large trees didn't say anything, either good or bad, and that's always the safe thing to do when you're stupid.'

The commandment about loving one's neighbour appears to apply in the animal world as well, though as in the human world only in theory. Flattered about her kindness a Portuguese duck replies: 'I've never given my kind heart a thought, but I do know that I love all other creatures except the cat, and no one can reasonably ask me to do that: he has eaten two of my young ones.' When in a fit of rage she has bitten off the head of a singing bird she says: 'What! Was that too much for him? Well, in that case he wasn't fit for this world. I've been like a mother to him, I know that. No one can doubt the kindness of my heart.'

The china shepherdess is a spoilt little bourgeois lady who thrives only in her indoor milieu. The moment she sees the world from the top of the chimney she feels homesick, lays her little head on the chimney-sweep's shoulder, crying and crying till the gold runs from her sash:

'This is too much!' she said. 'I can't bear it – the world's far too big. If only I were back on the little table under the looking-glass! I shall never be happy until I'm there again. I've come with you into the wide world; now I want you to take me home again, if you love me at all.'

She is disconsolate when on her return she finds that Grandpa, the old China-man, is broken; but the chimney-sweep comforts her by saying that when he has been riveted, 'he'll be as good as new again and able to say all sorts of nasty things to us'. – 'I do wish we had old Grandpa safely riveted,' she says. 'Do you think it'll be very expensive?'

The Danish rag is appalled at the bragging of the Norwegian rag:

'A Danish rag could never talk like that,' said the Dane. 'It isn't our nature to. I know myself, and all our Danish rags are like me; we're so amiable and modest, we've too little faith in ourselves, and that really doesn't get you anywhere. But it's a tempera-ment I quite like; I find it charming. Otherwise, I assure you, I'm well aware of my own good qualities, though I don't talk about them. That's a failing no one shall have the chance to accuse me of. I'm weak and yielding. I put up with everything, I envy no one and speak well of everybody, even though there isn't much to be said for most of the others; still, that's their look-out. I treat it all as a joke, being so talented myself.'

There are class distinctions, too, in the world of toys. The ball regards herself as belonging to a different world from that of the top. This is how the con-versation continues after the top has suggested that they might make a happy couple:

'Oh, you think that, do you?' answered the ball. 'You don't seem to realize that my father and mother were morocco slippers and that I have a cork inside me.'
'Ah, but I'm made of mahogany,' said the top. 'Why, the mayor turned me himself on his lathe, and he was so pleased about it.'
'Am I really expected to believe that?' asked the ball.
'May I never be whipped again, if I'm not telling you the truth!' answered the top.

In 'The Ugly Duckling' the mother duck points out to her young ones an old duck who is the aristocrat of the farmyard, and whom they must treat with respect: 'She's the most genteel of all these; she has Spanish blood, that's why she's so plump. And do you see that crimson rag she wears on one leg? It's extremely fine; it's the highest distinction any duck can win. It's as good as saying that there is no thought of getting rid of her; man and beast must take notice!' And to the new ducklings the old aristocratic duck says in her kind and condescending way: 'Make yourselves at home, my dears, and if you should find such a thing as an eel's head, you may bring it to me.'

A cucumber growing on a dunghill takes great pride in being a hot-bed growth: '"You're born to that!" it said to itself. "Not everybody can be born a cucumber, there have to be other breeds as well!"'

Talking about a dinner-party she attended the previous evening a mouse says: 'I sat twenty-first from the old Mouse King; that wasn't bad, when you come to think of it.'

'Naïvety is only one ingredient in the fairy tale,' Andersen writes; 'humour on the other hand is the salt in it.'

Humour is the most important element in many of Andersen's tales, but even where it isn't, it is often brought in by the back door. No one would classify 'The Snow Queen' as a humorous fairy tale, and yet it has many humorous passages. Think of the two crows, the wild one and his sweetheart, the tame crow, who has a free run of the palace, and who speaks to Gerda in a very refined manner: 'My betrothed had spoken so nicely of you, my dear young lady. Your biography, as they call it, is really most touching.' As a reward for having helped Gerda the princess offers them the choice of flying about on their own, or being given a permanent place as Court Crows, with all the scraps from the kitchen. 'Both crows curtsied and asked for a permanency; they had an eye to the time when they would be getting on in years, and they said it was best to have something laid by "for a rainy day", as the saying is.' When Gerda continues her journey in a coach provided by the princess she has company part of the way:

The wild crow, who was now married, went with Gerda for the first dozen miles, sitting beside her as he couldn't bear riding back to the horses. The other crow stood in the gateway flapping her wings; she didn't go with them because she suffered from headaches since getting a permanent place and too much to eat.

The end of the story is told by the robber girl, when Gerda asks her about the wild crow:

'Ah, the crow's dead,' she answered. 'The tame sweetheart's a widow now and goes about with a bit of black wool round her leg. She's terribly sorry for herself, but it's all put on.'

To the traditional folk tale Andersen often added an element of humour which was not there before. In the folk tale Simple Simon's two elder brothers are just stupid and arrogant, but in Andersen's version:

One of them knew the whole Latin dictionary off by heart, and also the local newspaper for the last three years, both backwards and forwards. The other son had learnt up all the by-laws of the city companies and the things every alderman is supposed to know; he thought this would help him to talk politics with the princess; and besides, he knew how to embroider braces, he was so very clever with his fingers.

Before going in to talk to the princess, 'they smeared their mouths with cod-liver oil, so that the words would come out pat'.

Since Andersen was writing primarily for children he took great pains not to use words which they might have difficulty in understanding, and he showed great ingenuity in paraphrasing complicated words and ideas. I have already mentioned how he referred to a microscope without using the word. In 'The High Jumpers' he speaks of 'the man who writes the almanac', meaning a professor of astronomy. He writes 'a student who was reading to become a parson' instead of 'a student of theology'. If he does use a word which children may not know he takes care to explain it; thus he says about one of his characters that 'he went in for conjuring and learnt to talk with his stomach, which is called being a ventriloquist.'

When, as he sometimes does, he uses French words or expressions in the dialogue, it is done deliberately:

'Superbe! Charmant!' exclaimed the maids-of-honour, for they all talked French, the one worse than the other.

Or:

'Prenez garde aux enfants!' said the father owl. 'Not in the children's hearing!'

Another of Andersen's special talents was that of giving abstract ideas a tangible reality. In 'The Tinder Box', after the soldier has lifted the third dog down on to the floor and seen the chest full of gold coins, the amount of money is explained in terms which are meaningful to a child: 'There was enough for him to buy the whole of Copenhagen, all the sugar-pigs that the cake-women sell, and all the tin soldiers and whips and rocking-horses in the world.'

In 'The Wild Swans' the young princes in their father's palace, 'wrote on gold slates with diamond pencils'; and the Elf King was so important that he had his gold crown polished with slate-pencil of a special kind – 'it was top-form slate-pencil, and it's very difficult for the Elf King to get top-form slate-pencil'.

Instead of saying of the merchant in 'The Flying Trunk' that he was very rich, Andersen says that 'he was so rich that he could pave the whole street, and most of a little alley as well, with silver money'. The addition about the little alley suggests precise information concerning his wealth.

We are told that Kay is clever, but we are told more than that; we hear 'how he could do mental arithmetic, even with fractions, and that he knew the number of square miles there were to the different countries and "what's the population?"'

The character of the information depends on the narrator. In 'The Snow Queen' the crow explains to Gerda: 'In the kingdom where we are now lives a princess who is tremendously clever. You see, she has read all the newspapers there are in the world and forgotten them again. She's as clever as that.'

Expressions like 'everybody' and 'the whole world' seemed too abstract to Andersen, so that he often added something more tangible to them. For their jumping competition the three high jumpers 'invited the whole world, and anyone else who liked, to come and watch the sport'; that really does give an impression of open admittance. The best example, however, is the reward which the Snow Queen promised Kay if he was able to combine the letters correctly; not only did she promise him his freedom but also 'the whole world and a pair of new skates'. This shows the kind of genius Andersen is; for behind that expression there is both humour and a deep understanding of children's minds.

In his review of Andersen's works Molbech spoke of 'nasty grammatical errors and orthographic carelessness', and he was right – but who cares today?

Molbech also asked: 'When will such a prolific writer, already quite well-known in his native country, learn to write his mother-tongue correctly?' The short answer is: never, in the sense Molbech meant. Andersen never learnt to use Molbech's language, and in his *Eventyr og Historier* he only very rarely used the literary language of the period in which he lived. Nevertheless he was a supreme master of the language and style he chose to use.

In view of the fact that Andersen has been so mutilated by most of his English translators it seems surprising that he should have survived at all. Why did he become so popular, and why did he survive? The answer must be, I think, that even in the dress his Victorian translators and translatresses gave his fairy tales and stories, there was nothing like them in English or American literature: Andersen's imagination was of a kind utterly unknown in European literature. But the badness of the translations, the constant tendency to moralize (which was mostly put in by the translators, rarely by Andersen himself), prevented a true appreciation of Andersen as a master of form.

It is true that even the best translations do not do full justice to Andersen's language and style, with its absurdities, its deliberate grammatical inconsistencies and its adherence to the oral rather than the written forms of expression, nor can they always do justice to his fine sense of humour. But good translations *are* available today, and it would be a pity if publishers of children's books continued to reprint his tales in versions which give an utterly false impression of his literary talent.

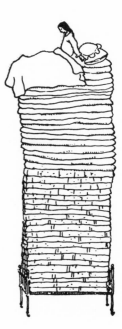

English illustration by Gilbert James to
'The Princess on the Pea' (London n.d.).

3 'A ray of sunshine, a drop of wormwood . . .'

IN A much quoted comment on his stories Andersen said: 'They lay in my thoughts like a seed-corn, requiring only a flowing stream, a ray of sunshine, a drop of wormwood, for them to spring forth and burst into bloom.'

In the biographical chapters several examples of immediate inspiration have already been given. Jenny Lind's visit to Copenhagen and Andersen's love for her was the background against which he wrote 'The Nightingale'; a casual meeting with a matronly Mrs Riborg Bøving, née Voigt, produced 'The Top and the Ball'; 'The Ugly Duckling' was begun at the manors of Gisselfeld and Bregentved in the summer of 1843, when he saw the swans and their cygnets swimming in the moats; for 'The Shadow' two different sources have been mentioned, the almost unbearable heat Andersen suffered in Naples in June 1846, and a long felt bitterness against Edvard Collin for not accepting the suggestion that they should say '*Du*' to one another; and for 'Auntie Toothache' the inspiration is obviously the author's own lifelong suffering from toothache.

In his book on *Andersen and his Fairy Tales* (1907) Hans Brix put forward the theory that the idea for 'The Princess on the Pea' is to be found in a letter which Andersen wrote to Henriette Wulff on 17 July 1834 following some disagreement between them. In this letter he wrote: 'Thank you, my most cordial thanks for your letter, though it made me sad. Made him sad? you say. Yes, indeed, my soul is a sensitive plant; when attacked by friends it is unable to put up with anything, however small and trivial.' Seeing himself as a sensitive plant, Brix suggests that Andersen then wrote the story of the ultimate example of sensitivity.

Brix also links 'The Little Mermaid' with Andersen's unrequited love for Louise Collin:

The unrequited love of the little mermaid for the prince represents the author himself and Louise Collin. But into this everything is drawn which this union might signify to Andersen: the bottom of the sea and the dry land represent the circle of people from which Andersen came and the one in which he tried to be accepted. Louise's love, which would give him the rank of a son in the Collin house and place him as the brother of his friend Edvard, is the goal aimed at but not achieved.

This would explain why Andersen admitted to having felt more deeply when writing this tale than when writing any of the previous ones.

A direct link between his relationship with Louise Collin and a particular incident in 'Willie Winkie' is revealed in Andersen's entry in his almanac on 11 January 1840: 'Louise C. intolerable. Wrote the ship with the stork.' What he meant by 'the ship with the stork' is the description of the tired stork landing on Hjalmar's ship in 'Willie Winkie' (Wednesday):

The ship's boy picked him up and put him in the hen-coop among hens, ducks and turkeys. The poor stork looked so sorry for himself amongst them.
'What a creature!' said all the hens.
And the turkey-cock puffed himself out as big as he could and asked who he was, and the ducks waddled backwards and nudged each other – 'Quick, get quacking!'
Then the stork told them about the warmth of Africa, and the pyramids, and the ostrich that ran like a wild horse through the desert; but the ducks never understood what he was saying and so they nudged each other again – 'We all agree, don't we, that he's stupid?'
'As stupid as can be!' said the turkey-cock with a gobble-gobble. At that the stork kept silent and thought about his beloved Africa.
'Those are nice lanky legs you have,' said the turkey. 'How much a yard?'
'Quack, quack, quack!' chuckled the ducks. But the stork pretended not to hear.
'You may well join in the laugh,' said the turkey to him; 'it was very neatly put. Or was it perhaps too low for him? Heigh-ho! He's a bit one-eyed; we must look to ourselves, if we want to have some fun.' And they clucked away, and the ducks kept quack-quacking – it was terrible how funny they seemed to think it was.

There can be no doubt that here the stork is meant to represent Andersen himself, and this particular episode is a characteristic example of the way in which he was able to work off his annoyance with the Collins.

There is also fairly convincing evidence that Andersen had Louise Collin and Lind, her prospective husband, in mind when he described the wedding of the two dolls in 'Willie Winkie' (Friday). This time Andersen appears in the guise of a swallow, and those who knew Jonas Collin's eldest daughter, immediately realized that the hen was both an amusing and malicious caricature of Ingeborg Drewsen.

This is the scene after the wedding ceremony is over, when the newly married couple discuss where to go on their honeymoon:

'Which do you think?' said the bridegroom to the bride. 'Shall we go and stay in the country, or shall we travel abroad?' They asked advice of the swallow, who was a great traveller, and of the old hen, who had hatched five broods of chicks. The swallow described the lovely warm countries, where the grapes hung in big heavy bunches and the air is so soft and the colour on the hills is something quite unknown to us here.
'Still, they haven't got our garden cabbage!' said the hen. 'I once spent the summer with all my chicks in the country; there was a gravel pit we could go and scratch in, and then we had the use of a garden where there were cabbages – such a green, they were! I can't imagine anything lovelier.'
'But one cabbage-stalk looks just like another,' said the swallow. 'And then again, the weather here is often so bad.'
'Oh, well, we're used to that,' replied the hen.
'But it's so cold. It freezes.'
'That just suits the cabbages,' said the hen. 'Besides, we get warm weather too, sometimes. Don't you remember, only four years ago, we had a summer that lasted five weeks! It was so hot here that you could hardly breathe. . . . And then we don't get all those poisonous creatures they have abroad; and we are free from brigands. Anyone who doesn't think our country is the best of all is a scoundrel; he doesn't

really deserve to live here' – and tears came into the hen's eyes. 'I've done a bit of travelling myself,' she added. 'I've ridden over fifty miles in a coop. There's no fun at all in travel.'

Like the old hen who had hatched five broods of chicks, Ingeborg Drewsen had given birth to five children at the time the story was written. She certainly did not believe in travelling abroad and kept on telling Andersen that he was stupid not to stay at home.

Two years later Ingeborg Drewsen once again found herself cast as a hen, this time in 'The Ugly Duckling'. The cottage in which the ugly duckling found refuge for a time, and which was inhabited by an old woman, a hen and a cat, is clearly based on elements both from the home of Captain and Mrs Wulff – 'a dear home where I was always being educated, though with the best of intentions,' – and that of Jonas Collin and his family. After the duckling has told the hen of his curious longing to swim in the water, the story continues, with the hen speaking:

'What's the matter with you?' she asked. 'You haven't anything to do – that's why you get these fancies. They'd soon go, if only you'd lay eggs or else purr.'
'But it's so lovely to swim in the water,' said the duckling; 'so lovely to duck your head in it and dive down to the bottom.'
'Most enjoyable, I'm sure,' said the hen. 'You must have gone crazy. Ask the cat about it – I've never met anyone as clever as he is – ask him if he's fond of swimming or diving! I say nothing of myself. Ask our old mistress, the wisest woman in the world! Do you suppose she's keen on swimming?'
'You don't understand me,' said the duckling.
'Well, if we don't understand you, I should like to know who would. Surely you'll never try and make out that you are wiser than the cat and the mistress – not to mention myself. Don't be silly, child! Give thanks to your Master for all the kindness you have met with. Haven't you come to a nice warm room, where you have company that can teach you something? But you're just a stupid, and there's no fun in having you here. You may take my word for it – if I say unpleasant things to you, it's all for your good; that's just how you can tell which are your real friends. Only see that you lay eggs and learn how to purr or give out sparks.'

'The Little Match Girl' was written after seeing a picture of a girl selling matches in the street; the original drawing was made in 1843 by J. T. Lundbye, a well-known Danish artist. Three years after the picture had been first used a Danish wood-engraver sent it, together with two other engravings, to Andersen, with a request that he write a story for whichever of the three he preferred. Having chosen the Lundbye picture Andersen then wrote the story, which was printed together with the illustration in 1846. This is, in fact, the only known case of a picture inspiring Andersen to write a story.

In his comments on the origin of his tales Andersen writes of 'The Drop of Water' that he wrote it for the benefit of H. C. Ørsted, and he prided himself on the fact that in it he had dealt with the new scientific techniques.

The story itself was written in November 1847, but the idea may be traced back to an experience which Andersen had in the summer of 1830 and which he described in a letter to a friend:

I had an experience which I truly enjoyed, namely seeing some animalcules. Just imagine: only a tiny drop of water on a piece of glass – and there was an entire world full of creatures, of which the largest seemed like grasshoppers, the smallest like pinheads; some of them really did look like grasshoppers, others had the most monstrous appearances, and they frisked among one another, and the bigger ones swallowed the smaller ones.

But it seems possible that a much later event may have had something to do with the tale as well. In a newspaper article in 1935 (quoted by H. Topsøe-Jensen in his book *Buket til Andersen*) Paul Læssøe Müller discussed the possible influence which one of Bulwer Lytton's novels might have had on the writing of 'The Drop of Water'. Immediately before leaving Denmark for England Andersen wrote in May 1847 to Edvard Collin how eager he was to learn English, and in this connection he wrote: 'Here, at the manor of Glorup, I have read almost the whole of the first part of *Night and Morning* and – understood it, well, of course, there were some gaps, but I know more of the language than I thought, and that pleases me.' Bulwer's novel *Night and Morning* (1841), which Andersen had previously read in a Danish translation, is divided into four books. This is how the first chapter of Book IV begins:

If, reader, you have ever looked through a solar microscope at the monsters in a drop of water, perhaps you have wondered to yourself how things so terrible have been hitherto unknown to you – you have felt a loathing at the limpid element you hitherto deemed so pure – you have half fancied that you would cease to be a water-drinker; yet, the next day you have forgotten the grim life that started before you, with its countless shapes, in that teeming globule; and, if so tempted by your thirst, you have not shrunk from the lying crystal, although myriads of the horrible Unseen are mangling, devouring, gorging each other, in the liquid you so tranquilly imbibe; so is it with that ancestral and master element called Life. Lapped in your sleek comforts, and lolling on the sofa of your patent conscience – when, perhaps for the first time, you look through the glass of science upon one ghastly globule in the waters that heave around, that fill up, with their succulence, the pores of earth, that moisten every atom subject to your eyes, or handled by your touch – you are startled and dismayed; you say, mentally, 'Can such things be? I never dreamed of this before! I thought what was invisible to me was non-existent in itself – I will remember this dread experiment.' The next day the experiment is forgotten. – The Chemist may rarify the Globule – can Science make pure the World?

It seems quite possible that, having once read Bulwer's entire novel in Danish, Andersen may well have turned to this particular passage once again in the spring of 1847; for it was in fact later in that year that he wrote 'The Drop of Water', one of the five stories which was first published in English in *A Christmas Greeting to My English Friends*. If anyone in Britain remembered Bulwer's *Night and Morning* while reading Andersen's tale, they must indeed have noticed the similarity of subject-matter, although Andersen's style is vastly superior to Bulwer's flowery rhetoric.

Andersen's diaries are often helpful to anyone interested in finding out how his mind and imagination worked. [20]

On 2 July 1842, while staying at Bregentved, he wrote in his diary: 'Count Moltke and his talk about V. who used to have nothing but a bootjack and a comb before, and who has now got his own homestead, a couple of cows and horses – it must be like being in heaven.' Six years later 'The Shirt Collar' was published, beginning: 'There was once a swell gentleman whose entire kit consisted of a bootjack and a comb.' Andersen had a talent for remembering and using much later in another context words and phrases which had been stored in his memory for years.

There is another example of this in the first part of 'Heartbreak', where the narrator tells an amusing story of the arrival of a widow who carries a fat pug-dog on her arm; the purpose of her visit is to invite people to take shares in her tannery. 'Heartbreak' was published in 1853, but the story of the widow, the pug-dog and the tannery is to be found almost verbatim in Andersen's diary for 26 May 1847, when he was staying at Glorup and was visited by the widow and her pug-dog.

Here is a case where the diary reveals the immediate inspiration for a tale. On 4 December 1860 Andersen noted: 'Changed my gold coins and lost on each *Napoleon* 14 *Skilling* compared with purchase price.' On 5 December: 'Stayed at home all evening and wrote the old story about the man who changed his horse for a cow, etc.' On 7 December: 'Finished the story of swapping.' In this case it is obvious that Andersen worked off his annoyance at the loss he had incurred when changing his French currency into Danish, by writing 'Dad's Always Right'.

During a visit to Paris in 1866 Andersen wrote in his diary on 13 April:

Outside my windows was a little open square with a fountain which was not working, a little bit of green grass with benches in front, where people sat staring at the greenness; there were also a couple of trees that had died, I think – like me they had suffered from the Parisian air, and since they weren't moved away they'd gone out. To help the situation one day two large trees, half burst into leaves, arrived from the countryside; they were heralding the spring. Two old trees were dug up and the new ones planted in their place; they stretched themselves up towards my window and let themselves be lit up by gas lamps, allowed themselves to be looked at by the Babylon of our time below. A fairy tale might be written about those trees, about their longing for the metropolis of the world and their premature death there. I shall probably write a fairy tale about it. I have also the idea of one from Holland, Saint Nicolas' Eve in Amsterdam, the Venice of the North.

The Dutch tale never materialized, and for a time it looked as if the fairy tale about the trees in Paris might never be written either. But the next year Andersen returned to Paris to see the World Exhibition, which made such an impression on him that he immediately wanted to write a tale about it – especially as a Danish journalist had stated that no one, except Charles Dickens, could give an adequate description of the World Exhibition. Looking for an idea Andersen remembered the newly planted trees outside his window in 1866 and wrote 'The Wood Nymph', which was first published in 1868 and which begins:

We are going to the Exhibition in Paris.
Now we are there! We went there speedily, like flying, yet without any witchcraft.

We went by steam, on sea as well as on land. Our age is the age of the fairy tale come true.

We are in the middle of Paris, in a great hotel. There are flower decorations up the staircase and soft carpets covering all the steps. We have a comfortable room, the door to the balcony is open, facing a large square. Down there lives Spring, she arrived on the same day as we did, in the shape of a young chestnut tree, newly burst into tender leaves. How lovely and springlike it is in contrast with the other trees in the square. One of them has gone out, ceasing to be a living tree; it lies, with its roots torn out, thrown across the ground. Where it used to stand the fresh chestnut tree is going to be planted and grow.

So in the end the story did materialize.

'"The Toad" came into being during my visit to Setubal in the summer of 1866,' Andersen writes. 'One day I saw an ugly toad approaching from one of the deep wells there, where the water is lifted in jars placed on a large rotating wheel. By regarding the animal more closely I noticed its clever eyes, and it wasn't long before I had a whole tale, which I rewrote later in Denmark, however, giving it a background of Danish scenery and homeliness.' The first part of this information is confirmed on reading an entry in Andersen's diary in Setubal on 26 June 1866, which ends with the words: 'Begun the tale of "The Toad".'

Occasionally it is possible to trace the origin of an incident in a tale to a personal experience. Here is one example: a little German boy, the son of the poet Julius Mosen, gave one of his tin soldiers to Andersen so that he should not feel 'too terribly lonely'. This incident has gone straight into 'The Old House'. And another example: in Andersen's diary for 30 July 1868 one finds the following information: 'I have put an artichoke, which I found lying cut off in the kitchen garden the other day, in water and it's blossoming beautifully.' It was clearly this incident which gave Andersen the idea of letting Larsen do exactly the same thing in 'The Gardener and the Squire'.

One finds in Andersen's diaries several references to ideas for tales which he intended to write but never did – though in some cases the ideas, or part of them, may have been worked into other tales. Thus he wrote in Italy on 27 March 1846: 'Thought of a fairy tale about Spring travelling through the country – thought of a tale about a stork travelling with its family to Egypt;' and on the following day: 'The idea of a tale about freedom and constitution in a farmyard.' In Switzerland he wrote on 1 July 1861 that on his way to Berne he had the idea of 'a story about a rat criticizing the human race'; and in Portugal he wrote on 16 June 1866: 'By seeing the mule plodding on the treadmill with bound eyes I thought of a tale about it.'

Some of Andersen's tales were written in a matter of hours, or in the course of a few evenings, others took him a long time. In a previous chapter it has been mentioned that he wrote to Ingemann in 1844 about 'The Snow Queen', 'that it came out dancing over the paper'. The extraordinary, almost unbelievable fact is that Andersen began writing 'The Snow Queen', one of his longest fairy tales, on 5 December 1844, and that it was published in book form (together

Russian illustration by G. A. V. Traugot
to 'The Ugly Duckling' (Leningrad
1969).

with 'The Fir Tree') on 21 December. The whole process of writing, setting
up type, printing, binding and publishing was done in the course of sixteen days.
   On the other hand Andersen wrote of another of his long fairy tales:

'The Marsh King's Daughter' belongs to the tales on which I have spent most time
and diligence; it may interest one or other person to see, almost as if through a microscope, the way in which it has grown, has unfolded itself and taken new shape. As
was the case with all the fairy tales the contents proper presented themselves immediately, as a well-known tune or song may come to one. I immediately told the
whole fairy tale to one of my friends, then it was written down, and again rewritten;
but even when it stood on paper for the third time I had to admit that there were still
whole sections of it which did not appear as lucid and colourful as they could and
must do. I then began reading some Icelandic sagas, which took me back in time, and
thus inspired the tale came nearer to the truth. I read a couple of contemporary travel
descriptions of Africa, was filled by its tropical glow and new strangeness; I visualized
the country and was able to talk about it more reliably. A few books on the flight of
birds also had their effect, they called forth new ideas, giving characteristic features
to the life of the birds as it unfolds itself in this fairy tale, which was thus rewritten
during a short span of time six or seven times until I was certain that now I could not
improve upon it any more.

I have already mentioned several times how important the autobiographical
element is in many of Andersen's tales. This, of course, is particularly obvious
in such tales as 'The Ugly Duckling' and 'The Gardener and the Squire'. When
Andersen told Georg Brandes that 'The Ugly Duckling' reflected his own life
story he said no more than most of his adult readers had realized ever since the

story first appeared in print. The farmyard, where the duckling is regarded as an oddity and suffers so much persecution and humiliation, represents both Odense and the stultifying atmosphere of Copenhagen, Slagelse and Elsinore; in the wild geese it is possible to identify the young Bohemian poets with whom he used to associate during his schooldays at Slagelse (the volume in which the story appeared is dedicated to one of them), and the wild ducks may possibly be intended to represent Edvard Collin and his brothers. I have already mentioned the old woman (Jonas Collin?), the hen (Ingeborg Drewsen) and the cat. The swans, of course, represent the great writers of Europe, and the new swan's words, 'I never dreamt of so much happiness when I was the ugly duckling', epitomise Aladdin's final monologue in Oehlenschläger's drama, which Andersen liked to interpret as a story about himself. 'The new one is the prettiest,' is the proud message of this tale, 'and the old swans bowed before him.'

It was not difficult either for Andersen's contemporaries to understand the irony of 'The Gardener and the Squire' and see Andersen as the gardener and Danish literary criticism as the squire and his wife. In the same way as Larsen often heard that his very first fruit, the apples and pears, were really his best, thus Andersen was often told that his very first tales were superior to anything he wrote later on. The melons, which were recognized as being 'no doubt extremely good, but they were of course something quite different', are probably meant to represent his travel books, and the strawberries, which 'might be called excellent, and yet no better than those to be found on other estates', his novels. The unfortunate radishes, a failure about which everybody talked, may well be interpreted as a reference to some of Andersen's several failures as a playwright.

Andersen had many different ways of putting himself into his tales. If, as an example, one examines his early tales, one will find that he appears in some form or another in eight of the first twelve. As already mentioned he identified himself with Aladdin, and the Aladdin-like soldier in 'The Tinder Box' may be regarded as an optimistic self-portrait, while 'The Princess on the Pea' may be interpreted as a tale about himself as a sensitive plant. In 'Little Ida's Flowers' he is easily recognizable as the student knowing the most lovely stories, and in 'Thumbelina' he is 'the man who can tell fairy tales', to whom the swallow chirps its 'tweet-tweet!' – 'And that's where the whole story comes from.' In 'The Naughty Boy' he is the kind-hearted poet lying weeping on the floor after Cupid has shot him through the heart. In 'The Little Mermaid' he has put all his own feelings of being an outsider into the description of the mermaid. In 'The Goloshes of Fortune' he is the poet who wrote the poem 'Would I were rich . . .', and in 'The Steadfast Tin Soldier' the title character is another outsider, different from the others by virtue of having been born with only one leg, a tragic-comic pocket-size *Orlando furioso*, as he has been called.

It is also worth noting that occasionally Andersen could be ironical at his own expense. Thus in 'Willie Winkie' (Tuesday) there is a scene in which the little dream god has touched the furniture with his magic squirt, with the result that it all immediately begins to chatter. The story then continues:

They all chattered about themselves, except the spittoon, which stood in silent annoyance that the others could be so conceited as to talk and think only of themselves and never have a thought for the one who, after all, stood so modestly in the corner and let himself be spat upon.

It is quite possible that Hans Brix is right in recognizing the author in the description of that spittoon.

It was not only himself Andersen put into his tales but also, as we have seen, his friends and enemies.

One thing he disliked intensely was Danish self-sufficiency and provincial self-glorification, and he resented being accused of lack of patriotism because he was fond of travelling abroad. To the previous examples of his satire directed against Danish super-patriots two more may be added (with Andersen cast in his favourite part as the swallow in both cases). The first is an extract from a conversation between two frogs in 'The Beetle':

'I should very much like to know,' said the other frog, 'whether the swallow – that gad-about creature – on its many journeys abroad has ever found a better climate than ours, with all its drizzle and damp. It's like lying in a soaking wet ditch. If you don't revel in that, you can't really love your native land.'

The other example is an extract from 'The Sprinters'. After the hare has been awarded the first prize and the snail the second prize as the fastest moving animals, the gate-post explains why the swallow could not be considered for a prize:

'You gad about too much. You always have to be off somewhere, right out of the country, as soon as it gets cold here. You've no love of the land you were born in. There can be no question of *you* for a prize.'
'Well, but suppose I stayed back in the marsh all winter,' said the swallow, 'and slept the time away, should I then be considered for a prize?'
'Get a certificate from the Marsh-Woman that you've slept half the time in your mother-country, and then you shall be considered.'

Andersen particularly disliked literary critics – except of course when they praised him – and his tales abound with sarcastic references to critics and literary scholars. The following are just some of the more obvious examples.

The Master of Music in 'The Nightingale' may be seen as a parody of the formalistic school of criticism, whose leading exponent was Johan Ludvig Heiberg. The man in 'The Bell' who had the theory that the mystic sound came from a big owl knocking its head against a hollow tree, while at the same time being unable to decide whether it was the owl's head or the hollow trunk that produced the sound, represents the kind of speculative philosophy for which Andersen had no use. The philosopher is rewarded and officially recognized, however; for on the basis of his theory he is appointed Universal Bell-ringer, 'and every year he wrote a little essay on the owl, but no one was any wiser than before'. Another obvious example is the fifth brother in 'Something', an ambitious person who wants to achieve something greater and higher than what his brothers plan to do. 'I'll stand aside and criticize what you do,' he says. 'There's always something wrong in everything; I'll pick that out and run it down – that'll be something!'

The donkey in 'The Sprinters' is another example of Andersen's view of the critic who pretends to believe in aesthetic ideas; he voted to give the hare the first prize, he says, because he believes in what is called 'the beautiful'. 'That is what I had an eye for in this case,' the donkey explains. 'I had an eye for the hare's beautiful, well-developed ears; it's a pleasure to see how long they are. I felt I was looking at myself when I was small, and so I voted for him.'

Georg Brandes was not quite wrong when he complained to Andersen in 1869 that he had given his support to every vulgar prejudice against literary criticism and brought it into contempt and disrepute.

I have dealt at length with some of the many personal elements to be found in Andersen's tales, because they may be of interest in the general context of a biography of Andersen. At the same time it should be stated unambiguously that to the large majority of readers all over the world, children as well as adults, who read Andersen's *Fairy Tales and Stories* with little or no knowledge of the author's life and background, all such information is irrelevant. One can, of course, enjoy Andersen's tales without ever having heard of the Collins, the Wulffs, Riborg Voigt, Jenny Lind, and all the others. If this were not so Andersen would never have been translated into most living languages, and even in Denmark he would have been largely forgotten by now.

'The Little Mermaid' is a deeply moving fairy tale in itself, and in order to appreciate it it is not necessary to identify the mermaid with Andersen, and her desire to become human with his longing to be accepted in the new world into which he had moved. 'The Nightingale' has a universal message about true art versus artificiality, which can be understood without in any way connecting it with events in Andersen's life at the time he wrote it. 'The Shadow' can be read and appreciated without knowing anything about his visit to Naples and without understanding the concealed message to Edvard Collin. Even 'The Ugly Duckling' is read by most children all over the world simply as a story about the sufferings and the ultimate reward of a fowl whose true identity as a swan is only revealed at the end.

The information given in this chapter may therefore be regarded as no more than footnotes to some of Andersen's tales, though in some cases it may add a further dimension to them.

It is hardly surprising that most of the serious research on Andersen and his work should have been done by Danish scholars. In addition to some of those already mentioned (Georg Brandes, Georg Christensen, Hans Brix, Helge Topsøe-Jensen) two others should be singled out for special mention, Paul V. Rubow, whose book on *Andersen's Tales* (with the sub-title 'Antecedents – Idea and Form – Language and Style') was published in 1927, and Bo Grønbech's book on *The Fairy-Tale World of Andersen*, a fascinating attempt at analysing the fairy-tale world on its own terms, without introducing any external material.

More recently an attempt has been made by Eigil Nyborg to interpret some of Andersen's tales according to the analytical method of the C. G. Jung school of psychology, and Arne Duve, a Norwegian psychoanalyst, has subjected each of Andersen's 156 tales to a more traditional Freudian interpretation.

There have also been some interesting and rewarding attempts by Harald Rue and Peer E. Sørensen to interpret Andersen's tales from a Marxist point of view. And young Danish scholars are today discussing Andersen's work against the background of modern sociological, linguistic and structuralist views.

Both in the Soviet Union and on the Continent generally there have been, and still are, more scholars seriously interested in Andersen than there are in Britain and America, where most adults have only had an eye for what W. H. Auden calls 'the Sensitive-Plantishness and rather namby-pamby Christianity of some of Andersen's heroes'; Auden adds, however, that 'one puts up with them for the sake of the wit and sharpness of his social observation and the interest of his minor characters'.

In the late 1840s Britain and America decided that Hans Christian Andersen belonged in the nursery, and as far as these countries are concerned he has remained there ever since – with the implication that he cannot be taken seriously as a literary figure. Or, as the Austrian writer Egon Friedell once put it: 'The great public had adopted the same attitude to Andersen as a certain Prussian lieutenant of the guard did to Julius Caesar when he said that he could not possibly have been a great man since he had only written for the lower Latin forms. Similarly, since Andersen is so great an author that even children can understand him, the grown-ups have concluded that he cannot possibly have anything to offer them.'

Andersen *has* something to offer both to children and grown-ups. What he called *Eventyr* covered, as I have tried to show, a much wider field than what is normally covered by the concept of 'fairy tales'. And it was a literary form he wanted to be taken seriously. One evening in 1860, after he had seen a play in Dresden, someone remarked condescendingly that the play they had just seen should not be taken too seriously; after all it was only a *Märchen*. 'I was indignant,' Andersen writes in his diary; 'as if *Eventyr* did not have any sense!'

Let me conclude by quoting Andersen's own definition of the literary genre in which he was, and still is, the unsurpassed master:

In the whole realm of poetry no domain is so boundless as that of the fairy tale. It reaches from the blood-drenched graves of Antiquity to the pious legends of a child's picture-book; it takes in the poetry of the people and the poetry of the artist. To me it represents all poetry, and he who masters it must be able to put into it tragedy, comedy, naïve simplicity, and humour; at his service are the lyrical note, the childlike narrative and the language of describing nature. . . . In the folk tale it is always Simple Simon who is victorious in the end. . . . Thus also the innocence of poetry, overlooked and jeered at by the other brothers, will reach farthest in the end.

Notes

Part one

1 In 1801 there were 1199 households in Odense, distributed as follows: 102 civil servants, 26 officers, 12 in the professions, 81 tradesmen of various descriptions, 36 publicans and caterers, 460 artisans, 39 employed in farming or gardening, 121 soldiers, 97 day labourers, 139 single women and paupers, and 28 pensioners. (A journeyman cobbler, such as Hans Christian Andersen's father, would rank as a day labourer.)

2 It has been possible to trace her ancestry and find out that her father was a Holsteinian glove maker who settled in Odense, where he and his wife ended their lives as paupers in the workhouse, and her maternal grandmother – Hans Christian's great-great-grandmother – was not a German noble lady but a poor Danish girl called Karen Nielsdatter, who did not elope with an actor but married a *Postrytter* (a mounted mail deliverer) in the town of Assens on Funen; he died in 1754 and left his wife and her eight children in extreme poverty.

3 When proposing a toast for a young lady in September 1868 Andersen explained that it was a popular belief that if one placed a St John's-wort in the chink of a beam and the sun was allowed to shine on it, then the person in whose name it had been placed would live a healthy and happy life.

4 In one of Andersen's last stories, 'Old Johanna's Tale', Maren, the tailor's wife, says that a deceased aristocrat is now having eternal life in the kingdom of heaven, whereupon the story continues:

" 'Who told you so, Maren?' said the tailor. 'Dead men are good manure. But this man was of course too well-connected to bring benefit to the soil; he's to be buried in a vault.'

'Don't talk so wicked,' said Maren. 'I tell you, he has eternal life.'

'Who told you so, Maren?' repeated the tailor. But Maren threw her apron over little Rasmus [their son]; he mustn't hear such talk. She carried him across to the peat shed and wept.

'Those words you heard over there, little Rasmus, they weren't your father's. It was Satan who went through the room and used your father's voice. Say "Our Father" – we'll both say it.' And she folded the child's hands.

'Now I'm happy again,' she said. 'Have faith in yourself and in God!' "

5 In *Levnedsbogen* this story is told in a context which clearly places the event before 1816. But in Andersen's later autobiographies it takes on a much more dramatic significance; there it is related to his mother's reluctance to allow him to go to Copenhagen in 1819, when she 'sent for an old, so-called "wise woman" from the hospital' and had her read the boy's future in a pack of cards and in coffee grounds. The old woman's verdict was, 'Your son will become a great man, and in his honour all Odense shall one day be illuminated.' Having heard this Mrs Andersen wept, and from then on did not object to her son leaving home.

6 In a letter to Jonas Collin, written on 27 March 1825, Andersen gave as his reason for leaving his job at Mr Madsen's that he could not pull the big saw.

7 This was written in 1832, and she did in fact die in 1830; for research has identified her as a person who called herself Mrs Christiane Jansen, though the alleged sea-captain, whose name she had taken, was not her husband but a bachelor boatswain, with whom she had lived until his death in 1806. She had two adopted daughters but no children of her own.

8 In his autobiography the Danish antiquarian J. M. Thiele relates how one

morning in June 1820 he was sitting at his desk in Copenhagen, with his back to the door, when he heard somebody knocking. When he lifted his eyes from the paper in front of him, Thiele writes, 'I was surprised to see a lanky boy, of a most extraordinary appearance, standing in the doorway, making a deep theatrical bow right down to the floor. He had already thrown his cap down by the door, and when he raised his long figure in a shabby, grey coat, the sleeves of which did not reach as far as his emaciated wrists, my glance met a couple of tiny, Chinese eyes, badly in need of a surgical operation to give them a free view, behind a large, protruding nose. Round his neck he wore a gaily coloured calico scarf, so tightly tied up that his long neck seemed to make an effort to escape: in short, a truly surprising figure, who became even more peculiar when, with a couple of steps forward and a repeated bow, he began his high-flown speech with these words: "May I have the honour of expressing my feelings for the stage in a poem written by myself?" ' It was only when the boy gave his name as Hans Christian Andersen that Thiele remembered that Weyse had mentioned his name and Guldberg opened a monthly subscription to keep him alive. Apparently, the boy was now going round to thank all his benefactors.

9 The earliest evidence of Andersen's desire to show off his talent for reciting in private homes in Copenhagen is given by the philologist N. C. L. Abrahams, who remembered visiting a schoolmaster and his wife in 1819: 'At the home of that family I saw for the first time a curious, long-legged, awkward boy of 14 or 15, who came rushing in occasionally with the question: 'May I read something to you?' or 'May I recite something to you?', and then he would recite either some verses of his own or a tirade from some tragedy. His entire appearance was undoubtedly ridiculous, at times he was even a nuisance, but all the same, behind his peculiar behaviour there was evidence that this boy wanted to achieve something, and occasionally there was in his immature poetry something which was not too bad. The boy's name was Hans Christian Andersen.'

10 Among other well-known Danes whose help Andersen tried to enlist during this period were Hans Christian Ørsted, the discoverer of electro-magnetism, and C. Gutfeld, dean of the naval church in Copenhagen. It was the latter who encouraged Andersen to submit *Alfsol* to the Royal Theatre and helped him to write a petition to the king.

11 Six years later, after Thorvaldsen had moved back to Denmark, he told Andersen that while sitting in his studio in Rome Byron talked gaily and happily, but as soon as Thorvaldsen began working on the statue Byron put on a melancholy expression. 'You mustn't change your facial expression,' Thorvaldsen said, 'you don't look natural that way.' 'Oh yes, this is my true nature,' Byron replied. When Thorvaldsen had finished the statue everybody admired the likeness, but Byron looked at it and shook his head: 'I don't look sad enough.' – Everything had to be sad, Thorvaldsen ended his story, which Andersen reported in a letter of 1839.

12 Inspired by Maria Felicita Malibran, the French-Spanish opera singer, whom Andersen had heard in Naples on several occasions.

13 Peppo, the Roman beggar, is the only character who appears under his own name in the novel. From Copenhagen Andersen wrote to Henriette Wulff in Italy: 'On the Spanish Steps there is a beggar with withered feet, he has a nasty, ingratiating grin and says his "buon giorno!" to everybody. He is the hero's uncle in my novel, so give him a bajok from me! Please don't forget it!'

14 In her letter of introduction to her colleague Erik Gustaf Geijer in Stockholm Fredrika Bremer wrote: 'Here is Herr Andersen, of a somewhat peculiar appearance, but simple, with a sensitive and warm heart, kind, pious like a child, and the author of some good books.' C. F. Dahlgren, another Swedish writer who met Andersen in Stockholm on this occasion, later described his appearance in a letter to a friend: 'I always called him *the Crane*, for I have never seen any human being more akin in appearance to a crane than him. Imagine a tall person, indeed taller than myself, with long, thin legs and a

long, thin neck on top of which a head has been placed like a knob; imagine this figure with a stooping, protruding back and in his gait never walking but hopping along almost like a monkey, or like a tripping crane; and finally, imagine his long arms hanging down like a couple of straps along his sides, and an ugly face, something in the manner of the late Lorenzo [the Swedish author Lars Hammarsköld]. Big lips, light-blue eyes, dark hair and long teeth, like tusks.'

15 Already in February 1839 Andersen had been fascinated by reading about Daguerre's invention; he wrote to Henriette Hanck: 'I have discussed it much and at great length with Ørsted; it is like the reflection in a mirror in which all objects are caught and retained; if you look through a microscope, then the smallest point will develop into a detailed object. A point representing a signpost on the copper plate will now show itself with its entire text; one sees the wetness of the tones, the hour of the day according to the light of the sun. Now we can get the most faithful reproductions of the remains of antiquity, the most brilliant prospects of tropical lands.'

16 As an example of what, on another occasion, Andersen called his ability to 'climb' through the French language, he mentions somewhere in his diaries that he wanted to speak about a hunch-backed lady he had met, and not knowing the French term he called her 'une dame avec un frontispiece sur le dot'.

17 In 1848 Jenny Lind and the Swedish tenor Julius Günther were in fact engaged for about six months.

18 The occupation of Jutland only lasted a few days, and the four million rixdollars were never paid. After diplomatic pressure from Russia the Prussian Commander-in-Chief was ordered by his government on 23 May to withdraw his troops from Northern Jutland. On 26 August an armistice was declared.

19 Fighting was resumed on 3 April 1849. The military campaign ended with the defeat of the Schleswig-Holstein troops at Fredericia on 6 July, and armistice was declared on 10 July.

20 What Andersen referred to as 'the proclamations of peace' was a protocol of preliminary peace between Denmark and Prussia, signed in July 1849; but not until 2 July 1850 was a final state of peace declared between Denmark and Prussia, the latter then leaving the insurgents in Schleswig-Holstein to carry on the war alone. On 25 July the decisive battle of Isted took place. Until the peace was final the relationship between the two friends remained strained. In January 1850 Carl Alexander wrote to Andersen: 'The fact that in every letter you threaten never to come here again, and that your letters will become more scarce in the future, makes me very sad indeed. What have I done to deserve this? Must I always, even among my friends, run my head against unhappy politics?'

21 441 letters exchanged between Andersen and Henriette Wulff, covering the years 1826–58, have been published by H. Topsøe-Jensen, and extracts from many of these are quoted in this book.

22 It is probably no coincidence that in June 1870, i.e. at the time he was writing *Lucky Peer*, Andersen should have written to J. P. E. Hartmann, the composer: 'It is strange how often, right up to the night before last, I relive the time I spent at Meisling's house: the pressure must have been very hard and my dependency on my surroundings unspeakably bitter according to my present ideas. Thus I dreamt two nights ago that I was being mentally tortured by Meisling but that I wouldn't put up with it any more and ran away; suddenly I found myself standing in 'Rosenvænget', where I told Viggo Drewsen what had happened. Anxiously he shook his head: 'What is Grandfather [Jonas Collin] going to say? And have you discussed it with Uncle Edvard?' Isn't it strange that at the age of 66 I can still suffer and feel these torments of my youth, live myself into the oppressing ties of dependency from which I have liberated myself? In my dreams I am still a schoolboy, and Meisling is rude but in recent years he always addresses me as "Herr Councillor of State".'

23 Ibsen, *Samlede Verker* (Centenary Edition), vol. XVI, p. 35.

24 In his book *Samliv med Ibsen* (1906)
John Paulsen relates that Ibsen told him
that on that evening at 'Rolighed' Andersen
appeared to be sulking in his room,
reluctant to come down and meet him, so
that the latter had to go up and fetch him.
Arm in arm they entered the sitting-room
where the Melchiors were waiting for
them. 'But what happened between you
and Andersen in his room?' John Paulsen
asked Ibsen, who replied: 'I embraced him
and paid him a casual compliment. He was
moved, and returning my embrace he asked
me, "So you really like me?"' In telling the
story Ibsen then added: 'It was one of the
pleasantest evenings I have ever
experienced. Andersen could be lovable and
entertaining as few other men if he wanted
to.'

25 Mrs Gatty's daughter, Juliana Horatia
Ewing, who was also a writer of children's
stories, wrote about her mother in 1880
that 'when Hans Andersen's fairy tales, with
all their sympathy for every corner of
creation, took her fancy quite by storm, she
complained that so many of them were
only quaint and taught nothing: imperfect
devices – the body without the soul.'

26 See *The Andersen-Scudder Letters*.

27 Andersen's mother must have called him
Christian, for some of her letters to him
begin: 'My dear Christian'.

28 A full English translation of the letter is
given in the notes of *The Andersen-Scudder
Letters*, pp. 175–6.

29 See Andersen's diary, Zurich, 20
November 1869: 'This morning, when I let
in the *Hausknecht* my purse was hanging
loosely round my neck, he looked at it, I
wonder if he will come in during the night
and strangle me to get it?'

30 The fact that Andersen himself was
acutely aware of being ugly is also evident
from the following story, told by William
Bloch.
   One evening Ludvig Phister, a
well-known Danish actor, met Andersen
in the Royal Theatre and said: 'My
goodness, Herr Andersen, how pleased I am
whenever I look at you; now you won't
mind me telling you that as an adolescent
you weren't very good-looking, but how

pleasant to see the change that has taken
place: now you are handsome.' Andersen
replied angrily: 'How can you, whom I
regard as a reasonable and intelligent person,
think for one moment that I would believe
what you are saying? I know perfectly well
that I'm ugly rather than handsome, but
you ought at least to respect in me that
which is worthy of respect and not make
fun of me to my face. Now you have
ruined my evening. Thank you very much
– I shall go home now.'
   Phister was not alone in going against the
general verdict that Andersen was ugly.
Kristian Zahrtmann, a Danish painter,
writes in his memoirs: 'People ought to say
that he had an impressive and good-looking
appearance. But it had become customary
to call him ugly and so this was generally
accepted. Later in life, when he got rid of
his long false teeth, his head took on an
extraordinarily beautiful shape, something
to which most people were blind.'
   In an article about Andersen Edvard
Brandes, who knew him well as an old
man, spoke of his 'magnificent head'.

31 G. W. Griffin, for a number of years
United States consul in Copenhagen, wrote
about Andersen: 'He is a remarkably fine
reader, and has often been compared in this
respect to Dickens. – Dickens was in truth a
superb reader, but I am inclined to think
that Andersen's manner is far more
impressive and eloquent. – Both of these
men have always read to crowded houses.
Dickens' voice was, perhaps, better suited
for the stage than the reading-desk. It was
stronger and louder than Andersen's, but
nothing like as mellow and musical. I
heard Dickens read the death-bed scene of
Little Nell in New York, and I was moved
to tears, but I knew that the author himself
was reading the story; but when I heard
Andersen read the story of the Little Girl
with the Matches, I did not think of the
author at all, but wept like a child,
unconscious of everything around me.'
(G. W. Griffin: *My Danish Days*,
Philadelphia 1875, pp. 208–9.)

Part two

1 The most recent English translation is
Hans Christian Andersen, *The Complete
Fairy Tales and Stories*. Translated from the

Danish by Erik Christian Haugaard. (New York, foreword by Virginia Haviland, and London, foreword by Naomi Lewis, 1974).

2 Sometimes called 'The Real Princess' or 'The Princess and the Pea'.

3 In Haugaard's translation called 'Inchelina'.

4 Sometimes called 'The Dauntless [or Constant or Staunch] Tin Soldier'.

5 Having failed to realize that 'Ole' in the title 'Ole Lukøie' is a Christian name, some of the English translators have called this story 'Old Luke' or 'Old Luke, the Sandman'. In other versions the title is given as 'The Sandman' or 'The Little Sandman' or 'Ole Lucköie', or 'The Dustman'.

6 Sometimes (as a correct translation of the Danish title, 'Kærestefolkene') called 'The Sweethearts' or 'The Lovers'.

7 Sometimes called 'The Pine Tree'.

8 Sometimes called 'The Hill of the Elves' or 'The Elfin Hill' or 'The Elfin Mound'.

9 Among the tales I would include in such a collection would be 'The Naughty Boy' (1835), 'The Goloshes of Fortune' (or 'The Magic Galoshes') (1838), 'The Bell' (1845), 'The High Jumpers' (or 'The Leaping Match' or 'The Jumping Competition') (1845), 'The Drop of Water' (1848), 'The Story of a Mother' (1848), 'There's a Difference' (1851), 'It's Perfectly [or Quite or Absolutely] True!' (1852), 'A Good Temper' (or 'A Happy Disposition') (1852), 'Heartbreak' (or 'Grief') (1852), 'Everything in its Right Place' (1852), 'The Goblin at the Grocer's' (or 'The Pixy and the Grocer') (1852), 'In a Thousand Years Time' (or 'The Millenium') (1852), 'She was no good' (1852), 'Simple Simon' ('Klods-Hans') (or 'Clod-poll' or 'Clumsy Hans' or 'Clod Hans' or 'Numskull Jack') (1855), 'Soup from a Sausage-Stick' (or 'How to Cook Soup on a Sausage Pin') (1858), 'The Marsh King's [or Bog King's] Daughter' (1858), 'Pen and Inkpot' (1859), 'The Beetle' (or 'The Dung Beetle') (1861), 'Dad's Always Right' (or 'What the Old Man Does is Always Right' or 'Father Always Does What's Right') (1861), 'The Snow Man' (1861), 'The Ice Maiden' (1861),

'The Snail and the Rose Tree' (1861), 'The Storm Moves Signposts' (or 'How the Storm Changed the Signs') (1865), 'Auntie' (1866), 'The Rags' (1868), 'Something to Write About' (or 'What One Can Invent' or 'Hitting on an Idea' or 'A Question of Imagination') (1869), 'The Gardener and the Squire' (or 'The Gardener and his Master') (1872), 'Old Johanna's Tale' (or 'The Story Old Johanna Told') (1872), 'The Cripple' (1872), and 'Auntie Toothache' (1872).

10 According to Andersen himself the tales in this category are 'The Tinder Box', 'Little Claus and Big Claus', 'The Princess on the Pea', 'The Travelling Companion', 'The Wild Swans', 'The Garden of Eden', 'The Swineherd', 'Simple Simon' and 'Dad's Always Right'.

The complicated question of Andersen's dependence on Danish folk tales has been dealt with in an important essay by Georg Christensen published in 1906. Since we are here dealing with an oral tradition it is not possible to know which particular versions Andersen heard as a child; we can only draw comparisons with versions recorded in other parts of Denmark.

11 Themes from Danish legends are incorporated in several tales, e.g., 'Mother Elder', 'The Elf Hill', 'Holger the Dane', 'The Goblin at the Grocer's' and 'The Bishop of Børglum'. Elements from some of Hoffmann's tales (especially 'Nussknacker und Mäusekönig', 'Meister Floh' and 'Abenteuer eines Sylvesternacht') are to be found in 'Little Ida's Flowers', 'The Snow Queen' (the devil's looking-glass), 'The Shepherdess and the Chimney-Sweep' and 'The Shadow'. There are loans from Musäus and *Njáls Saga* in 'The Marsh King's Daughter'. Chamisso's *Peter Schlemihl* has had an influence on both 'The Goloshes of Fortune' and 'The Shadow'; one of the inspirations for 'The Little Mermaid' is de la Motte Fouqué's *Undine*; features borrowed from Grimm and Brentano may be found in 'The Red Shoes', and elements in other tales may be traced back to Boccaccio's *Decameron* and to the *Arabian Nights*.

12 To the group of fairy tales proper also belong five of the tales previously

mentioned, 'The Tinder Box', 'The Travelling Companion', 'The Wild Swans', 'The Naughty Boy' and 'The Garden of Eden', and such tales as 'The Elf of the Rose', the sentimental 'The Angel', and the strange and to me unpleasant and cruel story of vanity, punishment and atonement, 'The Red Shoes'.

13 Others are: 'There's a Difference', a tale about class distinction in the plant world; the aristocratic apple blossom versus the despised dandelion; the message being that they are both beautiful but in different ways. 'Five Peas from one Pod' is the tale of five pea-siblings, one of which succeeds in bringing great happiness to a sick person. 'The Daisy' and 'The Flax' are stories of flowers whose attitude to life is exactly the opposite of that of the fir tree. The daisy enjoys every moment of its day and knows no envy. 'The sun shines upon me, and the wind kisses me. Oh! What gifts are given me!' The flax, too, is able to look on the best side of things in its transformation from a plant to linen which is woven and made into underwear, and finally discarded and burnt. 'The Buckwheat' is really a parable, and it could be said to illustrate one of the *Proverbs*, 'Pride goeth before destruction, and an haughty spirit before a fall.' (On 13 November 1845 Andersen noted in his diary that one of his acquaintances had drawn his attention to Jotham's parable of the trees in *The Old Testament* (Judges, IX): 'the only parable or what is similar to my fairy tales, the Greek *Einos*'.)

Trees and plants are also the main characters in 'The Last Dream of the Old Oak Tree', and 'What the Thistle Found Out'. The part flowers play in 'The Snow Queen' should be mentioned. While Gerda is staying with the old woman with the large sun hat, six flowers tell their stories – the tiger-lily, the convolvulus, the snowdrop, the hyacinth, the buttercup, and the narcissus. These six stories are really prose poems, in which Andersen has attempted to express in words the soul of each flower.

14 Included in *The Crimes of England* (London 1915).

15 For 'The Top and the Ball' see p. 162.

'The Shepherdess and the Chimney-Sweep' tells the story of how these two china figures elope, because an old nodding porcelain Chinaman who claimed to be the Shepherdess's guardian, wanted her to marry a carved satyr whom the children called 'Major-and-Minor-General-Company-Sergeant Billygoatlegs'. They escape to the top of the chimney but then return, and as he has been riveted after a fall the Old Chinaman is unable to nod his consent to the satyr any more, and so the two lovers are able to stay together.

A sad and lonely tin soldier is one of the main characters in 'The Old House'; unlike the other tin soldier this one does cry tin tears. The title character in 'The Snow Man' suffers from a longing for the warmth of the fireplace in the room into which he can see; and when he melts the reason is clear: there was a poker inside him, round which his snow body had been built. 'The Teapot' and 'The Rags' also belong to this category; the former being the reminiscences of a teapot who began her life as queen of the tea table and ended, her handle and spout broken off, as a flower-pot with a bulb in it. 'The Rags' records a dialogue between a Norwegian and a Danish rag, a witty satire on the presumed national characteristics of both nations. In 'Pen and Inkpot' the two characters quarrel about which of them is the real genius responsible for poetry being put on paper.

16 To this category of tales set in a kind of real, yet fantastic world belong some of those discussed previously in this chapter, 'The Princess on the Pea', 'The Emperor's New Clothes' and 'Simple Simon'. None of them contain any supernatural or magic elements, and they all take place in a human, though hardly in an ordinary or recognizable world.

'The Drop of Water' may also be regarded as belonging to this group, for though old Creepy-Crawley ('for that was his name') and his nameless colleague are both referred to as 'magicians', the point is, of course, that they are natural scientists, the drop of witch's blood ('the very finest kind at twopence a drop') a chemical substance, and the terrifying humans wrestling, wrangling, snapping and snarling which they see through the magnifying glass are in reality the kind of unicellular animals – the so-called animalcules – which could be seen at that time through a microscope.

'The Flea and the Professor' moves from Europe to Africa and back again, and however fantastic this amusing story is, it contains no elements which remove it from the real world.

Forty years before the invention of the first flying machines Andersen wrote the story he called 'In a Thousand Years Time', which must have appeared quite fantastic to his contemporaries, though in fact it foreshadowed, with a surprising amount of precision, the invention of the aeroplane, which, as he predicted, has enabled Americans to 'see Europe in one week'.

17 In spite of its title and the fact that the nightingale is capable of speaking (though its power lies in its singing) 'The Nightingale' certainly does not quite belong in the category of Andersen's animal tales. It would be possible to argue, on the other hand, that the appearance of Death as a character makes it into a fairy tale proper. However, it seems to me that the 'realistic' (though fantastic) elements in the tale are so important that in this, admittedly arbitrary, grouping of Andersen's tales I have found it reasonable to include this story here.

18 Two of the *fabliaux* belonging to this category have already been mentioned as having their origin in Danish folk tales, 'Little Claus and Big Claus' and 'Dad's Always Right'; in both of these the milieu is that of a Danish farming community.

Another well-known example is the sentimental story 'The Little Match Girl'. Here a poor little match girl in the streets of Copenhagen on a cold New Year's Eve lights one by one three of the matches she could not sell. Every time she lights a match she has a dreamlike vision, and with the last match she dies.

'A Good Temper' contains the quaint philosophy of a man whose favourite place for wondering about the strange ways of man is the churchyard; he has inherited his wonderful sense of humour from his father, whose profession was to drive a hearse. 'Heartbreak', a story in two parts, both of which are undoubtedly based on personal experience, contains a very

Andersenian mixture of humour and genuine emotion in its sympathy for the outsider. 'She was no good' and 'Old Johanna's Tale' are both clearly based on memories of Andersen's childhood in Odense; the former is an attempt to show his mother in a better and probably truer light in a description of a washerwoman who became addicted to alcohol. 'Auntie' is an amusing story of a spinster who was mad about the theatre. It is a composite picture, to some extent based on the memory of people Andersen knew.

Two stories fall into a group of their own within this category, 'The Wind Tells the Story of Valdemar Daa and his Daughters' and 'Chicken-Grethe's Family', for apart from the fact that Andersen has chosen to use the wind as the narrator in the former, they both relate stories based on historical facts. Valdemar Daa was a Danish seventeenth-century nobleman and alchemist, who spent everything he owned in his vain search for gold, and Marie Grubbe, the chief character in 'Chicken-Grethe's Family', was a noble lady of about the same period, whose life also ended in poverty, if for other reasons.

'The Cripple', one of Andersen's last tales, may be seen as a tribute to the art in which he himself became the supreme master; for it is a book of fairy tales which is the indirect cause that enables Hans, the paralysed cripple, to walk again.

19 Truisms with a humorous effect appear quite frequently in Andersen's tales, e.g., 'there were many people, and twice as many legs as heads'; 'when they travelled by train they went third class – that gets there just as quickly as first class'; 'two will-o'-the-wisps came hopping in, one faster than the other, and therefore he came in first'; '"The sixth comes before the seventh," said the Elf King, for he could do arithmetic.'

20 His own comments give some, if not reliable, information. He says 'Little Ida's Flowers' was written after telling the little Ida Thiele about the flowers in the Botanical Gardens and that her father suggested he write about a flute which could blow 'Everything in Its Right Place'. J. M. Thiele also gave the idea for 'The Bottleneck'.

Bibliography

Bibliographies, catalogues etc.

BIRGER FRANK NIELSEN *H. C. Andersen Bibliografi* Digterens danske værker 1822–75 (Copenhagen 1942)
SVEND LARSEN *H. C. Andersens Bøger* En Bibliografi (Copenhagen 1947)
ELIAS BREDSDORFF *Danish Literature in English Translation* With a special Hans Christian Andersen supplement. A bibliography (Copenhagen 1950)
Hans Christian Andersen Catalogue of a Jubilee Exhibition held at the National Book League, London. Arranged in association with the Danish government in cooperation with the Royal Library, Copenhagen, and Dr R. Klein, F.L.S. – Organizer: Elias Bredsdorff (London 1955)
AAGE JØRGENSEN *H. C. Andersen Litteraturen 1875–1968* (Aarhus 1970)
AAGE JØRGENSEN *H. C. Andersen Litteraturen 1875–1968. Tilføjelser og rettelser: Supplement 1875–1968. Fortsættelse 1969–72.* (Copenhagen 1973)

Editions of Andersen's works in Danish

H. C. ANDERSEN *Samlede Skrifter* Anden Udgave. I–XV (Copenhagen 1876–80)
H. C. ANDERSEN *Eventyr og Historier* I–V (Copenhagen 1918–20). Edited with notes and comments by Hans Brix and Anker Jensen
H. C. Andersens Eventyr Kritisk udgivet efter de originale Eventyrhefter med Varianter ved Erik Dal og Kommentar ved Erling Nielsen. I–VII (Copenhagen 1963–). By 1974 only volumes I–V had been published
H. C. ANDERSEN *Romaner og Rejseskildringer* Udgivet af Det danske Sprog- og Litteraturselskab under Redaktion af H. Topsøe-Jensen. I–VII (Copenhagen 1941–4)

Ungdoms-Forsøg af Villiam Christian Walter (Copenhagen 1956). Edited by Cai M. Woel
H. C. ANDERSEN *Et Besøg i Portugal 1866* (Copenhagen 1968). Edited with notes and introduction by Poul Høybye
H. C. ANDERSEN *Skyggebilleder* (Copenhagen 1968). Edited with a postscript by H. Topsøe-Jensen

Editions of Andersen's works in English

Among the innumerable English translations of Andersen's fairy tales and stories since 1846, the best ones are by Paul Leyssac (London 1937), Jean Hersholt (New York 1947), R. P. Keigwin (Leicester 1951–60), Reginald Spink (London 1960), L. W. Kingsland (London 1961) and Erik C. Haugaard (New York and London 1974)

Novels *(only first editions given)*

The Improvisatore, or, Life in Italy I–II. Translated by Mary Howitt (London 1845)
Only a Fiddler! and O.T., or Life in Denmark I–II. Translated by Mary Howitt (London 1845)
The Two Baronesses I–II. Translated by Charles Beckwith (London 1848).
To Be, or Not to Be? Translated by Mrs Bushby (London 1857)
Lucky Peer Translated by Horace E. Scudder (in *Scribner's Monthly*, New York, January, February, March and April, 1871)

Travel books

A Poet's Bazaar I–III. Translated by Charles Beckwith (London 1846)
Rambles in the Romantic Regions of the Hartz Mountains, Saxon Switzerland, etc. Translated by Charles Beckwith (London 1848)

Pictures of Sweden Translated by Charles
Beckwith (London 1851)
In Sweden Translated by K. R. K.
MacKenzie (London 1852)
In Spain Translated by Mrs Bushby
(London 1864)
A Poet's Bazaar Pictures of Travel in
Germany, Italy, Greece, and the Orient
(New York 1871)
Pictures of Travel In Sweden, Among the
Hartz Mountains, and In Switzerland, with
A Visit at Charles Dickens' House (New
York 1871)
In Spain, and A Visit to Portugal (New
York 1870)
A Visit to Portugal 1866 Translated, with
introduction, notes and appendices, by
Grace Thornton (London 1972)
A Visit to Spain Translated, edited and
introduced by Grace Thornton (London
1975)

Other works

Tales the Moon Can Tell ('Picture Book
without Pictures'). Translated by
R. P. Keigwin (Copenhagen 1955)
Seven Poems Translated by R. P. Keigwin
(Odense 1955)

Andersen's autobiographies

H. C. Andersens Levnedsbog 1805–1831
(Copenhagen 1962). An annotated edition
by H. Topsøe-Jensen of Andersen's first
autobiographical attempt, written in 1832,
though only intended for publication in
case of his premature death. For many
years the manuscript, which was left
incomplete by the author, was thought to
have been lost; it was found by Hans Brix
and first published by him in 1926. No
English translation exists.
Das Märchen meines Lebens ohne Dichtung
I–II (Leipzig 1847). Written for an edition
of Andersen's Gesammelte Werke
The True Story of My Life (London 1847).
Translated from the German edition of the
above by Mary Howitt
The True Story of My Life (London 1852).
A new translation by D. Spillan

Mit Livs Eventyr (Copenhagen 1855).
Andersen's definitive autobiography, partly
based on the unprinted Danish manuscript
of Das Märchen . . . (A revised edition was
published in 1859)
The Story of My Life Translated by
Horace E. Scudder (New York 1871). A
translation of Mit Livs Eventyr with
additional chapters covering the years
1855–67 which Scudder had induced
Andersen to write for this edition. (The
additional chapters were first printed in
Danish in 1877)
Mit eget Eventyr uden Digtning (Copenhagen
1942). Edited by H. Topsøe-Jensen. The
first publication of the original Danish
manuscript of Das Märchen . . .
Mit Livs Eventyr Revideret Tekstudgave
I–II (Copenhagen 1951). Edited by
H. Topsøe-Jensen. A fully annotated
edition of Mit Livs Eventyr, including the
additional chapters first published in The
Story of My Life
The Fairy Tale of My Life With illustrations
in colour by Niels Larsen Stevns
(Copenhagen 1954). A new translation by
W. Glyn Jones of Mit Livs Eventyr

Andersen's correspondence

Breve til Hans Christian Andersen
(Copenhagen 1877). Edited by C. S. A.
Bille and N. Bøgh
Breve fra Hans Christian Andersen I–II
(Copenhagen 1878). Edited by C. S. A.
Bille and N. Bøgh
H. C. Andersens Briefwechsel mit dem
Grossherzog Carl Alexander von
Sachsen-Weimar-Eisenach (Leipzig 1887).
Edited by Emil Jonas
Hans Christian Andersen's Correspondence
with the late Grand-Duke of Saxe-Weimar,
Charles Dickens, etc., etc. (London 1891).
Edited by Frederick Crawford
ELITH REUMERT H. C. Andersen og det
Melchiorske Hjem (Copenhagen 1924).
Includes most of the correspondence
between Andersen and Moritz and
Dorothea Melchior
J. BECK-FRIIS 'H. C. Andersens Breve til
Comtesse Mathilde Barck' (in Berlingske
Tidende, 6 April 1930)

H. C. Andersens Breve til Therese og Martin R. Henriques, 1860–75 (Copenhagen 1932). Edited by H. Topsøe-Jensen
H. C. Andersens Brevveksling med Edvard og Henriette Collin I–VI (1933–7). Edited by H. Topsøe-Jensen.
Hans Christian Andersen's Visits to Charles Dickens, as described in his letters, published with six of Dickens' letters in facsimile by Ejnar Munksgaard (Copenhagen 1937).
'H. C. Andersens Brevveksling med Henriette Hanck, 1830–46' (in *Anderseniana,* IX–XIII, 1941–6). Edited by Svend Larsen
H. C. Andersens Brevveksling med Jonas Collin den Ældre og andre Medlemmer af det Collinske Hus I–III (Copenhagen 1945–8). Edited by H. Topsøe-Jensen in cooperation with Kaj Bom and Knud Bøgh
H. C. Andersens Moder. En Brevsamling (Odense 1947). Edited by Svend Larsen.
'Riborgs Broder. H. C. Andersens Brevveksling med Christian Voigt' (in *Anderseniana,* Second Series, I.2, 1948). Edited by Th. A. Müller and H. Topsøe-Jensen
H. C. Andersen og Horace E. Scudder. En Brevveksling (Copenhagen 1948) Edited by Jean Hersholt, with a preface by H. Topsøe-Jensen and notes by Waldemar Westergaard
The Andersen-Scudder Letters. Hans Christian Andersen's correspondence with Horace Elisha Scudder. Edited by Jean Hersholt and Waldemar Westergaard. Introduction by Jean Hersholt and an essay by H. Topsøe-Jensen. Notes and translations by Waldemar Westergaard (Berkeley and Los Angeles 1949)
H. C. Andersen og Henriette Wulff. En Brevveksling. I–III (Copenhagen 1959–60). Edited by H. Topsøe-Jensen. Supplement in *Anderseniana,* Second Series, V. 1, 1962
H. C. Andersens Breve til Mathias Weber (Copenhagen 1961). Edited by Arne Portman
H. C. Andersens Breve til Carl B. Lorck (Odense 1969). Edited by H. Topsøe-Jensen.
'H. C. Andersens Breve til Robert Watt 1865–74', edited by H. Topsøe-Jensen (in *Fund og Forskning,* XVIII–XIX, Copenhagen 1971–2)

Important collections of letters are also included in the works with an asterisk in the sections: *Andersen's diaries* and *Other important source material*

Andersen's diaries

H. C. Andersens Dagbøger 1825–75 I–X. Udgivet af Det danske Sprog- og Litteraturselskab under ledelse af Kåre Olsen og H. Topsøe-Jensen (Copenhagen 1971–5). A complete, but unannotated, edition of all extant diaries, edited by Tue Gad, Helga Vang Lauridsen and Kirsten Weber. There will be a final index volume by H. Topsøe-Jensen. By 1974 the following volumes had been published: I (1825–34), II (1836–44), V (1861–3), VI (1864–5) and VII (1866–7)
H. C. Andersens sidste Leveaar. Hans Dagbøger 1868–75 (Copenhagen 1906) Edited by Jonas Collin junior. This unreliable and haphazard selection will be made superfluous when volumes VIII–X of Topsøe-Jensen's edition have been published

Among the previously published *annotated* extracts from Andersen's diaries the following are the most important:
*'H. C. Andersen og Odense 1866–75. Dagbøger og Breve' (in *Anderseniana,* I, 1933). Edited by C. M. K. Petersen and Svend Larsen
'H. C. Andersens Dagbog fra hans sidste Slagelse-Aar 1825–6' (in *Anderseniana,* IV, 1936). Edited by H. G. Olrik
H. C. ANDERSEN *Romerske Dagbøger* (Copenhagen 1947). Edited by Paul V. Rubow and H. Topsøe-Jensen
'H. C. Andersens Dagbog fra Pariser-Rejsen 1843' (in *Anderseniana,* Second Series, I.4, 1950). Edited by Poul Høybye.
'H. C. Andersens Norgesreise 1871' (in *Anderseniana,* Second Series, I.2, 1948). Edited by Christian Svanholm
'H. C. Andersens dagbog fra besøget hos Dickens i 1857'. Edited by Elias Bredsdorff. In *H. C. Andersen og Charles Dickens* (Copenhagen 1951)
'H. C. Andersens dagbog fra England og Skotland, 1874'. Edited by Elias Bredsdorff. In *H. C. Andersen og England* (Copenhagen 1954)
'Hans Andersen's Diary of his Visit to Dickens in 1847'. Edited by Elias Bredsdorff. In *Hans Andersen and Charles Dickens* (Cambridge 1956)

'H. C. Andersens Slagelse Dagbog, 4. marts – 11. april 1826' (in *Anderseniana*, Second Series, v.3, 1964). Edited by Helga Vang Lauridsen and Paul Raimund Jørgensen. (A supplement to VI.3, after a fragment sold by Hans Brix had been recovered)

Notebooks, draft material etc.

H. C. Andersens Optegnelsesbog (Copenhagen 1926). Edited by Julius Clausen
'Tre ufuldførte historiske Digtninge' (in *Anderseniana*, III, 1935). Edited by Tage Høeg
'Brudstykke af en Udflugt i Sommeren 1829' (in *Anderseniana*, VIII, 1940). Edited by C. M. K. Petersen, with a supplement by Harald Hatt
HANS BRIX *Det første Skridt. Drengen Hans Christian Andersens Skuespilarier* (Copenhagen 1943)
H. C. ANDERSEN *Reise fra Kjøbenhavn til Rhinen* (Copenhagen 1955). Edited by H. Topsøe-Jensen
POUL HØYBYE 'På opdagelsesrejse i H. C. Andersens papirer' (in *Anderseniana*, Second Series, III.2, 1956). (With a supplement in *Anderseniana*, Second Series, IV.2, 1958)
H. C. ANDERSEN 'Udsigt fra mit Vindue i Kjøbenhavn' (in *Anderseniana*, Second Series, IV.3, 1959). Edited by H. Topsøe-Jensen
H. TOPSØE-JENSEN 'Fra en Digters Værksted. H. C. Andersens Optegnelsesbøger' (in *Fund og Forskning*, IX–X, Copenhagen 1962–3)
H. C. ANDERSEN 'Et Kapitel af en paatænkt Sverigesroman' (in *Anderseniana*, Second Series, v.3, 1964). Edited by Morten Borup

Andersen's drawings, sketches, paper cuttings, etc.

Billedbog med Billeder af Hans Christian Andersen (Odense 1905)
POUL UTTENREITER *H. C. Andersen Billedbog* (Copenhagen 1924). Contains reproductions of Andersen's paper cuttings

POUL UTTENREITER *H. C. Andersens Tegninger* (Copenhagen 1925). Contains reproductions of Andersens sketches and pen drawings
Billedbog fra H. C. Andersen Samlingerne i Odense (Odense 1935)
H. C. ANDERSEN *Improvisatoren*. Med Digterens egne Tegninger (Copenhagen 1945)
ELIAS BREDSDORFF 'Hans Andersen as an Artist' (in *The Norseman*, XII, London 1955)
ERIK DAL 'Kristine Stampes billedbog' (in *Anderseniana*, Second Series, IV.4, 1961)
KJELD HELTOFT *H. C. Andersens Billedkunst* (Copenhagen 1969)
KJELD HELTOFT *H. C. Andersens tegninger til Otto Zinck* I–II (Odense 1972)

Other important source material

The journal *Anderseniana* was founded in 1933. First Series, I–XIII (Copenhagen 1933–46) was edited by C. M. K. Petersen and Svend Larsen. Second Series, I–VI (Copenhagen, later Odense, 1947–69) was edited by Svend Larsen (later: Niels Oxenvad) and H. Topsøe-Jensen. Third Series, I– (Odense 1970–) is edited by Niels Oxenvad and H. Topsøe-Jensen

N. C. L. ABRAHAMS *Meddelelser af mit Liv* (Copenhagen 1876)
WILLIAM ALLINGHAM *A Diary* Edited by H. Allingham and D. Radford (London 1907)
HARALD ÅSTRÖM *H. C. Andersens genombrott i Sverige* (Stockholm 1972)
*LADY BETTY BALFOUR (editor) *Personal and Literary Letters of Robert, First Earl of Lytton* Volume I (London 1906)
J. P. BANG *H. C. Andersen og Georg Brandes* (Copenhagen 1936)
WALTER A. BERENDSOHN *Fantasi og Virkelighed i H. C. Andersens Eventyr og Historier. Stil- og Strukturstudier* (Aarhus 1955)
WALTER A. BERENDSOHN *Phantasie und Wirklichkeit in den Märchen und Geschichten Hans Christian Andersens* (Wiesbaden 1973)
WILLIAM BLOCH 'Om H. C. Andersen. Bidrag til Belysning af hans Personlighed' (in *Nær og Fjern*, Copenhagen 1879)
WILLIAM BLOCH *Paa Rejse med H. C. Andersen* (Copenhagen 1942)

*LOUISE BOBÉ H. C. Andersen og Storhertug Carl Alexander af Sachsen-Weimar-Eisenach (Copenhagen 1905)

LOUIS BOBÉ 'H. C. Andersen og Weimar' (in Anderseniana, VIII, 1940)

*INGER BØGH H. C. Andersen og Nic. Bøgh I–II (Frederiksberg 1968–70)

N. BØGH 'H. C. Andersens sidste Dage' (in Illustreret Tidende, Copenhagen 1875)

N. BØGH 'Hvad H. C. Andersen fortalte' (in Danmark. Illustreret Kalender, Copenhagen 1887)

N. BØGH 'Fra H. C. Andersens Barndoms- og Ungdomsliv' (in Personalhistorisk. Tidsskrift, Copenhagen 1905)

N. BØGH 'Uddrag af en Dagbog paa en Rejse sammen med H. C. Andersen 1873' (in Julebogen, Copenhagen 1915)

A Book on the Danish Writer Hans Christian Andersen, his Life and Work (Copenhagen 1955)

FREDRIK BÖÖK H. C. Andersen. En levnadsteckning (Stockholm 1938)

FREDRIK BÖÖK Hans Christian Andersen: A Biography Translated by George C. Schoolfield (Norman, Oklahoma 1962)

EDVARD BRANDES 'H. C. Andersen. Personlighed og værk' (in Litterære Tendenser, Copenhagen 1968)

GEORG BRANDES 'H. C. Andersen som Eventyrdigter' (in Kritiker og Portraiter, Copenhagen 1870). Printed in English translation by R. B. Anderson in GEORG BRANDES Eminent Authors of the Nineteenth Century (New York 1886) and Creative Spirits of the Nineteenth Century (New York 1923)

L. YU. BRAUDE Zhizn i tvorchestvo Khansa Kristiana Andersena (Leningrad 1973)

*ELIAS BREDSDORFF H. C. Andersen og Charles Dickens Et venskab og dets opløsning (Copenhagen 1951)

*ELIAS BREDSDORFF 'Hans Andersen and Livingstone's Daughter' (in Blackwood's Magazine, Edinburgh 1955)

*ELIAS BREDSDORFF H. C. Andersen og England (Copenhagen 1954)

ELIAS BREDSDORFF 'Hans Andersen and Scotland' (in Blackwood's Magazine, Edinburgh 1955)

ELIAS BREDSDORFF 'Hans Andersen as seen through British Eyes' (in catalogue of National Book League exhibition, London 1955)

ELIAS BREDSDORFF 'H. C. Andersen set med engelske øjne' (in Anderseniana, Second Series, III.2, 1956)

*ELIAS BREDSDORFF Hans Andersen and Charles Dickens A Friendship and its Dissolution (Cambridge 1956)

ELIAS BREDSDORFF 'Hans Christian Andersen: A Bibliographical Guide to his Work' (in Scandinavica, VI.1, London 1967)

ELIAS BREDSDORFF 'A Critical Guide to the Literature on Hans Christian Andersen' (in Scandinavica, VI.2, London 1967)

HANS BRIX H. C. Andersen og hans Eventyr (Copenhagen 1907)

The Letters of Robert Browning and Elizabeth Barrett Volume I (London 1899)

The Letters of Elizabeth Barrett Browning Edited by F. G. Kenyon. Volume I (London 1897)

*FRANCIS BULL 'H. C. Andersen og Bjørnstjerne Bjørnson' (in Anderseniana, Second Series, III.2, 1956)

GEORG CHRISTENSEN 'H. C. Andersen og de danske Folkeeventyr' (in Danske Studier, Copenhagen 1906)

*EDVARD COLLIN H. C. Andersen og det Collinske Huus (Copenhagen 1882)

ERIK DAL 'Den lille Pige med Svovlstikkerne'. Træk af et Eventyrs forhistorie og skæbne (Copenhagen 1956)

ESTRID AND ERIK DAL Fra H. C. Andersens boghylde Hans bogsamling belyst gennem breve, kataloger og bevarede bøger (Copenhagen 1961)

The Recollections of Sir Henry Dickens (London 1934)

A. G. DRACHMANN 'E. B. Browning and Hans Andersen' (in Edda, Oslo 1933)

ARNE DUVE Symbolikken i H. C. Andersens eventyr (Oslo 1967)

Journals and Correspondence of Lady Eastlake Edited by Charles Eastlake Smith. Volume I (London 1895)

CARL ERLACHER Grimm und Andersen Eine Studie über Märchendichtung (Langensalza 1929)

N. L. FAABORG Grafiske portrætter af H. C. Andersen (Copenhagen 1971)

*FINN FRIIS H. C. Andersen og Schweiz (Copenhagen 1949)

*KJELD GALSTER H. C. Andersen og hans Rektor (Copenhagen 1933)

*KJELD GALSTER 'H. C. Andersens besøg i Lund 1840' (in Edda, Oslo 1959)

EDMUND W. GOSSE *Two Visits to Denmark* (London 1911)

CARSTEN HAUCH *Slottet ved Rhinen* (Copenhagen 1845)

J. L. HEIBERG 'En Sjæl efter Døden' (in *Nye Digte*, Copenhagen 1840)

HJALMAR HELWEG *H. C. Andersen. En psykiatrisk Studie* (Copenhagen 1927)

[HENRIK HERTZ] *Gengangerbreve* (Copenhagen 1830)

*TAGE HØEG *H. C. Andersens Ungdom* (Copenhagen 1934)

MARY HOWITT *An Autobiography* I–II. Edited by Margaret Howitt (London 1889)

POUL HØYBYE *H. C. Andersens franske ven Xavier Marmier* (Copenhagen 1950)

POUL HØYBYE 'H. C. Andersen og Frankrig' (in *Anderseniana*, Second Series, II.2, 1952)

POUL HØYBYE *H. C. Andersen et la France* (Copenhagen 1961)

ELISABETH HUDE *Henriette Hanck og H. C. Andersen* (Odense 1958)

*HANS HENRIK JACOBSEN *H. C. Andersen på Fyn 1819–75* (Odense 1968)

HENRY JAMES *William Wetmore Story and his Friends* Volume I (Edinburgh and London 1903)

ANKER JENSEN *Studier over H. C. Andersens Sprog* (Copenhagen 1929)

SØREN KIERKEGAARD *Af en endnu Levendes Papirer*. Om Andersen som Romandigter, med stadigt Hensyn til hans sidste Værk: 'Kun en Spillemand' (Copenhagen 1838)

NIELS KOFOED *Studier i H. C. Andersens Fortællekunst* (Copenhagen 1967)

KARL LARSEN *H. C. Andersen i Tekst og Billeder* (Copenhagen 1925)

SVEND LARSEN 'Barndomsbyen' (in *Anderseniana*, Second Series, III.1, 1955)

SVEND LARSEN AND H. TOPSØE-JENSEN *H. C. Andersens eget Eventyr i Billeder* (Copenhagen 1952)

FR. VON DER LEYEN 'H. C. Andersen und das deutsche Märchen' (in *Dänische Rundschau*, Copenhagen 1953)

FREDERICK J. MARKER 'H. C. Andersen as a Royal Theatre Actor' (in *Anderseniana*, Second Series, VI.3, 1968)

FREDERICK J. MARKER *Hans Christian Andersen and the Romantic Theatre* (Toronto 1971)

ERLING NIELSEN *H. C. Andersen* (Copenhagen 1963)

*ALFRED B. NILSSON: 'Sagoskalden och Malmöcomtessen' (in *Sydsvenska Dagbladet*, 3 March 1930)

EIGIL NYBORG *Den indre linie i H. C. Andersens eventyr En psykologisk studie* (Copenhagen 1962)

GEORG NYGAARD *H. C. Andersen og København* (Copenhagen 1938)

BJØRN OCHSNER 'H. C. Andersen-fotografier fra Frijsenborg' (in *Fund og Forskning*, II, Copenhagen 1955)

BJØRN OCHSNER 'Fotografier af H. C. Andersen' (in *Anderseniana*, Second Series, IV.1, 1957)

H. G. OLRIK *Undersøgelser og Kroniker 1925–44* (Copenhagen 1945)

H. C. ØRSTED *Aanden i Naturen* I–II (Copenhagen 1850)

H. A. PALUDAN 'H. C. Andersens Rejse i Portugal' (in *Edda*, Oslo 1933)

JØRGEN PAULSEN 'H. C. Andersen portrætter. Samtidige malerier og tegninger' (in *Anderseniana*, Second Series, III.2, 1955)

ARNE PORTMAN *H. C. Andersens sidste Dage* (Copenhagen 1952)

*ELITH REUMERT *H. C. Andersen som han var* (Copenhagen 1925)

*ELITH REUMERT *Hans Andersen the Man* Translated by Jessie Bröchner (London 1927)

HEINRICH ROHLFS 'Erinnerungen an Heinrich Heine aus dem Jahre 1851' (in *Die Gartenlaube*, Leipzig 1862)

PAUL V. RUBOW *H. C. Andersens Eventyr* (Copenhagen 1927)

PAUL V. RUBOW 'H. C. Andersens Pariserrejser' (in *Danske i Paris gennem Tiderne*, edited by Franz von Jessen. Volume I, Copenhagen 1936)

PAUL V. RUBOW 'Danske Guldalderforfattere i Rom' (in *Rom og Danmark gennem Tiderne*, edited by Louis Bobé. Volume II, Copenhagen 1937)

HARALD RUE 'H. C. Andersen' (in H. Rue, *Litteratur og Samfund*, Copenhagen 1937)

V. A. SCHMITZ *H. C. Andersens Märchendichtung* (Greifswald 1925)

H. SCHWANENFLÜGEL *Hans Christian Andersen. Et Digterliv* (Copenhagen 1905)

PEER E. SØRENSEN *H. C. Andersen & Herskabet* Studier i borgerlig krisebevidsthed (Copenhagen 1973)

REGINALD SPINK *Hans Christian Andersen and his World* (London 1972)

*RIGMOR STAMPE *H. C. Andersen og hans nærmeste Omgang* (Copenhagen 1918)
GLADYS STOREY *Dickens and Daughter* (London 1939)
CHR. SVANHOLM *H. C. Andersens ungdoms-tro* (Trondheim 1952)
HEINRICH TESCHNER *Hans Christian Andersen und Heinrich Heine* (Munich 1914)
The Letters and Private Papers of William Makepeace Thackeray volume II (London 1945)
J. M. THIELE *Af mit Livs Aarbøger 1795–1826* (Copenhagen 1873)
*H. TOPSØE-JENSEN 'H. C. Andersen paa Holsteinborg' (in *Anderseniana*, V–VI, 1937–8)
*H. TOPSØE-JENSEN *Mit eget Eventyr uden Digtning. En Studie over H. C. Andersen som Selvbiograf* (Copenhagen 1940)
*H. TOPSØE-JENSEN *Omkring Levnedsbogen. En Studie over H. C. Andersen som Selvbiograf 1820–45* (Copenhagen 1943)
H. TOPSØE-JENSEN 'Konferensraad A. L. Drewsens Optegnelser om H. C. Andersen (in *Personalhistorisk Tidsskrift*, Copenhagen 1943)
H. TOPSØE-JENSEN 'H. C. Andersen og U.S.A.' (in *Anderseniana*, Second Series, I.2, 1949)

H. TOPSØE-JENSEN 'Hvad H. C. Andersen fortalte. Optegnelser af Robert Watt' (in *Anderseniana*, Second Series, II.4, 1954)
*H. TOPSØE-JENSEN *H. C. Andersen i Livets Aldre. En Brevpotpourri* (Copenhagen 1955)
*H. TOPSØE-JENSEN 'H. C. Andersen og det augustenborgske Hertugpar' (in *Anderseniana*, Second Series, V.2, 1963)
H. TOPSØE-JENSEN 'H. C. Andersens Religion' (in *Anderseniana*, Second Series, V.2, 1963)
*H. TOPSØE-JENSEN *H. C. Andersen paa Glorup* (Copenhagen 1965)
*H. TOPSØE-JENSEN *H. C. Andersen og andre Studier* (Copenhagen 1966)
*H. TOPSØE-JENSEN *Buket til Andersen. Bemærkninger til femogtyve Eventyr* (Copenhagen 1971)
G. L. WAD *Om Hans Christian Andersens Slægt* (Odense 1905)
NIELS BIRGER WAMBERG *H. C. Andersen og Heiberg* (Copenhagen 1971)
[ANNIE WOOD] 'A Few Weeks with Hans Andersen' (in *Temple Bar*, London, February 1875)

Acknowledgements

Acknowledgement is due to Flensted's Forlag, Odense, for permission to quote from R. P. Keigwin's translation of Hans Christian Andersen's *Fairy Tales*, I–IV, first published 1958, edited by Svend Larsen, with an introduction by Elias Bredsdorff (also published by Edmund Ward, Leicester, and Scribner's, New York).

The following have kindly supplied photographs or given permission for items within their copyright to be reproduced:

Hans Christian Andersen Museum, Odense: 37, 43, 49, 97 top, 98, 101 top and bottom, 102 right, 104 top, 106, 107, 109, 136, 184, 192, 193 bottom, 194 bottom, 195, 196 top, 198 top left, 200, 245, 290 bottom right, 291 top, 294, 295, 296 bottom; *Det Kongelige Bibliotek, Copenhagen*: 73, 97 bottom, 99, 102 left, 103, 104 bottom, 120, 194 top, 196 bottom left, 197, 198 top right and bottom, 199, 204, 206, 208, 223, 289, 290 bottom left, 291 bottom, 292, 293; *Helsingør Bymuseum*: 100, 193 top; *Det Nationalhistoriske Museum, Frederiksborg*: 196 bottom right; *Punch*: 211; *National Travel Association of Denmark, London*: 296 top; *Laurence Whistler*: 306; *George G. Harrap & Co. Ltd*: 326.

Index